Escalation Dynamics in Cyberspace

BRIDGING THE GAP

Series Editors

James Goldgeier
Bruce Jentleson
Steven Weber

Escalation Dynamics in Cyberspace

ERICA D. LONERGAN AND
SHAWN W. LONERGAN

OXFORD
UNIVERSITY PRESS

OXFORD
UNIVERSITY PRESS

Oxford University Press is a department of the University of Oxford. It furthers the University's objective of excellence in research, scholarship, and education by publishing worldwide. Oxford is a registered trade mark of Oxford University Press in the UK and certain other countries.

Published in the United States of America by Oxford University Press
198 Madison Avenue, New York, NY 10016, United States of America.

Library of Congress Cataloging-in-Publication Data
Names: Lonergan, Erica D., author. | Lonergan, Shawn W., author.
Title: Escalation dynamics in cyberspace / Erica D. Lonergan, Shawn W. Lonergan.
Description: New York, NY : Oxford University Press, 2023. |
Series: Bridging the gap series | Includes index.
Identifiers: LCCN 2022050300 (print) | LCCN 2022050301 (ebook) |
ISBN 9780197550892 (paperback) | ISBN 9780197550885 (hardback) |
ISBN 9780197550915 (epub) | ISBN 9780197550922
Subjects: LCSH: Cyberspace operations (Military science) |
Escalation (Military science)
Classification: LCC U167.5.C92 L663 2023 (print) |
LCC U167.5.C92 (ebook) | DDC 355.40285—dc23/eng/20221213
LC record available at https://lccn.loc.gov/2022050300
LC ebook record available at https://lccn.loc.gov/2022050301

DOI: 10.1093/oso/9780197550885.001.0001

Paperback printed by Marquis Book Printing, Canada
Hardback printed by Bridgeport National Bindery, Inc., United States of America

To our students. Our greatest honor has been to play a small role in educating the next generation of cyber warriors.

Contents

Preface

This book speaks to one of the central questions of cyber strategy, namely, to what extent do cyberspace operations increase the risks of escalation between nation-state rivals? While scholars and practitioners have been concerned about escalation dynamics in cyberspace for decades, the question remains insufficiently answered. Moreover, the extent to which cyber operations lead to escalation has growing relevance for international politics as more states develop and employ offensive cyber capabilities and as the international system is increasingly characterized by emergent multipolarity.

We present a comprehensive theoretical framework to identify core characteristics of operating in cyberspace and assess the implications for when cyber operations may cause escalation—through both cyber and cross-domain means. We also extend our analysis to explore how these same factors may impact the utility of cyber operations for certain forms of signaling, which is inextricably linked to the process of escalation and escalation management in particular. Our theoretical analysis and case studies strongly suggest that cyber operations are not as escalatory as some observers might suggest and, instead, may serve de-escalation purposes. There are a number of critical aspects of planning and conducting cyber operations that mitigate the risks of escalation. Offensive cyber operations with strategic effects are difficult and complex to plan and conduct, have unreliable and unpredictable efficacy, and are limited in their abilities to generate meaningful costs against targets. Moreover, rather than make escalation risks more salient, the secrecy of cyber operations and their plausible deniability can create breathing room that dampens escalation risks and provide opportunity for cooler heads to prevail. Finally, the substantial intelligence value that cyber operations provide creates trade-offs that may make decision makers averse to conducting escalatory offensive cyber operations in lieu of other actions.

However, we also find that there is a narrow set of conditions under which cyber operations may trigger inadvertent escalation. This stems from the interdependence of conventional and nuclear weapon systems and the digital domain. Given the potentially high consequences of inadvertent escalation through these pathways, especially cyber threats to nuclear command, control, and communication systems, policymakers should prioritize measures that can promote transparency and stability around these types of cyber operations, as well as take action to reduce cyber vulnerabilities across these systems.

Furthermore, despite our conclusion that cyber operations are, in most instances, unlikely to trigger dangerous escalatory spirals, policymakers should nevertheless exercise care when employing cyber capabilities; ensure that actions taken in cyberspace are calibrated with intent; and deliberately and coherently communicate intent with external parties, including friendly and adversarial states. The absence of escalation thus far should not be perceived as granting a broad license for states to conduct any and all types of offensive cyber operations to satisfy a diversity of strategic objectives. In fact, our analysis suggests that skepticism is warranted about the overall efficacy of cyber operations for strategic ends.

We hope this book helps shape the ongoing rich and exciting dialogues around issues of cyberspace, national security strategy, and international politics.

Erica D. Lonergan
Shawn W. Lonergan

Acknowledgments

We are deeply grateful to the many individuals who directly and indirectly helped bring this book to fruition. This project was certainly a labor of love (and, sometimes, hate) and would not have been possible without the insights, feedback, thoughtful discourse, and disagreements of numerous friends and colleagues in the field of cyber strategy and policy. With so many people to thank, it is inevitable that we will unintentionally omit some. For this we sincerely apologize.

First, we are grateful to have had the opportunity to serve alongside the commissioners and staff of the U.S. Cyberspace Solarium Commission. The commission's willingness to tackle tough strategic challenges inspired our efforts and shaped our understanding of the policy applications of our research. We are especially lucky to have served under the leadership of co-chairs, Senator Angus King and Congressman Mike Gallagher; Executive Director, Rear Admiral (Ret.) Mark Montgomery; and the extraordinarily talented Task Force leads and Task Force One team. We also feel incredibly thankful to have worked alongside an amazing group of cyber scholars and friends, particularly Jacquelyn Schneider, Brandon Valeriano, and Benjamin Jensen.

We are also grateful to our former colleagues in the Cyber National Mission Force, where we both served in different capacities. We are fortunate to have served under the pioneering and visionary leadership of two commanders we worked for, Vice Admiral (Ret.) Timothy "TJ" White and Lieutenant General Timothy Haugh. In a relatively short, yet crucial, period of time we were lucky to have played a small role in helping to shape U.S. cyber strategy and operations.

Our academic histories are not only intertwined but also pivotal in our professional development. Columbia University will forever and always be our academic lodestar. We both received our PhDs from Columbia's Department of Political Science, and Erica is a graduate of Columbia College. We would not be the scholars we are today without the mentorship of the distinguished current and former faculty members of Columbia's Political Science Department and the Saltzman Institute of War and Peace Studies, especially Jack Snyder, Richard Betts, the late Robert Jervis, Austin Long, and Tanisha Fazal. We would also be remiss if we did not thank the United States Military Academy at West Point, where Shawn went to college. The initial seeds of this book project were first planted while we were both faculty members in the Department of Social Sciences at West Point. It reached maturity while we both held positions at the Army Cyber Institute at West Point.

We are deeply thankful to the incredible editors and team at Oxford University Press and Bridging the Gap, especially David McBride and James Goldgeier, for making this book possible and for creating opportunities for scholars who are passionate about doing policy-relevant research to share their ideas with the world.

Finally, we are forever grateful to our family for their unwavering support, particularly our parents and our children, Natalie and Oliver.

The views we express in this book are personal and do not reflect the policy or position of any U.S. government department, agency, or organization.

1

Why Is There No Escalation in Cyberspace?

Introduction

In the summer of 2021, a few months into his administration, U.S. President Joseph Biden warned in a speech that if a "real shooting war with a major power" were to take place, it would be caused by "a cyber breach of great consequence."[1] This is not the first time—nor will it likely be the last—that a senior policymaker publicly expressed fears of an impending conflict trigged by events in cyberspace. Indeed, for decades experts have presaged an imminent "Cyber Pearl Harbor" or "Cyber 9/11"—a decisive, devastating, and often surprise attack by a nefarious actor in cyberspace that would lead to instability and even war.[2] The problem with these fears is that they have simply not materialized, despite the fact that cyberspace is arguably growing more dangerous over time. More states are developing military cyber capabilities, criminal organizations are becoming more sophisticated, offensive tools are proliferating, and activity in cyberspace is increasing. And yet, to date, not a single cyber attack has resulted in a state responding with military force or caused an escalatory spiral. This begs the question: why has the international system not experienced meaningful cyber escalation?

Our book aims to answer this question, providing one perspective on why cyber operations are unlikely to trigger escalation. Specifically, we offer a theoretical framework that takes into account the unique characteristics of cyber operations and traces the mechanisms through which activities in cyberspace are more or less likely to lead to escalatory dynamics between states. In doing so, we distinguish between escalation in crisis situations short of war and potential escalation patterns during outright conflict. The overwhelming majority of cyber

---

[1] Nandita Bose, "Biden: If U.S. Has 'Real Shooting War' It Could Be Result of Cyber Attacks," *Reuters*, July 28, 2021.

[2] Elisabeth Bumiller and Thom Shanker, "Panetta Warns of Dire Threat of Cyberattack on U.S.," *The New York Times*, October 11, 2012. Brian Klaas, "Opinion: We're Sleepwalking toward a Cyber 9/11," *The Washington Post*, September 14, 2021. For a good discussion of various analogies that have been used to describe or categorize different offensive cyber operations see Gregory Rattray and Jason Healey, "Categorizing and Understanding Offensive Cyber Capabilities and Their Use," Proceedings of a Workshop on Deterring Cyber Attacks: Informing Strategies and Developing Options for U.S. Policy, 2010. But for a counterargument, see Thomas Rid, *Cyber War Will Not Take Place* (New York: Oxford University Press, 2013) .

Escalation Dynamics in Cyberspace. Erica D. Lonergan and Shawn W. Lonergan, Oxford University Press.
© Oxford University Press 2023. DOI: 10.1093/oso/9780197550885.003.0001

operations have occurred in the former context—strategic competition between states below the level of armed conflict. In these situations, there is little evidence that cyber operations lead to escalation. Instead, we find that the same properties that make cyber operations poor tools of escalation could also enable states to use cyber operations to diffuse crises. In contrast, we hypothesize that cyber operations may be more likely to contribute to escalation dynamics once conflict has already commenced—but that this is due to a very different logic than that which operates during routine competition or crisis between states.

Whether and how emerging technologies might contribute to international stability is a pervasive question for scholars and policymakers. Academic efforts to understand and make predictions about escalation dynamics crystallized during the Cold War and became particularly acute during the Cuban Missile Crisis when the threat of nuclear annihilation was suddenly made quite real. Richard Smoke notes that the concept of escalation "did not appear in dictionaries, in military or scholarly literature, or in the public statements of government officials, before about 1960."[3]

During the ensuing decades, the immensely destructive power inherent in nuclear weapons prompted scholars to consider the pathways along which this novel capability could contribute to or alleviate the risks of war, crisis stability, and escalation.[4] Deterrence and escalation were core frameworks to explain systemic stability or instability. On the one hand, mutual deterrence through the reciprocal and credible threat of catastrophic nuclear war was hypothesized to inject stability into relations between the two Cold War superpowers, preventing either from unleashing the devastating effects of nuclear weapons on the other.[5]

---

[3] Richard Smoke, *War: Controlling Escalation* (Cambridge, MA: Harvard University Press, 1977), p. 4.

[4] This is an enormous literature in the field that addresses questions pertinent to this broad statement that will be explored in significant depth over the course of this book. However, for some examples see Robert Jervis, "Why Nuclear Superiority Doesn't Matter," *Political Science Quarterly* 94, no. 4 (Winter 1979–1980): 617–633; Bernard Brodie, *War and Politics* (New York: Macmillan, 1973); Glenn Snyder, "The Balance of Power and the Balance of Terror," in Paul Seabury, ed., *The Balance of Power* (San Francisco: Chandler, 1965), pp. 184–201; Richard K. Betts, *Nuclear Blackmail and Nuclear Balance* (Washington, DC: Brookings Institute Press, 1977).

[5] See, for example, Thomas C. Schelling, *The Strategy of Conflict* (Cambridge, MA: Harvard University Press, 1960); Robert Jervis, "Rational Deterrence: Theory and Evidence," *World Politics* 41, no. 2 (January 1989): 183–207; Robert Powell, "The Theoretical Foundations of Strategic Nuclear Deterrence," *Political Science Quarterly* 100, no. 1 (Spring 1985): 75–96; Thomas Schelling, *The Reciprocal Fear of Surprise Attack* (Santa Monica, CA: RAND Corporation, 1958); Alexander George and Richard Smoke, *Deterrence in American Foreign Policy* (New York: Columbia University Press, 1974); Glenn Snyder, *Deterrence and Defense* (Princeton, NJ: Princeton University Press, 1961); Thomas Schelling, *Arms and Influence* (New Haven, CT: Yale University Press, 1966); Robert Jervis, *The Illogic of American Nuclear Strategy* (Ithaca, NY: Cornell University Press, 1984); Lawrence Freedman, *The Evolution of Nuclear Strategy* (London: Macmillan, 1989); Austin G. Long, *Deterrence: From Cold War to Long War: Lessons from Six Decades of RAND Deterrence Research* (Santa Monica, CA: Rand Corporation, Vol. 636, 2008); Francis J. Gavin, *Nuclear Statecraft: History and Strategy in America's Atomic Age* (Ithaca, NY: Cornell University Press, 2012).

On the other hand, the potential for inadvertent escalation risked undermining the very stability purportedly achieved through mutual strategic deterrence, often termed the stability-instability paradox.[6] Relatedly, the notion of deliberate escalation—most notably portrayed in Herman Kahn's iconic "escalation ladder"—envisioned a strategic interaction in which one state could deter undesirable behavior and achieve victory through maintaining "escalation dominance" over an adversary at every threshold of violence.[7]

But cyber weapons (if it is even appropriate to use the term weapon to refer to offensive cyber capabilities) are not comparable to nuclear weapons. Despite this, in the contemporary era scholars and policymakers alike have attempted to apply Cold War deterrence models to cyberspace, especially in the United States. Indeed, deterrence continues to serve as the underpinning conceptual framework for the U.S. government's cyber strategy.[8] However, while deterrence theory continues to play a central role in shaping academic and practitioner approaches to cyberspace, many also recognize that Cold War deterrence models are poor fits to account for behavior in cyberspace. Cyber deterrence is complicated by a number of factors, including the proliferation of a diverse set of cyber actors, problems of attribution, limits of credibility and signaling mechanisms, and challenges with demonstrating cyber capabilities for retaliation, to name a few issues.[9] Moreover, nuclear deterrence models define outcomes in binary terms, where success is the complete absence of nuclear use. This makes little sense when applied to cyberspace where, in contrast to the non-employment of nuclear weapons since 1945, interactions between cyber powers have been characterized by routine use of cyber capabilities to hold an adversary's critical infrastructure at risk, conduct espionage campaigns at scale, disrupt the functioning of critical systems, and even deliver destructive effects against strategic assets. For instance,

---

[6] Barry Posen, *Inadvertent Escalation: Conventional War and Nuclear Risks* (Ithaca, NY: Cornell University Press, 1991); Robert Jervis, *The Illogic of Nuclear Strategy* (Ithaca, NY: Cornell University Press, 1984).

[7] See, for example Herman Kahn, *On Escalation: Metaphors and Scenarios* (Praeger, 1965); Smoke, *War: Controlling Escalation*; Bernard Brodie, *Escalation and the Nuclear Option* (Princeton, NJ: Princeton University Press, 1966).

[8] "Summary: Department of Defense Cyber Strategy, 2018," Department of Defense; "National Cyber Strategy of the United States of America," The White House, September 2018; "Final Report," U.S. Cyberspace Solarium Commission, March 2020; "Remarks by Secretary of Defense Lloyd J. Austin III at the Reagan National Defense Forum (as Delivered)," U.S. Department of Defense, December 4, 2021.

[9] See, for example Joseph S. Nye, "Deterrence and Dissuasion in Cyberspace," *International Security* 41, no. 3 (Winter 2016–2017): 44–71; Robert Jervis, "Some Thoughts on Deterrence in the Cyber Era," *Journal of Information Warfare* 15, no. 2 (Spring 2016): 66–73; Martin C. Libicki, *Cyberdeterrence and Cyberwar* (Santa Monica, CA: RAND Corporation, 2009); Michael P. Fischerkeller and Richard J. Harknett, "Deterrence is Not a Credible Strategy for Cyberspace," *Orbis* 61 no. 3 (2017): 381–393; Erica D. Borghard and Shawn W. Lonergan, "The Logic of Coercion in Cyberspace," *Security Studies* 26, no. 3 (2017): 452–481; Thomas Rid and Ben Buchanan, "Attributing Cyber Attacks," *Journal of Strategic Studies* 38, nos. 1–2 (2015): 4–37; Erica D. Borghard and Shawn W. Lonergan, "Deterrence by Denial in Cyberspace," *Journal of Strategic Studies* (August 2021): 1–36.

the 2020 Verizon Data Breach Investigative Report, one of the authoritative sources that tracks annual trends in private sector data breaches across a range of industries in the United States, identified 157,525 cyber incidents, including 32,002 security incidents, in 2020 alone.[10] This represents only one subset of cases out of the total universe of cyber incidents.

If cyber deterrence is elusive or problematic in cyberspace, and if deterrence is generally accepted as a key determinant of strategic stability, it would be reasonable to infer that strategic interactions between rivals in cyberspace should be characterized by endemic instability and persistent risks of escalation. Indeed, there is a large and vocal group of scholars and practitioners who contend just that—cyberspace, they assert, is ripe for escalation and, if escalation has not yet occurred, it is just around the corner.[11] For example, Jason Healey asserts that "cyber conflict" is likely to be more escalatory than other types of conflict. He further contends that the ways in which states typically enhance deterrence and, therefore, promote stability—such as through brandishing capabilities to signal resolve—are likely to have destabilizing, escalatory effects in cyberspace by prompting targets to overreact rather than be deterred.[12] Others warn of the escalation risks stemming from unintended collateral damage and heightened risks of contagion from cyber operations, exacerbated by the loose command and control that states often exert over the actors conducting offensive actions on their behalf.[13] Martin Libicki argues that, holding constant the severity of interests at stake, crisis management is likely to be more difficult in cyberspace than in conventional domains. Libicki also posits that inadvertent escalation is more likely in cyberspace due to differences in how parties to a crisis define critical thresholds; the involvement of third parties in cyber disputes and ensuing attribution difficulties; and because of heightened problems of command and control.[14] Roger Hurwitz warns of the risk of conflict and escalation in cyberspace

[10] "2020 Data Breach Investigations Report, Executive Summary," Verizon, p. 4.

[11] For example, see Brandon Valeriano, Benjamin Jensen, and Ryan C. Maness, *Cyber Strategy: The Evolving Character of Power and Coercion* (Oxford: Oxford University Press, 2018) for an important critique of the belief that cyberspace is escalatory.

[12] Jason Healey, "The Cartwright Conjecture: The Deterrent Value and Escalatory Risks of Fearsome Cyber Capabilities," in Herbert Lin and Amy Zegart, eds., *Bytes, Bombs, and Spies: The Strategic Dimensions of Offensive Cyber Operations* (Washington, DC: Brooking Institute Press, 2019), pp. 173–194. In a keynote address, Jason Healey has also claimed that conflict in cyberspace is "the most escalatory kind of conflict we have ever come across," Keynote Address, CyberTalks, New York City, September 8, 2016.

[13] Lawrence J. Cavaiola, David C. Gompert, and Martin Libicki, "Cyber House Rules: On War, Retaliation and Escalation," *Survival: Global Politics and Strategy*, 57, no. 1 (February–March 2015): 84–94.

[14] Martin C. Libicki, *Crisis and Escalation in Cyberspace* (Santa Monica, CA: RAND Corporation, 2012), pp 10, 93–97, 106–108, 114–119. In an earlier piece, Libicki also argues that the factors that distinguish the cyber domain from conventional ones makes the former more escalatory, such as the uncertainty surrounding the effects of cyberattacks; the asymmetric nature of the vulnerability in the domain, which could prompt escalation to conventional kinetic attacks; and the greater credibility of

as a result of cyber arms races and perceptions that offense has an advantage over defense in cyberspace.[15] Nadiya Kostyuk et al., while acknowledging that cyber attacks do not currently present existential threats, warn that in the future there could be a "large-scale, long-lasting attack on the food production or supply distribution network once manual systems are sufficiently scarce [which] could create devastating casualties comparable to a small-scale nuclear strike."[16] In a 2017 joint statement to Congress senior U.S. intelligence and military leaders noted that "adversaries equipped with [offensive cyber capabilities] could be prone to preemptive attack and rapid escalation in a future crisis, because both sides would have an incentive to strike first."[17] Clearly, the view that cyberspace holds a palpable potential for escalation is widespread.[18]

The Puzzle: Where Is Cyber Escalation?

This strongly held notion among experts that cyberspace is escalatory presents a striking empirical puzzle. Namely, if cyberspace is in fact an environment that gives rise to escalatory dynamics between rivals, why is there so little evidence of escalation? Hundreds—if not thousands—of cyber incidents have occurred between enduring rivals with longstanding histories of crisis escalation. But not a single incident has triggered dangerous spirals, let alone escalation to war. As Brandon Valeriano noted in testimony to the U.S. Congress in May 2017, "There is a proliferating universe of cyber security incidents, threat actors, and perspectives that portend escalating danger in the domain. Yet, we also witness few incidents that involve escalation and there is rather limited severity evident

retaliatory threats. See Martin C. Libicki, *Cyberdeterrence and Cyberwar* (Santa Monica, CA: RAND Corporation, 2009), pp. 69–74.

[15] Roger Hurwitz, "Keeping Cool: Steps for Avoiding Conflict and Escalation in Cyberspace," *Georgetown Journal of International Affairs*, International Engagement on Cyber III: State Building on a New Frontier, 2013–2014, p. 17.
[16] Nadiya Kostyuk, Scott Powell, and Matt Skach, "Determinants of the Cyber Escalation Ladder," *Cyber Defense Review* 3, no. 1 (2018): 128.
[17] "Joint Statement for the Record to the Senate Armed Services Committee, Foreign Cyber Threats to the United States, The Honorable James R. Clapper, Director of National Intelligence, The Honorable Marcel Lettre, Undersecretary of Defense for Intelligence, Admiral Michael S. Rogers, USN, Commander, U.S. Cyber Command, Director, National Security Agency," January 5, 2017.
[18] In another example, Farrell and Glaser argue that U.S. cyber doctrine should incorporate the development of norms and saliencies around cyber operations to shape how adversaries perceive intent. While not explicitly arguing that cyberspace is dangerously escalatory, they do argue that the absence of these types of saliences and focal points could be determinants of escalation. See Henry Farrell and Charles Glaser, "The Role of Effects, Saliencies and Norms in US Cyberwar Doctrine," *Journal of Cybersecurity* 3 (2017): 7–17.

in each cyber incident to mark this arena as a critical threat to international stability."[19]

Rather than dangerous escalatory spirals that threaten to spill over into kinetic conflict, even the most heated interactions between rivals in cyberspace are characterized by limited, tit-for-tat retaliations that are often separated by significant periods of time and that remain far below any conflict or armed attack threshold. Indeed, in a survey of cyber incidents and responses between 2000 and 2014, Brandon Valeriano et al. find that "rivals tend to respond only to lower-level [cyber] incidents and the response tends to check the intrusion as opposed to seek escalation dominance. The majority of cyber escalation episodes are at a low severity threshold and are nonescalatory."[20] Similarly, Sarah Kreps and Jacquelyn Schneider conduct an original experiment to test different logics of cyber escalation and find that cyber attacks "create a threshold that restrains the escalation of conflict."[21] Specifically, they find that Americans are less likely to support using kinetic force to respond to a cyber attack, even when the effects of the latter are comparable to other types of kinetic attacks.[22]

Even the most destructive cyber attack in history, NotPetya, launched by Russia in the spring of 2017 (reportedly using a leaked National Security Agency tool, EternalBlue), did not cause escalation. NotPetya wreaked $10 billion worth of damage across the globe, including to large multinational companies such as Maersk, Merck, and FedEx.[23] If cyber operations are likely to cause escalation, NotPetya would be a prime contender, not only because of the extent of the damage inflicted, but also because it was carried out by a longstanding adversary of the nations it affected, which included some of the most powerful states in cyberspace.

Yet, the response on the part of the countries affected by NotPetya was rather restrained. In February 2018—nearly a year after the attack, seven allied nations (the United States, United Kingdom, Denmark, Lithuania, Estonia, Canada, and Australia) issued official statements attributing the NotPetya cyber attack

---

[19] "The International Cyber Conflict Threat Landscape," Statement of Brandon Valeriano, PhD, Donald Bren Chair of Armed Politics, Marine Corps University, Reader in Digital Politics, Cardiff University, Adjunct Fellow of Cyber Security, Niskanen Center, Cyber Threats Facing America, Testimony before the United States Senate Committee on Homeland Security and Government Affairs, May 10, 2017. Also see Valeriano et al., *Cyber Strategy*, p. 66, where the authors note: "While cyber incidents are increasing [between 2000 and 2014], this increase appears to be directly associated with espionage and disruption campaigns, not the more malicious degradation activities that many fear."

[20] Ibid.

[21] Sarah Kreps and Jacquelyn Schneider, "Escalation Firebreaks in the Cyber, Conventional and Nuclear Domains: Moving beyond Effects-based Logics," *Journal of Cybersecurity* 5, no. 1 (2019): 8.

[22] Ibid., 8–9.

[23] "Statement from the Press Secretary," The White House, February 15, 2018, https://trumpwhitehouse.archives.gov/briefings-statements/statement-press-secretary-25/; Andy Greenberg, "The Untold Story of NotPetya, The Most Devastating Cyberattack in History," *Wired*, August 22, 2018.

to Russia.[24] Concurrent with the coordinated attribution, Rob Joyce, then the White House cybersecurity czar, threatened other ambiguous consequences in remarks delivered at the Munich Security Conference in Germany. Joyce warned that the United States would "work on the international stage to impose consequences. Russia has to understand that they have to behave responsibly on the international stage . . . So we're going to see levers the U.S. government can do to impose those costs."[25] However, it took nearly a year for allied governments to organize a public, diplomatic attribution effort. The only observable costs that were imposed on Russia were sanctions targeting a limited number of individuals associated with the NotPetya attack as well as with the 2016 U.S. Presidential election interference and cyber penetration of the U.S. power grid.[26] Of course, it's possible that there were additional, covert measures taken to impose costs on Russia. But if so, there was no demonstrable effect on any escalation dynamic with Russia.

The NotPetya case is just one example. Nevertheless, the overall absence of any meaningful instances of cyber escalation raises questions about the extent to which the cyber domain is truly escalatory, let alone more dangerous than other domains of warfare or strategic competition. In other words, there is a significant mismatch between the cyber escalation views held by many prominent experts and the available evidence. Three factors could account for this gap.

First, differences between theoretical expectations and empirical reality may stem from definitional issues—specifically, how those who assert that the cyber domain is inherently escalatory define what "escalation" means. As we discuss in detail later in this chapter, we conceptualize escalation as something that changes the nature of a strategic interaction between parties in a way that makes war more likely or, if conflict is already taking place, more severe. According to this definition, neither the sheer volume of cyber incidents in the international system nor evidence of any type of response to a cyber incident necessarily constitutes escalation.[27] In contrast, some may point to the observation of a high volume of cyber incidents or any form of tit-for-tat dynamic (irrespective of the relative level of

---

[24] "Russian Military 'Almost Certainly' Responsible for Destructive 2017 Cyber Attack," National Cyber Security Centre, GCHQ, February 15, 2018, https://www.ncsc.gov.uk/news/russian-milit ary-almost-certainly-responsible-destructive-2017-cyber-attack; "Blaming Russia for NotPetya was Coordinated Diplomatic Action," ZDNet, April 12, 2018. "UK and US blame Russia for 'Malicious' NotPetya Cyber-attack," BBC, February 15, 2018; "Alert (TA17-181A) Petya Ransomware," US-CERT, Original Release: July 1, 2017, Revised: February 15, 2018, https://www.us-cert.gov/ncas/ale rts/TA17-181A.

[25] Natasha Turak and Hadley Gamble, "US Will Impose Costs on Russia for Cyber 'Acts of Aggression,' White House Cybersecurity Czar Says," CNBC, February 16, 2018.

[26] "Treasury Sanctions Russian Cyber Actors for Interference with the 2016 U.S. Elections and Malicious Cyber-Attacks," U.S. Department of the Treasury, March 15, 2018, https://home.treasury. gov/news/press-releases/sm0312.

[27] This approach is also consistent with how Valeriano et al. address "tit-for-tat" responses in Cyber Strategy, p. 76.

cost and risk they may generate) as forms of escalation. However, the mere presence of behavior or activity per se is not sufficient evidence of escalation.

Alternatively, some may acknowledge that cyber escalation has not yet occurred, but it could be lurking around the next corner. This reasoning has some parallels to academic debates about the success of nuclear deterrence during the Cold War. Deterrence optimists opined that the absence of nuclear war between the United States and Soviet Union was due to the success of the strategy, while others have argued that the world simply got lucky.[28] However, unlike the Cold War, where neither superpower ultimately chose to unleash its nuclear arsenal on the other, the offensive employment of cyber capabilities is hardly unthinkable. States have developed and employed offensive cyber capabilities since the 1980s and their use is only becoming more prevalent.[29] The sheer number of cyber incidents that has occurred over the course of multiple decades raises questions about how likely it is that cyber escalation would take place in the future, given the multi-decade track record of cyber incidents not causing that outcome. That said, as part of our analysis in this book we explore plausible hypothetical escalation scenarios, with a focus on cyber operations that take place during conflict.

Finally, there may simply be a mismatch between the conventional wisdom about cyber escalation and the empirical reality because the conventional wisdom is wrong. This is the core contention of our book.

Our Argument

We develop a theory of cyber escalation that extends traditional arguments about escalation in the security studies literature, taking into account the unique attributes of cyber operations. Escalation, whether deliberate or inadvertent, is ultimately a political decision carried out by human beings working inside organizations—it does not take place through the sheer force of technology alone. And, critically, what counts as an escalatory action, irrespective of the capabilities that may be employed, is always in the eye of the beholder.[30] This

---

[28] Kenneth Waltz, "The Spread of Nuclear Weapons: More May Better," in *Adelphi Papers*, Number 171 (London: International Institute for Strategic Studies, 1981); Scott D. Sagan, "The Perils of Proliferation: Organization Theory, Deterrence Theory, and the Spread of Nulcear Weapons," *International Security* 18, no. 4 (Spring 1994): 66–107; Frank C. Zagare, "Rationality and Deterrence," *World Politics* 42, no. 2 (January 1990): 238–260; Graham Allison and Philip Zelikow, *Essence of Decision: Explaining the Cuban Missile Crisis*, 2nd ed (New York: Longman, 1999).

[29] See Jason Healey, ed., *A Fierce Domain: Conflict in Cyberspace, 1986 to 2012* (Vienna, VA: Cyber Conflict Studies Association, 2013).

[30] Perhaps the singular exception to this statement is nuclear weapons, which is a capability that, in itself, is so overwhelmingly dangerous that its use (or even the credible threat of use) breaches a clear threshold. In all other instances, an action is escalatory when the target perceives it to cross some line that qualitatively changes the nature of the interaction itself.

makes political, organizational, and psychological variables essential to analyses of the conditions under which escalation is likely to occur. That said, the technology itself—the opportunities it offers and the limitations it contains—defines the contours of the possible. A capability that, for instance, "enables a military force to fight with more speed, range, and lethality will enable that force to cross escalation thresholds faster."[31] Conversely, one that is limited in its effects, or is only usable under a narrow set of conditions, may dampen escalation risks. In this book, we focus on the technical aspects of cyber operations and the constraints and opportunities they provide to leaders, because these are a necessary foundation to exploring the political aspects of decision-making around their employment.

Our analysis of escalation dynamics rests on four features of cyber operations: secrecy and plausible deniability; requirements for planning and conducting offensive operations; limitations on cost generation; and the role of intelligence. While each of these, individually, may not be unique to cyberspace, in the aggregate there are few comparable military capabilities that contain all of these features. These aspects of cyber operations give rise to several implications for escalation. First, cyber operations contain inherent restrictions and limitations on their employment, reducing the potential for cyber operations to trigger escalation during international crises. Second, these same factors may make cyber operations advantageous for diffusing, rather than ratcheting up, crisis situations. Finally, despite these limitations, there is a small but important number of plausible scenarios in which cyber operations could *indirectly* increase escalation risks.[32] These scenarios focus on the dependence of non-cyber military capabilities—ranging from nuclear command and control to fighter jets—on digital infrastructure. Along this escalation pathway, while the direct effects of cyber operations are still minor and transitory, the secondary implications for kinetic capabilities—those military capabilities that can actually inflict a level of damage sufficient to cause escalation—could result in escalation. The likelihood of this is greater during an ongoing conflict where the perceived cyber threats to key military assets are far more salient. However, even in these more dangerous instances, certain features of cyber operations mitigate escalation risks when compared to equivalent non-cyber escalation pathways.

Therefore, in this book, we not only seek to interrogate long-held assumptions about escalation in cyberspace, we also seek to reframe the conversation away

---

[31] Forrest E. Morgan, Karl P. Mueller, Evan S. Medeiros, Kevin L. Pollpeter, and Roger Cliff, *Dangerous Thresholds: Managing Escalation in the 21st Century* (Santa Monica, CA: RAND Corporation, 2008), p. xvi.

[32] See, for example, James M. Acton, "Escalation through Entanglement: How the Vulnerability of Command-and-Control Systems Raises the Risks of Inadvertent Nuclear War," *International Security* 43, no. 1 (Summer 2018): 56–99.

from binary debates about whether or not escalation is likely, and we identify the conditions under which escalation—or de-escalation—may be more or less likely as a result of cyber operations. Moreover, we clarify the scope conditions under which different escalation scenarios might occur, in particular distinguishing between cyber operations as tools of statecraft or coercion between rivals during international crises, and cyber operations as part of a state's military strategy during wartime. We ground these scenarios in existing arguments in the security studies literature about escalation and signaling, during crises and war, and then explore how characteristics of cyber operations shape, complicate, or extend these arguments. In doing so, we hope to shed light not only on how scholars should think about escalation and stability in cyberspace but also on the implications for theories of escalation in general.

In sum, the contention that cyber operations can easily trigger escalatory spirals and, therefore, that relations between cyber rivals are inherently unstable, misses the many factors that point in the direction of stability and deliberation.

Key Definitions

Given that some of the disagreements among experts about cyber escalation could be attributed to definitional issues, and to set a common baseline for our analysis, below we clarify definitions for the central concepts and terms we use throughout this book.

Escalation

Escalation involves a meaningful increase in the nature or intensity of a conflict or crisis situation. It occurs when at least one party crosses what it, the adversary, or both parties perceive to be a critical threshold such that the nature of their strategic interaction has changed.[33] The latter point is key to understanding escalation because the mere observation of an increase in military action, for example, does not constitute escalation per se. Rather, escalation occurs "when at least one of the parties involved believes there has been a significant qualitative change in the conflict as a result of the new development."[34] Escalation, put simply, is a function of perception.

---

[33] For foundational academic work on escalation see Kahn, *On Escalation*; Smoke, *War: Controlling Escalation*; Posen, *Inadvertent Escalation*; Bernard Brodie, *Escalation and the Nuclear Option* (Princeton, NJ: Princeton University Press, 1966).

[34] Morgan et al., *Dangerous Thresholds*, p. 8.

A meaningful change in the nature of an interaction could occur when one party ratchets up in quantitative terms the amount of pain one party is inflicting on the other using the same capabilities (such as increasing the scale of bombardment in a specific area of operations); or qualitatively changing the nature of a strategic interaction through introducing a new type of capability (such as weapons of mass destruction); or expanding the scope of a conflict (such as expanding the theater of operations to target the adversary's allies or homeland).[35] One example of a qualitative change leading to escalation is what Bernard Brodie dubbed the "firebreak" theory—the idea that there is a "profound difference in kind as well as in degree between nuclear and non-nuclear weapons."[36] Whether similar firebreaks exist in the context of cross-domain cyber escalation, where there are meaningful differences between offensive cyber capabilities and conventional kinetic ones, is a matter of debate.[37]

Deliberate versus inadvertent escalation

Escalation could occur as a result of deliberate action, where a state intends for its behavior to escalate a situation, or it could take place through inadvertent pathways, where the escalatory effect is neither intended nor desired. The concept of deliberate escalation became appealing for U.S. policymakers in the context of the Flexible Response doctrine during the Kennedy Administration, when the United States sought "seemingly numerous *possibilities* for *controlled* escalation, in deliberate gradations through an extended range of violence."[38] In this approach, it was assumed that policymakers would be able to deliberately manipulate the level of violence, increasing or decreasing it in a controlled manner and force an adversary to capitulate.[39] From an academic perspective, Herman Kahn conceptualized this type of controlled, deliberate escalation in the nuclear age as taking the form of an "escalation ladder," which involved "a linear arrangement of roughly increasing levels of intensity of crisis."[40] According to Kahn's

---

[35] Increasing intensity is often termed "vertical" escalation, while increasing scope is termed "horizontal" escalation. See, for example, the discussion in Morgan et al., *Dangerous Thresholds*, p. 18. In a prominent article that systematically reviews potential triggers of cyber escalation, Herbert Lin similarly defines escalation as, "a change in the level of conflict (where level is defined in terms of scope, intensity, or both) from a lower (perhaps nonexistent) to a higher level." See Herbert Lin, "Escalation Dynamics and Conflict Termination in Cyberspace," *Strategic Studies Quarterly* 6, no. 3 (Fall 2012): 52.

[36] Brodie, *Escalation and the Nuclear Option*, p. 104.

[37] See, for example, Kreps and Schneider, "Escalation firebreaks," or Farrell and Glaser, "The Role of Effects, Saliencies and Norms in US Cyberwar Doctrine."

[38] Smoke, *War: Controlling Escalation*, p. 13.

[39] Ibid., p. 4. Smoke also acknowledges that this represented something of a hubris on the part of U.S. practitioners and strategists, who believed that "escalation processes in war can be restrained and halted and war kept limited, and . . . that escalation can be deliberately managed to manipulate the ongoing level of violence," p. 13.

[40] Kahn, *On Escalation*, 38.

depiction of deliberate escalation, states could intentionally move up or down the escalation ladder to win in a crisis.[41] Victory is achieved through maintaining "escalation dominance," in which one side has a clear superiority at every level of escalation and therefore can prevent a crisis from spiraling out of control and achieve a desired political objective.[42]

The viability of deliberate escalation rests on states actually being able to control the level of violence they employ against an adversary. Yet, even in the era of nuclear deterrence, the feasibility of controlled escalation and escalation dominance was a contested issue.[43] The contention that either superpower could escalate in a rational, linear, and controlled manner to get its way in a crisis was met by skeptics who feared that misperceptions or accidents could spark inadvertent nuclear war.[44] This apprehension gave rise to an extensive literature on the causes of inadvertent escalation, which occurs not as a result of deliberate action on the part of the escalating state but, rather, because the latter's "intentional actions are unintentionally escalatory, usually because they cross a threshold of intensity or scope in the conflict or confrontation that matters to the adversary but appears insignificant or is invisible to the party taking the action."[45] Inadvertent escalation could result from a number of factors, such as security dilemma dynamics, perceptions of the offensive-defense balance, perceived windows of vulnerability, or domestic politics—we explore these in subsequent chapters.[46]

How relevant are these escalation concepts, developed during the Cold War, for understanding escalation risks in the cyber age? Most scholars largely agree that notions of deliberate escalation up and down a hierarchical escalation ladder and the notion of escalation dominance are mostly unrealistic or fantastical—although some military organizations still hold onto the idea of achieving

[41] Kahn's concept of escalation is akin to Thomas Schelling's notion of a "competition in risk-taking" in which, in the context of a crisis, one side attempts to increase its effort to match the other's, potentially producing an escalation that could lead to nuclear war—although Schelling places greater emphasis on the bargaining advantages gleaned from manipulating the risk that things might spiral out of control. See Schelling, *Arms and Influence*, ch. 3. For a critique, see Robert Pape's work on airpower and coercion.

[42] Schelling, *Arms and Influence*, 23–24.

[43] According to Kahn and other theorists, the structural condition of the nuclear balance of terror—the devastation that would occur from the use of strategic nuclear weapons—was likely to "induce some degree of restraint and prudent behavior on each side." Kahn, *On Escalation*, p. 13. But also see, for instance, Albert Wohlstetter, "The Delicate Balance of Terror," in Philip Bobbit, Lawrence Freedman, and Gregory F. Treverton, eds., *US Nuclear Strategy: A Reader* (London: Palgrave Macmillan, 1989), p. 211. Also see Robert Jervis, *The Meaning of the Nuclear Revolution* (Ithaca: Cornell University Press, 1989).

[44] See, for example, Scott D. Sagan, *The Limits of Safety: Organizations, Accidents, and Nuclear Weapons* (Princeton, NJ: Princeton University Press, 1993; for the rational deterrence debate, see Robert Jervis, "Rational Deterrence: Theory and Evidence."

[45] Morgan et al., *Dangerous Thresholds*, p. 23.

[46] See Robert Jervis, "Cooperation Under the Security Dilemma," *World Politics* 30, no. 2 (January 1978): 167–214; Posen, *Inadvertent Escalation*; Sagan, *The Limits of Safety*; Graham T. Allison, *Essence of Decision: Explaining the Cuban Missile Crisis* (Boston: Little, Brown, 1971).

"superiority" in cyberspace.[47] Instead, debates about cyber escalation flourish in the context of theories of inadvertent escalation—the idea that an action taken in cyberspace could have unintended, negative effects that increase the risk of crises spilling over into conflict. We therefore home in on in this debate to explore how well existing arguments about inadvertent escalation extend to cyberspace.

Cyberspace

Despite its current association with geopolitics and strategy, the term cyberspace was invented by the science fiction author William Gibson in the 1980s. Gibson described cyberspace as, "a consensual hallucination . . . . A graphic representation of data abstracted from the banks of every computer in the human system."[48] In the contemporary age, cyberspace is defined by global, interconnected networks of information and communications technology infrastructure and the data that resides in and transits through them. According to the U.S. military, cyberspace is "the domain within the information environment that consists of the interdependent network of information technology (IT) infrastructures and resident data."[49] Cyberspace is comprised of physical infrastructure—such as computers, undersea fiberoptic cables that traverse oceans to transmit signals between land stations, physical routers and servers dispersed around the world, etc.; the data that is transmitted between networks in the form of zeroes and ones, and the protocols that determine that interaction; and the actors operating within this complex environment.[50]

---

[47] Most scholars agree that cyber coercion is highly problematic. See, for example, Borghard and Lonergan, "The Logic of Coercion;" Valeriano et al. *Cyber Strategy*; Brandon Valeriano and Benjamin Jensen, "The Myth of the Cyber Offense: The Case for Restraint," *CATO Institute*, January 15, 2019; Jacquelyn Schneider, "Cyber and Cross Domain Deterrence" in Erik Gartzke and Jon R. Lindsay, eds., *Cross-Domain Deterrence: Strategy in an Era of Complexity* (New York: Oxford University Press, 2019), pp. 95–120. Fischerkeller and Harknett argue that that escalation dominance is "not sustainable" in cyberspace, see Michael P. Fischerkeller and Richard J. Harknett, "Persistent Engagement, Agreed Competition, and Cyberspace Interaction Dynamics and Escalation," *Cyber Defense Review* (2019 Special Edition): 279. There are some exceptions to this, such as Lawrence J. Cavaiola, David C. Gompert, and Martin Libicki, "Cyber House Rules: On War, Retaliation, and Escalation," *Survival* 57, no. 1 (2015): 81–104. U.S. Cyber Command identifies achieving and maintaining superiority in cyberspace as a core objective, in "Achieve and Maintain Cyberspace Superiority: Command Vision for US Cyber Command," U.S. Cyber Command, 2018.

[48] William Gibson, *Necromancer* (New York: Berkley Publishing Group, 1984), p. 51.

[49] "Joint Publication 3–12: Cyberspace Operations," U.S. Department of Defense, June 8, 2018, p. I–1.

[50] For alternative views, seeMartin C. Libicki, "Cyberspace Is Not a Warfighting Domain," *I/S: A Journal of Law and Policy* 8, No. 2 (2012): 321–336. Chris Demchak and Peter Dombrowski postulate that cyberspace is not a domain but, rather, a "substrate." See Chris Demchak and Peter Dombrowski, "Cyber Westphalia: Asserting State Prerogatives in Cyberspace," *Georgetown Journal of International Affairs* (March 2014): 29.

Nearly every aspect of modern life depends on cyberspace—from the clearing and settling of financial transactions around the world to the operation of power grids to advanced military weapon systems. And the cyber systems on which economies and societies depend were developed to prioritize efficiency and reliability rather than security. This provides an opportunity for malicious actors to exploit the vulnerabilities inherent in them, with the potential for systemic effects given the role of cyberspace in everyday life.[51]

How might threat actors actually do this? Signals transmitted in cyberspace between computers—via physical mediums (e.g., cables) or non-physical ones (e.g., radio frequency)—are digital. Therefore, the direct effect produced by an actor harnessing these signals for strategic purposes will occur to the data itself.[52] This could mean a host of things, ranging from disrupting the functioning of a government website for a period of time, making it difficult for citizens to access government services, to digitally wiping out the bank accounts of millions of customers.

Digital means could also produce secondary effects in the physical world because so many physical systems rely on and are tightly coupled with digital infrastructure. This includes critical infrastructure, industrial control processes, and the internet of things (IoT) devices—physical devices as basic as a toaster oven or thermostat that connect to the internet. Therefore, actions in cyberspace could, for instance, open up a dam's flood gate, raise and lower bridges, or divert a train—if the operational technologies that govern these functions are directly or indirectly connected to the internet. Additionally, digital means could generate psychological effects, which is where the cyber and information environments intersect. For cyber-enabled information operations, for instance, the immediate impact of the operations occurs in the digital world, but the ultimate objective is to affect the perception and cognition of the target.[53]

Additionally, cyberspace was designed by humans and, therefore, could conceivably be changed by them—although it is important not to exaggerate cyberspace's malleability.[54] In the words of General (Ret.) Michael Hayden, cyberspace is distinct from other domains (land, air, sea, space) because the latter "are natural, created by God, and this one is the creation of man. Man can actually change this geography, and anything that happens there actually creates a

---

[51] See Herbert Lin, "Offensive Cyber Operations and the Use of Force," *Journal of National Security Law and Policy* 4 no. 63 (August 2010): 65 for a technical discussion of vulnerabilities in the context of cyber operations and p. 86 for a chart of different types of vulnerabilities. On low barriers to entry see, for example, "The Digital Arms Trade," *The Economist*, March 30, 2013.

[52] Lin, "Offensive Cyber Operations and the Use of Force," pp. 67–68.

[53] Herbert Lin and Jaclyn Kerr, "On Cyber-Enabled Information Warfare and Information Operations," in Paul Cornish, ed., *The Oxford Handbook of Cyber Security* (Oxford: Oxford University Press, 2021), pp. 251–272.

[54] Max Smeets, "A Matter of Time: On the Transitory Nature of Cyberweapons," *Journal of Strategic Studies* 41, nos. 1–2 (2018): 12.

change in someone's physical space."[55] Yet, how cyberspace may change can be difficult to anticipate.[56] Because cyberspace has some degree of mutability, it's possible that the properties and architecture of cyberspace that we take as given may evolve or be radically different at some point in the future.[57] For instance, the trend toward internet balkanization—the splintering of the global internet into smaller, more self-contained systems largely spurred by the initiatives of states to exercise control over information and data within what they define as their sovereign cyber borders—may fundamentally change the structure of cyberspace in ways that could have implications for escalation.[58]

Cyber operations

Cyber operations span offensive, defensive, and intelligence activities. Our analysis focuses on the conditions under which offensive cyber operations are likely to trigger escalation. There are disagreements in the literature about how to define offensive cyber operations, especially regarding the distinction between computer network exploitation—gaining access to a targeted network—and computer network attack. Some scholars, such as Hebert Lin, define offensive cyber operations as encompassing both "military operations and activities in cyberspace for cyber attack against and (or) exploitation of adversary information systems and networks."[59] In other words, he classifies cyber exploitation as a subset of offensive cyber operations.

In contrast, we categorize exploitation itself as distinct from an offensive cyber operation, which we define as a cyber operation that causes some type of effect against a network or system. Our definition is consistent with many military definitions of offensive cyber operations. For instance, the U.S. Joint Publication for Cyberspace Operations defines offensive cyber operations as "missions intended to project power in and through foreign cyberspace . . . to target adversary cyberspace functions or create first-order effects in cyberspace."[60] Similarly,

---

[55] Michael V. Hayden, "The Future of Things 'Cyber,'" *Strategic Studies Quarterly* (Spring 2011): 4.

[56] Lucas Kello, *The Virtual Weapon and International Order* (New Haven, CT: Yale University Press, 2017), p. 128. Yet, Kello also notes in the same section that there have been significant and, thus far, insurmountable hurdles to redesigning the architecture of the internet away from TCP/IP protocols to prioritize security over the transmission of data packets.

[57] This is also the case for structural theories of international politics. Even Kenneth Waltz left the door open for a potential change in the structure of the international system itself were anarchy to be eclipsed by world government. See Kenneth Waltz, *Theory of International Politics* (New York: McGraw-Hill, 1979).

[58] Eric Schmidt, Google's former CEO, warned in September 2018 that over the course of the next decade it is likely that the global internet will bifurcate into a Chinese internet and an American internet. See Lora Kolodny, "Former Google CEO Predicts the Internet Will Split in Two—and One Part Will Be Led by China," *CNBC*, September 20, 2018. On cyber sovereignty, see Demchak and Dombrowski, "Cyber Westphalia," pp. 29–38.

[59] Lin, "Offensive Cyber Operations and the Use of Force," p. 64.

[60] Chairman of the Joint Chiefs of Staff, "Joint Publication 3-12, Cyberspace Operations," June 8, 2018, pp. II–5.

the United Kingdom defines it as "activities that project force to create, deny, disrupt, degrade, and destroy effects in and through cyberspace. These operations may transcend the virtual domain into effects in the physical and cognitive domains."[61] The Dutch Defence Cyber Strategy also distinguishes between "offensive cyber operations" and "intelligence cyber operations."[62]

From a theoretical perspective, including both cyber exploitation and attack within a larger umbrella of offensive cyber operations is problematic because it conflates espionage activities with military operations. While exploitation is a necessary condition for attack, when the former is conducted by nation-states for the purposes of espionage it is widely considered to be "not illegal" according to customary international law and is tacitly accepted by states.[63] Excluding exploitation from a definition of offensive cyber operations also enables us to assess the extent to which exploitation in itself, as distinct from offensive operations, might trigger escalation. Therefore, we exclude exploitation operations that lack a follow-on attack from our definition of offensive cyber operations, which enables us to explore the implications of the links between espionage and military action in cyberspace.

Offensive cyber operations are comprised of multiple steps. Broadly speaking, operations planning begins with intelligence collection against a targeted system or network (such as the manufacturer of the system, its operating system, or its most recent firmware update). This could be conducted through cyber methods (such as vulnerability scanning tools) or other intelligence methods (such as signals or human intelligence) to identify a vulnerability that an attacker can exploit. Having identified a vulnerability to serve as the attack vector, an attacker must then conduct activities that enable it to gain access. Once gained, access could function as a foothold that enables further intelligence collection or could serve as a keyhole or beachhead through which an offensive cyber capability could be launched against the targeted system. Additionally, the attacker must acquire or develop tools that will be employed against the target (exploits); having gained access, implant that exploit in the target's network/system; and, at the desired time, execute the malicious code against the target via the access

---

[61] U.K. Ministry of Defence, "Cyber Primer: Second Edition," Development, Concepts and Doctrine Centre, July 2016, p. 54.

[62] For an informative review of relevant cyber organizations and their roles and responsibilities in the Netherlands, see Alexander Claver, "Governance of Cyber Warfare in the Netherlands: An Exploratory Investigation," *The International Journal of Intelligence, Security, and Public Affairs* 20, no. 2 (2018): 155–180. The distinction between offensive cyber and espionage came from the 2015 Dutch cyber strategy, which was a revision of the 2012 strategy. A 2018 Dutch cyber strategy has also been published by the Ministry of Defence.

[63] Gary Brown and Keira Poellet, "Customary International Law of Cyberspace," *Strategic Studies Quarterly* (Fall 2012): 133.

provided. There may be additional follow-on operations executed by the exploit depending on the ultimate objective, such as surreptitiously exfiltrating information from a network.

Moving up another level of analysis, multiple cyber operations can be aggregated to comprise an offensive cyber campaign.[64] Campaign plans typically involve synchronizing a range of different types of operations to achieve an overall strategic objective. The U.S. military, for instance, defines campaigns as "a series of related military operations aimed at accomplishing strategic and operational objectives within a given time and space."[65] The operations that comprise a campaign can be carried out with relative simultaneity or over a period of time with various phases unfolding at different points.[66]

Conventional Wisdom about Cyber Escalation

Much of the literature on cyber strategy and conflict, even that which does not directly address questions of escalation, depicts an environment that is unstable, prone to escalation, and even dangerous. Proponents of the idea that cyberspace is escalatory generally rely on four types of arguments: offense has an advantage in cyberspace and security dilemmas proliferate; military organizations, defined by cultures that prioritize offense over defense, have militarized cyberspace and made it more dangerous; the secretive nature of cyberspace coupled with the proliferation of actors makes it hard to discern responsibility for cyber attacks, creating opportunities for inadvertent or catalytic escalation; and there is an absence of shared understandings or agreed-upon thresholds. Some of these assumptions—especially the argument that offense has a decisive advantage—are highly problematic. Other assumptions—like the lack of shared understandings—are partially correct but miss important nuances that have implications for escalation. Finally, some assumptions may be accurate—such as the inclination of military organizations to prefer offensive strategies or the "gray zone" nature of cyber operations—but are nevertheless not sufficient to account for patterns of behavior between states in cyberspace.

---

[64] Michael Sulmeyer, "Campaign Planning with Cyber Operations," *Georgetown Journal of International Affairs,* December 28, 2017.

[65] "Joint Publication 5-0, Joint Planning," June 16, 2017, pp. II–21.

[66] Gregory Rattray and Jason Healey, "Proceedings of a Workshop on Deterring Cyber Attacks: Informing Strategies and Developing Options for U.S. Policy," The National Academies, 2010.

The most problematic assumption: offense dominates in cyberspace

The most prominent—and, we argue, most problematic argument—about cyberspace is that it favors offense over defense, which are also difficult to distinguish. These factors are said to create particularly dangerous security dilemmas—a concept developed by Robert Jervis to describe situations in which "an increase in one state's security decreases the security of others"—which can lead to dangerous arms racing dynamics and spirals between states.[67] In Chapters 2 and 3, we conduct a more fulsome critique of the validity of this assumption, but briefly review some core elements below.

Jervis identifies two factors that contribute to the security dilemma: offensive versus defensive advantage; and the distinguishability between offense and defense. Security dilemmas occur when technology favors the defense, but states cannot distinguish between offense and defense; when offense dominates and offense and defense are indistinguishable, the world is "doubly dangerous" and security dilemmas become even more heightened.[68]

What makes for an offensive or defensive advantage? While these concepts have been hotly debated in the security studies literature, in general, factors that increase the distance, cost, or vulnerability as an attacker advances to the defender contribute to a defensive advantage, while factors that decrease these contribute to an offensive one.[69] For instance, the presence of geographic features that pose impediments to conquest, such as large bodies of water, is typically associated with a decreased risk of interstate war. When conquest is perceived to be easy, the allure of war and striking first is increased and the risk of disputes quickly escalating to conflict is amplified.[70]

In terms of distinguishability, it can be challenging to discern intent because states often have poor or incomplete information, or they are beset by cognitive biases that distort their perceptions of the environment.[71] But when offense and

---

[67] Jervis, "Cooperation Under the Security Dilemma," pp. 167–214, 186.

[68] Ibid., pp. 178, 211–212.

[69] Ibid., pp. 194–196; Sean M. Lynn-Jones, "Offense-Defense Theory and Its Critics," *Security Studies* 4, no. 4 (1995): 660–691; Michael E. Brown, Owen R. Cote, Jr., Sean M. Lynn-Jones, and Steven E. Millers, eds., *Offense, Defense, and War* (Cambridge, MA: MIT Press, 2004).

[70] See, for example, Stephen Van Evera, "Offense, Defense, and the Causes of War," *International Security* 22, no. 4 (Spring 1998): 5–43. Although, interestingly, the reverse may be the case with respect to causes of civil war and insurgency. See James D. Fearon and David D. Laitin, "Ethnicity, Insurgency, and Civil War," *American Political Science Review* 97, no. 1 (February 2003): 75–90.

[71] Incomplete information plays a prominent role in the literature on the cause of war. See, for example, James D. Fearon, "Rationalist Explanations for War," *International Organization* 49, no. 3 (Summer 1995): 379–414; Robert Jervis, *Perception and Misperception in International Politics* (Princeton, NJ: Princeton University Press, 1975), pp. 58–116. Also see Robert Jervis, "Signaling and Perception: Drawing Inferences and Projecting Images," in Kristen Renwick Monroe, ed., *Political Psychology* (Mahwah, NJ: Lawrence Erlbaum Associates, 2002), pp. 293–312. The focus of this

defense are distinguishable, states can more easily signal their "types" to others; status-quo states will arm themselves with defensive capabilities, while aggressive states will do the opposite.[72] Distinguishability also allows status-quo states to devise arms control agreements to limit offensive capabilities.[73] Therefore, if cyberspace is an environment where offense dominates and states fail to distinguish between offense and defense, then it should follow that "[a]rms races are likely. Incentives to strike first will turn crises into wars. Decisive victories and conquests will be common."[74]

The technology of cyberspace is often described in terms that suggest an offensive advantage, an argument we interrogate in much greater depth in subsequent chapters. Here, we briefly discuss the relationship between the geography of cyberspace and offensive advantage. Some experts argue that cyberspace's geography makes escalation more likely.[75] For instance, in contrast to physical boundaries between states, cyberspace's global and interdependent infrastructure means there are no boundaries or buffers between actors. Instead, everyone essentially shares a common, virtual border.[76] Ben Buchanan, for example, claims that "geography is minimally present in cyber operations . . . . The sort of natural barriers that normally aid defensive missions in physical space do not have exact parallels. Furthermore, all states virtually border one another."[77] Similarly, Chris Inglis describes cyberspace as a "systems of systems . . . that is largely devoid of physical boundaries or buffer zones that would afford some measure of time to detect and interdict oncoming threats to assets stored in or dependent on cyberspace."[78] The geography of cyberspace, therefore, is said to dramatically compress the time necessary to launch an attack and create heightened incentives to strike first.

However, there are reasons to be skeptical of these arguments. In reality, cyberspace is characterized by both physical and virtual geographic barriers. While the global internet is the most interconnected component of cyberspace, the internet is only one aspect of cyberspace. Many systems that support critical national infrastructure, such as nuclear power plants, are typically self-contained.

---

section, however, is on structural causes of the security dilemma and spirals, rather than individual psychology or cognitive biases.

[72] Jervis, "Cooperation Under the Security Dilemma," pp. 199–200.
[73] Ibid., p. 201.
[74] Ibid., p. 212.
[75] William J. Lynn, "Defending a New Domain: The Pentagon's Cyberstrategy," *Foreign Affairs* 89, no. 5 (2010): 97–108.
[76] Jack Goldsmith and Tim Wu, *Who Controls the Internet? Illusions of a Borderless World* (Oxford: Oxford University Press, 2016).
[77] Ben Buchanan, *The Cybersecurity Dilemma: Hacking, Trust, and Fear Between Nations* (Oxford: Oxford University Press, 2016), p 106.
[78] Chris Inglis, "Illuminating a New Domain," in *Bytes, Bombs, and Spies*, p. 20.

Moreover, even the internet relies on physical infrastructure, such as transoce-anic cables that connect to land-based stations erected in the sovereign territory of states or land-based cables that traverse sovereign borders, and these are in-herently tied to geography and territory.[79] The fact that cyberspace's physical and digital infrastructure does not perfectly map onto sovereign territorial borders has raised important questions about the definition of cyber sovereignty and therefore what constitutes a violation of it.[80] For instance, if one state gains access to another state's networks for the purposes of launching an offensive cyber op-eration against a third party, would the very fact of gaining access be considered a violation of sovereignty?

Regardless, states strive to exert sovereign control over their "borders" in cy-berspace.[81] Governments use the physical elements of cyber infrastructure to enforce digital borders through limiting, controlling, and monitoring the in-gress and egress of data at gateways and internet exchange points. Governments can also use international law and institutions to create and enforce rules and regulations concerning the use of cyberspace within and external to sovereign territorial borders, with varying degrees of success.[82] Therefore, the notion that cyberspace lacks any meaningful geography does not accurately reflect the nuances associated with how physical, digital, and governance worlds interact in cyberspace.

In addition to cyberspace favoring the attacker, many experts assert that it is even more difficult to distinguish between offense and defense in cyberspace

[79] See https://www.submarinecablemap.com/ for a map of global undersea cables that includes the physical location of landing points and gateways.

[80] See, for instance, the debate between Gary Corn, "Tallinn Manual 2.0—Advancing the Conversation," *Just Security*, February 15, 2017; and Michael Schmitt, "Tallinn Manual 2.0 on the International Law of Cyber Operations: What It Is and Isn't," *Just Security*, February 2, 2017. Also see Michael N. Schmitt and Liis Vihul, "Respect for Sovereignty in Cyberspace," *Texas Law Review* 95, no. 7 (2017), https://texaslawreview.org/respect-sovereignty-cyberspace/; Eric Talbot Jensen, "Cyber Sovereignty: The Way Ahead," *Texas International Law Journal* 50, no. 2 (2015); Michael Schmitt, "The Law of Cyber Warfare: Quo Vadis?" *Stanford Law and Policy Review* 25, no. 2 (2014); Michael N. Schmitt, ed., *Tallinn Manual on the International Law Applicable to Cyber Warfare* (Cambridge: Cambridge University Press, 2013); Michael N. Schmitt, ed., *Tallinn Manual 2.0 on the International Law Applicable to Cyber Operations*, 2nd ed. (Cambridge: Cambridge University Press, 2017).

[81] Demchak and Dombrowski, "Cyber Westphalia."

[82] Erica D. Borghard and Shawn W. Lonergan, "Confidence Building Measures for the Cyber Domain," *Strategic Studies Quarterly* (Fall 2018); James D. Fielder, "The Internet and Dissent in Authoritarian States," in Panayotis A. Yannakogeorgos and Adam B. Lowther, eds., *Conflict and Cooperation in Cyberspace: The Challenge to National Security* (Boca Raton, FL: Taylor and Francis, 2014), pp. 161–194; Daniel W. Drezner, "The Global Governance of the Internet: Bringing the State Back In," *Political Science Quarterly* 119, no. 3 (Fall 2004): 477–498; Stephen K. Gourley, "Cyber Sovereignty," in *Conflict and Cooperation in Cyberspace*, pp. 277–290; Dana Polatin-Reuben, and Joss Wright, "An Internet with Brics Characteristics: Data Sovereignty and the Balkanisation of the Internet." Paper presented at the 4th USENIX Workshop on Free and Open Communications on the Internet, San Diego, CA, August 18, 2014.

than in other domains.[83] In 2017 testimony to the House Armed Services Committee, Jason Healey, referencing Jervis's security dilemma, contends that "[c]yberspace may not just be 'doubly dangerous' but perhaps 'quintuply dangerous' and ripe for escalation and miscalculation."[84] These experts point to a litany of purported attributes of cyberspace that are said to complicate distinguishing between offense and defense. For instance, the role of secrecy in cyberspace can make it difficult to observe how states are arming themselves and complicate advance warning of an impending attack.[85] Moreover, problems of attribution mean that a targeted state may face significant barriers to identifying the adversary who committed an attack; and, even if attribution is possible, the true intentions of an attacking state may be difficult to discern.[86] In a similar argument, Ben Buchanan claims that network intrusions conducted for entirely defensive purposes can unexpectedly become threatening based on changes in a state's intentions.[87]

Others focus on the skills required for cyber operations and the implications for distinguishability. Rebecca Slayton points out that, beyond offensive versus defensive capabilities or technologies, skill is a crucial determinant of operational success in highly technical environments. Slayton asserts the overall skill set that supports offense and defense is largely congruent and, therefore, "[o]ffensive and defensive skills can be hard to distinguish."[88] For example, the skills needed to conduct penetration testing (often abbreviated as "pen testing"), which is a common defensive cybersecurity measure that involves approved efforts to test the security and vulnerability of a network or system by simulating an offensive actor, could also be used for an attack. As a result, practices that make defenders more adept at defense, in theory, also augment their offensive skills.

However, the contention that all, or even most, offensive and defensive measures or postures are difficult to distinguish in cyberspace is misguided. Most defensive measures are clearly identifiable as such. Libicki notes numerous examples of obviously defensive measures: "diligent patch management and

[83] See discussion in Keir Lieber, "The Offense-Defense Balance and Cyber Warfare," in Emily Goldman and John Arquilla, eds., *Cyber Analogies* (Monterey, CA: Naval Postgraduate School, 2014), pp. 100–103.

[84] Testimony of Jason Healey, Columbia University's School of International and Public Affairs, Saltzman Institute of War and Peace Studies, Before the United States House of Representatives Committee on Armed Services, Hearing on "Cyber Warfare in the 21st Century: Threats, Challenges, and Opportunities," March 1, 2017, p. 77.

[85] Erica D. Borghard and Shawn W. Lonergan, "Why Are There No Cyber Arms Control Agreements," *Net Politics*, January 16, 2018.

[86] Erik Gartzke and Jon R. Lindsay, "Weaving Tangled Webs: Offense, Defense, and Deception in Cyberspace," *Security Studies* 24, no. 2 (2015): 316–348; Borghard and Lonergan, "The Logic of Coercion in Cyberspace."

[87] Ben Buchanan, *The Cybersecurity Dilemma*, p. 113.

[88] Rebecca Slayton, "What is the Cyber Offense Defense Balance? Conception, Causes, and Assessment," *International Security* 41, no. 3 (2016): 86.

least privilege, multi-factor authentication, and intrusion detection systems." He emphasizes that these, "cannot be used to break into systems, in large part, because such actions take place within the computer networks being defended (aka *blue space*)."[89] Other examples of defensive measures that are clearly ascertainable include safeguarding the supply chain, air gapping (physically isolating networks and systems at a facility from the internet), facility physical security measures, training and personnel management, managing third party access (such as screening and limiting vendor and contractor access to networks), or controlling points of access of internal networks to the internet, to name a few.

Of course, some cybersecurity measures that are conducted for defensive purposes blur the distinction between offense and defense.[90] These include "active defense" measures that are typically conducted or initiated within the defender's networks (even if they may result in or trigger effects outside of them in some instances), such as employing beacons, honeypots, logic bombs, emulating networks, and other deceptive measures; as well as activities associated with "hacking back" in which defenders take actions outside of their own networks in response to identified attacker behavior to retrieve, corrupt, or degrade absconded data.[91] These are the types of defensive measures that are more difficult to distinguish from offensive ones.

Therefore, when scholars call attention to the "distinguishability" problem in cyberspace, what they are actually referring to is the difficulty states confront in discerning the intent behind a recognized adversary cyber *intrusion*. The indistinguishability in cyberspace is between espionage and military action, not between offense and defense—which poses a different challenge than that envisioned by the original architects of the security dilemma. Specifically, because both espionage and offensive cyber operations require the same initial steps—exploiting a vulnerability in a target's network or system to gain access to it—it is difficult to differentiate between cyber intrusions conducted for espionage (to exfiltrate data) and those that are laying the groundwork for an impending attack.[92] Moreover, even intelligence operations are not irrefutably defensive; they could support information requirements needed to target a network or specific systems connected to it.[93] Furthermore, some efforts to establish access could create escalation hazards.[94]

[89] Martin C. Libicki, "Is There a Cybersecurity Dilemma," *The Cyber Defense Review* 1, no. 1 (Spring 2016): 134.

[90] Buchanan, *The Cybersecurity Dilemma*, pp. 58–59.

[91] "Into the Gray Zone: The Private Sector and Active Defense against Cyber Threats," Center for Cyber and Homeland Security, George Washington University, October 2016; Wyatt Hoffman and Ariel (Eli) Levite, "Private Sector Cyber Defense: Can Active Measures Help Stabilize Cyberspace?" Carnegie Endowment for International Peace, June 14, 2017.

[92] Lin, "Offensive Cyber Operations and the Use of Force," p. 64.

[93] Buchanan, *The Cybersecurity Dilemma*, pp. 72–73.

[94] Austin Long, "A Cyber SIOP? Operational Considerations for Strategic Offensive Cyber Planning," in *Bytes, Bombs, and Spies*, p. 111.

There are numerous examples of this type of indistinguishability. For instance, in March 2018 the U.S. Department of Homeland Security released an alert indicating Russia had gained access to industrial control systems in multiple critical infrastructure sectors, including energy, nuclear, commercial, water, aviation, and critical manufacturing.[95] But it was not immediately apparent what Russia's objectives were—preparing for a forthcoming disruptive or destructive cyber attack against U.S. critical infrastructure, conducting espionage, or something else.[96] In theory, this type of indistinguishability could lead to inadvertent escalation if the United States mistook routine Russian intelligence collection activities as preparation for war, prompting the United States to launch a disproportionate response. Yet, it did not result in escalatory retaliation. In another example, when the United States discovered in December 2020 that Russia had gained access to the networks of dozens of government agencies and private companies through compromising SolarWinds, a software company that was a critical node in the cybersecurity supply chain, the government responded by publicly attributing the breach to Russia and imposing additional sanctions.[97] In turn, the Russian government denied its involvement in the SolarWinds breach, and no escalation took place.[98] The fact that it is indeed difficult to differentiate between espionage in cyberspace, but states have largely defaulted to nonescalatory responses to uncovered cyber intrusions, suggests analysts should be skeptical about distinguishability as a cause of escalation.

Military organizations and the cult of the cyber offense

Beyond the logic of the security dilemma, some scholars argue that cyber escalation is likely because of the growing role of military organizations. This draws on an extensive body of literature on the relationship between military organization, culture, and escalation.[99] Academic research has associated the heightened proclivity of military organizations to favor offensive strategies with the causes

[95] "Alert (TA18-074A): Russian Government Cyber Activity Targeting Energy and Other Critical Infrastructure Sectors," Cyber and Infrastructure Security Agency, Department of Homeland Security, March 15, 2018.

[96] Erica D. Borghard, "The 'Known Unknowns' of Russian Cyber Signaling," Net Politics, April 2, 2018.

[97] "FACT SHEET: Imposing Costs for Harmful Foreign Activities by the Russian Government," The White House, April 15, 2021.

[98] "'Flattered' Russia Spy Chief Denies SolarWinds Attack—BBC," Reuters, May 18, 2021.

[99] Jack Snyder, "Civil-Military Relations and the Cult of the Offensive, 1914 and 1984," International Security 9, no. 1 (Summer 1984): 108–146; Barry Posen, The Sources of Military Doctrine: France, Britain, and Germany between the World Wars (Ithaca, NY: Cornell University Press, 1986); Elizabeth Kier, Imagining War: French and British Military Doctrine between the Wars (Princeton, NJ: Princeton University Press, 1997); Scott D. Sagan, The Limits of Safety (Princeton, NJ: Princeton University, 1993).

of World War I.[100] Extending these ideas to cyberspace, some scholars claim that military organizations that operate in cyberspace also have an innate preference for the offense, and that cyberspace is becoming increasingly dominated by offensively inclined military organizations as more states pursue offensive programs.[101] Brandon Valeriano and Benjamin Jensen posit, for instance, that recent shifts in the U.S. strategic posture in cyberspace, particularly the "defend forward" concept that entails a more proactive approach to adversaries, "risks compounding common pathologies associated with strategic assessments and planning [such as] a cult of the offensive and the desire for officers to ensure their autonomy and resources."[102] Similarly, Healey decries a cyber "cult of the offense" in the United States dating back to the early days of cyber warfare in the 1990s.[103]

The proclivity of military organizations to pursue offensive strategies in cyberspace is not limited to the United States. For example, Chinese cyber doctrine reflects similar tendencies to prefer to strike first to secure an advantage in cyber warfare. As Jon Lindsay notes, "Chinese writers argue that a relatively weaker People's Liberation Army (PLA) can achieve information superiority against a stronger military only as long as it is able to launch paralyzing strikes at the beginning of a conflict."[104] Likewise, Russian General Valery Gerimasov, chief of the General Staff of Russia's armed forces, in a now-famous 2013 speech translated by Mark Galeotti and dubbed the Gerimasov Doctrine, described how new technologies of warfare (particularly in the information sphere) favor speed and agility and blur the boundaries between states of war and peace: "Military actions are becoming more dynamic, active, and fruitful. Tactical and operational pauses that the enemy could exploit are disappearing. New information technologies have enabled significant reductions in the spatial, temporal, and informational gaps between forces and control organs."[105]

Furthermore, civil-military relationships in cyberspace can exacerbate the tendency of military organizations to prefer offensive approaches. As Barry Posen notes in the context of conventional escalation to nuclear war, some civil-military configurations (such as divides between civilian leaders and military planners)

---

[100] Stephen Van Evera, "The Cult of the Offensive and the Origins of the First World War," *International Security* 9, no. 1 (Summer 1984): 58–107.

[101] Timothy J. Junio, "How Probable is Cyber War? Bringing IR Theory Back in to the Cyber Conflict Debate," *Journal of Strategic Studies* 36, no. 1 (2013): 130–131; Max Smeets, "NATO Members' Organizational Path toward Conducting Offensive Cyber Operations: A Framework for Analysis." 11th International Conference on Cyber Conflict, 2019.

[102] Valeriano and Jensen, "The Myth of the Cyber Offense," p. 8.

[103] Jason Healey, "Obama's Cyberwarfare Strategy Will Backfire," *U.S. News*, March 8, 2013.

[104] Jon R. Lindsay, "The Impact of China on Cybersecurity: Fiction and Friction," *International Security* 39, no. 3 (2017): 31.

[105] Mark Galeotti, "The 'Gerimasov Doctrine' and Russian Non-Linear War," https://inmoscows shadows.wordpress.com/2014/07/06/the-gerasimov-doctrine-and-russian-non-linear-war/.

could heighten the risk of inadvertent escalation when military planners possess significantly greater knowledge than civilians and closely hold war plans
to themselves and away from civilian leaders. This could also occur if civilian
leaders perceive some types of weapons (especially highly technical ones) as "ex-
otic," making it difficult for them to foresee the consequences of their use and
more likely to take actions that risk escalation.[106] In the cyber domain, lack of
expertise among civilian leaders about the nature of cyber warfare and an aversion to understanding what is perceived to be a highly technical field may make
it difficult for civilian policymakers to understand and appreciate the escalatory
risks of war plans, potentially empowering the military and playing into the cult
of the offensive logic. In one example of this, a Japanese cybersecurity minister
admitted in November 2018 that he does not use computers.[107] Moreover, for
highly technical environments, there may also be variation within military organizations with respect to cyber skill level and competence, resulting in a small,
elite cadre of cyber warriors to whom both civilian and military leadership delegate significant autonomy and decision-making authority, further enhancing the
risk of inadvertent escalation.[108]

The idea that military cyber organizations prefer offensive strategies holds inherent plausibility and is consistent with evidence that more states are building
organizational capacity for their militaries to conduct offensive cyber operations. For example, since 2008 within the North Atlantic Treaty Organization
(NATO), a growing number of member states have developed organizations and
strategies for military cyber operations.[109] In tandem, states have grown more
public about conducting offensive cyber operations. For instance, U.S. cyber
policy underwent a significant shift in 2018 when the Department of Defense
and Cyber Command issued updated strategy and policy documents that articulated a more expansive role for the military in conducting offensive cyber operations below the level of armed conflict outside of U.S.-controlled cyberspace.
And the United States has reportedly conducted a number of offensive cyber operations, such as dropping "cyber bombs" on the Islamic State in 2016 to disrupt
their communications and command and control; the 2018 cyber operation to

[106] Posen, *Inadvertent Escalation*, pp. 13–14.

[107] Justin McCurry, "System Error: Japan Cybersecurity Minister Admits He Has Never Used a
Computer," *The Guardian*, November 14, 2018.

[108] Herbert S. Lin, "Reflections on the New Department of Defense Cyber Strategy: What It Says,
What It Doesn't Say," *Georgetown Journal of International Affairs* 17, no. 3 (Fall/Winter 2016): 5–13.
Also see Valeriano and Jensen, "The Myth of the Cyber Offense." But see Erica D. Borghard and Shawn
W. Lonergan, "What Do the Trump Administration's Changes to PPD-20 Mean for U.S. Offensive
Cyber Operations?" *Net Politics*, September 10, 2018. For variation across services in approaches
to cyber capabilities, see Sarah P. White, "Subcultural Influence on Military Innovation: The
Development of U.S. Military Cyber Doctrine," PhD diss., Harvard University, Graduate School of
Arts & Sciences, 2019.

[109] Smeets, "NATO Members' Organizational Path," pp. 3, 7.

disrupt the Russian-linked Internet Research Agency's ability to interfere in the midterm elections; and disrupting ransomware groups targeting U.S. critical infrastructure in 2021.[110] The U.S. military has also worked bilaterally with other NATO allies, such as Estonia[111] and Montenegro,[112] to conduct "hunt forward" cyber operations on allied and partner networks to uncover and disrupt malicious cyber activity.

But the United States is not alone among NATO allies in leaning into more offensive approaches to cyber strategy. In 2020, the United Kingdom announced a significant investment in its National Cyber Force, its organizational arm for offensive cyber operations.[113] Moreover, UK leaders have become increasingly public in discussing Britain's role in offensive cyber operations, such as the recent announcement by Government Communications Headquarters (GCQH) that it was working with the United States to "impose consequences" in cyberspace to disrupt adversary operations.[114] The United Kingdom's recently released National Cyber Strategy 2022 points to the government's "responsible use of offensive cyber capabilities" and highlights that it has "significantly invested in our offensive cyber capabilities."[115] Other NATO members, such as the Netherlands, have also publicly alluded to conducting offensive cyber operations.[116]

These patterns only underscore the puzzle motivating this book: even with increasing assertiveness of military organizations in cyberspace, there has not been a commensurate increase in escalation. This suggests that cult of the offensive arguments are not sufficient to account for escalation dynamics in cyberspace.

The cyber "gray zone": secrecy, attribution, and false flags

A third set of arguments about cyber escalation focus on the "gray zone" attributes of cyberspace—the role of non-state actors, plausible deniability, and operations

---

[110] Erica D. Borghard, "What a U.S. Operation against Russian Trolls Predicts about Escalation in Cyberspace," *War on the Rocks*, March 22, 2019; David E. Sanger, "U.S. Cyberattacks Target ISIS in a New Line of Combat," *The New York Times*, April 24, 2016; Sean Lyngaas, "US Military's Hacking Unit Publicly Acknowledges Taking Offensive Action to Disrupt Ransomware Operations," *CNN.com*, December 5, 2021.

[111] "Hunt forward Estonia: Estonia, US Strengthen Partnership in Cyber Domain with Joint Operation," U.S. Cyber Command, December 3, 2020.

[112] Julian Barnes, "U.S. Cyber Command Expands Operations to Hunt Hackers from Russia, Iran and China," *The New York Times*, November 2, 2020.

[113] Joe Devanny and Tim Stevens, "What Will Britain's New Cyber Force Actually Do?" *War on the Rocks*, May 26, 2021.

[114] "UK and US Join Forces to Strike Back in Cyber-space," *BBC.com*, November 18, 2021.

[115] "National Cyber Strategy 2022," United Kingdom, December 15, 2021.

[116] Max Smeets, "The Netherlands Just Revealed its Cybercapacity. So What Does That Mean?" *The Washington Post*, February 8, 2018.

short of war.[117] While there is no unanimous definition, gray zone conflicts typically occur below the level of armed conflict. Furthermore, operations in the gray zone tend to leverage ambiguity, plausible deniability, and proxy actors as a means of reducing the likelihood that they cross that threshold into outright conflict.[118] A paradigmatic example of gray zone conflict is Russia's combined use of "little green men"—groups affiliated with the Russian government but not formally incorporated into the military's command and control—offensive cyber capabilities, and disinformation operations as part of its annexation of Crimea in 2014.[119]

While actors who maneuver in the gray zone typically seek to contain escalation, some scholars assert that the nature of these operations nevertheless risks provoking escalation. This could manifest in cyberspace in a variety of ways. For example, third parties could provoke conflict between rivals through "false flag" cyber operations to take advantage of secrecy and ambiguous attribution, a concept Herbert Lin terms "catalytic escalation."[120] More generally, attribution difficulties could lead to miscalculations and misperceptions, prompting states to inadvertently retaliate along escalatory pathways in response to cyber attacks.[121] Attribution issues may also undermine deterrence and, by extension, enhance instability through "reducing an assailant's expectation of unacceptable penalties."[122]

Relatedly, the proliferation of proxy groups in cyberspace—actors who conduct plausibly deniable cyber operations on behalf of state patrons—is also said to contribute to escalation dynamics.[123] States find cyber proxies appealing because they provide technical expertise, can augment indigenous state capabilities, and offer political cover for states. This has become increasingly important as the technical ability to assign attribution improves.[124] When proxy

---

[117] Michael J. Mazarr, *Mastering the Gray Zone: Understanding a Changing Era of Conflict* (Carlisle, PA: U.S. Army War College, 2014), p. 59. Also see Francis G. Hoffman, "The Contemporary Spectrum of Conflict: Protracted, Gray Zone, Ambiguous, and Hybrid Modes of War," The Heritage Foundation, Index of Military Strength, 2016, p. 30; Joseph L. Votel, Charles T. Cleveland, Charles T. Connett, and Will Irwin, "Unconventional Warfare in the Gray Zone," *Joint Force Quarterly* 80 (2016): 101–109.

[118] For an excellent discussion of the nature of gray zone conflict, see Hal Brands, "Paradoxes of the Gray Zone," *Foreign Policy Research Institute* (February 2016): 1–6.

[119] Alexander Lanoszka, "Russian Hybrid Warfare and Extended Deterrence in Eastern Europe," *International Affairs* 92, no. 1 (2016): 175–195.

[120] Lin, "Escalation Dynamics and Conflict Termination in Cyberspace," pp. 53–55. Also see Charles L. Glaser, "Deterrence of Cyber Attacks and U.S. National Security," The George Washington University Cyber Security Policy and Research Institute, June 1, 2011, p. 4.

[121] Cavaiola et al., "Cyber House Rules," p. 89.

[122] Lucas Kello, "The Meaning of the Cyber Revolution: Perils to Theory and Statecraft," *International Security* 38, no. 2 (2013): 33.

[123] See Erica D. Borghard and Shawn W. Lonergan, "Can States Calculate the Risks of Using Cyber Proxies?" *Orbis* 60, no. 3 (2016): 395–416.

[124] On the distinction between technical and political attribution, see Lin, "Escalation Dynamics," pp. 49–50.

actors are inserted into a crisis the probability increases that they may intentionally (if proxy actors go rogue) or inadvertently (if command, control, and communications become attenuated during an operation) exceed their mandate and escalate a crisis beyond what is intended.[125] For instance, Patrick Allen and Chris Demchak posit that patriotic hackers—citizens who engage in cyber attacks against perceived enemies of the state for nationalistic motivations—can escalate crisis situations because their motivations may diverge from those of the government.[126]

In addition to delegating authority to conduct cyber operations to other political actors, authority could be delegated in a technical sense to computers as a form of automaticity. This is another way that command and control could be removed from a decision maker, creating an additional source of potential escalation. For example, when Estonia came under a sweeping cyber attack in 2007 following its removal of a Soviet war monument, over 128 botnet control nodes were registered.[127] This means that the perpetrator of the attack, Russia, had delegated authority to proxy actors in a technical fashion such that the Russian government absconded control over the botnet's actions. There are other technical methods to create automatic cyber responses, such as leveraging artificial intelligence to develop capabilities for automatic cyber counterattacks. For example, the Defense Advanced Research Projects Agency's 2015 Cyber Grand Challenge demonstrated that super computers can be used to find vulnerabilities and attack another computer while they are themselves under attack.[128] Advancements in artificial intelligence and machine learning are likely to make automaticity even more common. And some types of malware contain inherent automaticity, such as worms that self-replicate and propagate while inside an adversary's network.

Despite the presence of actors with delegated operational authorities, whether technical or political, operating in an ambiguous and secret environment, evidence of escalation is lacking. This too suggests that arguments focused on the "gray zone" and cyber proxies fall short in accounting for strategic interactions between states in cyberspace.

---

[125] Kello, "Cyber Revolution," p. 36.

[126] Patrick D. Allen and Chris C. Demchak, "The Palestinian-Israeli: CYBERWAR," *Military Review* 83, no. 2 (March/April 2003). Also see Lin, "Escalation Dynamics," pp. 59–61. For further discussion of cyber proxies, see Borghard and Lonergan, "Can States Calculate the Risks of Using Cyber Proxies?" and Tim Maurer, *Cyber Mercenaries: The State, Hackers, and Power* (Cambridge, UK: Cambridge University Press, 2018) .

[127] Andreas Schmidt, "The Estonian Cyberattacks," in Jason Healey, ed., *A Fierce Domain: Conflict in Cyberspace, 1986 to 2012* (Vienna, VA: Cyber Conflict Studies Association, 2013), p. 182.

[128] Kelsey Atherton, "DARPA's Cyber Grand Challenge Ends in Triumph," *Popular Science*, August 5, 2015, http://www.popsci.com/machines-win-darpas-cyber-grand-challenge; Merit Janow, Gregory Rattray, and Phil Venables, co-chairs, "Building a Defensible Cyberspace," New York Cyber Task Force, Columbia University School of International and Public Affairs (2017), p. 21.

Blurred lines: the absence of mutual understandings and clear thresholds in cyberspace

During the Cold War, mismatches between U.S. and Soviet understandings about limited nuclear operations and intra-war restraint created escalation risks.[129] In a similar vein, some scholars assert that the absence of clear thresholds, firebreaks, red lines, or mutually agreed upon understandings of acceptable behavior in cyberspace heightens the probability of escalation.[130] According to this logic, escalation could occur as a result of divergent understandings between states about what type of cyber behavior would violate critical thresholds, especially because escalation is ultimately a function of perception.[131] And while effective signaling could ameliorate disagreements about thresholds, communication in cyberspace may be more fraught than in other domains due to the absence of an "agreed-upon language that guides policymakers to a common understanding."[132] Lucas Kello, for instance, presents a range of examples of "escalatory ambiguity" that he argues make the development of common thresholds difficult and therefore undermine stability. These include "rudimentary" shared norms of acceptable behavior and the lack of common "conversion tables" that would help states understand what constitutes proportionate responses to cyber actions.[133] Efforts by states to come to agreements about norms of behavior in cyberspace through international fora, such as at the United Nations, have been met in the past by some setbacks.[134]

Yet, while cyber governance is far from perfect, the notion that cyberspace is bereft of norms or shared understandings is incorrect.[135] For instance, multiple international bodies are responsible for setting technical standards that govern critical aspects of cyberspace's functioning, such as the International Corporation for Assigned Names and Numbers (ICANN), a non-profit organization responsible for the interoperability of the internet, and the United

---

[129] Jack L. Snyder, *The Soviet Strategic Culture: Implications for Limited Nuclear Operations* (Santa Monica, CA: RAND Corporation, 1977).

[130] Morgan et al., *Dangerous Thresholds*.

[131] Lin, "Escalation Dynamics," p. 52. Libicki, *Crisis and Escalation in Cyberspace*, p. 78. Although see Max Smeets for an argument that there are too many red lines in cyberspace; Max Smeets "There Are Too Many Red Lines in Cyberspace," *Lawfare*, March 20, 2019.

[132] Borghard and Lonergan, "The Logic of Coercion in Cyberspace," p. 456. For a discussion of how to develop a framework for building international cyber norms, see Martha Finnemore and Duncan B. Hollis, "Constructing Norms for Global Cybersecurity," *The American Journal of International Law* 110, no. 3 (July 2016): 425–479.

[133] Kello, "The Meaning of the Cyber Revolution," p. 35.

[134] Borghard and Lonergan, "Confidence Building Measures," pp. 16–18; Alex Grigsby, "The United Nations Doubles Its Workload on Cyber Norms, and Not Everyone Is Pleased," *Net Politics*, November 15, 2018.

[135] Jeanette Hoffman, "Multi-stakeholderism in Internet Governance: Putting Fiction into Practice," *Journal of Cyber Policy* 1, no. 1 (2016): 29–49.

Nation's International Telecommunication Union (ITU), which is responsible for setting global standards for information and communications technologies. Furthermore, from a norms perspective, states have formally agreed to shared standards of acceptable behavior in cyberspace, working through UN processes such as the Group of Government Experts or the Open Ended Working Group—even as there have been gaps between these agreements and actual state practice.[136] Moreover, there is evidence that some implicit norms have emerged as a result of strategic interactions between states, such as a norm against using kinetic military force to respond to cyber operations. In particular, researchers have found that there is indeed a "firebreak" between cyber and conventional military operations—a clear, recognizable, and mutually understood threshold that draws a defined distinction between cyber operations, which exist below it, and kinetic military operations above it.[137] Finally, states do agree that international law applies to cyberspace (even as they may disagree about how precisely it applies), and customary international law has also shaped how states operate, particularly below the level of armed conflict.[138]

It is clear that there are challenges with respect to the robustness of cyber norms and shared understanding about what constitutes acceptable behavior, especially between rivals. However, arguments about cyber escalation that hinge on stark assessments of the absence of cyber norms and governance misconstrue or exaggerate the nature of the latter.

What should we make of existing arguments?

As the discussion here notes, many of the factors that scholars identify as pathways to or correlates of escalation dynamics in cyberspace do in fact exist. Strategic interactions in cyberspace are complicated by difficulties of

---

[136] Martha Finnemore, "Cybersecurity and the Concept of Norms," Carnegie Endowment for International Peace, November 30, 2017; Mark Raymond, "Managing Decentralized Cyber Governance: The Responsibility to Troubleshoot," *Strategic Studies Quarterly* 10, no. 4 (2016): 123–149; Michael Schmitt, "The Sixth GGE and International Law in Cyberspace," *Just Security*, June 10, 2021; Michael Schmitt and Liis Vihul, "The Nature of International Law Cyber Norms," CCDCOE, Tallinn Papers (2014).

[137] Schneider and Kreps, "Escalation Firebreaks;" Farrell and Glaser, "The Role of Effects, Saliencies and Norms in US Cyberwar Doctrine."

[138] Duncan Hollis, "A Brief Primer on International Law and Cyberspace," Carnegie Endowment for International Peace, June 14, 2021; Oona Hathaway et al., "The Law of Cyber-Attack," *California Law Review* 100, no. 4 (2012): 817–885; Robert Chesney, "Cybersecurity Law, Policy, and Institutions," Version 3.1, University of Texas Law, Public Law Research Paper No. 716, 2021; Gary Brown and Keira Poellet, "The Customary International Law of Cyberspace," *Strategic Studies Quarterly* 6, no. 3 (2012): 126–145.

discerning intent, offensively oriented military cultures, proxies, and limitations of norms. However, this only makes the empirical puzzle more salient—despite all of these escalation risk factors, there are few, if any, instances of escalation.

We argue that the absence of cyber escalation, despite many attributes of strategic interaction in cyberspace that would otherwise predict it, indicates that there are fundamental aspects of cyber operations that dampen the potential for escalation. Specifically, we argue that this absence of escalation stems from the fact that, contrary to the conventional wisdom, the technology of cyberspace is not offense dominant. Instead, developing offensive cyber capabilities requires significant investments in time, resources, and building skills; and efforts to employ them in the context of a single operation or a larger campaign often cause unpredictable and dissatisfying results, are limited in their ability to generate costs at scale, and are defined by operational requirements that inject breathing room into crisis situations. Put simply, the types of offensive operations that would generate sufficient costs against a target to provoke a potentially escalatory response are hard to execute, while those that are easy to conduct are not likely to be escalatory.

Plan of the Book

The remainder of the book proceeds as follows. In Chapter 2 we explore core characteristics of cyber operations and in Chapter 3 we leverage those to develop a theory of escalation in cyberspace that accounts for the conditions under which cyber operations may lead to escalation between rivals. We argue that cyber operations are unlikely to trigger dangerous escalatory spirals due to the role of secrecy and plausible deniability; the technical requirements for operating in cyberspace; trade-offs between the uses of cyberspace for espionage and military purposes; and limits on the cost generation of cyber operations. In Chapter 4, we extend our argument about escalation to evaluate the implications for cyber signaling during international crises. We posit that many of the same factors that make cyber operations poor tools of escalation also make them useful for accommodative signaling and enable crisis de-escalation. We test our arguments about escalation and signaling through a series of "least likely" case studies in Chapters 5 and 6. In Chapter 7 we explore potential pathways through which cyber operations may indirectly lead to escalation to war or further exacerbate an ongoing conventional conflict, given the interdependence of modern warfighting and nuclear capabilities on digital infrastructure. Finally, Chapter 8 concludes by applying the logic of our theory to evaluate and make specific recommendations for U.S. policymaking. If it is indeed the case that cyberspace is not as escalatory as some experts suggest, and cyberspace could provide an avenue for signaling to de-escalate crises, then there are significant implications for how the United States should approach strategic interactions with allies, adversaries, and competitors in cyberspace.

2

Four Attributes of Cyber Operations

Technical Realities of Cyberspace

Do cyber operations cause escalation, either within or outside of cyberspace? How dangerous are cyber operations for international stability? Longstanding fears of cyber escalation have not materialized. We argue that this is due to four crucial characteristics of cyber operations that most states confront—despite important differences in their strategies, capabilities, and force postures. Cyber operations are not likely to lead to escalatory responses—either with cyber or non-cyber means—because the secret, plausibly deniable nature of cyber operations, coupled with limitations on generating costly effects, dampens pressure for escalation. Instead, states are likely to rely on proportionate, tit-for-tat cyber or non-cyber responses, which may be separated by temporal buffers between action and reaction. Moreover, the difficulties of conducting strategic cyber operations at desired moments in time and trade-offs between intelligence and military utilities for cyber operations further limit escalatory dynamics. In this chapter, we systematically identify and explore the nature of these characteristics.

Given the pace of technological change in cyberspace, it may seem deeply problematic, or even obtuse, to claim that there are "fixed" characteristics of cyber operations. However, while there is indeed considerable flux and rapid innovation in cyber capabilities and adversary tactics, techniques, and procedures, it is nonetheless possible to identify several fundamental properties that have defined the development and employment of cyber operations. These are unlikely to change absent a momentous transformation of the underlying architecture of cyberspace itself or other significant technological innovations. The four attributes of cyber operations that are central to our analysis are: the importance of secrecy and related characteristics, such as plausible deniability; the technical challenges of planning and conducting strategic cyber operations; the limited effects in generating costs from cyber operations; and the relationship between espionage and military cyber operations. These attributes serve as the backbone of our theory, and in the ensuing chapters we explore their implications for escalation—and the prospects of de-escalation—during international crises and in wartime.

Escalation Dynamics in Cyberspace. Erica D. Lonergan and Shawn W. Lonergan, Oxford University Press.
© Oxford University Press 2023. DOI: 10.1093/oso/9780197550885.003.0002

Secrecy, Deception, and Plausible Deniability in Cyber Operations

Secrecy is important for cyber operations from an operational success perspective and it can provide strategic utility for states that seek to deny their involvement in cyberspace activities. In terms of the former, secrecy is less of a political decision and more of a requirement for an operation to achieve its desired objective while, in the case of the latter, maintaining a certain level of secrecy is more of a choice driven by strategic and political calculations.[1] Unpacking the different manifestations of secrecy in cyber operations, therefore, demands taking these nuances into account.

Operational requirements for secrecy

Operational security is important for all military operations, but it is particularly salient in cyberspace. This is in large part due to the malleable, non-physical nature of cyber capabilities and the cyber environment that together enable network defenders to alter the terrain on which attackers operate and potentially render their tools useless. Therefore, successfully operating in cyberspace often demands that states conceal their activities.[2] Revealing information about operations to gain access to a target and efforts to develop tools (particularly highly tailored ones) prior to or during the course of an operation can negate their efficacy because it permits defenders to take concrete steps to render the threat inert.[3]

In particular, secrecy is essential to maintaining access once a vulnerability has been discovered and an exploit built for it, especially once an attacker has already gained a foothold in a network but has not yet fully executed the mission. Attackers must keep their behavior secret from networks defenders who are employing multiple layers of methods to uncover and defeat the former at each

---

[1] For a discussion of the political aspects in the United States of maintaining the secrecy of cyber programs in general, see David Sanger, "Cyber, Drones, and Secrecy," in George Perkovich and Ariel Levite, eds., *Understanding Cyber Conflict: 14 Analogies* (Washington, DC: Georgetown University Press, 2017).

[2] Erik Gartzke and Jon Lindsay, "Weaving Tangled Webs: Offense, Defense, and Deception in Cyberspace," *Security Studies* 24, no. 2 (2015): 316–348.

[3] As applied to deterrence, Gartzke and Linsday term this the "cyber commitment problem." See "The Cyber Commitment Problem," in Herbert Lin and Amy Zegart, eds., *Bytes, Bombs, and Spies: The Strategic Dimensions of Offensive Cyber Operations* (Washington, DC: Brookings Institute Press, 2019), p. 204. An interesting theoretical extension of this is to explore the implications for rationalist explanations for war. In this line of reasoning, war occurs because states disagree about the balance of power and, as information is revealed over the course of fighting about the true balance of capabilities and resolve, they should arrive at the outcome that reflects these. However, in cyberspace, revealing information about capabilities can actually *change* the balance of power as it removes those capabilities from the table for future use.

stage of an operation. Employing obfuscation techniques, for example, prevents defenders from detecting an attacker's presence.[4] Network defenders can employ intrusion detection approaches to uncover adversaries attempting to gain access to a network, such as deploying perimeter sensors to detect activity at all ingress and egress points in a network. Sophisticated defenders will also collect and analyze data about anomalous behavior within a network perimeter, after a hypothetical adversarial breach, such as identifying novel or remote executables.[5] If the target uncovers an adversary on its networks and has information about the attack vector it can marshal defenses and take measures to patch vulnerabilities, rendering the attacker's access (and therefore whatever subsequent effects might be caused) moot.

This is why military and intelligence organizations, for instance, typically maintain secrecy about zero-day exploits—those that exist "in the wild" and are not previously known to the network defender—and why markets for zero-days on the Dark Web proliferate.[6] From a defensive perspective, cyber hunt teams—defensive teams that conduct threat hunting on networks to identify and mitigate potential malicious activity—exist because attacker obfuscation is so integral to offensive missions, particularly when attempting lateral movement or privilege escalation within a network. Secrecy is also critical to preserving the tool itself because revealing that information allows the target to develop defenses against it and may also reveal the attacking state's targeting strategy and broader set of capabilities. Maintaining this type of operational secrecy, particularly at scale in a strategic environment of multiple, ongoing offensive cyber operations against important targets, requires advanced tradecraft.

Attribution and political decisions about secrecy

States also take advantage of the plausible deniability that cyberspace enables to avoid being held responsible for cyber attacks. This is not an absolute requirement to ensure operational effectiveness but, rather, a strategic decision.[7] This gives rise to what is termed the "attribution problem" in the cyber literature—that is, the fact that it can be difficult for targets of a cyber attack to quickly

<hr/>

[4] For a thorough discussion of different types of adversaries, OPSEC tactics, techniques, and procedures, see MITRE, https://attack.mitre.org/techniques/pre/.

[5] Blake E. Strom et al., "Finding Cyber Threats with ATT&CK-Based Analytics," *MITRE* (June 2017), pp. 17–21.

[6] Lillian Ablon, Martin C. Libicki, and Andrea A. Golay, *Markets for Cybercrime Tools and Stolen Data: Hackers' Bazaar* (Santa Monica, CA: RAND Corporation, 2014), ch. 4.

[7] Poznansky and Perkoski make the important distinction between clandestine and covert operations and secrecy as an operational imperative versus as a choice. Michael Poznansky and Evan Perkoski, "Rethinking Secrecy in Cyberspace: The Politics of Voluntary Attribution," *Journal of Global Security Studies* 3, no. 4 (2018): 402–416.

identify the party responsible for carrying them out. Even if they can locate the source of an attack, they may not be able to ascertain with sufficiently high confidence whether it was ordered by a government or conducted without its knowledge or approval.[8] Of course, the opportunity for secrecy in this sense is also linked to the technical design of cyberspace, which enables actors to more easily conceal their responsibility for cyber attacks by facilitating the obfuscation of points of departure for attacks through the use of spoofing, proxy servers, third party infrastructure, compromised certificates, and other anonymizing capabilities.[9] Moreover, technical methods to avoid attribution—which may be easier for targets to determine—are confounded by deliberate efforts to obscure command and control for cyber attacks, such as employing cyber proxies with varying degrees of connection to the state to conduct offensive operations on the latter's behalf.[10]

States leverage plausible deniability in different ways, with governments varying in the level of direct or explicit authority they choose to exert over their cyber proxies. These ambiguities in the extent of state control further complicate political attribution. Governments can coopt unwitting proxy actors into targeting enemies of the state (for instance, by distributing malware in patriotic hacker forums, as was the case during the Russian-Georgian conflict in 2008), or they can establish more direct relationships with organized groups that knowingly act on the behalf of state military or intelligence agencies (such as the relationship between Russian intelligence agencies and the various advanced persistent threat groups they work with).[11]

For all of these reasons, political attribution of a cyber attack may take weeks or months and only result in a degree of confidence about the true decision-making behind an attack—even as the time to technical attribution with confidence continues to rapidly improve. The speed with which the United States publicly attributed the 2014 Sony hack to North Korea reflects this latter trend.[12]

---

[8] See, for example, Thomas Rid and Ben Buchanan, "Attributing Cyber Attacks," *Journal of Strategic Studies* 30, nos. 1–2 (2015): 4–37. For how secrecy can aid defenders, see Gartzke and Lindsay, "Weaving Tangled Webs."

[9] For further reference see Clement Guitton and Elaine Korzak, "The Sophistication Criterion for Attribution: Identifying the Perpetrators of Cyber-Attacks," *The RUSI Journal* 158, no. 4 (2013): 62–68.

[10] Rid and Buchanan argue that, at the strategic level, "attribution is a function of what is at stake politically," Thomas Rid and Ben Buchanan, "Attributing Cyber Attacks," *Journal of Strategic Studies* 38, nos. 1–2 (2015): 7. Also see Erica D. Borghard and Shawn W. Lonergan, "Can States Calculate the Risks of Using Cyber Proxies?" *Orbis* 60, no. 3 (May 2016): 395–416 for a discussion of why states delegate authority to proxy actors to conduct cyber attacks on their behalf; and see Tim Maurer, *Cyber Mercenaries: The State, Hackers, and Power* (Cambridge: Cambridge University Press, 2017).

[11] Jeffrey Carr, *Inside Cyber Warfare: Mapping the Cyber Underworld* (Sebastopol: O'Reilly Media, Inc., 2011), pp. 15–19; Andreas Hagen, "The Russo-Georgian War 2008," in Jason Healey, ed., *A Fierce Domain: Conflict in Cyberspace, 1986 to 2012* (Vienna, VA: Cyber Conflict Studies Association, 2013), p. 201. "Who Is Fancy Bear?" *CrowdStrike*, September 12, 2016.

[12] Indeed, Deputy Undersecretary Alejandro Mayorkas of the Department of Homeland Security remarked on October 7, 2015, that the U.S. government has the ability to attribute cyber attacks to

Furthermore, beyond identifying the physical source of an attack—the location of the originating IP address and its association with a particular owner—the decision to go public with this information about responsibility for a cyber attack depends on a strategic, political calculus.

Understanding why some actors may find it appealing to evade attribution requires an analysis that goes beyond the technical factors. Avoiding attribution will likely remain attractive for political and strategic reasons that will persist even as technical abilities to attribute are increasingly perfected. States may find plausible deniability appealing because it enables them to reduce the chance of retaliation by the target; to refrain from setting precedents regarding permissible types of operations or to preclude the target from interpreting ambiguous norms to justify action against the perpetrator; to maneuver around domestic political or bureaucratic issues, especially if there are internal debates within a government about who "owns" offensive cyber operations or if the domestic public or veto players are risk-averse.[13]

One illustration of how plausible deniability about responsibility for cyber operations reflects a political calculus is the fact that governments sometimes do decide to go public with their involvement in cyber operations (with varying degrees of formality). For example, in December 2021, U.S. Cyber Command publicly acknowledged that the military had conducted cyber operations to counter ransomware groups, although the statement left out critical details such as the nature of the targets, the types of cyber operations that took place, and their timing.[14] Similarly, then-Secretary of Defense Ash Carter acknowledged during a press conference in February 2016 that the United States had conducted cyber attacks against the Islamic State in Mosul; this was followed by the release of several official accounts and assessments of this effort.[15] Through more informal channels, in September 2017, a senior official in the Trump Administration leaked to the press that Cyber Command had conducted a sustained distributed denial of service attack against North Korea's Reconnaissance General Bureau.[16]

state actors and that these abilities are growing. Alejandro Mayorkas, interview by Jason Healey, Managing Our Nation's Cyber Risk, Christian Science Monitor, October 7, 2015, http://www.csmoni tor.com/World/Passcode/2015/1006/Watch-live-Managing-our-nation-s-cyber-risk.

[13] It is also reasonable to surmise that the instances of accurate attribution are grossly underestimated because we can only observe the cases where a government or private entity chose to publicly reveal information to support attribution. However, the cost of public attribution—such as losing valuable intelligence assets—can often outweigh the political benefits.

[14] Julian E. Barnes, "U.S. Military Has Acted against Ransomware Groups, General Acknowledges," The New York Times, December 5, 2021.

[15] "Department of Defense Press Briefing by Secretary Carter and Gen. Dunford in the Pentagon Briefing Room," News Transcript, Department of Defense, February 29, 2016; "Joint Task Force ARES and Operational GLOWING SYMPHONY: Cyber Command's Internet War Against ISIL," National Security Archive, George Washington University.

[16] Karen DeYoung, Ellen Nakashima, and Emily Rauhala, "Trump Signed Presidential Directive Ordering Actions to Pressure North Korea," The Washington Post, September 30, 2017.

While avoiding attribution reflects a political calculus, it is related to the operational requirement for secrecy in a broad sense. Attribution of a cyber operation after the fact does not negate the mission that was just executed. However, information linking an event to an actor can provide a target with more information about the actor's overall capabilities, skill level, and tactics, techniques, and procedures; it can also provide insight into the actor's broader military or political strategy. This is particularly true if the operation at hand is only one component of a larger cyber campaign.

High Barriers to Entry: The Difficulty of Some Cyber Operations

Cyberspace is often described as having low barriers to entry, and cyber operations are depicted as relatively easy to conduct, even for unsophisticated actors. This is certainly true for some types of cyber operations. However, we define a category, strategic cyber operations, that comprises operations that are difficult to plan and execute and demand a level of operator skill, organizational maturity, and strategic patience to successfully implement. Moreover, these types of operations are typically required to create significant cyber effects against hardened, well-defended assets, networks, and systems that are essential to a state's economic or national security. The requirements states often face in endeavoring to gain access to these types of networks, maintain that access over time, achieve the intended effect against a specific target set, and at the desired time of employment pose a significant challenge. Below, we describe in greater detail some of the hurdles associated with gaining access, obtaining effects, and timing.

Gaining access to a target

Offensive cyber capabilities cause effects against targets through exploiting a vulnerability to gain access (through an attack vector) to a target's network or system and deliver a payload that is activated by communicating back with a host or triggered by a command order written into the code.[17] Therefore, the employment of offensive cyber power depends on gaining access through exploiting a vulnerability in a network or system prior to launching an attack.[18] An implication

[17] William A. Owens, Kenneth W. Dam, and Herbert S. Lin, eds., *Technology, Policy, Law, and Ethics Regarding U.S. Acquisition and Use of Cyberattack Capabilities* (Washington, DC: National Academies Press, 2009), pp. 83–89.

[18] See Erica D. Borghard and Shawn W. Lonergan, "The Logic of Coercion in Cyberspace," *Security Studies* 26, no. 4 (2017): 452–481 for an additional discussion of access-dependence.

of this is that, even if an actor has a capability to attack an adversary's network, without the right access to deploy it, the capability might as well not exist.[19] The initial penetration of a target network or system can be resource-intensive and net unpredictable results, which is why the employment of cyber capabilities that rely on access to a targeted network require prior planning and resource allocation and development. Indeed, according to Chris Inglis, the planning staff at U.S. Cyber Command found that "the first 90 percent of cyber reconnaissance (i.e., ISR [intelligence, surveillance, and reconnaissance]), cyber defense, and cyberattack consisted of the common work of finding and fixing a target of interest in cyberspace."[20]

While nearly all offensive cyber capabilities require exploiting some kind of vulnerability to gain access to a target and cause an effect, there are some exceptions.[21] Distributed denial of service (DDoS) attacks, for instance, produce disruptive effects by overwhelming the target's processing capacity (typically through overloading its bandwidth via the sheer volume of requests). However, at scale, the process of building large botnet armies to carry out DDoS attacks involves exploiting vulnerabilities in infected devices that are then harnessed as part of the botnet.

The difficulties associated with gaining, maintaining, and escalating access can vary depending on the means required to gain access, the type of target, and the shelf-life of access.

Means of gaining access

How an actor gains access to a target will depend on the type of network, time constraints, and available capabilities, affecting the level of difficulty of gaining access. Table 2.1 depicts various means of gaining access to a targeted network or system and evaluates them along a spectrum of cost, risk, and reliability. The table is not meant to be a comprehensive review of all of the ways in which an operator could gain access. Rather, it provides some critical illustrative examples. Cost concerns the resource requirements necessary to acquire access; risk includes physical as well strategic risks of different means of access; and reliability pertains to the likelihood of achieving a desired outcome.

The vast majority of efforts to gain access involve creative means to emplace malicious software, known as malware, on a targeted system. In general terms,

---

[19] Steven M. Bellovin, Susan Landau, and Herbert S. Lin, "Limiting the Undesired Impact of Cyber Weapons: Technical Requirements and Policy Implications," *Journal of Cybersecurity* 3, no. 1 (2017): 60.

[20] Chris Ingis, "Illuminating a New Domain," in *Bytes, Bombs, and Spies*, p. 25.

[21] Zero days are vulnerabilities in hardware or software that are unknown and, therefore, patches have not yet been developed for them. Zero day vulnerabilities are often not revealed until they have been used to carry out an attack and, even then, it may take considerable time before network defenders ascertain that a zero-day was used to carry it out.

Table 2.1 Common Means of Gaining Access

Means of Gaining Access	Cost	Risk	Reliability	Feasibility against Target Sets
Remote Access				
Hacking: Using a computer to gain unauthorized access to a system using a suite of tools.	Low to High	Low to Medium	Low to High	Can be resource-intensive depending on the target.
Phishing: Mass and indiscriminate dissemination of email containing malware.	Low	Low	Low	Not feasible against air-gapped networks.
Spear-Phishing: Tailored dissemination of email containing malware.	Low	Low	Medium. More targeted than phishing, so more reliable, but depends on the sophistication of social engineering. Ability to deliver the effects also depends on controls within a network.	Not feasible against air-gapped networks.
Whaling: Similar to spear-phishing, but targets a high-profile individual.	Low to Medium	Low	Medium. Tends to be more reliable compared to spear-phishing given the highly targeted nature of the operation. Can be resource intensive, however, as it requires increased social engineering and target development and is often deployed against a hardened target.	Not feasible against air-gapped networks.
Pharming: Directing internet users to a cloned but bogus website that prompts them to provide user credentials.	Low	Low	Low	Not feasible against air-gapped networks.
Man in the Middle: A common hacking operation that can rely on remote or physical access to essentially eavesdrop on communication between two parties.	Low to High	Low to High	Low to High	Varies depending on remote or close access.

Table 2.1 Continued

Means of Gaining Access	Cost	Risk	Reliability	Feasibility against Target Sets
Close Access				
Supply Chain Interdiction: Intercepting and compromising a software or hardware component of the targeted network prior to delivery.	Medium to High	Low to Medium	Low to Medium. Attacker has no guarantee when the infected systems will be brought online, how they will react in the targeted environment, or if they will even be used in the targeted environment.	May be one of the only viable means to gain access to a closed system but requires extensive planning and intelligence collection.
Physical Access: Emplacing an operator on the ground to gain physical access to the targeted system and infecting via a software or hardware implant.	High	High	Medium to High. Varies depending on what capabilities the operator has for the operation. It may be difficult to engineer solutions for data exfiltration if required.	May be one of the only viable means to gain access to a closed system. Often requires a trained operator surreptitiously gaining access to a targeted system or finding a person with access to wittingly or unwittingly deliver the exploit.
Wireless Access: Associating wirelessly, typically via Wi-Fi or Bluetooth, to inject a software capability or harvest credentials. Standoff distance can vary greatly depending on the frequency the attacker is exploiting and the power emitted by the transmitter.	Medium	Medium to High	Low to High. Varies depending on what capabilities the operator has for the operation.	Feasibility varies depending on the standoff distance necessary to deliver the exploit and the permissibility of the environment of the operation.

experts often distinguish between remote access (such as using the internet) and close access (which requires some degree of physical proximity to a target, such as gaining access through a human agent or supply chain interdiction). Remote access is typically the safest for an attacker, as there is a lower threat of attribution or apprehension by a defender—especially if an operator gains access from the safe harbor of their homeland. In contrast, close access requires a witting or unwitting human to be stationed in proximity to the targeted system or conducting an operation to interdict some part of the supply chain while in production or transit.

As Table 2.1 depicts, most of the low-cost and low-risk means of gaining access to a target are not particularly useful against more hardened (and therefore more strategically valuable) targets, such as the air-gapped networks that are common in critical infrastructure systems and some military and defense systems. However, they are useful against softer targets, such as private sector firms that rely on global internet infrastructure to conduct routine business. The most reliable type of access, physical access through a human intermediary on the ground, is also the riskiest and costliest.

Type of target and implications for access

Implicit in Table 2.1 is the notion that the type of network or system being targeted affects the means through which an attacker may be able to gain access and, as a result, the level of difficulty involved. We identify three dimensions along which variation in the type of target has implications for access: the distinction between Operational Technology (OT) and Information Technology (IT) targets; the specific level of access within a network; and targeting hardware, software, and networks.

Information Technology versus Operational Technology Targets

In general, gaining access to OT networks and systems is significantly more costly and complex and less scalable than gaining access to IT networks and systems, although this may be changing over time as IT and OT systems converge.[22] OT is comprised of both the hardware and software that is responsible for monitoring and controlling physical devices, most notably those that administer Industrial Control Systems that are used in critical infrastructure (such as water treatment and filtration plants, electric grids, or nuclear power plants). OT networks tend to be closed (ideally, they should not touch the internet, although there are some exceptions). They also usually run unique protocols that

---

[22] A potential source of change is IT/OT convergence, which may reduce barriers to gaining access to OT networks and systems. See, for example, https://www.cisco.com/c/dam/en_us/solutions/ind ustries/manufacturing/ITOT-convergence-whitepaper.pdf.

are used to control highly specific processes and systems.[23] Typically, this also means that they require very specific knowledge because the programs that they run are customized to their specific systems and the networking protocols they employ may not be widely proliferated. In contrast, IT networks are comprised of any computer that stores and transmits digital information, as well as the underlying infrastructure that supports the exchange. They tend to be connected to the internet, which means that access to IT networks is typically remotely gained.

Level of Access
The relative ease of access also depends on the level of access needed to conduct a particular operation. The mere fact of "gaining access" to a target network does not guarantee that an attacker has gained the *correct* type of access from which to launch an offensive operation. From a network engineering perspective, networks are layered in what is termed the Open Systems Interconnection (OSI) model. In general, the lower level of access, the greater the control and persistence a potential cyber capability can have over a compromised system. For instance, gaining access at the kernel level via an Operating System (OS) exploit (commonly layer 3 or 4, depending on the OS) is far more significant and potentially devastating than gaining access at the application layer (layer 7). Kernel level access also provides a more persistent foothold—even if a savvy defender were to conduct an OS update, this would be unlikely to eject an attacker's kernel access—whereas access at the application level can be vitiated through OS updates. This is why most access operations are followed by operations that enable persistence through privilege escalation prior to the ultimate action on the objective.

Hardware, Software, and Network Access
Finally, gaining access to a target via a hardware implant—the actual, physical components of a computer (such as the motherboard, USB and other flash memory devices, or routers)—is appreciably costlier and more difficult than gaining access to software (the digital programs on a computer, from the OS to applications such as Microsoft Word).[24] Hardware access almost by definition

[23] There are exceptions to each model. IT networks can indeed be closed and not connected to the open internet and OT networks can have access to the internet. That said, OT networks having access to the open internet is considered poor cybersecurity and the convergence of the two networks is something most cyber security practitioners try to avoid. In one study, Twist et al., found maritime systems connected to the internet. For further information see Jim Twist, Blake Rhoades, and Ernest Wong, "Navigating the Cyber Threats to the U.S. Maritime Transportation System," in Joseph DiRenzo III, Nicole K. Drumhiller, and Fred S. Roberts, eds. *Maritime Cyber Security* (Westphalia Press, 2017), ch. 4.

[24] For our purposes it is not theoretically necessary to distinguish between software and firmware, but it is important to note that, from a technical perspective, they are different. Firmware is a type of software that is placed in hardware and is responsible for controlling some of the hardware's basic functions. Like software, firmware can (and should, from a cybersecurity perspective) be updated.

requires physical access to a target and, therefore, incurs greater cost and risk and is comparably rare. This type of access is typically less vulnerable and can persist over time, with the potential for significant implications depending on the extent of the distribution of a compromised piece of hardware.

Software vulnerabilities are relatively easier to detect and to patch and manufacturers routinely disseminate information about known vulnerabilities and remediation protocols.[25] However, there is also a large and continuously growing number of these vulnerabilities. Indeed, as computing processing power and storage capacity have increased over time by orders of magnitude, the software they have the capacity to run has also grown in size and increased in complexity. For instance, Windows 95 had roughly 15 million lines of code when it debuted in 1995, compared to 35 million lines of code in the 2001 release of Windows XP and the reportedly 50 million lines of code in Windows 10 released in 2015. Of course, these pale in comparison to the reportedly 2 billion lines of code that comprise Google.[26] Microsoft typically finds 10–20 defects per 1000 lines of code during in-house testing, but releases software with 0.5 per 1000 lines.[27] That may seem like a low defect ratio, but it implies that Windows XP, for example, likely contains over 17,500 vulnerabilities.[28] While not every one of these bugs necessarily provides a means for a hacker to take over a machine, some of course do. Recognizing this, governments have adapted over time to protect their own supply chains and develop or purchase highly customized programs. China, for instance, has worked with Microsoft through its Government Security Program to gain access to the source code, conduct security reviews, and have Microsoft customize programs to meet their security requirements.[29]

Beyond hardware and software, attackers can also seek to gain access to network vulnerabilities.[30] Vulnerabilities in network protocols—the rules that manage how data is transmitted between networked devices (such as TCP/IP versus UDP, or Border Gate Protocol that routes data across the internet)—and network infrastructure—the routers, servers, and gateways that carry out data transmission (such as Domain Name System root servers[31])—can be exploited

[25] Max Smeets, "A Matter of Time: On the Transitory Nature of Cyber Weapons," *Journal of Strategic Studies* 41, nos. 1–2 (2018): 18.
[26] Steve Lohr and John Markoff, "Windows Is So Slow, but Why?" *The New York Times*, March 26, 2007, sec. Technology, http://www.nytimes.com/2006/03/27/technology/27soft.html; Cade Metz, "Google Is 2 Billion Lines of Code—and It's All in One Place," *Wired*, September 16, 2015.
[27] Steve McConnell, *Code Complete*, 2nd ed. (Redmond, Washington: Microsoft Press, 2004), p. 521.
[28] Ibid. However, Windows is beating the industry average of 1–25 errors per 1000 lines of code for delivered software
[29] Sumner Lemon, "China Gets Access to Microsoft Source Code: Move Comes after Similar Pact with Taiwan," *InfoWorld*, March 3, 2003.
[30] Smeets, "A Matter of Time," p. 18.
[31] ICANN is the entity responsible for the global management of all root servers, which are an essential component of the internet's infrastructure and contains the IP addresses for all top-level domains, see https://www.iana.org/domains/root/servers.

to deliver more widespread effects, particularly depending on the connectivity of the targeted network. For instance, a 2015 DDoS attack targeted almost all of the internet's root servers for several hours, flooding the domain name system with billions of queries.[32]

Taken together, there are manifold challenges to gaining access to the appropriate target within a network from which to launch a cyber attack. The sheer complexity of these targets means that success often depends on an accurate understanding of how multiple and diverse functions and processes relate to and depend on each other.[33]

The shelf life of access
Finally, even if an attacker has successfully gained access to a target, it often has to preserve that access for a period of time. Yet, accesses do not have an infinite shelf-life.[34] In many cases, an attacker may wish to maintain persistent access to a target so that a particular cyber tool can be employed at the precise time desired by a decision maker. This requires a certain level of tradecraft for an attacker to conceal its presence on a target's network and for information about the attack vector to remain secret. However, preserving persistent access over time can be highly unpredictable and evaporate unexpectedly based on unanticipated and often unintended behavior by the target. As mentioned above, routine software or firmware updates can render an attacker's access moot, removing the latter from the defender's system. A target can "transition from vulnerability (to a particular attack) to invulnerability in, literally, minutes."[35]

Additionally, third party disclosure about software vulnerabilities, either by governments through vulnerabilities equities processes or by private actors, can also unintentionally precipitate the loss of access, as exposure about vulnerability information enables network defenders to take measures to remedy them.[36] For

---

[32] Dan Goodin, "Attack Floods Internet Root Servers with 5 Million Queries a Second," *ArsTechnica*, December 9, 2015. In a different type of example, NATO leaders have recently expressed concerns about Russia's ability to target the global undersea cable system, see "Russia a 'Risk' to Undersea Cables, Defence Chief Warns," *BBC*, December 15, 2017.

[33] Martin C. Libicki, "Second Acts in Cyberspace," in Herbert Lin and Amy Zegart, eds., *Bytes, Bombs, and Spies: The Strategic Dimensions of Offensive Cyber Operations* (Washington, DC: Brookings Institute Press, 2019), p. 137.

[34] For research on the lifecycle of zero-day exploits, see Lillian Ablon and Andy Bogart, *Zero Days, Thousands of Nights: The Life and Times of Zero-Day Vulnerabilities and Their Exploits* (Santa Monica, CA: RAND Corporation, 2017).

[35] Libicki, "Second Acts in Cyberspace," in *Bytes, Bombs, and Spies*, p. 133. Also see Max Smeets, "A Matter of Time: On the Transitory Nature of Cyber Weapons," *Journal of Strategic Studies* 41, nos. 1–2 (2018): 6–32.

[36] Within the U.S. government, for example, there is a Vulnerabilities Equities Process (VEP) that articulates standards for when the government discloses information about zero-day vulnerabilities. See, "Vulnerabilities Equities Policy and Processes for the United States Government," November 15, 2017, https://www.whitehouse.gov/sites/whitehouse.gov/files/images/External%20-%20Uncla ssified%20VEP%20Charter%20FINAL.PDF. Governments and other actors must balance trade-offs between the public security goods associated with information sharing about vulnerabilities (which

instance, the disclosures by the group Shadow Brokers, beginning in 2016, of purportedly pilfered U.S. National Security Agency exploits and zero-days ostensibly put U.S. government accesses at risk.[37] In a different example, when the U.S. government was made aware of a compromise of the software vendor SolarWinds, which enabled Russia to gain access to dozens of Federal and private sector networks, it released an emergency directive in December 2020 providing information about how affected entities across the federal government should implement mitigation measures.[38] Put simply, a vulnerability upon which an access relies may in theory be only one update or disclosure away from being patched.

The non-universal lethality of offensive cyber capabilities

Once an attacker has established a foothold in a target's network, it must deliver a payload—a piece of malicious code or malware—to achieve the desired effect. But, unlike conventional weapons, where the same capability could be deployed against a range of targets (such as a stealth bomber dropping a bomb against an aircraft hangar, a massed enemy formation, a munitions factory, or a hospital), many cyber payloads lack what we call universal lethality. In other words, an operator may not be able to employ a particular cyber tool against a range of targets—and may not even be able to reuse it. Other types of cyber capabilities are more modular, can be repeatedly used in roughly the same form, or can be repurposed in a slightly different and new form against a range of potential targets. For example, an attacker could repurpose an exploit and sufficiently alter it so that it evades detection capabilities that rely on known signatures.

But because cyber tools are comprised of computer code written to produce some kind of effect against another computer, they can't be employed against *any* desired target. As Martin Libicki notes, "A piece of malware that brings one system down may have absolutely no effect on another. The difference between the two may be as simple as which patch version of a piece of software each system runs."[39] The 2017 WannaCry ransomware attack that wreaked billions of dollars in damage and was attributed to North Korea's Lazarus Group, for

would enhance the overall security of information technology networks and systems) and the potential national security/intelligence benefits that come with stockpiling zero-days. Although, it is important to note that there is considerable variation in the time it takes different organizations to patch vulnerabilities.

[37] Scott Shane, Nicole Perlroth, and David E. Sanger, "Security Breach and Spilled Secrets Have Shaken the N.S.A. to Its Core," *The New York Times*, November 12, 2017.

[38] "Emergency Directive 21-01," Department of Homeland Security, December 13, 2020.

[39] Libicki, "Second Acts in Cyberspace," in *Bytes, Bombs, and Spies*, p. 133.

instance, targeted hundreds of thousands of computers around the world across a range of industries that were running an older version of Windows.[40] The widespread nature of the damage actually belies the highly specific and targeted nature of the malware—almost all of the affected systems were running a version of Windows 7; the same strain of malware had no effect on computers running more up-to-date operating systems, such as Windows 10.

Moreover, asset owners of targets of strategic significance, such as critical infrastructure owners and operators, typically employ customized software (such as custom-developed supervisory control and data acquisition, SCADA, software) and very specific hardware with tailored configurations that are unique to those systems and usually only intimately understood by the original developers and manufacturers. It has been reported, for example, that the malware employed in the Stuxnet cyber attacks against the Iranian nuclear program was tailored to target the specific model of Siemens-brand programmable logic controllers used at the enrichment facility at Natanz.[41] Indeed, while Stuxnet was discovered in computers around the world, it only caused destructive effects against the centrifuges in Natanz.[42] The non-substitutability of entire classes of offensive cyber capabilities also increases the cost of developing an arsenal of them. Indeed, Herbert Lin notes that, "the cost of a cyber weapon, which is almost entirely in R&D, cannot be amortized over as many targets as would be the case for a kinetic weapon. This fact necessarily increases the cost-per-target destroyed."[43]

The role of time in cyber operations

There is a common conception that time is highly—even dangerously—compressed in cyberspace operations. Lucas Kello, for instance, asserts that, "strategic depth in the new domain barely exists . . . . The speed at which code can travel and execute eliminates temporal limitations to the infliction of harm across national borders."[44] Matthew Miller et al. suggest that, in cyberspace, "[a]ttacks can transit the globe at near the speed of light. Battles can be won or lost in milliseconds."[45]

[40] "Cyber-attack: US and UK Blame North Korea for WannaCry," *BBC*, December 19, 2017.
[41] Kim Zetter, "An Unprecedented Look at Stuxnet, the World's First Digital Weapon," *Wired*, November 3, 2014.
[42] Steven M. Bellovin, Susan Landau, and Herbert Lin, "Limiting the Undesired Impact of Cyber Weapons," in *Bytes, Bombs, and Spies*, p. 269.
[43] Herbert Lin, "Oft-Neglected Cost Drivers of Cyber Weapons," Council on Foreign Relations-Net Politics (blog), December 14, 2016, https://www.cfr.org/blog/oft-neglected-cost-drivers-cyber-weapons.
[44] Lucas Kello, *The Virtual Weapon and International Order* (New Haven, CT: Yale University Press, 2017), pp. 138–139.
[45] Matthew Miller, Jon Brickley, and Gregory Conti, "Why Your Intuition about Cyber Warfare is Probably Wrong," *Small Wars Journal*, November 29, 2012.

This fundamentally misunderstands the temporal nature of offensive cyber operations. Rather than occurring at "lightning speed," some crucial aspects of cyber operations take time.[46] While it is true that, at the tactical level, a line of code can indeed be executed at "network speed," at the operational level cyber operations (and, in the aggregate, campaigns) are distinguished by slower-paced and unpredictable operational tempos—even as individual events may occur immediately and without apparent warning to the target. Specifically, there are three mechanisms that slow operational tempo, pausing the pace at which operations and campaigns unfold. The first is the time required to conduct reconnaissance and gain access to a target as part of operational preparation of the environment (OPE). The second is the development timelines for tailored offensive capabilities. And the final mechanism is the shelf life of both of these over the course of an operation or campaign.

As Troy Mattern et al. describe, OPE requires a significant investment in time prior to the moment at which an attacker causes an cyber effect:

> Days, weeks, months or even years may be required to: decide to take action; determine objectives; select an avenue of approach to use (through the network, an insider, or the supply chain); collect the required information on what to specifically target; acquire the appropriate capability; develop the appropriate access and then, finally commit the action itself, before assessing the effects and determining if further actions are needed.[47]

The initial penetration of a target network or system can be resource intensive and net unpredictable results, requiring prior planning and resource allocation and development. There are certainly long research and development timelines for sophisticated conventional weapons systems (in the case of the F-35 or V-22 Osprey, for instance, this process can take over a decade). However, once most conventional capabilities are developed they can be manufactured at scale, employed against a target when desired, and stay operational for years if not decades. In contrast, in cyberspace, operational planning and execution must consider that a given capability may not be usable or even exist at the desired time of employment. Therefore, the continuous and often time-intensive requirements for exploit development is an important consideration for cyber operations

---

[46] Jason Healey, "Claiming the Lost Cyber Heritage," *Strategic Studies Quarterly* 6, no. 3 (Fall 2012): 14.

[47] Troy Mattern, John Felker, Randy Borum, and George Bamford, "Operational Levels of Cyber Intelligence," *International Journal of Intelligence and Counterintelligence* 27, no. 4 (2014): 706.

planning in a way that is distinct from development timelines for conventional capabilities.[48]

The role of time is perhaps most striking when considering the implications of access and capability development in the context of carrying out an offensive operation or campaign. As in any other military campaign, in cyberspace this occurs under dynamic conditions in which a strategic adversary can take measures to blunt the effectiveness and impact of an attack. But because the virtual world is changeable in a way that the physical world is not, actions taken by defenders during a crisis between rivals can radically and unpredictably change an attacker's ability to deliver and sustain effects against a target over time.[49] Footholds into a target's network that were time-intensive to develop can unexpectedly disappear as vulnerabilities in a network are patched. Also, exploits may have a short shelf life as revealing information about them enables targets to identify indicators of compromise to prevent further damage from specific malware strains or quarantine malicious traffic using known malware signatures.

Thus, in the context of an iterative interaction between an attacker and defender in cyberspace, the former's operational tempo is likely to be interrupted by the latter's behavior, forcing the attacker to devote additional time to develop or acquire new vulnerabilities and exploits in the middle of an offensive operation or campaign. The ability to build or acquire new accesses and capabilities "in real time" during a crisis is highly limited.[50] Indeed, General Paul Nakasone, commander of U.S. Cyber Command, remarked in a January 2019 interview on the radical difference in shelf life between conventional and cyber capabilities:

> Compare the air and cyberspace domains. Weapons like JDAMs [Joint Direct Attack Munitions] are an important armament for air operations. How long are those JDAMs good for? Perhaps 5, 10, or 15 years, sometimes longer given the adversary. When we buy a capability or tool for cyberspace . . . we rarely get a prolonged use we can measure in years. Our capabilities rarely last 6 months, let alone 6 years. This is a big difference in two important domains of future conflict.[51]

---

[48] From a defensive/cybersecurity perspective, the pace of DevOps (a conjunction of "development"—building computer programs—and "operations"—testing those programs) in a dynamic and continuous process reflects the dynamism of the environment.

[49] Libicki, "Second Acts in Cyberspace," in *Bytes, Bombs, and Spies*, p. 133.

[50] Austin Long, "A Cyber SIOP? Operational Considerations for Strategic Offensive Cyber Planning," in Herbert Lin and Amy Zegart, eds., *Bytes, Bombs, and Spies* (Washington, DC: Brookings Institution Press, 2018), p. 120.

[51] William T. Eliason, "An Interview with Paul M. Nakasone," National Defense University Press, January 17, 2019.

Therefore, as a 2013 Defense Science Board report notes, "offensive cyber will always be a fragile capability" when pitted against network defenders who are "continuously improving network defensive tools and techniques."[52]

Moreover, the pace of offensive operations may also be limited by the complexity and sophistication of IT systems, which can impede attackers from causing intended effects. Many systems are "built to avoid single points of failure, and typically, many things have to fail for a cyberattack to succeed."[53] This makes persisting over time against a dynamic defender even more imperative—yet also immensely difficult. As Chris Inglis notes, "The dynamism of cyberspace cuts both ways, challenging the aggressor attempting to prosecute a sustained *campaign* (measured by success that is sustained beyond the initial opening tactic) in the face of a now alerted and often unpredictable defender . . . maintaining the precision and staying power of an attack beyond the opening phase . . . is a daunting proposition."[54]

Finally, the limits on decisive effects of a given cyber operation (which we discuss in greater detail below) implies that attackers may often have to carry out a series of attacks as part of a cyber campaign. In the initial salvo, the attacker may have a momentary advantage—provided the attacker was able to maintain an enduring, stealthy presence in the target's network to execute the ultimate objective at the desired time. But that advantage is likely to quickly reverse as the target takes measures to reduce its vulnerabilities to follow-on attacks (which can include technical fixes as well as shifting toward more redundant, resilient systems) and as the attacker is forced to invest time and resources to gain new accesses and develop new exploits or shift to less costly capabilities. To succeed in an offensive cyber campaign that unfolds over time, attackers must be able to sustain "the efficacy of tools under varying conditions caused by the defender's response and the natural variability and dynamism of cyberspace."[55] Altogether this suggests that, rather than occurring at rapid speed, cyber operations and campaigns take time in the development stage and even as they unfold.

More Bark than Bite: Limitations on Costly Effects

The effects of cyber operations are often portrayed in harrowing terms, especially by some policymakers and media in the United States who describe a

---

[52] Department of Defense Defense Science Board, "Task Force Report: Resilient Military Systems and the Advanced Cyber Threat," *Office of the Undersecretary of Defense for Acquisition, Technology and Logistics*, Washington, DC, January 2013, p. 49.

[53] Libicki, "Second Acts," in *Bytes, Bombs, and Spies*, p. 137.

[54] Chris Inglis, "Illuminating a New Domain," in *Bytes, Bombs, and Spies*, p. 21.

[55] Ibid., p. 29.

potential for cyber attacks to have disastrous implications for targeted societies and economies.[56] But, as then-Director of National Intelligence James Clapper noted in Congressional testimony in 2015, these fantastical scenarios are divorced from reality: "[r]ather than a 'Cyber Armageddon' scenario that debilitates the entire US infrastructure [w]e foresee an ongoing series of low-to-moderate level cyber attacks from a variety of sources over time, which will impose cumulative costs on US economic competitiveness and national security."[57]

Actors face significant limitations in leveraging cyberspace to impose decisive and meaningful costs against a target, particularly at a magnitude comparable to that of offensive operations that employ conventional or, certainly, nuclear munitions.[58] Moreover, sustaining costly effects over time is likely to be even more difficult and unreliable, given the confluence of a number of other attributes of cyber operations discussed at length above.

The utility of military power for the purposes of coercion or brute force inheres in its abilities to inflict—or credibly threaten to inflict—significant damage and harm against a target to achieve a political objective.[59] Cyber operations could be (and have been) used to cause disruption of an adversary's networks and systems—overwhelming them such that they temporarily lose the ability to function or the target loses confidence in their reliability; to produce destructive effects by destroying data resident on these systems; or, in rarer circumstances, causing effects in the physical realm.[60] However, cyber operations do not produce direct, physical violence against their targets. This is consistent with how actors have behaved in cyberspace; "the vast majority of malicious cyber activity has taken place far below the threshold of armed conflict between states, and has not risen to the level that would trigger such a conflict."[61] This is why, in Herbert Lin's parlance, "going cyber is pre-escalatory" and countervalue cyber attacks (those that target civilian, rather than military, assets) occur "all the time now and are at the BOTTOM of the escalation ladder."[62] Rather than their ability to

---

[56] Sean T. Lawson, *Cybersecurity Discourse in the United States: Cyber-Doom Rhetoric and Beyond* (New York: Routledge, 2019). Also see Brandon Valeriano and Ryan C. Maness, *Cyber War versus Cyber Realities: Cyber Conflict in the International System* (Oxford: Oxford University Press, 2015).

[57] James Clapper, "Statement for Record: Worldwide Cyber Threats," House Permanent Select Committee on Intelligence, September 10, 2015, p. 2.

[58] See Erik Gartzke, "The Myth of Cyberwar," *International Security* 38, no. 2 (Fall 2013): 41–73; and Thomas Rid, *Cyber War Will Not Take Place* (Oxford: Oxford University Press, 2013).

[59] For a discussion of the distinction between brute force and coercion, see Thomas C. Schelling, *Arms and Influence* (New Haven, CT: Yale University Press, 1967). Also see Robert J. Art, "To What Ends Military Power?" *International Security* 4, no. 4 (Spring 1980): 3–35.

[60] For a more detailed discussion of this point see Borghard and Lonergan, "The Logic of Coercion in Cyberspace," pp. 452–481, 461–463.

[61] Eric Talbot Jensen, "The Tallinn Manual 2.0: Highlights and Insights," *Georgetown Journal of International Law* 48, no. 3 (2017): 736.

[62] Herbert Lin, "Thinking about Nuclear and Cyber Conflict: Same Questions, Different Answers." Presentation, Hoover Institution/Center for International Security and Cooperation, Stanford

wreak permanent, destructive effects, cyber operations are often prized for their temporary and reversible nature.[63]

Measuring the costs of cyber operations in terms of violence—physical destruction or loss of life—reveals the relatively minimal harm that stems from them in comparison to other military tools. Relatedly, psychological factors may play a role in shaping how decision makers and domestic publics are likely to perceive the "cost" of physical versus virtual destruction.[64] Non-physical effects may not generate the kind of visceral urge for retaliatory or escalatory responses as physical violence.

While theoretically possible, no one has reportedly died to date as a direct result of a cyber attack despite over 30 years of recorded cyber operations.[65] Even in hypothetical catastrophic scenarios, the cost in terms of human casualties is minimal. For instance, common "worst case" scenarios of cyber attacks involve a cyber attack a power grid.[66] However, even in this instance, the conceivable damage from the loss of power over an extended period of time is far less than that which could be wreaked using basic conventional capabilities. To draw a comparison, when Hurricane Sandy hit the U.S. eastern seaboard in late October 2012 over 8.5 million people were left without power, with many going weeks and even months before it was brought back on line.[67] Yet, a U.S. National Hurricane Center postmortem of Hurricane Sandy reported that of the 159 people in the United States killed either directly or indirectly from Hurricane Sandy only "[a]bout 50 of these deaths were the result of extended power outages during cold weather, which led to deaths from hypothermia, falls in the dark by senior citizens, or carbon monoxide poisoning from improperly placed generators or cooking devices."[68]

University, CA, May 15, 2015, https://sipa.columbia.edu/sites/default/files/Thinking%20about%20 Nuclear%20and%20Cyber%20Conflict-Columbia-2015-05-14.pdf.

[63] Max Smeets and Herbert S. Lin, "Offensive Cyber Capabilities: To What Ends?" 10th International Conference on Cyber Conflict (CyCOn), Tallinn, Estonia, 2018.

[64] For work on the role of emotion in decision-making during cyber crises, see Rose McDermott, "Some Emotional Considerations in Cyber Conflict," *Journal of Cyber Policy* 4, no. 3 (2019): 309–325.

[65] Some might claim that there have been indirect deaths associated with cyber attacks, such as the WannaCry ransomware attack in May 2017 that crippled the UK's National Health Service. However, a 2018 National Audit Investigation by the British government does not even mention indirect casualties that may have resulted from the impact of the cyber attack on UK hospital and medical providers. Comptroller and Auditor General, Department of Health, "Investigation: WannaCry Cyber Attack and the NHS," National Audit Office, April 25, 2018. Similarly, in 2020 *Wired* reported that a German woman may have died in a hospital as a result of a ransomware attack, but this was also an indirect effect of the cyber attack. See William Ralston, "The Untold Story of a Cyberattack, a Hospital and a Dying Woman," *Wired*, November 11, 2020.

[66] See for example, Joseph Marks, "Pentagon Researchers Test 'Wort-Case Scenario' Attack on U.S. Power Grid," *Nextgov*, November 13, 2018.

[67] Eric S. Blake et al., "Tropical Cyclone Report- Hurricane Sandy (AL182012) 22–29 October 2012," National Hurricane Center, February 12, 2013, 14–15, http://www.nhc.noaa.gov/data/tcr/AL1 82012_Sandy.pdf.

[68] Ibid., 14.

If a cyber attack took out power of a similar magnitude and duration of Hurricane Sandy, it is conceivable that an equivalent number of casualties would result. The 2015 synchronized cyber attacks against Ukrainian power companies, attributed to Russia, is the first known example of an offensive cyber operation targeting a state's power grid. Its cost was ultimately low. Service was temporarily disrupted to 225,000 customers for several hours and energy providers operated at a limited capacity for some period of time after service was restored.[69] There were no reported casualties from this power outage. While any casualty resulting from a cyber attack would certainly be lamentable, even worst-case scenario figures are minor in comparison to the cost in human lives stemming from other, even limited, conventional military operations. Moreover, the targets of cyber attacks have demonstrated a consistent ability to recover from them relatively quickly. For example, in the case of two destructive cyber attacks attributed to North Korea, the 2013 South Korean banks attack and the 2014 Sony attack, "despite the destruction of files, all are still in business, and none spent more than an inconsequential amount of time recovering."[70]

Finally, a target may not even perceive the costs being imposed against it. Depending on the nature of the cyber incident, the sheer volume of cyber activity against a particular target may mean that an operation itself could go entirely unrealized. In other words, a target may not even comprehend that it is being attacked. While this may seem implausible, in the case of a cyber attack against North Korea, for instance, local internet service may already be so unreliable that a temporary disruption could be interpreted as a routine technical malfunction rather than an intentional attack by a strategic actor.[71] Moreover, when an adversary employs sophisticated tradecraft and is able to obscure its presence on a network, it could take months or even years for a breach to be detected. For example, while Russian threat actors compromised SolarWinds's systems in January 2019, the hack was not discovered until December 2020. Moreover, the breach was uncovered by a private cybersecurity firm, not the U.S. government—despite the fact that dozens of government networks had already been compromised.[72]

---

[69] "Cyber-Attack against Ukrainian Critical Infrastructure," IR-ALERT-H-16-056-01, ICS-CERT, Department of Homeland Security, February 25, 2016; "Analysis of the Cyber Attack on the Ukrainian Power Grid," E-ISAC, March 18, 2016.

[70] Bellovin et al., "Limiting the Undesired Impact of Cyber Weapons," in *Bytes, Bombs, and Spies*, p. 272.

[71] See Erica D. Borghard, "Lost in Cyber Translation? U.S. Cyber Signaling to North Korea," *NetPolitics*, October 16, 2017.

[72] Tim Starks, "SolarWinds CEO Reveals Much Earlier Hack Timeline, Regrets Company Blaming Intern," *Cyberscoop*, May 19, 2021.

Relationship between Intelligence and Military Cyber Operations

Some experts have described strategic interactions in cyberspace as characterized by an intelligence contest where states aim to collect and exploit information, undermine adversary morale, conduct sabotage, and emplace intelligence assets in the event of military conflict.[73] In our analysis, we focus on the operational aspects of intelligence in cyberspace, as distinct from debates about whether cyberspace provides greater strategic utility for intelligence versus military objectives. Specifically, we are concerned with the interplay of and relationship between intelligence and offense at an operational level and the implications for escalation.

A core characteristic of cyber operations is the inextricable link between intelligence (including cyber intelligence, surveillance, and reconnaissance) and military cyber operations.[74] This is where the terminological distinction between exploitation and attack becomes relevant. While both require taking advantage of a vulnerability to gain access to a target, exploitation involves clandestinely gaining access for the purposes of observing and exfiltrating private information, while attack entails causing some kind of effect against data at rest or in transit (e.g., disrupt, degrade, destroy, etc.).[75]

Intelligence operations are "an *essential predicate* and enduring component to mission success in the cyber realm."[76] Intelligence forms the foundation of offensive cyber operations due to the tailored and specific nature of access and capabilities and the ensuing collection requirements against targets to plan and execute offensive operations. As Martin Libicki notes, "[s]uccess at operational cyberwar depends to a great extent on knowing where the target is vulnerable."[77] The time and resource requirements for intelligence about a target may exceed by orders of magnitude those to conduct an operation—potentially at a ratio of 100 to 1.[78] Intelligence operations can be conducted to gather information as part of laying the groundwork for a forthcoming offensive operation.[79] For instance, an attacker might conduct an initial intelligence operation to "map the

---

[73] Joshua Rovner, "Cyber War as an Intelligence Contest," *War on the Rocks*, September 16, 2019. Also see Gartzke and Lindsay, "Weaving Tangled Webs."

[74] Although other sources of intelligence, such as human intelligence (HUMINT) and open source intelligence (OSINT), can contribute to preparatory efforts.

[75] Herbert S. Lin, "Offensive Cyber Operations and the Use of Force," *Journal of National Security Law & Policy* 4, no. 63 (2010): 63–64.

[76] Inglis, "Illuminating a New Domain," in *Bytes, Bombs, and Spies*, p. 24.

[77] Martin C. Libicki, *Cyberdeterence and Cyberwar* (Santa Monica, CA: RAND Corporation, 2009), p. 154.

[78] Ibid., p. 155.

[79] Andru E. Wall, "Demystifying the Title 10-Title 50 Debate: Distinguishing Military Operations, Intelligence Activities & Covert Action," *Harvard National Security Journal* 3 (2011): 118–120.

network and make inferences about important and less important nodes on it simply by performing traffic analysis to determine what the organizational structure is and who holds positions of authority," for the purposes of identifying the key nodes to attack.[80]

The intelligence operations that support and enable offensive cyber operations involve collecting information about a target through a variety of intelligence sources; it is not confined to collection via cyber means alone.[81] For example, collecting intelligence on an opponent's integrated air defense system may begin with human intelligence or imagery intelligence that then drives cyber capability development to disrupt that system in the future.

The relative ease of collection is conditional on the complexity of the target; "[t]he more sophisticated the target, the more effort it will take to find usable vulnerabilities and understand the effects of exploiting them on adversary capabilities."[82] In Libicki's words:

> The search for vulnerabilities is usually a search for specific vulnerabilities in specific systems that can be exploited in specific ways. Intelligence is also needed on network architecture, the relationships between various defense systems (e.g., what information from the target system feeds into which other systems?), and influence relationships (what information affects which types of decisions?).[83]

For example, the Stuxnet attacks that targeted Iranian centrifuges in Natanz reportedly relied on extensive intelligence collection about the particular characteristics of the systems used at Natanz that could have been acquired "through a human operator (an insider, for example); it could have been electronic (obtained by hacking into Siemens systems, the supplier of the specific programmable logic controllers [PLCs] used in Natanz and that signaled to Stuxnet that it was at the target system); or some other methods or combination of methods."[84] Intelligence is therefore vital at every step of an operation, from collecting information about the specifications of a target's network or system and identifying vulnerabilities to serve as a foothold for an attack, to developing means of access and the exploit itself.

---

[80] Lin, "Offensive Cyber Operations," p. 69.
[81] Matthew M. Hurley, "For and from Cyberspace: Conceptualizing Cyber Intelligence, Surveillance, and Reconaissance," *Air & Space Power Journal* 26, no. 6 (November–December 2012): 14.
[82] Libicki, "Cyberdeterrence," p. 154.
[83] Ibid., p. 155.
[84] Bellovin et al., "Limiting the Undesired Impact of Cyber Weapons," in *Bytes, Bombs, and Spies*, p. 270.

Therefore, intelligence operations are not only necessary and fundamental to any offensive operation but can also be time- and resource-intensive. As Austin Long notes, "the intelligence requirements for cyber options are immense, as the delivery mechanism is entirely dependent on intelligence collection."[85] Laying the intelligence groundwork for an offensive cyber operation "can be extraordinarily difficult, even for advanced cyber actors."[86] This is because states typically secure the critical systems that might be targeted through cyber means because of their importance to social and economic functioning and national security. This means that developers of offensive cyber capabilities must not only collect intelligence on a target that is likely to be well defended and not connected to the internet, but they must also possess intimate knowledge of the specific information or operational technology on which a particular system is built, which is often customized and not publicly known. Developing a capability that can interface with a custom-built system is difficult, but it is by orders of magnitude more arduous to develop the mastery necessary to manipulate the system to do something that it may have been designed to resist—to understand, for instance, how complex processes relate to one another or to identify key nodes that could be targeted to produce cascading failures.

Finally, intelligence collection is vital not only prior to gaining access to a target's network or system (identifying vulnerabilities and developing exploits for them), but is also important even after an actor has established a foothold in a network. It is often the case that cyber capabilities themselves have built-in intelligence collection functions to gather information about a target's network subsequent to penetration. Intimate knowledge of a network's structure and how different components relate to one another can often be gained only after breaching the network itself.[87]

Conclusion

This chapter explores four important attributes of cyber operations: the importance of secrecy for operational success and, relatedly, the role of plausible deniability; the technical challenges in planning and conducting offensive cyber operations, especially the role of gaining access, the unpredictability and temporal nature of effects, and the non-universal lethality of cyber capabilities; the limitations of cyber operations in causing costly effects at scale and, especially, sustaining these over time; and the relationship between intelligence and

---

[85] Long, "Cyber SIOP," p. 117.
[86] Ibid.
[87] Bellovin et al., "Limiting the Undesired Impact of Cyber Weapons," in *Bytes, Bombs, and Spies*, p. 274.

military operations in cyberspace. These attributes stem from fundamental aspects of cyberspace and are separate and distinct from the political calculations and decision-making associated with the development and employment of cyber capabilities. Put simply, all cyber actors confront these technical realities, even if they may be defined by different regime types and strategic cultures, force postures and strategies for force employment, levels of risk tolerance, civil-military relations, or other factors that may impact escalation dynamics. Of course, this does not mean that these political, organizational, and cultural factors are unimportant. In the following chapter, we explore the implications of these four characteristics for escalation.

3

A Theory of Cyber Escalation

Problematic Assumptions about Cyberspace

Two prominent viewpoints within practitioner and academic communities are that strategic rivalries that play out in cyberspace are likely to be characterized by escalatory dynamics and that the potential risk of escalation may be greater in cyberspace than in other environments. Cyberspace is said to be conducive to escalation for a plethora of reasons, such as the covert, secretive manner in which capabilities are developed and employed; the difficulties of discerning the intent behind observed behavior on a network and the limited ability to send credible signals of resolve, heightening the likelihood of misperception; the potential for cyber operations to hold civilian populations and economies at risk by targeting critical infrastructure; the danger that responding to a cyber attack based on poor attribution could catalyze unintended escalation; the ambiguous command and control of governments over cyber proxies that empower the latter to ratchet up tensions with state rivals without the knowledge or approval of their sponsors; and so on. However, if escalation dynamics between cyber rivals are so overdetermined, why have we failed to observe numerous—if any—cyber escalatory spirals triggered by cyber incidents?

This chapter builds on the key attributes of cyber operations discussed in Chapter 2 to present a theory of cyber (non)escalation. These realities of cyber operations affect how states use offensive cyber power for strategic purposes—both to conduct and respond to cyber operations. Moreover, these operational factors dampen escalatory pressure even when there are other variables present that might otherwise exacerbate it. This takes place through three mechanisms. First, most offensive cyber operations of strategic significance are costly, complex, unpredictable, difficult to sustain over time, and limited in their ability to impose costs on a target. This means they are not offense dominant in the way the cyber literature assumes.[1] Second, the reliance of cyber operations on secrecy

---

[1] For foundational work on offense-defense theory see, Robert Jervis, "Cooperation Under the Security Dilemma," *World Politics* 30, no. 2 (1978): 167–214; Stephen van Evera, "Offense, Defense, and the Causes of War," *International Security* 22, no. 4 (Spring 1998): 5–43; Charles L. Glaser and Chaim Kaufmann, "What Is the Offense-Defense Balance and How Can We Measure It?" *International Security* 22, no. 4 (Spring 1998): 44–82; George H. Quester, *Offense and Defense in the International System* (New York: Wiley, 1977); Sean M. Lynn-Jones, "Offense-Defense Theory and Its Critics," *Security Studies* 4, no. 4 (Summer 1995): 665–666; Jack S. Levy, "The Offense/Defense

Escalation Dynamics in Cyberspace. Erica D. Lonergan and Shawn W. Lonergan, Oxford University Press.
© Oxford University Press 2023. DOI: 10.1093/oso/9780197550885.003.0003

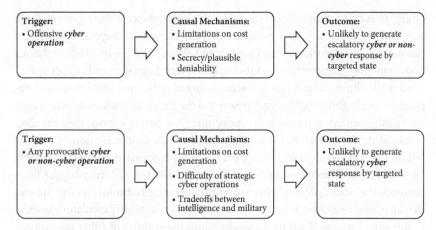

Figure 3.1 Relationship between Cyber Operations and Escalation

and plausible deniability creates breathing space that can reduce the urgency of crisis situations. And finally, the utility of cyberspace for intelligence operations creates trade-offs that decision makers must weigh. All actors in cyberspace, regardless of political organization or individual leadership, from nation-states to criminal entities to individual hackers, confront these same operational realities and constraints.[2]

Altogether, these factors generate an environment in which interactions between rivals are likely to be characterized by relative stability and limited (if any) escalatory dynamics, even as rivals compete with one another in and through cyberspace. The logic of our argument is summarized in Figure 3.1, which distills how states evaluate the use of cyber operations in response to potential cyber and non-cyber triggers. Essentially, we claim that cyber operations are unlikely to cause escalation—either in cyberspace or beyond it—and that states are not likely to turn to cyber operations as a tool of escalation in response to actions that take place within or outside of cyberspace.

This framework provides a structural explanation for the overall absence of escalatory dynamics between cyber rivals. Specifically, the four core characteristics of cyber operations narrowly circumscribe the instances in which states may

Balance of Military Technology: A Theoretical and Historical Analysis," *International Studies Quarterly* 28, no. 2 (June 1984): 219–238; Stephen Biddle, "Rebuilding the Foundations of Offense-Defense Theory," *Journal of Politics* 63, no. 2 (August 2001): 741–774; Michael E. Brown, Owen R. Cote, Jr., Sean Lynn-Jones, and Steven E. Miller, *Offense, Defense, and War* (Cambridge, MA: MIT Press, 2004).

[2] By extension, we would expect that if these properties change in a way that favors offense and reduces impediments to building and sustaining offensive cyber operations of consequence, then there should be an increase in the risk of instability and escalation.

be able to escalate with cyber means. And this accounts for why, in general, there is so little evidence of cyber escalation. At the same time, beyond these broad claims, this framework serves as a guide to help explore the specific conditions under which escalation risks are more or less severe. Even if, overall, cyber operations are not linked to escalation, the feasibility of cyber operations is context dependent. If a highly capable cyber power has the ability to retaliate against a rival with significant cyber means at an opportune time during a crisis, then the risks of escalation are greater. But satisfying all of these conditions is, more often than not, a rare event. And even for states that are more inclined to accept risk and rely on strategies and doctrines that are offensively oriented with hair-trigger force postures, the lack of physical violence from cyber attacks diminishes the chances that an offensive approach in cyberspace will seed or intensify escalatory spirals.

But what happens if a state misunderstands the realities of cyber operations? In other words, even if cyber operations have characteristics that make them poor tools of escalation, what if leaders act as though cyberspace is a perilous environment? Leaders have made similar miscalculations in the past, sometimes with disastrous implications. For instance, in the lead-up to World War I experts believed that the technologies of warfare favored the offense and conferred first strike advantages. Instead, they found that the combination of the lethality of machine guns, artillery, and trench warfare favored the defense, but only after all parties sustained extraordinary levels of battlefield casualties.[3] The good news is that because cyber operations can't kill people or cause physical destruction in the same way that the weapons of World War I could, the consequences of contemporary miscalculations are less severe. But holding on to wrong assumptions about the dangers of cyberspace does have negative strategic implications, which we explore later in this book.

Does Cyberspace Actually Favor the Offense?

Part of our argument rests on the reality that the cyber operations most likely to cause escalation are also those that are more difficult to plan and carry out. Additionally, even these operations rarely cause significant costs, let alone violent, physical effects. In this sense, how we conceptualize cyber operations starkly contrasts with the idea that offense has an advantage in cyberspace. Offensive advantage is an important cause of escalation in the security studies literature. Specifically, when offense has the advantage, escalation is likely to occur

---

[3] Van Evera, "Offense, Defense, and the Causes of War"; Jack Snyder, *The Ideology of the Offensive: Military Decision Making and the Disasters of 1914* (Ithaca, NY: Cornell University Press, 1984); Biddle, "Rebuilding the Foundations of Offense Defense Theory."

regardless of whether an actor is status quo or revisionist because aggression and conquest are perceived to be relatively cheap and easy in comparison to defense.[4] In contrast, when defense is purported to be dominant, the probability of conflict escalation decreases.

Therefore, in this section we go back to basics, plumbing the traditional offense-defense literature to investigate whether the conventional wisdom is right that offense has an advantage over defense in cyberspace. We assess how the traditional literature has measured offensive advantage in the past and extend this to cyberspace.[5] Specifically, we evaluate how traditional measures of the offense-defense balance map onto some of the characteristics of cyber operations that we identified as important in the previous chapter. We find compelling evidence in favor of our claim that cyber operations do not lend themselves to an offensive advantage.

In the next section, we move beyond debates about offensive advantage, which only get us part of the way toward an explanation for why there has not been cyber escalation. Specifically, we show why just focusing on the purported offensive advantages of cyber operations misses other, important features of cyber operations that contribute to escalation dynamics.

False assumptions: conventional wisdom about offensive advantage in cyberspace

The prevailing wisdom in the discipline is that cyberspace is offense dominant and that the supposed advantages accruing to the attacker create an environment that increases the risk of escalation.[6] For instance, Lucas Kello describes cyberspace as a "perfect breeding ground for political disorder and strategic instability

---

[4] Van Evera, "Offense, Defense, and the Causes of War," pp. 5–43.

[5] Our analysis sets aside the question of measuring the relative utility of a given dollar spent on offensive versus defensive cyber capabilities. We do this for three reasons. First, most budgets on offensive (and even defensive) cyber capabilities are secret, and even rough or aggregate numbers do not adequately capture the distinctions in budgetary allocations for offensive versus defensive forces and capabilities. Second, Rebecca Slayton has already done fantastic work on this particular question and, indeed, her results demonstrate that offensive cyber operations are actually quite costly and difficult in comparison to defense (see Rebecca Slayton, "What Is the Cyber Offense-Defense Balance? Conceptions, Causes, and Assessment," *International Security* 41, no. 3 (2016): 72–109). Finally, as we will discuss in much greater detail later in the chapter, the non-universal lethality and non-substitutability of many cyber capabilities that target critical military and civilian networks and systems pose significant measurement problems for developing a generalizable or aggregate measure of the cost of these capabilities and operations.

[6] P.W. Singer and Allan Friedman, *Cybersecurity and Cyberwar* (New York: Oxford University Press, 2014), p. 154; Keir Lieber, "The Offense-Defense Balance and Cyber Warfare," in Emily O. Goldman and John Arquilla eds., *Cyber Analogies* (Monterey, CA: Naval Postgraduate School, 2014), pp. 100–101; Lucas Kello, "The Meaning of the Cyber Revolution: Perils to Theory and Statecraft," *International Security* 38, no. 2 (Fall 2013): 7–40; Gregory J. Rattray, *Strategic Warfare in Cyberspace*

[because] cyberspace is an offense-superior domain."[7] Kello attributes this to the "enormous costs of cyber defense."[8] Jason Healey claims that "powerful defense and resilience is difficult in cyber conflict, as the offense tends to have so many tactical advantages over the defense."[9] The New York Cyber Task Force posited in 2017 that "attackers in cyberspace have for decades held fundamental advantages over defenders,"[10] while a January 2013 Defense Science Board report asserts, "it is not possible to defend against the most sophisticated cyber attacks."[11] Martin Libicki claims that "[o]ffense-defense curves at levels that characterize today's cyberspace favor the offense."[12] P.W. Singer and Allan Friedman describe a widespread belief across military organizations in the advantages of the offense in cyberspace, driving them to invest in offensive cyber capabilities.[13] Ilai Saltzman explicitly links cyber offense dominance with escalation, positing that the technology of cyberspace "allows states to take greater risks and thus adopt more vigilant or offensive positions vis-à-vis their adversaries. Cyber capabilities [make] the decision to escalate armed conflict easier and considerably cheaper."[14] In a discussion of U.S.-China crisis stability, Avery Goldstein notes that, with respect to cyber capabilities, "the advantages that the attacker enjoys in these realms and the integration of such assets with both nuclear and conventional forces generate distinctive but still unknown 'cross-domain' escalation risks."[15]

But, even beneath the surface of these stark pronouncements of an offensive advantage in cyberspace, there are some glimmers of reality that challenge these assumptions. For instance, the very same Defense Science Board report that proclaims cyberspace as nearly indefensible also describes sophisticated attacks as being solely within the purview of a handful of states who must "invest large

---

(Cambridge, MA: MIT Press, 2001); Dale Peterson, "Offensive Cyber Weapons: Construction, Development, and Employment," *Journal of Strategic Studies* 36, no. 1 (2013): 120–124. For critiques, see Rebecca Slayton, "What Is the Cyber Offense-Defense Balance?" and Erik Gartzke and Jon R. Lindsay, "Weaving Tangled Webs: Offense, Defense, and Deception in Cyberspace," *Security Studies* 24, no. 2 (2015): 316–348.

[7] Kello, "The Meaning of the Cyber Revolution," p. 32.
[8] Ibid., p. 27.
[9] Jason Healey, "The Cartwright Conjecture," in Herbert Lin and Amy Zegart, eds., *Bytes, Bombs, and Spies: The Strategic Dimensions of Offensive Cyber Operations* (Washington, DC: Brooking Institute Press, 2019), p. 174.
[10] "Building A Defensible Cyberspace: New York Cyber Task Force," Columbia University School of International and Public Affairs, 2017, p. 4.
[11] Defense Science Board, "Resilient Military Systems and the Advanced Cyber Threat," January 2013, p. 1.
[12] Martin C. Libicki, *Cyberdeterrence and Cyberwar* (Santa Monica, CA: RAND Corporation, 2009), p. 32.
[13] Singer and Friedman, *Cybersecurity and Cyberwar*, p. 154.
[14] Ilai Saltzman, "Cyber Posturing and the Offense-Defense Balance," *Contemporary Security Policy* 34, no. 1 (2013): 41.
[15] Avery Goldstein, "First Things First: The Pressing Danger of Crisis Instability in U.S.-China Relations," *International Security* 37, no. 4 (Spring 2013): 87.

amounts of money (billions) and time (years) to actually create vulnerabilities in systems."[16] As Austin Long notes, "if an attack requires years of work and billions of dollars to overcome a defense that cost (only) millions of dollars, political scientists would characterize the environment as highly defense-dominant."[17] In concordance with Long's intuition, our analysis will demonstrate how the characteristics of cyber operations do not actually lend themselves to an offensive advantage. We also argue that, even if states misperceive the nature of the offense-defense balance in cyberspace, the technical realities—and limitations— of offensive cyber capabilities dampen pathways to escalation.[18]

Measuring offensive advantage

In Robert Jervis's classic formulation, the advantage of offense versus defense stems from a relative economic efficiency calculus—whether, in a context of limited resources, a state gets more out of investing in offensive or defensive forces— or from an assessment about a likely path to victory through exploiting windows of opportunity. In Jervis's words:

> First, does the state have to spend more or less than one dollar on defensive forces to offset each dollar spent by the other side on forces that could be used to attack? If the state has one dollar to spend on increasing its security, should it be put into offensive or defensive forces? Second, with a given inventory of forces, is it better to attack or to defend? Is there an incentive to strike first or to absorb the other's blow?[19]

Focusing on this latter question—whether it is "better" to go on the offensive or defend—there are generally three ways in which the literature has attempted to measure offensive advantage: the relative ease of conquest; mobility and maneuver; and firepower.[20] A challenge in extending these measures to cyberspace is that they were developed to assess offensive advantage for conventional

---

[16] Defense Science Board, "Resilient Military Systems," p. 2.

[17] Austin Long, "A Cyber SIOP? Operational Considerations for Strategic Offensive Cyber Planning," in *Bytes, Bombs, and Spies*, pp. 118–119.

[18] For an example of perceptions of the cyber offense-defense balance in the U.S. and China, see James D. Ryseff, "The Maliciously-Formed Packets of August: Cyberwarfare and the Offense-Defense Balance," *Center for Strategic & International Studies*, September 2017. For a discussion of the "cult of the offensive" and World War I, see Stephen Van Evera, "The Cult of the Offensive and the Origins of World War I," *International Security* 9, no. 1 (Summer 1994): 58–107.

[19] Jervis, "Cooperation Under the Security Dilemma," p. 188. Also see Lynn-Jones, "Offense-Defense Theory and Its Critics," pp. 665–666 for a discussion of the offense-defense investment ratio, as well as Glaser and Kaufmann, "What is the Offense-Defense Balance and Can We Measure It?"

[20] Jack S. Levy, "The Offensive/Defensive Balance of Military Technology: A Theoretical and Historical Analysis," *International Studies Quarterly* 28, no. 2 (June 1984): 223–225; Glaser and

(typically land-based) warfare. What "conquest" means in cyberspace, where there is no physical territory for an invading army to take and hold, is fundamentally different than what the original architects of the offense-defense literature likely envisioned. We take this into account in evaluating how measurements that were developed for one form of conflict could apply to a new one.

The ease of cyber "conquest"

An axiom of offense-defense theory is that "war is far more likely when conquest is easy."[21] As Jervis describes, "[w]hen we say that the offense has the advantage, we simply mean that it is easier to destroy the other's army and take its territory than it is to defend one's own. When defense has the advantage, it is easier to protect and hold than it is to move forward, destroy, and take."[22] In a similar vein, Sean Lynn-Jones describes how one would evaluate the offense-defense balance: "[it] can be assessed by asking whether existing technology makes it relatively easy for a state to use an offensive strategy to conquer another state of roughly equal strength."[23] When conquest is easy, war is more likely because both status-quo and revisionist states will find offensive action appealing. Even "security-seeking states will find war more attractive; and the advantage of striking first grows with offensive advantage, which increases the risk of crises escalating via preemptive attacks and accidents."[24]

Applying the concept of "conquest" to cyberspace is complicated by the absence of physical territoriality; this is also the case when assessing territorial conquest in the context of air or sea power.[25] It is also complicated by the nature of tactical engagements and interactions between offensive and defensive cyber forces. Offensive cyber operations are not used to defeat the adversary's armed forces but, rather, at the tactical level to cause effects against data (disrupt, degrade, destroy, manipulate) and at the strategic level to attempt to coerce, deter, or confuse a target state, its military, or its population.[26] That said, in the past scholars have reconceptualized conquest in light of new technologies. With the advent of nuclear weapons, academics were forced to grapple with how those novel capabilities affected "the concept of the offensive/defensive balance

Kaufmann "What Is the Offense-Defense Balance and How Can We Measure It?" p. 64. Although, in the context of nuclear weapons, their destructive power created conditions of deterrence dominance.

[21] Evera, "Offense, Defense, and the Causes of War," p. 5.

[22] Jervis, "Cooperation Under the Security Dilemma," p. 187.

[23] Lynn-Jones, "Offense-Defense Theory and Its Critics," pp. 666–667.

[24] Glaser and Kaufmann, "What Is the Offense-Defense Balance and How Can We Measure It?," p. 45.

[25] See Levy's discussion of air and sea power in "The Offense/Defense Balance of Military Technology," p. 226.

[26] Erica D. Borghard and Shawn W. Lonergan, "The Logic of Coercion in Cyberspace," *Security Studies* 26, no. 3 (2017): 452–481.

of military technology [which] may mean entirely different things in the two different situations."[27]

In a similar vein, we must reassess how the "ease of conquest" notion of the offense-defense balance applies in cyberspace. While territorial conquest per se does not occur in cyberspace, offensive cyber operations do have analogous logics. The ultimate objective of conquest is to take control of an enemy's territory. This requires physically defeating its armed defenders. In the case of offensive cyber operations, the objective is to manipulate the enemy's networks or systems in some way to achieve a desired military or political objective. This requires surmounting enemy network defenses. Therefore, we extend the logic of ease of conquest to assess the extent to which offensive cyber operations are "easy" in cyberspace. We find that, simply put, offensive cyber operations are much harder than typically depicted. Specifically, access dependence, prior intelligence collection requirements to carry out offensive operations, and the non-universal lethality of cyber capabilities make cyber "conquest" difficult.

As described in the previous chapter, a successful offensive cyber operation rests on identifying a vulnerability that an attacker can exploit to gain access to a target's system and cause desired effects. Causing sustained effects against an adversary over time requires that the attacker replicate this process across potentially diverse and unique target sets with different vulnerabilities, access requirements, and tool specifications. The argument that the technology of cyberwar is offense dominant and, therefore, that escalation is likely rests in part on the notion that there are numerous vulnerabilities that could be exploited, making defenders always one step behind attackers and enabling the latter to always find means of gaining access. However, setting aside the relative skill level of any particular cyber power, the "ease" of a given offensive cyber operation varies considerably depending on two characteristics particular to the desired target. The first is whether causing an effect against a target requires gaining access and the relative difficulty and cost of that process (see Table 2.1 in Chapter 2). The second is how tailored the tool needs to be to the target (in other words, if the attacker can use off-the-shelf or easily modified, modular tools) and the extent to which a tool can be reused over time against the same or other targets.

In fact, there are few truly "easy" offensive cyber operations. Some of these, like DDoS attacks, rely on access-independent and non-tailored capabilities while others, like ransomware-as-a-service capabilities, may be easy to acquire in illicit marketplaces but difficult to employ with effect against strategic targets. These types of capabilities are unlikely to trigger escalatory responses because they do not generate costly and long-lasting effects against a target—their limited utility

---

[27] Levy, "The Offensive/Defensive Balance of Military Technology," p. 229. Also see Thomas C. Schelling, *Arms and Influence* (New Haven, CT: Yale University Press, 1967), ch. 2.

in imposing costs means they are unlikely to represent a qualitative or quantitative increase in the intensity of a crisis. Against those targets that are strategically
valuable and, therefore, more likely to provoke or signify an escalatory action,
offensive cyber operations are hard, unreliable, and difficult to scale. Moreover,
in addition to access requirements, the development of offensive tools can require extensive intelligence support and high research and development costs.
This cost cannot be amortized over numerous targets because cyber weapons,
particularly those against the most critical targets, lack universal lethality.

How might this unfold in the context of an ongoing crisis between cyber
rivals? States are unlikely to turn to cyber operations as a way of retaliating in
an escalatory fashion in response to some provocative action taken by a rival
state. That's because cyber "conquest" is not easy. The non-universal lethality of
cyber weapons and access requirements limit the utility of offensive cyber operations as tools of escalation because a state may not possess escalatory cyber
responses in their arsenal at the moment of desired use. Moreover, they may not
have time during an unfolding crisis or contingency to develop custom accesses
and capabilities to employ against an adversary. Therefore, waging an effective
long-term cyber campaign is difficult and costly under these conditions as actors
are likely to exhaust their arsenals over time and cannot replenish them with sufficient rapidity.

Moreover, the difficulty is compounded by the dynamic nature of cyber
defenses, as access and capabilities can be rendered inert through vulnerability patching, shifts to redundant systems, and other defensive measures. The
target is a strategic actor who can act to mitigate existing vulnerabilities once the
attacking state's tools and accesses are revealed as they are employed. Therefore,
as states conduct cyber operations over time as part of a series of interactions
with a rival, they are likely to use their most decisive, strategic capabilities at
the outset and will be less effective and/or precise over time, generating effects
against the most vulnerable or easiest, rather than more deliberate, targets.
Moreover, targets that are easier to hit may also be less likely to be perceived as
escalatory; states are more likely to harden targets they perceive to be strategically significant. Thus, cyber escalation is likely to be self-dampening, because a
tit-for-tat exchange in cyberspace may only iterate in an escalatory fashion a limited number of times—if at all—given access limitations, capability constraints,
and evolving target defensive measures.

Mobility and maneuver in cyberspace

Conventional mobility and maneuver are inextricably related to the relative
ease of conquest (in fact, the former is often used as an observable indicator of
the latter). As Charles Glaser and Chaim Kaufmann note, "[t]he most widely
agreed proposition is that improvements in mobility favor offense. Only offense

inherently requires mobility; a force that cannot move cannot attack, and a defender that can hold its positions need not move."[28] Mobility in conventional terms can be measured as "the ability of troops and equipment to move from one place to another."[29] A key component of mobility is breakthrough, which is a prerequisite to routing the defender's forces and achieving offensive territorial gains. Glaser and Kaufmann identify two stages of an offensive:

> The attacker must first achieve a breakthrough by defeating or destroying a section of the defender's front; the attacker must then exploit this breakthrough to advance into the defender's rear. Breakthrough is logically and temporally prior to exploitation, and substantively more important because the issue of exploitation arises only if and when breakthrough succeeds.[30]

Innovations in mobility that confer an offensive advantage should therefore facilitate breakthrough in addition to exploitation. Mobility intensifies the risks of escalation because it creates windows of opportunity and first strike incentives; if technology lends itself to mobility, then both attackers and defenders have an incentive to rush to the front lines to be the first to capitalize on an offensive advantage.

A predominant belief among experts is that cyberspace grants an advantage in mobility to the attacker. This is encapsulated in the notion that cyber offenses occur "at the speed of light" and that attackers can rely on stealth and maneuver to rapidly and without warning cause offensive effects against an unexpecting target. As General Keith Alexander, then-Commander of U.S. Cyber Command, noted in a Congressional testimony in 2012, cyber attacks "happen at lightning speed."[31] Similarly, Chris Inglis claims that mobility favors the attacker, who possesses "agility derived from choosing, without advance notice, the means, time, and place of exploitation to surprise, outmaneuver, and out-run victims."[32] Kier Lieber directly applies the precepts of offense-defense theory to cyber warfare, contending that "[c]yber offense is highly 'mobile' in the sense that attacks

[28] Charles L. Glaser and Chaim Kaufmann, "What Is the Offense-Defense Balance and Can We Measure It?," *International Security* 22, no. 4 (1998): 62. Also see Levy, "The Offensive/Defensive Balance of Military Technology," p. 225 and Keir A. Lieber, "Grasping the Technological Peace: The Offense-Defense Balance and International Security," *International Security* 25, no. 1 (Summer 2000): 78–80.

[29] Ibid., p. 78.

[30] Glaser and Kaufmann, "What Is the Offense-Defense Balance and How Can We Measure It?," p. 62.

[31] House Committee on Armed Services, Budget Request for Information Technology and Cyber Operations Programs: Hearing Before the Subcommittee on Intelligence, Emerging Threats, and Capabilities, Committee on Armed Services, House of Representatives, 112th Congress, March 20, 2012.

[32] Chris Inglis, "Illuminating a New Domain: The Role and Nature of Military Intelligence, Surveillance and Reconnaissance in Cyberspace" in Lin and Zegart, *Bytes, Bombs, and Spies*, p. 26.

can be carried out almost instantaneously. Cyber defenders may have little (if any) warning of a cyber attack, may not even detect an attack as it is underway and inflicting damage, and may be quickly outflanked or overwhelmed . . . . Mobility in cyberspace appears to favor offense in spades."[33]

It is true that some aspects of cyber operations enhance mobility and, therefore, may favor the offense. Much of this stems from the inherently non-physical, digital nature of cyber capabilities and the networks with which they interact (though there are of course physical components of cyber infrastructure). A command to execute a line of code to deliver a payload can be instigated instantaneously and without warning. Moreover, the virtual nature of cyberspace means that there are no physical impediments to producing an offensive effect—provided an attacker has already gained access to a network. According to a CrowdStrike report, the average breakout time, "how long it takes for an intruder to jump off the initial system (beachhead) they had compromised and move laterally to other machines within the network," was just under two hours for incidents it investigated in 2017, and is likely getting shorter each year.[34] Nevertheless, lateral movement—maneuvering within a network to find a desired target or data—is not perfectly frictionless; it can be hindered through defensive measures such as access controls, user and entity behavior analysis, and micro-segmentation, among other measurers.

However, considerable friction also limits an attacker's mobility prior to establishing a beachhead on a network. Identifying a vulnerability and discerning a means of gaining access to exploit it are prerequisites for any offensive cyber attack. This is the cyber equivalent of "breakthrough" in Glaser and Kaufmann's conventional terminology. The process of gaining access to a target, as noted in the previous chapter, can be costly in terms of time and resources.

Moreover, even in response to a skilled and well-resourced attacker there is a plethora of defensive measures that a state can take to increase the costs to an attacking force and impede its ease of mobility.[35] Attackers must overcome a range of buffers and measures that defenders employ to protect against attacking cyber forces trying to gain access to strategically important targets and, if those fail, increase the costs to them of doing so. The defense of networks and systems in cyberspace is layered, as illustrated in Table 3.1. However, it is important to note that Table 3.1 represents an abridged list of different types of security

---

[33] Lieber, "The Offense-Defense Balance and Cyber Warfare," p. 101.

[34] "2018 Global Threat Report: Blurring the Lines between Statecraft and Tradecraft," CrowdStrike, p. 5, https://go.crowdstrike.com/2018ThreatReport.html.

[35] These defensive measures are distinct from active defenses, to be discussed in the next section on the distinguishability of offense and defense, which are directed at attributing the adversary's offensive capabilities rather than defending one's own networks and systems.

Table 3.1 Examples of Defensive Measures That Counter Access

Type of Defensive Measure	Description	Means of Access It Counters
Physical Security of the System		
Secure and approved wireless access points	Ensure there are no "rogue" wireless access points.	Physical and on-net
Safeguarding supply chain	Prevent adversaries from interdicting the supply chain that provides hardware and software components.	Physical
Air gapping	Physically isolate networks and systems at a facility from the internet.	Physical and on-net
Facility security	Physically secure facilities on which networks and systems reside.	Physical
Training and personnel management	Ensure all personnel are screened and practicing proper cybersecurity practices.	Physical and on-net
Network Architecture and Management		
Intranet versus internet	Control points of access of internal networks to the internet.	On-net
VPN technology	End-to-end securing of remote user's access to a network.	On-net
Third party access	Screen and limit vendor and contractor access to a network.	Physical and on-net
Firewalls and other network-based intrusion prevention systems	Filters network traffic to scan for known attack signatures and/or anomalous activity and preclude access to blocked content; firewalls are typically emplaced at a gateway between a network and the internet.	On-net
Network-based intrusion detection systems	Programs that scan network traffic looking for signs of an attack and alert network administrators if they detect indications of one.	On-net
Compartmentalization	Identifying and segregating sensitive data assets.	On-net
Routine network maintenance	Ensuring firmware is updated on networked infrastructure (e.g., routers, switches).	On-net
Quarantining traffic	Create a "DMZ" for suspect traffic to facilitate identification and early warning of malicious activity.	On-net

(*continued*)

Table 3.1 Continued

Type of Defensive Measure	Description	Means of Access It Counters
Honeypots[a]	Appealing traps to distract and isolate potential attackers.	On-net
Network obfuscation	Prevent attackers from mapping entire network through constructing false network typologies.	On-net
Host Security		
Passwords and advanced forms of identification	Security protocol that limits unauthorized access to the network and the end user's computer.	Physical and on-net
Host-based encryption	Encrypting work stations and data storage.	Physical and on-net
Host-based intrusion detection systems	Similar to network detection systems, but based on host machines.	On-net
Personal firewalls	Programs that block malware access to/from the individual computer and the network.	On-net
Anti-malware tools	Programs that run on a host that hunt for known malware.	On-net
Application Security		
Routine software updating	Ensure regular and time-sensitive patch management.	On-net

[a] Honeypots could also be used for the purposes of disinformation, to undermine an attacking state's confidence in the integrity of stolen data if information is revealed regarding the use of honeypots.

controls; a more comprehensive depiction can be found in sources such as the Center for Internet Security, MITRE, and the National Institute of Standards and Technology.

This type of "defense in depth" in cyberspace, as Table 3.1 illustrates, encompasses physical, human, network, and host security measures to thwart an attacker's efforts to gain a launching point from which to deploy a payload. Of course, given sufficient time, resources, and skill, a dedicated attacker can almost always find a means of gaining access, but defensive measures that increase any of the three former factors force attackers to pay significantly greater costs and undermine the efficiency of offense.

Moreover, gaining access to a network and then stealthily maintaining persistent presence on a network until the desired execution of a payload requires that attacking forces prioritize stealth, careful tradecraft, and deliberate actions over speed. Because gaining access to a network requires secrecy for operational success, "the cyber operation involved must only minimally disturb the normal operating state of the computer involved. In other words, the intelligence collectors need to be able to maintain a clandestine presence on the adversary computer or network."[36] To do so, therefore, the attacker must first know what "normal" looks like on a particular network, so that its activities do not manifest as anomalous to defenders.

The twin requisites of access and stealth for operational success, coupled with the variety of physical and virtual impediments that defenders can erect to hamper attackers in their efforts to secure a foothold in a network, militates against the otherwise mobility enhancing nature of cyber capabilities in the wake of securing access. In the context of a single-shot iteration, the aggregate effect of these competing factors on mobility may be neutral. However, in an environment of multiple offensive cyber operations carried out against an adversary during an ongoing crisis, it is likely that the impediments to mobility will increasingly outweigh its facilitators. In other words, as an attacking state shifts resources from executing payloads at the "speed of light" using pre-positioned accesses against targets already being held at risk, to scrambling to acquire or build new means of access in the face of a responsive and calculating network defender, mobility will likely give way to the temporal requirements for capability and access development described in detail above. Therefore, these obstacles to mobility should dampen the potential for states to escalate using cyber means in the context of an ongoing crisis.

Cyber "firepower"

Similar to applying the concept of "conquest" to cyberspace, there are challenges with evaluating what "firepower" means in cyberspace because cyber operations take place in a virtual environment and rarely cause physical destruction. As originally conceived in the context of conventional warfare, firepower is defined as "the destructive power of the weapons or array of weapons available to sides in a conflict. Firepower consists of not only explosive power, but also range, accuracy, and rate of fire."[37] Unlike mobility, conventional firepower is typically

---

[36] Herbert Lin, "Offensive Cyber Operations and the Use of Force," *Journal of National Security Law and Policy* 4, no. 63 (August 2010): 64.

[37] Lieber, "Grasping the Technological Peace," p. 80

hypothesized to favor defenders over attackers because the defender's employ-ment of overwhelming firepower against advancing attacking forces undermines the latter's mobility, compelling the attacker to slow down, disperse, and seek cover.[38] However, there are exceptions. If there is a distinction between how fire-power is employed against attackers versus defenders, then there can be instances where improvements in the destructive potential of weapons could aid attackers. Glaser and Kaufmann note this, pointing to the examples of siege artillery used during the 20th century to attack fixed positions and anti-radiation missiles that target air defense systems as instances where differentially employed firepower favored the attacker.[39]

Conventional firepower generally favors defenders because the deployment of firepower against an attacking force is something that can hinder the attacker's advance and make it more difficult for them to take and hold territory. In cyber-space, beyond the more static defensive measures described in Table 3.1, there are numerous "active defense" measures that a defender could employ, compel-ling attackers to reduce their speed or employ obfuscation measures, or poten-tially even cut off an attack vector at its source. These defensive measures occur within and outside of the defender's network.

For example, defenders could directly target the attacker's attack infrastruc-ture, which refers to the infrastructure that enables a cyber attack to be delivered through the internet. These include but are not limited to servers and routers that are strategically emplaced or conscripted, potentially external to the attacking state's sovereign borders. While these are replaceable, destroying them could serve a delaying function. Another temporary advantage that a defender could impose on an attacker is to target command and control infrastructure used to monitor and deploy malware to points of presence in conscripted machines. If these could be decapitated at a strategic time then an adversary's employment of a capability, at least theoretically, could be prevented until communication is reestablished.[40] A defender could also conduct activities such as engaging with a third party (such as telecommunications providers) to cut off the origin of an attack. Or a defender could emplace a "logic bomb," which is malicious

---

[38] Glaser and Kaufmann, "What Is the Offense-Defense Balance and How Can We Measure It?," p. 64. However, Biddle notes that the innovations in firepower in the first half of the 20th century were initially perceived to benefit attackers, rather than defenders and it took some time for leaders to recognize the defensive benefits of firepower as part of a combined-arms, modern system of force employment. See Biddle, "Rebuilding the Foundations of Offense-Defense Theory."
[39] Glaser and Kaufmann, "What Is the Offense-Defense Balance and How Can We Measure It?," p. 64. Also see Lieber, "Grasping the Technological Peace," p. 80.
[40] The conditions under which offensive cyber authorities can and should be delegated is an area that needs further research. A good starting point is C. Robert Kehler, Herbert Lin, and Michael Sulmeyer, "Rules of Engagement for Cyberspace Operations: A View From the USA," *Journal of Cybersecurity* 3, no. 1 (February 28, 2017): 69–80.

code that resides on the defender's network that an attacker takes back to its own network, triggering a negative impact such as wiping files. Additionally, defending states could engage in "hacking back," which entails operating outside of its own networks. This could include penetrating an attacker's networks during the course of or following an attack for the purposes of destroying information with which the attacker absconded, stealing adversary information, wiping their networks, or other retaliatory measures. Finally, a defender could also employ counter-computer network exploitation, which involves going after the adversary's toolkit and developing custom defenses against it; or revealing information about the threat such that others can develop patches against the vulnerability that the cyber weapon exploits and, in effect, degrading the attacking state's offensive capabilities by rendering them useless.[41]

Yet, the underlying issue that the above discussion does not directly address is the reality that what "firepower" means in cyberspace—and if it even makes sense to conceptualize offensive advantage in this way for cyber operations—is fundamentally different from conventional conflict. Cyber "firepower" simply does not contain the inherent physical violence of conventional firepower. These constraints strongly suggest that any application of offensive cyber firepower will be limited. Despite this, there are experts who use the language of firepower to describe the effects of cyber operations. For example, Ilai Saltzman coined the term "byte power" to describe how firepower applies to cyberspace, stating that "in cyberspace firepower actually relates to the degree of technological damage that can be inflicted on the enemy's ICT-based infrastructure at the strategic, operational, and tactical levels."[42] At a 2011 RSA Conference, former U.S. Deputy Defense Secretary William Lynn characterized cyber operations as having significant firepower potential: "[a] couple dozen talented programmers wearing flip-flops and drinking Red Bull can do a lot of damage."[43]

But, as the discussion in the previous chapter on the limitations of cost generation of cyber operations illustrates, most of the time, "cyber weapons have far less firepower than is commonly assumed."[44] And, certainly, offensive cyber

---

[41] Andrew Wichmann and Elmar Gerhards-Padilla, "Using Infection Markers as a Vaccine Against Malware Attacks," 2012 IEEE International Conference on Green Computing and Communications, November 20–23, 2012; Erica D. Borghard and Shawn W. Lonergan, "U.S. Cyber Command's Malware Inoculation: Linking Offense and Defense in Cyberspace," Council on Foreign Relations, April 22, 2019.

[42] Saltzman, "Cyber Posturing," p. 44. Also see John Arquilla and David Ronfeldt, Cyberwar is Coming! (Santa Monica, CA: RAND Corporation, 1993); and Arquilla, "Cyberwar is Already Upon Us," Foreign Policy, February 27, 2012.

[43] U.S. Department of Defense, Office of the Assistant Secretary of Defense (Public Affairs), "Remarks on Cyber at the RSA Conference as Delivered by William J. Lynn, III," San Francisco, California, February 15, 2011.

[44] Thomas Rid, Cyber War Will Not Take Place (New York: Oxford University Press, 2013), p. 39.

capabilities simply cannot bring to bear a level of firepower that is comparable to any conventional munition. In fact, we would submit that to describe offensive cyber as representative of an innovation in firepower verges on the nonsensical. As Bart Groothuis, former chief cyber policy official for the Netherlands, remarked about cyber operations taking place during the crises between Russia and Ukraine in the winter of 2021–2022: "Cyber warfare doesn't exist, it's nonsense . . . .Warfare, we have to reserve that term for other things."[45] Therefore, while it is the case that cyberspace affords attackers—particularly those that are well-resourced, patient, and skilled—the ability to overwhelm a target's defenses, the magnitude of cyber power in general (whether it comes from an attacker or defender) raises questions about how useful firepower is as a metric of offensive or defensive advantage in cyberspace. In other words, while a dedicated attacker may ultimately, at some point, be able to gain access and cause an effect against a target's network, the strategic implications of this advantage to the attacker may be limited when taking into account the overall effects of cyber operations.

Taken together, when extending measures of offensive advantage to cyberspace, there are reasons to be skeptical of prominent arguments in the literature that cyberspace confers an offensive advantage. Cyber operations are more complex, difficult, and time-consuming to plan and implement than proponents of an offensive advantage acknowledge. Moreover, cyber operations may not even be reliable at the desired moment of employment. Even when they are, most do not create significant costs for targeted entities when compared to other types of military capabilities. The implications of cyber firepower for offensive advantage are more mixed—given sufficient time and resources, an attacker can typically overwhelm a defender. But what this means in a broader context, incorporating all of the other limitations of cyber operations, suggests that the offensive advantages of cyber operations have been highly exaggerated.

Beyond Offensive Advantage: The Role of Secrecy and Espionage

Moreover, offensive advantage is not the only aspect of cyber operations that is important for assessing their escalatory potential. We argue that two other mechanisms play a role in dampening the escalatory impact of cyber operations: the centrality of secrecy and the value cyber operations have for intelligence purposes. These factors are not typically considered in the context of conventional operations because they are not relevant for that form of conflict.

---

[45] Laurens Cerulus, "Don't Call It Warfare. West Grapples with Response to Ukraine Cyber Aggressions," *POLITICO*, January 18, 2022.

Yet it is these aspects of cyber operations—more analogous to covert and intelligence operations or subversion than to outright military conflict—that also shape the dynamics of escalation.[46]

The dampening effects of secrecy

At first glance, it may seem that the characteristics of cyberspace that enable governments to obfuscate their role in offensive cyber operations—the fact that they can avoid attribution—would cause attackers to perceive that they could get away with a first strike, putting rivals on a pathway to escalation. Or, secrecy could cause escalation through creating the conditions for false flags, catalyzing escalation between rivals where it would not otherwise have occurred. However, the literature on traditional covert operations has convincingly demonstrated that, rather than prompting escalation, secrecy is more likely to be an effective tool of escalation management in situations that would otherwise be conducive to triggering escalatory spirals. For conventional covert operations, even those that are "open secrets" where responsibility is de facto understood and assumed (though not admitted), plausible deniability serves as a form of escalation control as rivals engage in "tacit collusion" to diminish potential escalation.[47] Secrecy can mitigate the risk of escalation in contexts where it might otherwise be high through reducing domestic political pressure and allowing states to privately communicate to resolve disputes short of escalation.[48] There is no a priori theoretical reason to suspect that secrecy would not serve a similar function in non-attributed or ambiguously attributed cyber operations. We explore the signaling and de-escalation implications of this in greater detail in the next chapter.

There are additional reasons why we would expect secrecy to dampen the potential for escalation between rivals in cyberspace. Specifically, secrecy is inextricably linked to the role of time in cyber operations, compounding the other temporal aspects described above that can put the brakes on any inexorable route to escalation. The operational requirement for secrecy—the fact that, in many

---

[46] Lennart Maschmeyer, "The Subversive Trilemma: Why Cyber Operations Fall Short of Expectations," *International Security* 46, no. 2 (Fall 2021): 51–90.

[47] Austin Carson, "Facing Off and Saving Face: Covert Intervention and Escalation Management in the Korean War," *International Organization* 70, no. 1 (Winter 2016): 103–131.

[48] See, for example, Austin Carson, *Secret Wars: Covert Action in International Politics* (Princeton, NJ: Princeton University Press, 2018); Austin Carson and Keren Yarhi-Milo, "Covert Communication: The Intelligibility and Credibility of Signaling in Secret," *Security Studies* 26, no. 1 (2017): 124–156. This is similar to the dynamics of "gray zone" conflicts which, as Hal Brands notes, are meant to "reap gains, whether territorial or otherwise, that are normally associated with victory in war . . . *without* escalating to overt warfare, *without* crossing established red-lines, and thus *without* exposing the practitioner to the penalties and risks that such escalation might bring." See Hal Brands, "Paradoxes of the Gray Zone," *Foreign Policy Research Institute*, February 5, 2016.

cases, attackers must maintain a stealthy presence on a network for some period of time, potentially for the entire duration of an operation—means it not only takes time for an operation to unfold but it may also take time for an affected entity to even discern that it has been the target of an offensive cyber operation and ascertain the extent of the damage inflicted. Moreover, plausible deniability means that it may take time for an entity to assign attribution at a confidence level that is sufficiently high to warrant or justify an escalatory response, or for a state to be willing to share potentially sensitive attribution information with domestic publics and allies. If attribution requirements place a pause on response times, they inject a break into a potential escalatory cycle.

Crises are defined by temporal pressure—the exigency of having to make rapid decisions in high-stakes situations, often within the view of domestic and international audiences. The extension of time, therefore, creates breathing room for parties to ratchet down potential escalatory tensions. Therefore, those factors that lengthen time horizons reduce the salience of these crisis pressures, producing space for decision makers to discern the nature of the situation, for alternative policy options to be considered and, potentially, for cooler heads to prevail.

The intelligence value of cyber operations

Finally, a unique aspect of cyber operations that is outside of the scope of traditional measures of offensive versus defensive advantage is the relationship between intelligence and military operations. This relationship is twofold. First, cyber operations have a critical intelligence function. The overwhelming majority of cyber incidents associated with nation-states is conducted for the purpose of espionage.[49] In fact, a significant body of the cyber literature argues that strategic interactions in cyberspace should be primarily understood as an intelligence contest.[50] Beyond espionage as an objective of most cyber operations, intelligence is also an essential component of offensive cyber operations as it is a critical prerequisite of successful attack, especially those conducted against strategic, hardened targets requiring tailored access and custom exploits.

---

[49] Brandon Valeriano, Benjamin Jensen, and Ryan C. Maness, *Cyber Strategy: The Evolving Character of Power and Coercion* (Oxford: Oxford University Press, 2018).

[50] See debate in, "Policy Roundtable: Cyber Conflict as an Intelligence Contest," *Texas National Security Review*, September 17, 2020, https://tnsr.org/roundtable/policy-roundtable-cyber-conflict-as-an-intelligence-contest/. This builds on earlier work by Gartzke and Lindsay, "Weaving Tangled Webs," which focuses on the role of deception in cyber operations; Joshua Rovner, "The Intelligence Contest in Cyberspace," *Lawfare*, March 26, 2020, https://www.lawfareblog.com/intelligence-cont est-cyberspace; Joshua Rovner, "Cyber War as an Intelligence Contest," *War on the Rocks*, September 16, 2019, https://warontherocks.com/2019/09/cyber-war-as-an-intelligence-contest/.

Gaining access to an adversary's network or system can serve dual military and intelligence purposes, creating trade-offs. Specifically, it forces states to conduct intelligence gain-loss calculations when engaging in military actions that could result in burning valuable intelligence accesses and assets.[51] How a decision maker ultimately weighs these trade-offs is a function of a number of factors beyond the scope of our analysis. Nevertheless, as Michael Sulmeyer notes, "[t]he challenge is that the potential for operational gain may be fleeting, as the adversary may be able to adapt its defenses quickly or the effectiveness of the cyberattack may be less than anticipated. Given these caveats, decision makers are likely to err on the side of caution by preferring to maintain intelligence collection and not risk exposing sources and methods."[52] Jon Lindsay, in analyzing this trade-off in the context of U.S.-China relations in cyberspaces, notes that strategic interactions between them are likely to remain "in a relentlessly irritating but indefinitely tolerable stability" because both sides are incentivized to "moderate the intensity of their exploitation in order to preserve the benefits that make exploitation worthwhile in the first place."[53]

This presents decision makers with what we term a "use it *and* lose it" conundrum (rather than the typical "use it *or* lose it" trade-off that the escalation literature depicts). The decision to conduct an offensive cyber operation—the choice to "use it"—may preclude other intelligence operations on which an access relies—to "lose it." This is distinct from the "use it or lose it" trade-off because the latter implies pressure to employ a capability or squander it. In contrast, the trade-off in cyberspace is between using a capability for one purpose (offensive operations) in comparison to a different purpose (espionage). If a state chooses the former, it forfeits the latter. However, choosing not to use a capability for offensive purposes still preserves it for other strategic ends. Compounding this choice is the fact that, if cyber operations have relatively limited utility to impose costs against adversaries, states may be more likely to balk at risking prized intelligence accesses for evanescent offensive cyber benefits. In other words, the intelligence value associated with having penetrated an adversary network may, in many cases, far outweigh the value of an offensive cyber operation. Therefore, in a scenario in which a state seeks to escalate in response to some provocative maneuver by an adversary (the second causal pathway in Figure 3.1), the intelligence

---

[51] James A. Lewis, J.D. McCreary, and Maren Leed, "Offensive Cyber Capabilities at the Operational Level: The Way Ahead," *Center for Strategic and International Studies*, September 2013, p. 6.

[52] Michael Sulmeyer, "Campaign Planning with Cyber Operations," *Georgetown Journal of International Affairs* 18, no. 4 (Fall 2017): 136.

[53] Jon R. Lindsay, "The Impact of China on Cybersecurity: Fiction and Friction," *International Security* 39, no. 2 (Winter 2014/2015): 9.

trade-offs provide an additional reason beyond the difficulty of cyber operations and their limitations in obtaining costly effects to choose other, non-cyber response tools.

This dual-use nature of cyber operations presents alternatives to the employment of cyber power for offensive purposes alone. The gains a state may perceive from prioritizing the intelligence value of cyber operations over the limited, transient effects they typically produce is yet another factor that diminishes the efficacy of cyber operations as tools of escalation.

What Does This Mean for State Behavior and Escalation?

The characteristics of cyber operations we describe above shape how states make decisions about the use of cyber power—both their willingness to escalate and their ability to do so with cyber means. Most of the time, even when a state may desire to escalate a situation, cyber operations present limited options for doing so. Offensive cyber operations are challenging, unreliable, and limited in their decisiveness, making a decision to escalate a crisis through employing them unlikely to net the desired returns. The nature of cyber operations can also affect the desire to escalate. The temporal aspects of cyber operations can ameliorate the heightened political pressure of crises by creating breathing space, reducing the willingness of decision makers to escalate, either with cyber or non-cyber options. And the utility of cyber operations for strategic objectives outside of military force—especially intelligence—affects the proclivities of decision makers to choose cyber operations as part of an escalatory response.

These dynamics should be reflected in how states actually behave in cyberspace. Therefore, in this section, we derive a number of observable predictions about state behavior as well as patterns of interactions between cyber rivals. Specifically, in Table 3.2 we identify potential scenarios that specify the conditions under which we should expect to observe deliberate cyber escalation, inadvertent cyber escalation, failed cyber escalation, cross-domain escalation, or the absence of any escalation. This allows us to consider the full scope of potential scenarios, including cyber and non-cyber responses.

As noted earlier, the core logic of our theory rests on the technical foundations of offensive cyber operations, rather than on theorizing about the sources or determinants of political calculations about the willingness of states to use some types of capabilities against certain types of targets, engage in greater risk-taking, or prioritize military over intelligence uses of cyberspace. Russia, for instance, may be inclined to pursue strategies that are offensive, decentralized, opportunistic, and risk-acceptant. This may derive from cultural and organizational

Table 3.2 Observable Predictions for State Behavior

	Possesses the Ability to Escalate Using Cyber Means at the Desired Time	Lacks the Ability to Escalate Using Cyber Means at the Desired Time
State Seeks to Escalate in Response to a Cyber or Non-Cyber Action by a Rival	*Deliberate Cyber Escalation:* State may choose to conduct escalatory offensive cyber operations against a rival. Time is compressed (attribution occurs quickly; rapid, strategic response options are available and in place). Military priorities supersede intelligence ones.	*Failed Cyber Escalation:* State may attempt failed or ineffective cyber escalation as it finds itself limited by technological realities. The state may "hit what it can get" in cyberspace based on capabilities at the time. *Cross-Domain Escalation:* If the stakes are sufficiently high, states will likely eschew a cyber response in favor of escalating with non-cyber means.
State Does Not Seek to Escalate in Response to a Cyber or Non-Cyber Action by a Rival	*No Escalation:* State may have escalatory offensive cyber capabilities but chooses not to escalate. Time diffuses crisis pressure (attribution is slow or uncertain). Intelligence priorities supersede military ones. *Inadvertent Cyber Escalation:* Loose command and control over offensive cyber capabilities, including relying on cyber proxies, leads to an escalatory response despite a lack of political will.	*No Escalation:* State lacks both willingness and capabilities, so escalation should not occur. State will engage in tit-for-tat responses, if at all, using proportionate cyber or cross-domain means.

legacies, regime type, geography, or simply relative power position.[54] Exploring these origins requires its own research initiative. However, we cannot ignore the fact that, while all political actors confront the same technological realities of operating in cyberspace, variation in the political factors that drive willingness to engage in more or less risky behavior also shapes the strategic environment in which cyber rivals interact.

[54] Erica D. Borghard and Jack Snyder, "Strategic Culture in the Cyber Age," working paper; Nathan Leites, *A Study of Bolshevism* (Glencoe, IL: The Free Press, 1953); Maria Snegovaya, "Putin's Information Warfare in Ukraine: Soviet Origins of Russia's Hybrid Warfare," *Institute for the Study of War*, September 2015.

Most of the time, strategic interactions in cyberspace take place across the three scenarios in the right-hand column, because it is difficult and unpredictable to engage in offensive cyber responses. Two out of the three scenarios in that column are non-escalation scenarios. The one escalation scenario, cross-domain escalation, is contingent on the target of an offensive cyber operation perceiving that the stakes are sufficiently high to justify an escalatory response and, lacking appropriate cyber capabilities, choosing to escalate using conventional means. As of this writing, this scenario is purely hypothetical; no state has ever perceived a cyber event to be of such significant consequence that it chose to retaliate in an escalatory fashion using conventional military capabilities. However, later in this book we explore possible contexts where states might breach the cyber-kinetic military threshold.

The scenarios described in Table 3.2 represent expectations for how an individual state might behave. But escalation is, by its very nature, a dyadic interaction. Therefore, we pair together different scenarios of individual state behavior to generate hypotheses about when we might expect to see escalation dynamics between rivals. In particular, we focus on the most dangerous of these combinations, which are summarized in Table 3.3.

We should only expect to observe patterns of deliberate escalation dynamics between cyber rivals under the rare circumstance in which both states have the ability during a crisis to escalate and the political willingness to do so (the top,

Table 3.3 Escalation Scenarios between Cyber Rivals

Deliberate Cyber Escalation Dynamics	Both states are in the top, left-hand box of Table 3.2. Rivals deliberately escalate against each other using offensive cyber capabilities.
Inadvertent Cyber Escalation Dynamics	Both states are in the bottom, left-hand box of Table 3.2; or one state is in the bottom, left-hand box and the other is in the top, left-hand box. Inadvertent escalation occurs between rivals using offensive cyber capabilities when both parties have poor command and control, or when one seeks to escalate deliberately and the other has poor command and control.
Cross-Domain Escalation Dynamics	Both states are in the top, right-hand box of Table 3.2; or one state is in the top, right-hand box and the other is in the top, left-hand box. In other words, one party to a rivalry lacks the ability to escalate with cyber means but has the willingness to escalate in general; the other party mirrors the latter or has the willingness to escalate and the ability to escalate with cyber means. It is sufficient for only one party to cross the cyber-conventional threshold to generate cross-domain escalation dynamics.

left-hand box of Table 3.2). These types of situations are inherently dangerous; both parties are already committed to taking a strong stance. When interactions between them begin in cyberspace, both states are likely to quickly find that cyber operations provide limited efficacy in achieving escalation dominance. Instead, the escalatory effects of cyber operations are likely to dissipate over time due to the temporal requirements for gaining and maintaining accesses and capabilities as part of a sustained engagement. As each state reveals its accesses and capabilities, the other will gain increasing information to take measures to mitigate the costs and effectiveness of the adversary's offensive cyber actions, producing limited (at best) cyber escalatory spirals. It will take time for states to regain or gain new accesses and capabilities. Under these circumstances, an escalatory dynamic that started in cyberspace may spill over into the use of kinetic military force if a state is determined to escalate but finds that cyber operations are suboptimal for doing so.

Similar dynamics are likely to unfold through inadvertent escalation pathways. These occur when at least one state has the ability to escalate, but neither wants or intends to. This is most risky when a state has loose command and control structures over the employment of offensive cyber power and/or when a state relies on cyber proxies. However, even under these conditions, the limited effects of cyber operations and the constraints on sustained employment over time help to limit pathways to escalation. In fact, the breathing room that cyber operations create is particularly important in arresting inadvertent spirals, because it allows time for states to signal their true intentions and walk back from the precipice.

Finally, in a dyad where both parties seek to escalate but at least one lacks the ability to do so using cyber means, we should expect to observe states either engaging in failed endeavors to escalate using cyber capabilities (if they misunderstand the implications of their own technologies) and then shifting to cross-domain means of escalation or escalating in initial stages using non-cyber capabilities. Therefore, interactions in this case are likely to resemble the first scenario, but with states turning more rapidly to non-cyber means of escalation.

The first and third escalation scenarios—where states more or less quickly turn to the use of military force—may seem highly speculative because they are. Nevertheless, as part of our analysis we explore plausible scenarios that resemble these patterns and assess the conditions that may be more or less likely to trigger them.

Alternative Explanations

We offer one explanation for the absence of cyber escalation grounded in the features of offensive cyber operations. But there are other potential arguments beyond our theoretical framework. For instance, drawing on balance of power theory and arguments about the relationship between power preponderance and stability, one alternative explanation for the absence of escalation between cyber rivals is that the cyber system is characterized by escalation dominance or hegemony by a status quo power.[55] According to this logic, one state possesses such a clear and decisive preponderance of cyber power—an overmatch over all other prospective cyber rivals—that escalation does not occur because no revisionist state would risk the consequences or incur the costs of challenging the dominant cyber state. This is perhaps the least plausible alternative explanation because even the United States, the ostensible preponderant military power in conventional and nuclear domains of warfare, acknowledges that the cyber environment is characterized by competition with capable rivals rather than dominance. In 2019 Congressional testimony, General Paul Nakasone, commander of U.S. Cyber Command, explicitly describes a strategic environment in cyberspace in which the United States confronts "near-peer competitors conducting sustained campaigns below the level of armed conflict to erode American strength and gain strategic advantage."[56] Similarly, writing in 2010, Joseph Nye notes that, "a few states like the United States, Russia, Britain, France, and China are reputed to have greater capacity than others [but] it makes little sense to speak of dominance in cyber space as in sea power or air power."[57] In the ensuing years other nation-states have joined that list, most notably North Korea and Iran.[58] While it is implausible that, at a systemic level, a preponderance of power accounts for the absence of escalation dynamics, we incorporate the relative balance of power between rivals in our case study analysis.

---

[55] See Herman Kahn, *On Escalation: Metaphors and Scenarios* (New York: Routledge, 2017), pp. 23–24 on escalation dominance. For literature on unipolarity, hegemony, and stability see, William C. Wohlforth, "The Stability of a Unipolar World," *International Security* 24, no. 1 (Summer 1999): 5–41; John G. Ikenberry, Michael Mastanduno, and William C. Wohlforth, "Unipolarity, State Behavior, and Systemic Consequences," *World Politics* 61, no. 1 (2009): 1–27; Robert Jervis, "Unipolarity: A Structural Perspective," *World Politics* 61, no. 1 (2009): 188–213; Randall L. Schweller, *Unanswered Threats: Political Constrains on the Balance of Power* (Princeton, NJ: Princeton University Press, 2008); Duncan Snidal, "The Limits of Hegemonic Stability Theory," *International Organization* 38, no. 4 (Autumn 1985): 579–614. For arguments that escalation dominance is possible in cyberspace, see Stephen J. Cimbala, "Cyber War and Deterrence Stability: Post-START Nuclear Arms Control," *Comparative Strategy* 33, no. 3 (2014): 279–286; Cavaiola et al., "Cyber House Rules," 84, 99.

[56] "Statement of General Paul M. Nakasone, Commander United States Cyber Command, before the Senate Armed Services Committee," February 14, 2019, p. 2.

[57] Joseph S. Nye, Jr., "Cyber Power," Belfer Center for Science and International Affairs, May 2010, p. 4.

[58] See, for example, David E. Sanger, David D. Kirpatrick, and Nicole Perlroth, "The World Once Laughed at North Korean Cyberpower. No More." *The New York Times*, October 15, 2017; "M-Trends 2019: FireEye Mandiant Services Special Report," https://content.fireeye.com/m-trends; "2019 Global Threat Report: Adversary Tradecraft and the Importance of Speed," CrowdStrike, https://www.crowdstrike.com/resources/reports/2019-crowdstrike-global-threat-report/.

Second, escalation may not occur because there is mutual deterrence between cyber rivals that is highly credible and is clearly understood by both parties.[59] In this world, both parties to a cyber rivalry possess the capabilities to inflict escalatory costs against the other but are deterred from doing so out of the reciprocal fear of painful or costly retaliation. This form of deterrence does seem to exist at high thresholds—those cyber attacks that would rise to a level of war or conflict.[60] In this sense, the apparent robustness of strategic-level cyber deterrence may account for why states contest their rivals in cyberspace short of war; in an effort to avoid direct military confrontation, states conduct cyber operations below a level that would risk escalation. A corollary of this argument is that there are intrinsic incentives in the cyber environment that are conducive to "agreed competition" between powers in which all mutually (even if only implicitly) accede to the shared understanding that parties to a cyber crisis will avoid escalating beyond the use of force threshold.[61] This draws from Kahn's notion of "mak[ing] use of features of the particular 'agreed battle' that is being waged in order to gain an advantage."[62] In other words, parties to a crisis may have a threshold or limit beyond which they will not escalate and will instead focus on achieving objectives within a predetermined sphere.

However, the problem with these arguments is that they cannot account for the absence of *inadvertent* cyber escalation—which is what most of the cyber escalation literature is concerned with. In other words, just because states may prefer to keep strategic interactions in cyberspace contained to the competitive space below conflict does not mean they are precluded from unintentionally taking actions that nevertheless put them on an escalation pathway. The lack of both deliberate and inadvertent escalation, therefore, suggests a deeper theoretical explanation is warranted.

Third, escalation may be absent because strategic interactions in cyberspace are a form of Kahn's "subcrisis maneuvering" in which interactions do not escalate beyond a low-level threshold, not due to any "agreed competition" but, rather, because cyberspace operations in themselves are simply insufficiently

---

[59] But see, for example, Libicki, *Cyberdeterrence and Cyberwar*; Joseph S. Nye Jr., "Deterrence and Dissuasion in Cyberspace," *International Security* 41, no. 3 (Winter 2016/17): 44–71; Michael Fischerkeller and Richard Harknett, "Deterrence Is Not a Credible Strategy for Cyberspace," *Orbis* 61, no. 3 (Summer 2017): 381–393; and Dorothy Denning, "Rethinking the Cyber Domain and Deterrence," *Joint Forces Quarterly* 77, no. 2 (April 2015).

[60] Erica D. Borghard and Shawn W. Lonergan, "Deterrence by Denial in Cyberspace," *Journal of Strategic Studies* (2021): 1–36.

[61] Michael P. Fisherkeller and Richard J. Harknett, "Persistent Engagement, Agreed Competition, Cyberspace Interaction Dynamics, and Escalation," *Institute for Defense Analyses*, May 2018. But see Max Smeets, "There Are Too Many Red Lines in Cyberspace," *Lawfare*, March 20, 2019 for a critique of the concept of agreed competition.

[62] Kahn, *On Escalation*, p. 7.

costly to generate escalatory responses.[63] According to Brandon Valeriano and Benjamin Jensen, "[l]ow-level responses beget low-level counter-responses as states constantly engage in a limited manner . . . . Rarely does a response include an increase in severity."[64] This is consistent with similar arguments in the literature that cyber operations should be conceived as distinct from other forms of coercion and warfare that, through their violence, provoke crisis escalation.[65] Our argument is not inconsistent with this logic and explicitly draws from it. However, our argument is not only about the limited effects of cyber operations. We also posit that there are additional factors that mitigate escalation risks beyond the relative costs a state can impose on a rival through cyber operations, especially through the mechanisms of secrecy and intelligence considerations and the ways these shape decision-making and the role of time in interactions between states in cyberspace.

Conclusion

Our argument that cyberspace is not likely to be characterized by dangerous escalatory spirals between rivals is grounded in some of the core arguments of offense-defense theory and their application to cyberspace. Put simply, we argue that cyberspace does not confer a clear offensive advantage. Instead, the types of cyber operations that are likely to cause escalation are difficult to plan and execute and are unreliable and unpredictable in their effects. Moreover, even when these barriers are surmounted, they have limited cost-generation potential.

However, this is only one strand of our argument. We also incorporate other, distinct elements of cyber operations that provide additional mechanisms that dampen escalatory risks. These include the role of secrecy and plausible deniability in cyber operations, as well as their intelligence functions. These aspects of cyber operations have a temporal effect that stifles what might otherwise be escalatory situations, creating breathing room that defuses the time-based pressure that characterizes crises. They also generate trade-offs for decision makers that may cause them to prefer to respond (if at all) to perceived adversary

---

[63] Kahn, *On Escalation*, pp. 41–42.

[64] Brandon Valeriano and Benjamin Jensen, "The Myth of the Cyber Offense: The Case for Restraint," *Cato Institute*, January 15, 2019, p. 5. For further elaboration of the point and corresponding data, see Valeriano et al. *Cyber Strategy*.

[65] Erik Gartzke, "The Myth of Cyberwar: Bringing War in Cyberspace Back Down to Earth," *International Security* 38, no. 2 (Fall 2013): 41–73. Also see Borghard and Lonergan, "The Logic of Coercion in Cyberspace."

aggression with non-cyber means. In the next chapter, we further explore the implications of these arguments for signaling and de-escalation. Specifically, we posit that some of the same characteristics of cyber operations that reduce escalation risks can also make cyber operations useful tools for accommodative signaling and create opportunities for crises to de-escalate.

4

Restraint and Accommodation

How Cyber Operations Can Defuse Crises

Cyber Operations and De-Escalation

In Chapter 3, we presented our theory of why cyber operations are not likely to cause escalation. But one even more striking aspect of cyber operations is that not only do they not lead to conflict, in some situations they may even help defuse crises. Therefore, in this chapter, we extend the logic of our argument to explore how cyber operations can play a role in facilitating crisis de-escalation and stability, specifically through acting as signals of a willingness to avoid escalation. Offensive cyber operations are taking place more frequently in the context of international crises caused by events that happen outside of cyberspace.[1] In fact, since states first started using cyber operations during international crises in the late 1990s—such as when Chinese patriotic hackers defaced U.S. government websites after the United States and NATO accidentally bombed the Chinese embassy in Belgrade during the war in Kosovo—there is evidence that cyber operations are associated with crisis de-escalation.

We argue that cyber operations can help in crisis de-escalation because they allow states to "do something" during a crisis—defacing websites, disrupting traffic to a network, or even degrading military capabilities—that is visible but not clearly linked to the government. These types of cyber operations are also appealing because they do not cause such costly effects that they would prompt the other side to retaliate in a painful way, escalating the situation. For instance, experts expressed concerns about potential Iranian conventional retaliation after the United States withdrew from the nuclear agreement in May 2018, as Iran has a history of retaliating against the United States and its interests in the region.[2]

---

[1] For a review of data on cyber operations, see Brandon Valeriano, Benjamin Jensen, and Ryan C. Maness, *Cyber Strategy: The Evolving Character of Power and Coercion* (New York: Oxford University Press, 2018). For a historical account of cyber operations, see Jason Healey, ed., *A Fierce Domain: Conflict and Competition in Cyberspace, 1986–2012* (Vienna, VA: Cyber Conflict Studies Association, 2013).

[2] See, for example, Suzanne Maloney, "After Dumping the Nuclear Deal, Trump Has no Strategy for Iran," *Brookings*, May 9, 2018.

Escalation Dynamics in Cyberspace. Erica D. Lonergan and Shawn W. Lonergan, Oxford University Press.
© Oxford University Press 2023. DOI: 10.1093/oso/9780197550885.003.0004

But Iran appeared to respond in cyberspace, with observers noting an uptick in Iranian cyber activity against U.S. government and private sector entities.[3]

Therefore, rather than serving as a perilous playing field for states, cyberspace holds opportunities for international stability through facilitating crisis management and de-escalation. Actions in cyberspace do not cause war; instead, they can sometimes act as an alternative to military force. Specifically, during international crises the use of cyber operations can signal a desire not to escalate—what Glenn Snyder and Paul Diesing, in their work on coercive diplomacy, refer to as accommodative signaling.[4] Below, we discuss how the traditional international relations literature has approached the concept of signaling and then show how these insights may extend to cyberspace.

The Role of Signaling in International Politics

Signaling is a core element of international crisis bargaining and coercive diplomacy. To succeed in crises, states must convey to targets that they possess the capability to impose an advantageous outcome and that they are resolved to do so, while also managing the risks of unintended escalation and war.[5] Successful coercion rests on clearly communicating to a target what the coercing state expects of it—if you do X, then Y will follow.[6] As Alexander George notes in the context of coercive diplomacy, "both the threat and employment of force should be coupled with (that is, preceded, accompanied, or followed by) appropriate communications to the opponent."[7] And, the target must perceive these communications to be credible, rather than merely "cheap talk."[8]

Much of the literature on signaling in international politics focuses on how to communicate resolve—a state's commitment to follow through on a threat.[9]

[3] Nicole Perlroth, "Without Nuclear Deal, U.S. Expects Resurgence in Iranian Cyberattacks," *The New York Times*, May 11, 2018.

[4] Glenn H. Snyder and Paul Diesing, *Conflict among Nations: Bargaining, Decision Making and System Structure in International Crises* (Princeton, NJ: Princeton University Press, 1977), p. 107.

[5] Richard Smoke, *War: Controlling Escalation* (Cambridge, MA: Harvard University Press, 1977); Glenn H. Snyder and Paul Diesing, *Conflict Among Nations: Bargaining, Decision Making, and System Structure in International Crises* (Princeton, NJ: Princeton University Press, 1977); Paul Huth and Bruce Russett, "What Makes Deterrence Work? Cases from 1900 to 1980," *World Politics* 36, no. 4 (1984): 496–526; Thomas C. Schelling, *The Strategy of Conflict* (Cambridge, MA: Harvard University Press, 1960) and *Arms and Influence* (New Haven, CT: Yale University Press, 1966).

[6] Ibid., pp. 3–4.

[7] Alexander L. George, "Coercive Diplomacy: Definition and Characteristics," in Alexander L. George and William E. Simons, eds., *The Limits of Coercive Diplomacy*, 2nd ed. (Boulder, CO: Westview Press, 1990), p. 10.

[8] James D. Fearon, "Signaling Foreign Policy Interests: Tying Hands Versus Sinking Costs," *Journal of Conflict Resolution* 41, no. 1 (1997): 69; Schelling, *Arms and Influence*, 150.

[9] For instance, see Schelling, *The Strategy of Conflict* and *Arms and Influence*; Snyder and Diesing, *Conflict among Nations*; Alexander L. George and Richard Smoke, *Deterrence in American Foreign*

States can convey how resolved they are by engaging in different forms of costly signaling, allowing resolute states to distinguish themselves from irresolute ones.[10] In addition to signaling resolve, states can also try to make it clear to adversaries that they possess the military capabilities to carry out a threat through brandishing them, conducting military demonstrations, or engaging in military exercises.[11] Even in a traditional environment not defined by secrecy in the way cyberspace is, the nature of the international system means that other states may not be completely aware of their adversaries' abilities to take military action against them. There are information asymmetries about relative capabilities; states have private information about their own military capabilities and incentives to misrepresent them.[12] In turn, states can attempt to overcome these asymmetries by signaling their capabilities.[13]

Less studied in the signaling literature is how states can use signals for the purposes of managing escalation risks or even de-escalating crises. But crisis management is an essential aspect of coercive diplomacy. Even when one side is seeking to maximize its strategic objectives, it will also simultaneously seek to reduce escalation risks.[14] This is for a straightforward reason: no state wants a crisis escalating beyond its control, even when it is putting pressure on a rival to capitulate to its demands. The traditional literature on escalation also discusses the role of signaling in facilitating de-escalation. Herman Kahn, for example, argues that states can de-escalate a situation through engaging in "concessions and conciliation," but acknowledges that this process can be quite difficult because it "is even more sensitive to accurate communication and shared understandings than escalation is."[15] This is because, to de-escalate, adversaries in the context of a crisis situation—when tensions are already heightened—must be able to coordinate de-escalation moves.[16]

Policy: Theory and Practice (New York: Columbia University Press, 1974); Fearon, "Signaling Foreign Policy Interests," pp. 68–90; Kenneth A. Schultz, *Democracy and Coercive Diplomacy* (Cambridge, UK: Cambridge University Press, 2001).

[10]   Fearon, "Signaling Foreign Policy Interests," 69.
[11]   Evan Braden Montgomery, "Signals of Strength: Capability Demonstrations and Perceptions of Military Power," *Journal of Strategic Studies* 43, no. 2 (2020): 309–330.
[12]   James D. Fearon, "Rationalist Explanations for War," *International Organization* 49, no. 3 (1995): 379–414.
[13]   Montgomery, "Signals of Strength." Of course, states can also conduct intelligence collection against adversary military capabilities to reduce this information gap.
[14]   Snyder and Diesing, *Conflict among Nations*, 207.
[15]   Herman Kahn, *On Escalation: Metaphors and* Snyder *Scenarios*, 2nd ed. (New Brunswick, NJ: Transaction Publishers, 2010), 230–231.
[16]   Ibid., p. 231.

What are signals?

Robert Jervis defines signals as "statements or actions the meanings of which are established by tacit or explicit understandings among the actors . . . signals are issued mainly to influence the receiver's image of the sender."[17] Signals do not have to constitute literal messages (although Jervis identifies diplomatic notes as a paradigmatic type of signal); they can also include actions such as military maneuvers that convey meaning.[18] Signaling is important because actions in themselves may not clearly convey meaning or intent. Moreover, because signaling is not an inherent component of military strategy, a broader strategy of coercive diplomacy must also entail "the signaling, bargaining, and negotiating that are built into the conceptualization and conduct of any military alerts, deployments, or actions."[19] In other words, actions (particularly military ones) should be coupled with messages to communicate intent to an opponent. In Jervis's words, "[f]ew actions are unambiguous. They rarely provide anything like proof of how the state plans to act in the future."[20]

Signals rely on implied, shared agreements about the meaning behind different types of statements or actions. In this way, "signals are not natural; they are conventional. That is, they consist of statements and actions that the sender and receiver have endowed with meaning in order to accomplish certain goals."[21] Similarly, George notes that signaling in coercive diplomacy not only includes "military actions or political-diplomatic moves," but also contains "explicit verbal warnings."[22]

Challenges of signaling

Numerous factors complicate signaling in international politics. The recipient of the signal must not only discern the specific message the signaling state desires to convey but also assess its credibility.[23] Indeed, the bulk of the signaling

---

[17]   Robert Jervis, *The Logic of Images in International Relations* (New York: Columbia University Press, 1970), p. 18. Jervis further distinguishes between signals and indices, whereby indices are "statements or actions that carry some inherent evidence that the image projected is correct because they are believed to be inextricably linked to the actor's capabilities or intentions," p. 18.

[18]   Ibid., 113–114. For more on diplomatic signaling see, Anne E. Sartori, *Deterrence by Diplomacy* (Princeton, NJ: Princeton University Press, 2013); and Robert F. Trager, "Diplomatic Calculus in Anarchy: How Communication Matters," *American Political Science Review* 104, no. 2 (2010): 347–368.

[19]   George, "Coercive Diplomacy: Definition and Characteristics," p. 10.

[20]   Jervis, *The Logic of Images*, pp. 9, 19.

[21]   Ibid., p. 139

[22]   Alexander L. George, "Theory and Practice," in *The Limits of Coercive Diplomacy*, p. 17.

[23]   Jervis, *The Logic of Images*, pp. 24–25. On intelligibility of signals, particularly covert signals, see Austin Carson and Keren Yarhi-Milo, "Covert Communication: The Intelligibility and Credibility of Signaling in Secret," *Security Studies* 26, no. 1 (2017): 124–156.

literature focuses on how states can make their signals credible, particularly signals of resolve.[24] Thomas Schelling, for instance, exhaustively assesses the various mechanisms through which states can credibly communicate resolve in the context of international crises and strategic interactions, such as through strategies of brinksmanship, games of chicken, the "threat that leaves something to chance," trip wire forces, and so forth.[25]

Rationalist approaches to crisis bargaining and coercive diplomacy also home in on the question of how states can credibly communicate resolve. In James Fearon's formulation, states face dual information challenges: resolve is private information and states have incentives to exaggerate it. To overcome this, a resolved state must send costly signals because such actions separate resolute states from irresolute ones. States can do this through tying their hands with public signals to create costs ex post for failing to follow through on commitments, which Fearon posits is more effective. Or, states can sink costs, such as mobilizing military forces, which creates costs ex ante (but, as some critics note, also increases the probability of war).[26]

Extensions in the literature explore related aspects of costly signaling of resolve, such as the role of the domestic political opposition;[27] how non-democratic states can effectively signal resolve;[28] the role of reputation-building in coercive diplomacy;[29] how alliances can communicate resolve and commitment;[30] and empirical testing of tying hands versus sinking costs.[31] There is also a number of important caveats, critiques, and limitations of the rationalist approach to

[24] Joshua D. Kertzer, *Resolve in International Politics* (Princeton, NJ: Princeton University Press, 2016), p. 3.

[25] Schelling, *The Strategy of Conflict; Arms and Influence.* Also see Robert Powell, *Nuclear Deterrence Theory: The Search for Credibility* (Cambridge, UK: Cambridge University Press, 1990).

[26] Fearon, "Signaling Foreign Policy Interests." Also see James D. Fearon, "Signaling versus the Balance of Power and Interests: An Empirical Test of a Crisis Bargaining Model," *Journal of Conflict Resolution* 38, no. 2 (1994): 236–269. And see Todd S. Sechser and Abigail Post, "Hands-Tying versus Muscle-Flexing in Crisis Bargaining," Paper presented at the Annual Meeting of the American Political Science Association, San Francisco, CA, September 5, 2015. For critiques, see Jack Snyder and Erica D. Borghard, "The Cost of Empty Threats: A Penny, Not a Pound," *American Political Science Review* 105, no. 3 (2011): 437–456. For sinking costs increasing the risk of war, see Shuhei Kurizaki, "Efficient Secrecy: Public versus Private Threats in Crisis Diplomacy," *American Political Science Review* 101, no. 3 (2007): 543–558.

[27] Kenneth A. Schultz, "Domestic Opposition and Signaling in International Crises," *American Political Science Review* 92, no. 4 (1998): 829–844.

[28] Jessica L. Weeks, "Autocratic Audience Costs: Regime Type and Signaling Resolve," *International Organization* 62, no. 1 (2008): 35–64.

[29] Todd S. Sechser, "Reputations and Signaling in Coercive Bargaining," *Journal of Conflict Resolution* 62, no. 2 (2018): 318–345. Also see Dale C. Copeland, "Do Reputations Matter?," *Security Studies* 7, no. 1 (1997): 33–71; and Jonathan Mercer, *Reputation and International Politics* (Ithaca, NY: Cornell University Press, 2010).

[30] Brett Ashley Leeds, Jeffrey M. Ritter, Sara McLaughlin Mitchell, and Andrew G. Long, "Alliance Treaty Obligations and Provisions, 1815–1944," *International Interactions* 28, no. 3 (2002): 237–260.

[31] Keren Yarhi-Milo, Joshua D. Kertzer, and Jonathan Renshon, "Tying Hands, Sinking Costs, and Leader Attributes," *Journal of Conflict Resolution* 62, no. 10 (2018): 2150–2179.

costly signaling. For instance, while rationalist theories tend to focus on signals of resolve, equally important for coercive diplomacy is conveying military capability.[32] Military threats and demonstrations of capability that act not as costly signals, but as meaningful demonstrations of military power, are often sidelined in rationalist approaches.[33] Other lines of criticism challenge assumptions in the literature about rationality, cognition, and perception.[34]

However, as we will demonstrate later in this chapter, two important critiques of the costly signaling literature are most relevant for cyberspace. The first is the substantial emphasis on resolve as the primary objective of signaling at the expense of other signaling objectives, such as de-escalation, accommodation, and crisis stability. The second is the assumption that signaling is an inherently public endeavor—that the act of going public with an action or a message is what imbues that signal with credibility.[35] Our theory of signaling in cyberspace merges and builds on these two critical assessments within the signaling literature to account for why cyber operations have limited utility as costly signals of resolve but nevertheless have unique properties that can make them advantageous for accommodative signaling and crisis de-escalation.

Signaling for accommodation and de-escalation—not just resolve

Even though most of the international relations literature focuses on signaling resolve, signaling has other purposes. That's because, while states generally want to get their way in international crises, they also want to do so at an acceptable cost, avoid unwanted conflict, and minimize the risk of things spiraling out of control. The challenge "is to find the optimum mix or trade-off between coercion and accommodation in the particular crisis context, given the distribution of values and military power among the participants."[36] Therefore, Snyder and Diesing's foundational work on coercive diplomacy emphasizes that almost all

[32] Brendan Rittenhouse Green and Austin Long, "Conceal or Reveal? Managing Clandestine Military Capabilities in Peacetime Competition," *International Security* 44, no. 3 (2020): 48–83.

[33] Branislav L. Slantchev, *Military Threats: The Costs of Coercion and the Price of Peace* (Cambridge, UK: Cambridge University Press, 2011); Montgomery, "Signals of Strength."

[34] See, for example, Todd Hall and Keren Yarhi-Milo, "The Personal Touch: Leaders' Impressions, Costly Signaling, and Assessments of Sincerity in International Affairs," *International Studies Quarterly* 56, no. 3 (2012): 560–573, on the role of personal impressions in assessing signals of resolve. For the role of legitimacy, see Christopher Gelpi, *The Power of Legitimacy: Assessing the Role of Norms in Crisis Bargaining* (Princeton, NJ: Princeton University Press, 2002).

[35] This is despite the fact that, in his original discussion of signaling, Jervis identifies all secret diplomatic correspondences as the most prominent example of signaling. Jervis, *The Logic of Images*, p. 21.

[36] Snyder and Diesing, *Conflict among Nations*, p. 207. Also see David Hall, "The Laos Crisis of 1960–1961," in *The Limits of Coercive Diplomacy*.

international crises contain elements of coercion *and* accommodation.[37] And for accommodation, the type of signaling that matters is less oriented around resolve than it is around more conciliatory objectives. These include a willingness to make concessions, compromise, save face, and avoid war. Similarly, George notes that coercive diplomacy not only encompasses threats but also includes "rational persuasion and accommodation . . . to encourage the adversary either to comply with the demands or to work out an acceptable compromise."[38]

The distinction between coercion and accommodation in the context of international crises rests on the relative emphasis on winning versus mitigating the risks of war. Coercion weighs the former more heavily, while accommodation seeks to "reach some settlement that promises to defuse the issue as a potential source of future crises"—without making too many painful concessions.[39] Nevertheless, each contains elements of the other—coercive strategies may include accommodative tactics meant to address controlling the risks of escalation, while accommodative strategies may include coercive tactics that seek to minimize losses.[40] Characteristics of accommodation or reassurance include actions that demonstrate an exercise of restraint, the provision of better or more reliable information, clarifying shared expectations and norms regarding limits on conflict, or creating space for negotiations and diplomacy.[41]

Public versus secret signaling

Much of the signaling literature assumes that signaling occurs in the open. This is because the public nature of a signal is said to make it more credible.[42] However, there is a burgeoning literature on secret, covert signaling that shows that signaling occurring in the shadows of international politics may be equally,

---

[37] For seminal work on signaling and reputations for honesty (rather than resolve), see Anne E. Sartori, *Deterrence by Diplomacy* (Princeton, NJ: Princeton University Press, 2013) and "The Might of the Pen: A Reputational Theory of Communication in International Disputes," *International Organization* 56, no. 1 (2002): 121–149. Also see Andrew Kydd, "Trust, Reassurance, and Cooperation," *International Organization* 54, no. 2 (2000): 325–357, for work on how states can send costly signals for reassurance that persuade a target that the signaler is trustworthy. See Scott Wohlford, "Showing Restraint, Signaling Resolve: Coalitions, Cooperation, and Crisis Bargaining," *American Journal of Political Science* 58, no. 1 (2014): 144–156.

[38] George, "Coercive Diplomacy: Definition and Characteristics," p. 7.

[39] Snyder and Diesing, *Conflict among Nations*, p. 207.

[40] Ibid., p. 208.

[41] Stein, "Reassurance," 434. Restraint is usually conceived of in more systemic terms as part of grand strategy, rather than as a tool of crisis bargaining. See, for example, Barry R. Posen, *Restraint: A New Foundation for U.S. Grand Strategy* (Ithaca, NY: Cornell University Press, 2015); G. John Ikenberry, *After Victory: Institutions, Strategic Restraint, and the Rebuilding of Order after Major Wars* (Princeton, NJ: Princeton University Press, 2001).

[42] Fearon, "Rationalist Explanations for War." Also see Kurizaki, "Efficient Secrecy," p. 543.

if not more, effective than public signaling.[43] For example, Austin Carson and Keren Yarhi-Milo find that covert action "contains a range of salient, qualitative thresholds that are mutually meaningful as symbols of a sponsor's resolve," especially when leaders face domestic constraints.[44]

Beyond conveying resolve, secret signaling can be an effective tool of escalation management. Indeed, Synder and Diesing explicitly link the decision to signal in public versus in private with coercive versus accommodative strategies. While they argue that public threats may enhance credibility, these threats also increase the risks of escalation through creating mutual public commitments and invoking prestige. Conversely, private threats enable risk-avoidance because they are more deniable, although they lack the coercive heft of public threats.[45] Similarly, private communication increases the probability of a settlement that avoids war, but it also reduces the chances that any one actor will maximize its own objectives.[46] Therefore, Snyder and Diesing argue that private communication lends itself to accommodative strategies while public communication lends itself to coercive strategies.[47] More recent research uncovers similar findings: privacy and secrecy can enable signalers to save face, avoid paying potential domestic costs, and reduce escalation risks.[48]

What Does This Mean for Signaling in Cyberspace?

The prevailing consensus within the field of academic research on cyber signaling is that cyber operations are poor signaling tools. This is because the application of signaling to cyberspace has largely centered on whether cyber operations could function as costly signals of resolve in support of coercive strategies.[49] But there is a growing recognition that, instead of being used to signal resolve, cyber operations could be useful for accommodation and de-escalation.[50] Martin Libicki,

---

[43] On how private diplomatic communications can shape threat perception, see Trager, "Diplomatic Calculus in Anarchy."

[44] Carson and Yarhi-Milo, "Covert Communication," pp. 132, 136.

[45] Snyder and Diesing, *Conflict among Nations*, p. 251.

[46] Ibid., p. 252.

[47] Ibid. As noted by Snyder and Diesing, states can also pursue a "public-private mixture," which involves "perhaps a public but ambiguous statement of implied demands and hinted sanctions, combined with a more specific spelling out of one's own position through private channels."

[48] Kurizaki, "Efficient Secrecy," pp. 551, 553; Austin Carson, "Facing Off and Saving Face: Covert Intervention and Escalation Management in the Korean War," *International Organization* 70, no. 1 (2016): 104–105.

[49] Herbert Lin, "Escalation Dynamics and Conflict Termination in Cyberspace," *Strategic Studies Quarterly* 6, no. 3 (2012): 46–70; Erica D. Borghard and Shawn W. Lonergan, "The Logic of Coercion in Cyberspace," *Security Studies* 26, no. 3 (2017): 452–481.

[50] See Brandon Valeriano and Benjamin Jensen, "The Myth of the Cyber Offense," *Cato Institute Policy Analysis* no. 862 (Winter 2019) and "De-escalation Pathways and Disruptive Technology: Cyber Operations as Off-Ramps to War," working paper, November 10, 2020.

for example, suggests that brandishing cyber capabilities could serve accommodative strategies by prompting a target to speculate whether a cyber signal may have been chosen in lieu of a more costly response in other domains. He concludes that the target may surmise that "brandishing a cyberattack capability was meant to signal that more violent responses are off the table."[51] Similarly, Brandon Valeriano and Benjamin Jensen posit that cyber operations may provide "a means of signaling future escalation risk as well as a cross-domain release valve for crises. Rival states use cyber operations as a substitute for riskier military operations."[52] Drawing on their prior empirical findings about the relative absence of meaningful escalation dynamics in cyberspace, Valeriano and Jensen suggest that this could be because cyber operations "offer great powers escalatory offramps."[53]

We argue that cyber operations can act as accommodative signals, creating the conditions for crises to peacefully resolve, for some of the same reasons that they do not cause escalation. Like our claims about cyber escalation, this argument does not only rest on the limited effects of cyber operations and how an adversary may perceive cyber operations in comparison to other military operations that may be on the table during a crisis. In addition, the strategic use of secrecy—specifically, plausible deniability—plays an important role in making cyber operations a good tool for accommodative signaling. We argue that this is especially the case when a state is faced with more hawkish domestic political audiences that may be pushing for a more aggressive stance during a crisis. In this context, a state can leverage the ambiguity around responsibility for cyber operations to take low-cost, but visible, actions in cyberspace to placate domestic veto players while not exacerbating the crisis.

The limitations of cyber signaling for resolve

Just as the technical requirements for planning and conducting cyber operations make them poor tools of escalation, these same characteristics also give cyber operations marginal utility for brandishing capabilities or credibly signaling resolve.[54] Because many cyber operations are characterized by perishable and exquisite capabilities, a decision to employ them typically means that an attacker is

---

[51] Martin C. Libicki, *Brandishing Cyberattack Capabilities* (Santa Monica, CA: RAND Corporation, 2013), p. 4.

[52] Valeriano and Jensen, "The Myth of the Cyber Offense."

[53] Ibid.; Valeriano et al., *Cyber Strategy*. Also see Jacquelyn Schneider, "Deterrence in and through Cyberspace," in Jon R. Lindsay and Erik Gartzke, eds., *Cross-Domain Deterrence: Strategy in an Era of Complexity* (New York: Oxford University Press, 2019).

[54] Libicki, "Brandishing Cyber Capabilities," pp. 2–3. Also see Montgomery, "Signals of Strength."

foregoing a future opportunity to do so.[55] As Libicki notes, "[c]yber capabilities exist only in relationship to a specific target, which must be scoped to be understood. Cyber warriors can illustrate their ability to penetrate systems, but penetration is not the same as getting them to fail in useful ways. Since cyberattacks are essentially single-use weapons, they are diminished in the showing."[56] In other words, if cyber capabilities cannot be easily reused against multiple targets, especially once they are revealed, brandishing that capability inevitably reduces its effectiveness as a signal of resolve because the capability itself is rendered less effective by that very act. Similarly, Brendan Rittenhouse Green and Austin Long note that offensive cyber capabilities "could have a tremendous military utility, yet may be difficult to signal to adversaries without exposing the capability to relatively inexpensive countermeasures (e.g., updating software)."[57]

Moreover, cyber operations are less than ideal as signals of capability and resolve because they are not universally transferable across different target sets. Even if conducting a complex and sophisticated cyber operation may send a general signal about a state's capabilities (distinguishing between advanced and unsophisticated actors) and its willingness to employ them (distinguishing between resolute and irresolute actors), the signal itself is nevertheless weak because there is no guarantee that the state will be able to repeat the operation against other states or target sets. Furthermore, with sufficient information, the target can learn about the signaling state's tactics, techniques, procedures, capabilities, and organization to enable it to be better prepared for potential follow-on operations or to blunt the effectiveness of the threatened operation. Paradoxically, the strength of a hands-tying signal in cyberspace is inversely related to its ultimate coercive effectiveness; the more specific a state is about the types of actions it will take, against what targets sets, within a certain timeframe, the more information the target has to render the threatened action impotent. Indeed, Green and Long hypothesize that states are less likely to use cyber operations for signaling purposes when they are one-off capabilities.[58]

Of course, this does not characterize the full scope of cyber operations. There are off-the-shelf capabilities with interfaces that enable novices with limited to no programming knowledge to exploit well-known vulnerabilities. These capabilities can be used and reused, and may not diminish in the same way as more exquisite capabilities. But, even if cyber capabilities are not ephemeral, they are still poorly suited for coercive signals because of the inherent limits on cost generation discussed in extensive detail in prior chapters.

[55] Max Smeets, "A Matter of Time: On the Transitory Nature of Cyberweapons," *Journal of Strategic Studies* 41, nos. 1–2 (2018): 6–32.
[56] Libicki, "Brandishing Cyber Capabilities," p. xi.
[57] Green and Long, "Conceal or Reveal?," p. 82.
[58] Ibid., pp. 82–83.

Underscoring this point, Dorothy Denning and Bradley Strawser even argue that states have a moral obligation to use cyber weapons in lieu of other weapons, provided the former can accomplish comparable objectives, precisely because cyber capabilities reduce the harm inflicted on both target and perpetrator.[59] Because effective coercive signals rely on generating some level of pain for the target state (to make them credible) or some level of cost for the coercer (to convey resolve), cyber operations are a poor fit for this form of signaling.[60]

Cyber Operations as Accommodative Signals

While counterproductive for signaling resolve, the inherent restraint made possible by cyber operations makes them useful for accommodative signaling and crisis de-escalation. An important part of this is the relatively limited scale of effects that cyber operations can produce. In Chapter 2, we discussed how cyber operations have inherent limitations in the magnitude of damage they can inflict: the effects of cyber operations are often fleeting, reversible, and rarely cause damage in the physical world. Crucial for signaling, though, are not only the inherent constraints of cyber operations, but also the likelihood that states will evaluate and understand cyber operations in the context of an international crisis. In these situations, states are not assessing the implications of a particular cyber operation in isolation. Instead, they are apt to situate cyber operations within a broader circumstance and evaluate how the choice to employ cyber capabilities during a crisis compares to other plausible retaliatory or offensive options available to the adversary. Because even the most costly cyber operations lack the physical violence and destruction associated with other military instruments—and may even be less painful than some economic instruments (such as sanctions)—they can be interpreted as a signal of restraint relative to other options.[61]

---

[59]   Dorothy E. Denning and Bradley J. Strawser, "Moral Cyber Weapons," in Luciano Floridi and Mariarosaria Taddeo, eds., *The Ethics of Information Warfare* (Cham: Springer, 2014).

[60]   See Sarah Kreps and Jacquelyn Schneider, "Escalation Firebreaks in the Cyber, Conventional, and Nuclear Domains: Moving beyond Effects-Based Logics," *Journal of Cybersecurity* 5, no. 1 (2019): 1–11, for a review of arguments about how the effects of cyber operations impact perceptions of escalation. Also see Henry Farrell and Charles Glaser, "The Role of Effects, Saliencies, and Norms in US Cyberwar Doctrine," *Journal of Cybersecurity* 3, no. 1 (2017): 7–17.

[61]   The early cyber literature was rife with proclamations about the dangerous advent of this new class of weaponry. A particularly good example of this is John Arquilla and David Ronfeld's "Cyberwar is Coming!," *Comparative Strategy* 12, no. 2 (1993): 141–165. Also see Martin Libicki's early monograph, *Cyberdeterrence and Cyberwar* (Santa Monica, CA: RAND Corporation, 2009). Similarly, early work by Chris Demchak, for instance, describes cyber power, in part, as the ability to inflict "violent effects," *Wars of Disruption and Resilience: Cybered Conflict, Power, and National Security* (Athens: University of Georgia Press, 2011), p. ix. However, as the literature on cyber conflict has evolved, a scholarly consensus has emerged that cyber capabilities lack the violence associated with most weapons and that concerns about cyber war are overblown. See, for example, Thomas

This extends of the logic of the substitutability of foreign policy. Benjamin Most and Harvey Starr posit that there is "a set of alternative modes of response by which decisions makers could deal with some situation."[62] Most and Starr claim that theories that endeavor to explain foreign policy behavior must take into account the fact that a state could make alternative foreign policy choices or employ different tools to achieve a given objective and, conversely, a single instrument could be employed in a variety of contexts for different purposes. Applied to international crises that involve the use of cyber operations, the relative coercive or accommodative strength of a cyber signal could be understood in comparison to other potential actions that a state could take during a crisis. It could also be assessed in terms of its timing in the context of a crisis; for instance, if a state responds to a kinetic attack with a cyber operation, it could help defuse a crisis because it could be perceived as a de-escalatory choice.

Evaluating cyber operations in comparison to alternative courses of action may provide a signaling advantage to states that are highly capable across a range of military operations, because the deliberate choice to employ cyber rather than kinetic capabilities could send a strong signal of restraint. For instance, in the summer of 2019 the United States reportedly launched a cyber attack to degrade the functioning of Iranian missile launch systems in the middle of a regional crisis, including Iranian attacks on oil tankers and the downing of a U.S. drone. The purported cyber attacks were an alternative to conventional kinetic strikes against Iran, which the Trump administration threatened but ultimately did not pursue.[63] Particularly in the shadow of an explicit threat to employ kinetic capabilities, the choice of a cyber operation with narrowly targeted and non-deadly effects can be a signal that provides a means for crises to de-escalate.[64] Conversely, cyber operations may be murkier accommodative signals

---

Rid, *Cyber War Will Not Take Place* (Oxford, UK: Oxford University Press, 2013); Erik Gartzke and Jon R. Lindsay, "Weaving Tangled Webs: Offense, Defense, and Deception in Cyberspace," *Security Studies* 24, no. 2 (2015): 316–348; Brandon Valeriano and Ryan C. Maness, *Cyber War versus Cyber Realities: Cyber Conflict in the International System* (New York: Oxford University Press, 2015) .

[62] Harvey Starr, "Substitutability in Foreign Policy: Theoretically Central, Empirically Elusive," *Journal of Conflict Resolution* 44, no. 1 (2000): 128. Also see Benjamin A. Most and Harvey Starr, "International Relations Theory, Foreign Policy Substitutability, and 'Nice' Laws," *World Politics* 36, no. 3 (1984): 383–406; Benjamin A. Most and Harvey Starr, *Inquiry, Logic and International Politics* (Columbia: University of South Carolina Press, 1989); and T. Clifton Morgan and Glenn Palmer, "A Model of Foreign Policy Substitutability: Selecting the Right Tools for the Job(s)," *Journal of Conflict Resolution* 44, no. 1 (2000): 11–32.

[63] Julian E. Barnes, "U.S. Cyber Attack Hurt Iran's Ability to Target Oil Tankers, Officials Say," *The New York Times*, August 28, 2019, https://www.nytimes.com/2019/08/28/us/politics/us-iran-cyber-attack.html; "US 'Launched Cyber Attacks on Iran Weapons Systems,'" *BBC*, June 23, 2019, https://www.bbc.com/news/world-us-canada-48735097; Robert Chesney, "A Cyber Command Operational Update: Clarifying the June 2019 Iran Operation," *Lawfare*, September 3, 2019, https://www.lawfareblog.com/cyber-command-operational-update-clarifying-june-2019-iran-operation.

[64] A cyber operation could contribute to crisis de-escalation without necessarily serving as an accommodative signal.

for weaker states. It is likely to be more difficult for the recipient of a signal to discern—absent the synchronous employment of additional tools (such as private diplomatic communications)—whether a state that may be asymmetrically disadvantaged is using cyber capabilities for the purposes of accommodation or attempted coercion.[65]

Plausible deniability and accommodative cyber signaling

Our argument about the signaling value of cyber operations goes beyond the costliness of effects. A state may conceivably choose a range of non-lethal actions to take during a crisis to convey to its adversary that it does not want to escalate a crisis, such as diplomatic overtures. What is unique about cyber operations, however, is that they give states an opportunity to leverage their ambiguity and be strategic about the extent of their visibility. But unlike covert military operations, which also take place with some level of plausible deniability, cyber operations do not cause death and physical destruction. In other words, it is the combination of relatively constrained effects and the role of secrecy that together give cyber operations distinctive signaling properties.

The literature on covert action and secret signaling has shown that interactions that occur in the shadows of international politics can widen the bargaining space between adversarial states. Consistent with this literature, we argue that when cyber operations are employed during a crisis, both perpetrator and recipient can be strategic about attribution and the relative plausible deniability of cyber operations. Making these choices about the public or private nature of attribution and the extent to which a cyber operation is designed to be deniable can serve as a signal during a crisis and can enable or impede de-escalation, as depicted in Table 4.1.[66]

---

[65] Leveraging preexisting direct communication mechanisms can increase the likelihood that the signal will be perceived as legitimate, such as the 2013 agreement between Russia and the United States to use their respective Nuclear Risk Reduction Centers to communicate about cyber crises and the Organization for Security and Co-operation in Europe (OSCE) Communication Network, which can be leveraged to communicate about cyber events and crises. See Alex Grigsby, "OSCE Agrees to New Confidence Building Measures. Pop the Champagne?," *Council on Foreign Relations-Net Politics*, March 31, 2016, https://www.cfr.org/blog/osce-agrees-new-confidence-building-measures-pop-champagne,. An important drawback of existing mechanisms is that they are generally limited to European states, plus Russia.

[66] This assumes that the choice of a public versus private signal is deliberate. However, information could also be inadvertently made public by third parties. This is often the case with private cybersecurity firms that publish reports on attribution and threat actor profiles. Additionally, this mechanism is distinct from public attribution that takes place long after a crisis has occurred. A further factor to take into account, which we explore in the case studies, is the extent to which the cyber operation itself is visible to public audiences.

Table 4.1 Strategic Secrecy and Accommodative Signaling

	Attacking State Conceals Responsibility	Attacking State Reveals Responsibility
Target Conceals Attribution	Mutual plausible deniability prevails (even if states privately communicate knowledge about responsibility); both parties implicitly coordinate to keep attribution of cyber operations private, creating conditions for de-escalation.	Self-attribution by the attacking state creates political costs for the target; may make it more difficult for the latter to offer concessions.
Target Reveals Attribution	Public attribution by the target state creates political costs for the attacking state; may make it more difficult for the latter to offer concessions.	Public attribution by both parties makes it difficult for either side to offer public concessions; de-escalation is least likely following a cyber operation in this scenario.

As we discussed in Chapter 2 regarding the role of secrecy in cyber operations, the extent to which a state is willing to be associated with a cyber operation is a choice, as distinct from the operational requirement to maintain secrecy around accesses and capabilities. In addition, the target of a cyber operation is also presented with a choice about the extent to which it should openly attribute a cyber attack to a rival during a crisis, or keep that information out of the public view.[67] Furthermore, one way governments create ambiguity about attribution is to use proxy groups. In crisis situations, proxies can simultaneously serve domestic and international objectives, particularly when governments seek to defuse a crisis with an adversary but also need to placate nationalistic groups or domestic veto players who may seek more aggressive action.[68] In these circumstances, so-called "patriotic hackers," "hacktivists," or other proxy actors could be encouraged or allowed to conduct cyber operations against certain adversary targets, even as the state may seek to deescalate the overall situation.[69] Proxy groups do not necessarily have to be non-state actors. For example, in tandem with a significant buildup of conventional Russian military forces along

---

[67] For a discussion of attribution see Jon R. Lindsay, "Tipping the Scales: The Attribution Problem and the Feasibility of Deterrence against Cyber Attack," *Journal of Cybersecurity* 1, no. 1 (2015): 53–67; also see David D. Clark and Susan Landau, "Untangling Attribution," *Harvard National Security Journal* 2, no. 2 (March 2011): 25–40.

[68] Jessica Chen Weiss, "Authoritarian Signaling, Mass Audiences, and Nationalist Protest in China," *International Organization* 67, no. 1 (2013): 1–35.

[69] For further discussion on patriotic hackers and their relationship with a state see, Tim Maurer, *Cyber Mercenaries* (Cambridge, UK: Cambridge University Press, 2018), pp. 146–149.

the border with Ukraine in January 2022, Ukrainian government agencies were struck with a spate of website defacements, and Microsoft also revealed that it had discovered destructive malware in some Ukrainian government systems.[70] Ukrainian officials have linked the malware to the Belarusian group, GhostWriter.[71] Belarus has close ties to Russia and observers have speculated that Belarus may have been operating in cyberspace on Russia's behalf.[72] These kinds of noisy, nationalist demonstrations can alleviate domestic pressure, but are not sufficiently costly to prompt an escalatory retaliation by the target.

These strategic choices about the level of secrecy versus publicity for both parties to a crisis have various implications for signaling. As depicted in the top-left box of Table 4.1, during a crisis the target of a cyber attack may choose to preserve the plausible deniability associated with attribution—even when it has some degree of confidence that its rival is responsible—to prevent further escalation and enable crisis resolution.[73] In these cases, adversaries share a mutual incentive to keep the bargaining dynamic private. Therefore, the choice to not go public, or even to issue vague and ambiguous public statements in response to a cyber attack, can create the conditions for crises to de-escalate. This is especially the case if the target perceives domestic political dynamics within its own or the rival state (such as ongoing nationalist protests or vocal, hawkish veto players) that may increase the risks of unwanted escalation.

Conversely, if one party goes public with attribution while the other seeks to maintain plausible deniability, depicted in the top-right and bottom-left boxes, it can make it more difficult for the latter to offer concessions. There are scant instances of states taking responsibility for their own cyber operations. In addition to the examples discussed in Chapter 2, another example is the decision of a number of U.S. government leaders to publicly discuss the efforts by the Russia Small Group to disrupt Russian threat actors' efforts to interfere in the 2018 U.S. midterm elections, which reportedly included U.S. cyber operations.[74] In the limited cases where states have taken responsibility for cyber operations, it has been to support coercion and deterrence, rather than de-escalation, which is consistent with our expectations.

---

[70] Kim Zetter, "What We Know and Don't Know about the Cyberattacks Against Ukraine—(updated)," January 17, 2022, https://zetter.substack.com/p/what-we-know-and-dont-know-about; "Destructive Malware Targeting Ukranian Organizations," Microsoft, January 15, 2022, https://www.microsoft.com/security/blog/2022/01/15/destructive-malware-targeting-ukrainian-organizations/.

[71] Pavel Polityuk, "EXCLUSIVE Ukraine Suspects Group Linked to Belarus Intelligence over Cyberattack," *Reuters*, January 15, 2022.

[72] "Ukraine Cyber-attack: Russia to Blame for Hack, Says Kyiv," *BBC*, January 14, 2022.

[73] There may be instances where technical attribution is infeasible within a reasonable timeframe, but a target nevertheless chooses to politically attribute given the concurrent geopolitical crisis.

[74] Sean Lyngaas, "NSA Chief Confirms He Set Up Task Force to Counter Russian Hackers," *Cyberscoop*, July 23, 2018, https://www.cyberscoop.com/russia-small-group-paul-nakasone-nsa-aspen/. "An Interview with Paul M. Nakasone," *Joint Force Quarterly* 92 (1st Quarter 2019): 4–9.

Finally, if attribution is mutually made public during a crisis, it is unlikely that cyber operations can create pathways for crises to de-escalate because both sides will perceive a disadvantage in appearing to back down. This framework illustrates that secrecy is not necessarily a defining characteristic of operating in cyberspace and, in fact, both parties to a crisis can be strategic about their relative levels of secrecy to create opportunities for accommodative signaling and de-escalation.

Revealing Operational Information to Reassure in Cyberspace

The preceding discussion of cyber signaling focused on scenarios where cyber operations are considered in comparison to other tools a state may employ during a crisis. In this context, states may use cyber operations to palliate broader geopolitical crises that take place outside of cyberspace. Separately, there may also be crises where a state perceives a need to reassure a rival that it will *not* take actions in cyberspace that unduly exacerbate the situation. This is the inverse of the previous scenario—the issue in this case is how a state might be able to credibly convey that it will not further aggravate a crisis through cyber means. A state could feel vulnerable to a cyber attack during a crisis if, for example, it knows that its adversary has already gained access to its critical infrastructure networks and may fear the adversary could exploit that access to conduct a cyber attack at a critical moment during a crisis. For example, in the context of Russia's conventional invasion and occupation of Ukraine, in December 2022 the U.S. government revealed that cyber actors associated with the Russian government had gained access to a U.S. satellite network earlier that year—an important part of U.S. critical infrastructure with dual civilian and military uses—which means the Russian government was also made aware of the fact that the United States knew its critical infrastructure networks were compromised.[75] Mutual awareness of these vulnerabilities could, in theory, shape the dynamics of future crises between states.

In these kinds of circumstances, if a state aims to signal reassurance or restraint *within* cyberspace during a crisis, it could take measures that tie its hands in credible ways that are communicable to the adversary. Specifically, a state could do this by strategically or selectively revealing information that would allow the adversary to improve its defenses or by sharing information that would constrain the ability of the would-be attacking state to operate—without necessarily even

[75] Christian Vasquez, "CISA Researchers: Russia's Fancy Bear Infiltrated US Satellite Network," *Cyberscoop*, December 16, 2022, https://www.cyberscoop.com/apt28-fancy-bear-satellite/.

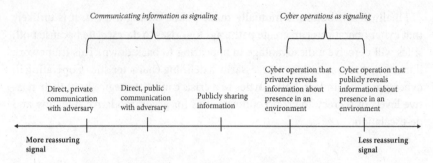

Figure 4.1 Signaling Reassurance through Revealing Information

carrying out a cyber operation. For instance, revealing information about the vulnerabilities a state could exploit against a target, illuminating the means of gaining access to a targeted system, or the tools and techniques it has developed to cause effects could serve as a gesture of conciliation with varying degrees of reassurance. The more specific and actionable the information, and the more the communication of it can be kept out of the purview of domestic and international audiences, the more it could help reassure a rival about a state's intentions in cyberspace. Figure 4.1 depicts different categories of this signaling mechanism along a spectrum, from more to less accommodative.

For most cyber operations, if information is revealed about its various components (the specific vulnerability used to gain access, malware source code, etc.), defenders could, in theory, take action to thrust attackers out of their networks, mitigate the effects of operations, and/or prevent an attacker from reusing an exploit or a capability for a future operation. That is why certain types of information that aid in network defense, such as Yara and Snort rules,[76] and indicators of compromise (to include malware hashes, malicious domain names and IPs, signatures of malicious tactics, techniques, and procedures, etc.) are valuable for defenders. Therefore, the choice by a state to reveal some of the information that would enable a rival to better defend itself and would also constrain its own ability to operate could serve as a powerful signal of deliberate cyber restraint during a time of crisis.

As depicted in Figure 4.1, at the most accommodating end of the spectrum a state could communicate with its adversary for the purposes of sharing exquisite and meaningful information about its own cyber capabilities and operations,

---

[76] Koen Van Impe, "Signature-Based Detection with YARA," *Security Intelligence*, June 24, 2015, https://securityintelligence.com/signature-based-detection-with-yara/; "Understanding and Configuring Snort Rules," *Rapid 7*, December 9, 2016, https://blog.rapid7.com/2016/12/09/unders tanding-and-configuring-snort-rules/. These are scripts (lines of code) that a network defender would run in their environment to identify malicious activity.

effectively burning them. As keeping this kind of information secret is essential to operational success, sharing it could serve as a tool of reassurance because it effectively equips the defender with the information to blunt the effectiveness of a state's capabilities. Furthermore, revealing this type of information has an additional accommodative signaling purpose because the signaling state would forfeit the intelligence value of access to an adversary's networks and systems, including the intelligence function necessary for the *signaler's* own reassurance that the adversary is not defecting from agreements or concessions. This opens up the signaling state to the additional risk that derives from losing access that may serve multiple strategic intelligence purposes.

These types of signals could come in several forms. For instance, a state could "burn" a vulnerability that it is exploiting for access by alerting others, either publicly or privately. This enables defenders to implement compensating controls. Relatedly, a state could also burn hardware exploits that it has prepositioned. Furthermore, a state could share the malware's original source code that could be in its own network or on a host network, promoting a shared understanding of the situation and allowing the targeted state to more rapidly engineer a means to thwart the attack and patch vulnerabilities rather than having to wait for an in-depth forensic analysis. A state could also share information about the capabilities of a third party. This protects the signaler as it does not come at the expense of losing one's own capabilities. Moreover, if signaled covertly, there is a potential that the third-party tools could be misrepresented as the signaler's own. This could include a mixture of activities such as sharing source code, intelligence on mutual threat actors and their campaigns, or libraries of threat signatures to aid in early warning and contribute to an opponent's overall defensive posture.

A state could also share information to stop or reverse the effects of its own cyber operation or one carried out by a proxy group. An operation that encrypts a target's hard drive, for instance, could be reversed by providing the decryption key.[77] One example of this took place in May 2021 when a ransomware group Wizard Spider, which has links with Russia, provided the decryption keys to Ireland's Health Service Executive, despite the fact that the Irish government said it did not pay a ransom to the group.[78] While it is not likely that Wizard Spider was seeking to reassure Dublin in this case, it serves as an illustrative example of what this could look like in practice.[79] Cyber operations could also be

[77] Neil C. Rowe, "War Crimes from Cyber-Weapons," *Journal of Information Warfare* 6, no. 3 (2007): 15–25.
[78] Shawn Pogatchnik, "Hackers Who Stole Ireland's Hospital Records Offer Decryption Key," *Politico*, May 20, 2021.
[79] Conor Lally, "Wizard Spider Profile: Suspected Gang behind HSE Attack Is Part of World's First Cyber-Cartel," *Irish Times*, May 18, 2021.

deliberately engineered with a back door that enables an operator to remotely disable an ongoing attack. For instance, the May 2017 WannaCry ransomware attack, which encrypted the data on systems around the world, including FedEx and the United Kingdom's National Health Services, contained a "kill switch" that was accidentally discovered by a researcher, stopping the spread of the ransomware.[80] In a slightly different example, in January 2021 Europol, the law enforcement agency for the European Union, and the U.S. Department of Justice released information that an international coalition of law enforcement agencies had participated in a successful takedown of the Emotet botnet, which had been distributing malware for nearly a decade.[81] The botnet takedown involved the use of a kill switch to disable it from continuing to propagate malware. These instances involve the targets themselves employing a kill switch. However, as part of an effort to signal reassurance, a state could also choose to share details about a kill switch with an opponent.

Across all of these potential examples of signaling to demonstrate reassurance or restraint within cyberspace, a core challenge is whether any action will be perceived by the target as such. States have mechanisms to directly communicate about cyber operations, including in private ways. Leveraging these mechanisms can increase the likelihood that the signal will be perceived, linked to the signaling state, and seen as legitimate. For example, in 2013 Russia and the United States struck an agreement to use their respective Nuclear Risk Reduction Centers—the nuclear hotline created during the Cold War—to communicate about cyber crises. Also, the Organization for Security and Co-operation in Europe (OSCE) has a Communication Network states can use to communicate about cyber events and crises.[82]

Information can also be indirectly communicated to an adversary through disclosing it in public venues used by security researchers to share cybersecurity information. However, indirect public signaling is less accommodative than direct communication because the signal may not be immediately perceived by the intended target if it is not delivered by a prominent figure or in an outlet in which garnering the attention of the target is ensured. An example of this kind of indirect communication is U.S. Cyber Command's recent initiative to conduct

---

[80] Nadia Khomami and Olivia Solon, "'Accidental Hero' Halts Ransomware Attack and Warns: This Is Not Over," *The Guardian*, May 13, 2017, https://www.theguardian.com/technology/2017/may/13/accidental-hero-finds-kill-switch-to-stop-spread-of-ransomware-cyber-attack. However, in this example it is unlikely that the attackers intended for the kill switch to be uncovered.

[81] "World's Most Dangerous Malware EMOTET Disrupted through Global Action," Europol, January 27, 2021; "Emotet Botnet Disrupted in International Cyber Operation," U.S. Department of Justice, January 28, 2021.

[82] See Grigsby, "OSCE Agrees to New Confidence Building Measures." An important drawback of existing mechanisms is that they are generally limited to European states, plus Russia. The United States, in particular, lacks similar types of institutionalized mechanisms for communication with China.

"malware inoculation," although it's important to note that there is no public evidence that this has been done for reassurance signaling purposes. Nevertheless, it provides a use case for how states may apply these operations for signaling purposes.

When U.S. cyber forces conduct threat hunting—proactively searching for cyber threats on assets and networks—they could uncover information that can aid in network defense. In turn, the United States could elect to "inoculate" adversary malware through publicizing information that can help network owners and operators better defend their systems against those malware strains in information-sharing venues, such as VirusTotal.[83] This effort began in 2018 when Cyber Command publicly posted information about adversary malware, including malware associated with APT28, linked to Russia's Main Intelligence Directorate (GRU).[84] This particular release occurred in conjunction with the 2018 midterm elections and the synchronous campaign by Cyber Command to disrupt the Internet Research Agency's efforts to conduct cyber-enabled information operations against the U.S. midterm elections.[85] In being deliberate about the timing of disclosing this information, public exposure of Russian malware could have been a signal by the United States to Russia that its networks are compromised, generating uncertainty about the viability of ongoing and future operations and campaigns. The United Kingdom engaged in similar efforts around that time as well. In October 2018 the National Cyber Security Centre publicly disclosed attribution information as well as indicators of compromise and Snort rules to enable network defenders to search for evidence of an APT28 compromise.[86] This release was also conducted in coordination with a statement

---

[83] This release was advertised on Twitter and via a formal press release—"#USCYBERCOM Cyber National Mission Force as kicked off an initiative to upload malware samples it discovers to @virustotal. #CNMF is proud to prevent harm by malicious cyber actors by sharing with the global cybersecurity community," @CNMF_Virus Alert, *Twitter*, November 5, 2018, https://twitter.com/ CNMF_VirusAlert/status/1059512606212476931; and "New CNMF Initiative shares malware samples with cybersecurity industry," USCYBERCOM, *Twitter*, November 5, 2018, https://www. cybercom.mil/Media/News/News-Display/Article/1681533/new-cnmf-initiative-shares-malware-samples-with-cybersecurity-industry. The technical artifacts released by U.S. Cyber Command are posted to @CYBERCOM_Malware_Alert, *VirusTotal*, https://www.virustotal.com/en/user/CYB ERCOM_Malware_Alert/.

[84] For further background on the Russia APT28 aspect of the malware release, see "Who is FANCY BEAR (APT28)?" *Crowdstrike*, February 12, 2019, https://www.crowdstrike.com/blog/who-is-fancy-bear/; Joseph Cox, "The US Military Just Publicly Dumped Russian Government Malware Online," *Vice*, November 9, 2018, https://www.vice.com/en_us/article/8xpa7k/us-military-cyber com-publicly-dumped-russian-government-malware-fancy-bear-apt28.

[85] Ellen Nakashima, "U.S. Cyber Command Operation Disrupted Internet Access of Russian Troll Factory on Day of 2018 Midterms," *The Washington Post*, February 27, 2019.

[86] "Reckless Campaign of Cyber Attacks by Russian Military Intelligence Service Exposed," National Cyber Security Centre, October 3, 2018, https://www.ncsc.gov.uk/news/reckless-campa ign-cyber-attacks-russian-military-intelligence-service-exposed; "Indicators of Compromise for Malware Used by APT28," National Cyber Security Centre, October 4, 2018, https://www.ncsc.gov. uk/news/indicators-of-compromise-for-malware-used-by-apt28.

from the UK ambassador to the Netherlands, who detailed a joint Dutch-UK effort to identify and remove GRU officers targeting several international organizations.[87] Of course, the objective in these examples was to share information aimed at blunting the effectiveness of Russian cyber operations, rather than as a form of reassurance. However, a state could conceivably use the same type of mechanism for more conciliatory signaling purposes as well.

A state also faces the choice of how much information it may seek to disclose and, in doing so, calibrate the desired strength of the signal by narrowing or widening the scope and magnitude of the type and quality of information it chooses to reveal. For instance, revealing a limited amount of one's own offensive capabilities can serve as a signal of accommodation (because it helps the adversary better defend itself against the signaling state), but it simultaneously leaves unanswered the question of the other potential targets the signaling state may also hold at risk. At the same time, revealing this kind of information can leave open a window of opportunity for the signaling state to continue to take advantage of a vulnerability before a patch is developed or prior to defensive controls being emplaced. Due to this, the signal could retain a coercive edge because of the mutually understood vulnerability that exists for the target between the time a compromise is revealed and a remedy is implemented.

Moving from disclosing information to conducting a cyber operation reduces the accommodative nature of a signal because it increases the target's vulnerability. However, some operations can also convey restraint or reassurance through revealing information that enables defense. This could include, for example, cyber operations that do not disrupt a network's functions and processes or destroy data but, rather, reveal an adversary's presence on a network. For instance, a state could conduct cyber operations intended to reveal presence in a compromised system or network, such as an operation that defaces a website or system interface or that forces a system to beacon in a way that would alert network defenders to the state's presence. Beaconing occurs when malicious code within a compromised system communicates back to a command and control server; it may occur repeatedly over time at standardized intervals. Typically, a skilled attacker with advanced tradecraft would seek to reduce the likelihood that a defender is alerted to its presence. Operations that alert network defenders to a hostile presence may garner increased vigilance, detection, and mitigation efforts to ultimately identify and neutralize the opponent. However, for this behavior to be discerned by the target as a form of signaling, it would have to be coupled with other forms of communication. Otherwise, the target could just as easily interpret the discovered presence as malicious or as an indication of poor tradecraft, rather than as a signal.

Conclusion

Cyber operations are problematic as signaling devices for a variety of reasons—states may not have shared understandings about what specific cyber behaviors mean; their limited effects and tailored nature make them difficult for signaling resolve; and cyber signals may not even be perceived by the target and understood to be a form of communication by an adversary. Despite this, cyberspace does afford states opportunities for certain forms of signaling, especially signals that aim to convey restraint, reassurance, and conciliation. In fact, we argue that it is precisely the same reasons that cyber operations are not effective signals of strength or resolve that make them useful for accommodation. The limited, often temporary, effects of cyber operations mean they can be perceived as less costly than alternative actions that a state may pursue during a crisis. Therefore, in carrying them out a state could implicitly convey that it deliberately chose a less escalatory course of action compared to other means at its disposal. And plausible deniability and secrecy, which are hallmarks of cyber operations and are typically depicted as detrimental to stability between rivals; they could in fact enable states to maneuver outside of the public sphere and therefore reduce pressure to escalate that often stems from external audiences. Moreover, a state can make choices about strategically revealing information to convey restraint around its own employment of cyber power, such as communicating information that enables a rival to improve its cyber defenses or demonstrating that it is constraining its own ability to operate in cyberspace. In the following two chapters, we explore how these patterns unfold across a number of cases of cyber operations that take place in the context of enduring international rivalries and during geopolitical crises to assess whether there is evidence to support our argument.

5

Patterns of Escalation in Cyberspace

Evaluating Evidence of Escalation

In this chapter, we explore patterns of state behavior in cyberspace through a number of different case studies to assess the extent to which cyber operations may lead to dangerous escalatory spirals between rivals. Specifically, we explore patterns of behavior over time between pairs of rival states, with a focus on cases where factors suggest escalation would be more likely to take place. In other words, we examine cases that are more difficult for our argument because they are conducive to escalation. In addition to evaluating patterns of cyber behavior, we also conduct a deep dive into the strategic interactions between the United States and four rival states. Overall, we find that there is little evidence of cyber operations causing escalation.

To identify cases to assess patterns of state behavior in cyberspace, we aggregated a comprehensive dataset of cyber incidents from August 2005 to May 2020. We took this approach to reduce the likelihood of creating undue bias in our case selection. Of course, there is an inherent selection bias in this universe of cases, as it relies on observed, publicly reported instances of cyber operations. In other words, these are the cases about which we know something. There are surely other cases about which researchers do not yet have any reliable information—if they ever will—because the information about them has been kept secret or because a state may not have even realized it has been subjected to a cyber operation. Therefore, it is important to assess the implications of this potential selection bias—whether and how it may distort or skew the cases in a way that disproportionately favors our argument over countervailing ones.

While there is certainly bias in the data, we argue that it actually works against our argument, which assuages much of our concerns. That's because it is precisely the *observable* instances of cyber operations that are most likely to create escalation risks. Observable cyber operations are the "noisiest" cases—those that have the most significant, direct impact on their targets as well as involving some level of public knowledge. This raises the potential for nationalism, prestige, and reputation to shape decision making, which can make de-escalation more difficult. If researchers know about cyber operations, then domestic and

Escalation Dynamics in Cyberspace. Erica D. Lonergan and Shawn W. Lonergan, Oxford University Press..
© Oxford University Press 2023. DOI: 10.1093/oso/9780197550885.003.0005

international publics are likely to know about them as well. Therefore, if anything, these cases are biased toward being more likely to involve escalation.

We created our universe of cases by merging and deconflicting three different existing datasets on cyber incidents: the Council on Foreign Relation's (CFR) Cyber Operations Tracker; Ryan Maness, Brandon Valeriano, and Benjamin Jensen's Dyadic Cyber Incident and Campaign Dataset (DCID) Version 1.5; and the Center for Strategic and International Studies (CSIS) list of significant cyber incidents. We also cross-referenced these datasets against a list of cyber disruption events produced by Jason Healey, Neil Jenkins, and J.D. Work.[1] We use this data to provide some basic descriptive information about patterns of behavior and trends in cyberspace and, importantly, to help inform the selection process for our case studies. This enables us to employ systematic criteria for case study selection and avoid choosing cases with the highest profile and avoid selecting on the dependent variable.

As of June 8, 2020, the CFR Cyber Operations Tracker identified 425 distinct cyber operations that occurred from 2005 to 2020, which includes "all instances of publicly known state-sponsored cyber activity since 2005."[2] This cyber activity encompasses a range of actions, including DDoS attacks, espionage, defacement (such as website defacement), data destruction, sabotage, doxing, and financial theft. Out of this universe of cases, there are 12 cases of data destruction; 3 of defacement; 18 of DDoS; 6 of doxing; 338 of espionage; 20 of sabotage; 1 of financial theft; and the remaining 27 are uncategorized in the data but, according to the descriptions, represent additional instances of cyber espionage. The DCID dataset identifies 266 cyber incidents between 2000 and 2016, coded according to four different types: vandalism, denial of service, intrusion, and infiltration. The DCID definition of intrusion is similar to CFR's coding of espionage. Importantly, while "infiltration" may seem to suggest intrusion, Maness et al. define this category as "malware that is usually worms or viruses, but can also be logic bombs and keystroke logs."[3] Finally, the CSIS published a list of significant cyber incidents from 2006 to 2018. While it does not code for particular

[1] CFR Cyber Operations Tracker, https://www.cfr.org/cyber-operations/; Ryan C. Maness, Brandon Valeriano, and Benjamin Jensen, "Dyadic Cyber Incident and Campaign Dataset (DCID) Version 1.5," https://drryanmaness.wixsite.com/cyberconflict/cyber-conflict-dataset; Center for Strategic and International Studies, "Significant Cyber Incidents," https://www.csis.org/programs/technology-policy-program/significant-cyber-incidents; Jason Healey, Neil Jenkins, and J.D. Work, "Defenders Disrupting Adversaries: Framework, Dataset, and Case Studies of Disruptive Counter-Cyber Operations," 12th International Conference on Cyber Conflict, 2020.
[2] CFR Cyber Operations Tracker, "Our Methodology," https://www.cfr.org/cyber-operations/#OurMethodology.
[3] Ryan C. Maness, Brandon Valeriano, and Benjamin Jensen, "Codebook for the Dyadic Cyber Incident and Campaign Dataset (DCID) Version 1.5," June 2019, p. 3.

variables or attributes of cyber operations, the list contains "cyber attacks on government agencies, defense and high tech companies, or economic crimes with losses of more than a million dollars."[4]

To explore whether escalation dynamics may be characterized by different logics during conflict in contrast with competition below the level of war, as well as to assess when cyber operations may trigger escalation from crisis to conflict, we added a category to the dataset to account for whether the reported cyber operation took place during an armed conflict using the UCDP/PRIO Armed Conflict Dataset, Version 19.1. This dataset defines armed conflict as follows: "[a] state-based armed conflict is a contested incompatibility that concerns government and/or territory where the use of armed force between two parties, of which at least one is the government of a state, results in at least 25 battle-related deaths in one calendar year."[5] This allows us to evaluate potential differences between escalation dynamics below the threshold of warfare versus above it (we explore the latter later in this book).[6] The remainder of this chapter is organized into two sections, each of which explores a different set of case studies to test various aspects of our argument about the relationship between cyber operations and escalation.

Does Cyber Escalation Happen between Rival States?

If cyber operations increase the risk of escalation, then it would be reasonable to expect that this would be most likely to occur between rival states, especially those with rivalries that could be characterized as enduring. Rivalries are dyadic relationships between states that involve "conflicts that governments conduct using the military means of foreign policy." Rivalries that are enduring persist over time.[7] The international relations literature has shown that there is a

---

[4] "Significant Cyber Incidents," Center for Strategic International Studies, last updated November 2020, https://www.csis.org/programs/cybersecurity-and-governance/technology-policy-program/other-projects-cybersecurity.

[5] Nils Petter Gleditsch, Peter Wallensteen, Mikael Eriksson, Margareta Sollenberg, and Håvard Strand, "Armed Conflict 1946–2001: A New Dataset," *Journal of Peace Research* 39, no. 5 (2002): 615–637; Therese Pettersson, Stina Högbladh, and Magnus Öberg, "Organized Violence, 1989–2018 and Peace Agreements," *Journal of Peace Research* 56, no. 4 (2019): 589–603. We selected this dataset based on the fact that it focuses on state-based armed conflict, consistent with our focus on state-sponsored cyber activity; the relatively low battle death threshold for armed conflict as compared to similar datasets, such as the Correlates of War dataset; and the fact that the latest version of the dataset has been completed up to the year 2018, as compared to, for instance, the Militarized Interstate Disputes dataset that ends in 2010.

[6] This threshold is not unambiguous, and states may have different approaches to how they define where precisely the threshold exists. Indeed, as we discussed earlier in this book, differences between and misperceptions about thresholds are one of the factors hypothesized to contribute to escalation risks.

[7] Paul F. Diehl and Gary Goertz, *War and Peace in International Rivalry* (Ann Arbor: University of Michigan Press, 2001), p. 28.

strong link between rivalries, crisis escalation, and the onset of war—arms races are more likely to occur in the context of rivalries, and crises between interstate rivals are more dangerous and more likely to escalate to war.[8] The evidence from the public record of cyber operations strongly indicates that states use cyber operations as a tool of foreign policy—cyber operations typically take place in the context of geopolitical events or are carried out with the aim of achieving a strategic edge over other states.[9] Moreover, the sheer volume of cyber operations that take place in the context of international rivalries suggests that cyberspace provides states with a fruitful avenue to pursue strategic objectives in the context of rivalries.

Nevertheless, there is no evidence that cyber operations have triggered escalation between rivals—even in pairs of states with a history of crisis escalation and military conflict.[10] This is true for rival dyads that have otherwise been plagued by recurring crises and conflicts. For instance, North Korea and South Korea have a longstanding rivalry that dates back to the Korean War, and tensions between them have persisted into the contemporary environment with numerous recurring crises between the two states.[11] Escalation on the Korean Peninsula would be particularly precarious given the confluence of a number of factors: the potential unpredictability of the deeply isolated and personalist regime in Pyongyang; U.S. security guarantees to South Korea; the presence of tens of thousands of U.S. troops stationed on the peninsula, as well as over one million North Korean and South Korean troops; North Korea's weapons programs, including its nuclear weapons program, chemical and biological weapons capabilities, and ballistic missiles; and the sheer number of long-range artillery emplaced along the demilitarized zone.[12]

Offensive cyber capabilities are an important component of Pyongyang's investments in asymmetric warfighting capabilities and also serve as a means of circumventing sanctions and illicitly generating revenue. Threat actors affiliated with North Korea, particularly the Lazarus Group, have carried out a range

---

[8] See, for example, ibid.; Toby J. Rider, Michael G. Findley, and Paul F. Diehl, "Just Part of the Game? Arms Races, Rivalry, and War," *Journal of Peace Research* 48, no. 1 (January 2011): 85–100; Michael Colaresi and William R. Thompson, "Strategic Rivalries, Protracted Conflict, and Crisis Escalation," *Journal of Peace Research* 39, no. 3 (May 2002): 263–287.

[9] Brandon Valeriano, Benjamin Jensen, and Ryan C. Maness, *Cyber Strategy: The Evolving Character of Power and Coercion* (Oxford: Oxford University Press, 2018).

[10] For further empirical work on this, see Brandon Valeriano and Ryan C. Maness, "The Dynamics of Cyber Conflict between Rival Antagonists, 2001–11," *Journal of Peace Research* 51, no. 1 (May 2014): 347–360.

[11] Glenn Palmer, Vito D'Orazio, Michael Kenwick, and Matthew Lane, "The MID4 Dataset, 2002–2010," *Conflict Management and Peace Science* 32, no. 2 (2015): 222–242.

[12] See, for example, James Hackett and Mark Fitzpatrick, eds., "The Conventional Military Balance on the Korean Peninsula," The International Institute for Strategic Studies (June 2018); and Chung Min Lee and Kathryn Botto, "Korea Net Assessment 2020: Politicized Security and Unchanging Strategic Realities," Carnegie Endowment for International Peace, March 18, 2020.

of cyber operations, such as destructive malware attacks, DDoS attacks, and cyber crime and financial theft operations.[13] South Korea has been the primary target of North Korean cyber operations, ranging from government and defense targets, the financial and media sectors, and cryptocurrency exchanges. South Korea's economy, deeply reliant on advanced information and communications technology, is an especially vulnerable target.[14]

Indeed, out of the 36 cyber incidents we identified that have been linked to the government in Pyongyang from 2009 to 2020, 16—almost half—were carried out against South Korean entities in the government or private sector. Most of these were espionage operations against government and private sector targets as well as cyber operations for the purposes of financial theft, where escalation might be less likely. However, North Korea has also been associated with four different denial of service campaigns against South Korean targets that took place in the context of heightened political tensions: the July 2009 cyber attack against government and private sector websites in South Korea and the United States, which began on the same day that Pyongyang launched a ballistic missile;[15] the Ten Days of Rain denial of service attack against South Korean government websites, financial institutions, and critical infrastructure in March 2011 at the same time that the United States and South Korea were conducting joint military exercises in the region;[16] a denial of service attack against South Korean banks a few weeks later in April 2011;[17] and the Dark Seoul cyber attack in March 2013, which employed malware that led to denials of service across the financial services and media sectors and took place at the same time as joint U.S.-South Korean military exercises.[18]

[13] "Sanctions Programs and Country Information," U.S. Department of the Treasury, accessed November 2020, https://www.treasury.gov/resourcecenter/sanctions/Programs/Documents/dprk_cyber_threat_advisory_20200415.pdf; "'Lazarus Group' MITRE ATT&CK," accessed November 2020, https://attack.mitre.org/groups/G0032/.

[14] "Hotspot Analysis: Cyber Disruption and Cybercrime: Democratic People's Republic of Korea," Center for Security Studies (CSS), June 2018.

[15] Choe Sang-Hun and John Markoff, "Cyberattacks Jam Government and Commercial Web Sites in U.S. and South Korea," The New York Times, July 8, 2008, https://www.nytimes.com/2009/07/09/technology/09cyber.html; "North Korea Launched Cyber Attacks, Says South," Associated Press, July 2009, https://www.theguardian.com/world/2009/jul/11/south-korea-blames-north-korea-cyber-attacks.

[16] "Denial of Service Incident against South Korean and U.S. Targets," The Council on Foreign Relations, April 2011, https://www.cfr.org/cyber-operations/denial-service-incident-against-south-korean-and-us-targets; "South Korea Government Websites Targeted in Cyber Attack" Associated Press, March 4, 2011, https://www.theguardian.com/world/2011/mar/04/south-korea-websites-cyber-attack; "The Sony Hackers Were Causing Mayhem Years Before They Hit the Company," Wired, February 24, 2016, https://www.wired.com/2016/02/sony-hackers-causing-mayhem-years-hit-company/#slide-3.

[17] "North Korea Behind Cyber Attack on S.Korea Bank—Prosecutors," Reuters, May 3, 2011, https://www.reuters.com/article/korea-north-cyber-idUSL3E7G31BT20110503.

[18] Choe Sang-Hun "Computer Networks in South Korea Are Paralyzed in Cyberattacks," The New York Times, March 20, 2013, https://www.nytimes.com/2013/03/21/world/asia/

Nevertheless, none of these cyber campaigns resulted in escalation, despite the fact that assessments of North Korean campaign plans for war on the peninsula include "a simultaneous and multifarious cyber offensive on the Republic of Korea's society and basic infrastructure, government agencies, and major military command centers."[19] Public reporting indicates the South Korean response was minimal and limited to either direct, official attribution to North Korea by government officials or more indirect public suggestions that Pyongyang was likely behind the cyber attacks. Attribution challenges existed across all of these cases, which may have constrained Seoul's ability to respond and damped the temporal pressure that might have otherwise prompted more immediate action.[20]

Moreover, even the more sophisticated instances of North Korean-affiliated attacks only resulted in short-term disruption to services in the affected entities. This is not only consistent with our argument regarding the challenges and complexities of strategically significant offensive cyber operations, it also supports our contention that the effects of cyber operations are relatively minor. In this case, the costs imposed by these campaigns were likely not sufficient to generate the level of political pressure that may have prompted political leaders to respond in a more forceful manner. In fact, in comparison to other actions taken by Pyongyang in the context of these events, such as ballistic missile and nuclear tests, the consequences of disruptive cyber operations are relatively minor.

The only public information about an alleged response to any of North Korea's cyber campaigns is in March 2013, when Pyongyang accused the United States and South Korea of conducting a cyber attack that disrupted internet access for two days.[21] Experts are skeptical about the veracity of this claim, but even if one were to hypothetically accept Pyongyang's accusations at face value, this type of disruptive cyber operation would be proportionate to North Korean denial of service operations; if anything, it would be of a lesser magnitude given the extremely limited nature of internet access in North Korea and, therefore, the narrow scope and impact of the purported operation. Therefore, even when responses may have occurred in cyberspace, they were limited and proportionate.

There are similar patterns in cyber relations between India and Pakistan, whose rivalry dates to the partition of British India into the Dominion of India

---

south-korea-computer-network-crashes.html.   https://www.sans.org/reading-room/whitepapers/critical/tracing-lineage-darkseoul-36787.

[19] Duk-Ki Kim, "The Republic of Korea's Counter-asymmetric Strategy," *Naval War College Review* 65, no. 1 (Winter 2012): 4.
[20] Stephan Haggard and Jon R. Lindsay, "North Korea and the Sony Hack: Exporting Instability through Cyberspace" *Asia Pacific Issues* no. 117 (May, 2015): 5.
[21] Steve Herman, "North Korea Blames US, South for 'Cyber Attack,'" *VOA News*, March 15, 2013, https://www.voanews.com/east-asia-pacific/north-korea-blames-us-south-cyber-attack.

and the Dominion of Pakistan in 1947 and is one of the most dangerous in the international system. Political disputes between India and Pakistan are rooted in the violence that followed partition, especially in the newly divided Punjab, as Muslims fled India for Pakistan and Hindus fled to India. Since then, relations between the two states have been characterized by recurring disputes that have generated serious risks of crisis escalation.[22] Some of these have precipitated conventional conflict, such as in 1947, 1965, 1971, and 1999—a particularly perilous dynamic given the nuclear arsenals of both states. State sponsored terrorist attacks have also exacerbated relationships between the two countries, such as the November 2008 Mumbai terrorist attacks carried out by Lashakr-e-Taiba, likely at the behest of Pakistan's intelligence services, which killed 166 people.[23] A more recent example of crisis dynamics between these states dates from February 2019 when the Indian Air Force crossed the Line of Control (LoC) between the two countries in the state of Kashmir to bomb an alleged militant training camp in retaliation for a terrorist attack against Indian forces in Kashmir, which India claimed had been perpetrated by a Pakistani-sponsored group. In response, Pakistan shot down at least one Indian fighter jet and took a pilot hostage. Both India and Pakistan mobilized tens of thousands of troops along the LoC. While the crisis was ultimately resolved following Pakistan's offer to release the captured pilot, the situation generated a real risk of military conflict between two nuclear-armed regional powers.[24]

In contrast, India-Pakistan relations in cyberspace have remained relatively muted. Despite numerous interactions between Indian and Pakistani-backed groups in cyberspace, no cyber incident or even series of incidents between these rivals has broached any meaningful threshold that would trigger escalatory risks. Rather, beginning as early as 2008, Pakistani and Indian cyber actors, mostly "hacktivists," have engaged in tit-for-tat website defacement campaigns targeting government and military websites using known vulnerabilities. Groups associated with both governments have also carried out espionage campaigns.[25] The former types of cyber operations are relatively unsophisticated and low-cost with transient effects, which are unlikely to rise to a level warranting major retaliation. It is notable that, in the context of a rivalry that has produced numerous

---

[22] T.V. Paul, "Why Has the India-Pakistan Rivalry Been so Enduring? Power Asymmetry and an Intractable Conflict," *Security Studies* 15, no. 4 (2006).

[23] Stephen Tankel, *Storming the World Stage: The Story of Lashkar-e-Taiba* (New York: Columbia University Press, 2011).

[24] "India Demands Pakistan Release Pilot as Kashmir Crisis Intensifies," *BBC*, February 28, 2019; Salman Masood, Jeffrey Gettleman, and Maria Abi-Habib, "Imran Khan Says Pakistan Will Release Captured Indian Pilot," *The New York Times*, February 28, 2019.

[25] "Hotspot Analysis: Regional Rivalry between India-Pakistan: Tit-for-tat in Cyberspace" CSS Cyber Defense Project, ETH Zurich, August 2018.

disputes and crises that have escalated along dangerous pathways, reciprocal cyber incidents have thus far failed to produce any significant crises.

If one were to conduct a closer examination of similar dynamics in other regional rivals such as, for example, the rivalries between China and Southeast Asian nations, China and Japan, or Israel, the Gulf States, and Iran, similar patterns obtain.[26] In the following sections, we explore strategic interactions between the United States and four enduring rivals more deeply.

The U.S. Dogs That Didn't Bark

To test our argument that characteristics of cyber operations make it unlikely they will lead to escalation, we conduct process tracing across a set of case studies in which we hold one party to a rivalry constant, while varying the states it interacts with. Specifically, we explore four examples of interactions between the United States and rivals in cyberspace: China, North Korea, Iran, and Russia. There are, of course, limitations to the generalizability of our analysis given our focus on the United States. Later in the chapter, we discuss our motivations for taking this approach and acknowledge that some of the insights may not apply to other contexts (such as pairs of non-democratic rival states or rivalries involving states with less mature cyber capabilities).

We are specifically interested in assessing a state's behavior in response to a range of different types of cyber operations conducted by various adversaries, under conditions in which one might have expected to observe escalation take place. Therefore, this set of case studies represents a hard test of our argument that cyber operations are unlikely to trigger dangerous escalatory spirals.[27] A core part of our argument rests on the minimal effects of most cyber operations, on the one hand, and the challenges associated with those cyber operations that may have more significant effects, on the other. While many types of cyber operations are relatively unsophisticated and easy to conduct. They also are more likely to have temporary, disruptive effects against soft, vulnerable targets. We expect these to carry minimal risks of escalation. Moreover, the level of skill and capability required to plan and conduct the types of cyber operations that may be more likely to lead to an escalatory response limits the availability

---

[26] "Hotspot Analysis: Use of Cybertools in Regional Tensions in Southeast Asia," CSS Cyber Defense Project, ETH Zurich, August 2018. "Hotspot Analysis: A One-sided Affair: Japan and the People's Republic of China in Cyberspace," CSS Cyber Defense Project, ETH Zurich, January 2020; "Hotspot Analysis: Iranian Cyber Activities in the Context of Regional Rivalries and International Tensions," CSS Cyber Defense Project, ETH Zurich, May 2019.

[27] For a discussion of case selection strategies, see Alexander L. George and Andrew Bennett, *Case Studies and Theory Development in the Social Sciences* (Cambridge, MA: MIT Press, 2005), pp. 120–123.

of those options to only the more powerful cyber actors. Therefore, one of the motivations behind exploring dynamics between the United States and its rivals is to assess how more capable powers in the international system—those that one might expect would have the capability to escalate in cyberspace and across other domains—respond to cyber attacks by rival states.

But we are not only evaluating the potential for escalation within the cyber domain. In fact, a key concern of some experts is the risk that cyber operations may spill over into kinetic conflict. Therefore, in our case studies we explore the full range of responses to cyber operations, which could include military and non-military tools (such as diplomatic action, economic sanctions, or legal measures). This raises the question of how to evaluate whether a response to a cyber action that takes places outside of cyberspace is escalatory. We measure the extent to which a response is escalatory based on two observed outcomes: first, in the immediate sense, whether the scale or effects of the target's response are pro-portionate to the scale or effects of the initial cyber action; and second, whether there is a meaningful change in the nature of the interaction between rival states, such that the risk of conflict is heightened. The former measure follows from long-standing approaches in international law concerning the definition of the use of force, which legal scholars have extended to cyberspace.[28] The latter captures the political nature of escalation and the role of perception in shaping the strategic interaction between states. In other words, what might on its face look like a tit-for-tat, proportionate response to a cyber attack may neverthe-less escalate a crisis if either party perceives that a key threshold or line has been crossed, misinterprets the intent or underlying strategic context, or otherwise perceives some interest in escalating despite one party's failure to do so.

By a number of measures, the United States is one of the most cyber-capable powers, with a mature strategy and doctrine for cyberspace operations, a robust military organization dedicated to offensive and defensive cyber operations, clear command and control of military cyber capabilities, and demonstrated capability for coercion.[29] Additionally, the United States possesses substantial

---

[28] See Michael N. Schmitt, ed., *Tallinn Manual 2.0 on the International Law Applicable to Cyber Operations* (New York: Cambridge University Press, 2017), ch. 14, for a fulsome discussion of definitions of the use of force in cyberspace. However, it is important to note that not all states agree about how international law applies in cyberspace, and the United States does not recognize the distinction between the "use of force" and "armed attack" thresholds in the United Nations charter. See, for example, Michael N. Schmitt, "International Law in Cyberspace: The Koh Speech and Tallinn Manual Juxtaposed," *Harvard International Law Journal* 54 (December 2012): 13–37. Also see Catherine Lotrionte, "Reconsidering the Consequences for State-Sponsored Hostile Cyber Operations Under International Law," *Cyber Defense Review* 3, no. 2 (Summer 2018): 73–114.

[29] International Institute for Strategic Studies, *The Military Balance: The Annual Assessment of Global Military Capabilities and Defence Economics* (New York: Routledge, 2020), pp. 515–518. Also see Brandon Valeriano, Benjamin Jensen, and Ryan C. Maness, *Cyber Strategy: The Evolving Character of Power and Coercion* (New York: Oxford University Press, 2018).

non-cyber military capabilities that rival or exceed those of its adversaries.[30] Given these factors, it would be reasonable to infer that it is among the states most capable of escalating in response to a cyber operation, either in cyberspace or with non-cyber instruments of power.

Moreover, while this should not be the sole factor driving case study selection, there is a significant amount of publicly available information about U.S. behavior in cyberspace, in contrast to the relative scarcity of information about closed regimes. In a field where much of the relevant information is not public, the existence of multiple corroborating sources to substantiate a particular finding gives greater confidence in the overall results and interpretation of a case. Additionally, the United States provides a wealth of variation to our analysis because it is among the most targeted states in cyberspace and has experienced a range of different types of cyber operations, including disruptive attacks, destructive malware, ransomware, cyber-enabled espionage and theft, and cyber-enabled information operations.

The evidence overwhelmingly demonstrates that, across the range of different types of cyber attacks that the United States has experienced, stemming from different rivals with different degrees of capability and varying salience of interests at stake, the United States has consistently chosen not to escalate. Instead, it has relied on tit-for-tat, proportionate responses to observed adversary cyber activity, including responses outside of cyberspace.[31]

The United States and China

In this section, we explore interactions between the United States and China caused by sustained cyber-enabled espionage and data theft conducted by threat actors associated with the Chinese government. Some experts have argued that a particular challenge of cyberspace is the inability to distinguish between offensive cyber operations and espionage, given that the initial steps of a cyber operation are analogous for both. As we discussed earlier in this book, this has led academics to hypothesize that security dilemmas are likely to pervade cyberspace and be especially dangerous.[32] Therefore, we set out to explore whether

[30] International Institute for Strategic Studies, *The Military Balance: The Annual Assessment of Global Military Capabilities and Defence Economics* (New York: Routledge, 2020), pp. 21–27.

[31] Some have attributed this to successful deterrence on the part of the United States, suggesting that, because its economy and society are highly reliant on information technology and are more vulnerable to adverse cyber activity, it is hesitant or unwilling to escalate. Setting aside empirical challenges of measuring successful deterrence—ascertaining what accounts for a non-observed outcome—this line of reasoning nevertheless supports our argument that cyber operations generally do not lead to escalatory responses. Jason Healey, "Not the Cyber Deterrence the United States Wants," *Net Politics*, June 11, 2018.

[32] See, for example, Ben Buchanan, *The Cybersecurity Dilemma: Hacking, Trust, and Fear Between Nations* (New York: Oxford University Press, 2017).

espionage campaigns do in fact cause escalation. We find little evidence that they do. Interactions between the United States and China demonstrate how even long-term cyber-enabled espionage campaigns—including those conducted both for economic gain and national security purposes—do not prompt escalatory behavior on the part of their targets.

The patterns apparent in this case highlight two aspects of our theoretical framework. First, cyber operations contain immense intelligence value, which weigh against the strategic utility of conducting offensive operations that may jeopardize those accesses. This is an important factor that keeps interactions that begin in a cyber espionage context more contained and that incentivizes policymakers to reach for other tools to respond to cyber espionage. There is no evidence that the United States conducted offensive cyber operations in response to Chinese cyber activity, even as it turned toward diplomatic, legal, and economic measures. Second, this case illustrates how states perceive the costs of cyber operations, especially those that do not cause disruptive or destructive effects against networks, and how this shapes what constitutes a proportionate response.

It is well documented that the Chinese government and affiliated threat actors have engaged in a systemic campaign of cyber-enabled economic espionage and intellectual property theft targeting private and government entities in the United States.[33] Indeed, China has conducted cyber-enabled espionage campaigns since at least 2005, when it was made public that hackers said to be affiliated with the Chinese government gained access to a range of U.S. government networks in a campaign dubbed Titan Rain.[34] A number of other cyber espionage campaigns have been made public, such as the targeting of U.S. information technology firms in Operation Aurora in 2010 or theft of data from U.S. defense contractors in 2011, as well as extensive reports by cybersecurity firms such as McAfee in 2011, Mandiant in 2013, and CrowdStrike in 2014 about Chinese cyber espionage campaigns against U.S. industries.[35] The cumulative economic impact of these campaigns has been significant. In 2016 Congressional testimony, General Keith Alexander, former director of the National Security

---

[33] For a review of major Chinese cyber operations, see Senator Angus King and Representative Mike Gallagher, co-chairs, "United States of America Solarium Commission Final Report," March 2020, p. 10, https://cybersolarium.org/march-2020-csc-report/march-2020-csc-report/. Also see "Two Chinese Hackers Associated with the Ministry of State Security Charged with Global Computer Intrusion Campaigns Targeting Intellectual Property and Confidential Business Information," Department of Justice, December 20, 2018, https://www.justice.gov/opa/pr/two-chinese-hackers-associated-ministry-state-security-charged-global-computer-intrusion; "How China's Elite Hackers Stole the World's Most Valuable Secrets" *Wired*, December 20, 2018, https://www.wired.com/story/doj-indictment-chinese-hackers-apt10/.

[34] "Titan Rain," CFR Cyber Operations tracker.

[35] "Hotspot Analysis: Strategic Stability between Great Powers: The Sino-American Cyber Agreement," CSS Cyber Defense Project, ETH Zurich, December 2017, pp. 7–8.

Agency and commander of U.S. Cyber Command, described how cyberspace has enabled the greatest transfer of wealth in history.[36] Indeed, estimates of economic losses stemming from Chinese cyber espionage range from $30 to $50 billion annually.[37] Despite these economic costs, however, the way that U.S. policymakers chose to respond to Chinese cyber behavior is consistent with the idea that states do not perceive cyber operations—especially those oriented around theft of data rather than disruptive or destructive effects—as rising to a level warranting escalatory, especially military, responses. This form of cyber behavior seems to be conceptualized as qualitatively different from even other ways of operating in cyberspace, despite some scholars' concerns about the indistinguishability of espionage and offense leading to escalation.

Out of the set of cases in our aggregated dataset, some clear trends emerge regarding patterns of behavior between the United States and China in cyberspace. China has been associated with 110 distinct cyber incidents between 2005 and 2020, a disproportionate share of which involved cyber operations targeting the United States for the purposes of cyber-enabled espionage. Specifically, 54 cyber incidents linked to China targeted U.S. public sector or private entities, and all but two were espionage campaigns. In contrast, of the 14 incidents associated with the United States, none were directly aimed at Chinese public or private entities.[38] Rather, the United States has largely responded to Chinese behavior in cyberspace by leveraging diplomatic, economic, and law enforcement instruments of power.

Furthermore, there is little evidence of meaningful escalation trigged by cyber operations, even as the U.S. government has become more vocal and public in addressing cyber behavior it attributes to the Chinese government.[39] With some notable exceptions, which we discuss further below, U.S. responses have been at a far lesser magnitude in terms of scope and effects than the precipitating cyber

[36] Keith B. Alexander, "Prepared Statement of GEN (Ret) Keith B. Alexander on Digital Acts of War: Evolving the Cybersecurity Conversation before the Subcommittees on Information Technology and National Security of the Committee on Oversight and Government Reform," U.S. House Oversight Committee, July 13, 2016, https://oversight.house.gov/wp-content/uploads/2016/07/Gen-Alexander-Statement-Digital-Acts-of-War-7-13.pdf.

[37] James Andrew Lewis, "How Much Have the Chinese Actually Taken?" The Center for Strategic and International Studies, March 22, 2018, https://www.csis.org/analysis/how-much-have-chinese-actually-taken. Also see "The Cost of Malicious Cyber Activity to the U.S. Economy," Council of Economic Advisers, February 2018, https://www.whitehouse.gov/wp-content/uploads/2018/03/The-Cost-of-Malicious-Cyber-Activity-to-the-U.S.-Economy.pdf.

[38] There are a few incidents in the dataset where cyber incidents reported to have been linked to the United States had inadvertent effects against Chinese entities. Of course, it is possible that there has been U.S.-sponsored cyber activity against China that has not been publicly reported.

[39] A more recent response not captured by the dataset due to the time period it covers is the joint public attribution in July 2021 by the United States and multiple allies and partners of Chinese responsibility for the Microsoft Exchange Server hack, among other cyber incidents. See "The United States, Joined by Allies and Partners, Attributes Malicious Cyber Activity and Irresponsible State Behavior to the People's Republic of China," The White House, July 19, 2021.

action. Figure 5.1 contains a timeline of major, publicly known Chinese cyber campaigns and U.S. policy responses. The timeline does not detail every single Chinese cyber incident; rather, it highlights some of the most significant ones for illustrative purposes.

As Figure 5.1 illustrates, there has been a conspicuous shift over time in the U.S. approach, with the Obama Administration predominantly exercising diplomatic instruments of power, coupled with limited indictments and the threat of sanctions, to bring China to a diplomatic agreement about cyber behavior. In contrast, the Trump Administration relied far more heavily on indictments and economic instruments. Despite this apparent shift, escalation did not take place.

Initial diplomatic efforts

Initially, the U.S. government was reticent to even publicly acknowledge cyber incidents associated with the Chinese government. Despite China being linked to cyber espionage from the early 1990s, the first time a U.S. government figure publicly named the Chinese government as being behind the cyber-enabled theft of intellectual property was in a 2011 National Counter Intelligence Executive report, which noted that "Chinese actors are the world's most active and persistent perpetrators of economic espionage."[40] This was a significant step because, prior to this report, the United States had been reticent to publicly chastise state actors for economic cyber espionage.[41]

While it is difficult to ascertain the reasons for this reluctance, the events surrounding the decision to be more public about Chinese cyber behavior suggests some plausible explanations. In February 2013, the New York Times published an article that directly named the Chinese People's Liberation Army (PLA) as one of the sources of a series of cyber operations targeting private corporations in the United States.[42] The article was based on a foundational investigatory report issued by the U.S. cybersecurity firm Mandiant.[43] Though the Chinese government immediately disavowed any involvement or responsibility, its denial was largely perceived to lack credibility given the technical nature of China's internet infrastructure, which is known for widespread government monitoring and filtering, as well as the detail of the evidence that Mandiant had collected

[40] "Foreign Spies Stealing US Economic Secrets In Cyberspace," Office of the National Counter Intelligence Executive, October 2011, p. i.
[41] Thom Shanker, "U.S. Report Accuses China and Russia of Internet Spying," The New York Times, November 3, 2011, http://www.nytimes.com/2011/11/04/world/us-report-accuses-china-and-russia-of-internet-spying.html.
[42] David E. Sanger, David Barboza, and Nicole Perlroth, "China's Army Is Seen as Tied to Hacking Against U.S.," The New York Times, February 18, 2013, sec. Technology, http://www.nytimes.com/2013/02/19/technology/chinas-army-is-seen-as-tied-to-hacking-against-us.html.
[43] "APT1- Exposing One of China's Cyber Espionage Units," Mandiant, February 2013, https://www.fireeye.com/content/dam/fireeye-www/services/pdfs/mandiant-apt1-report.pdf.

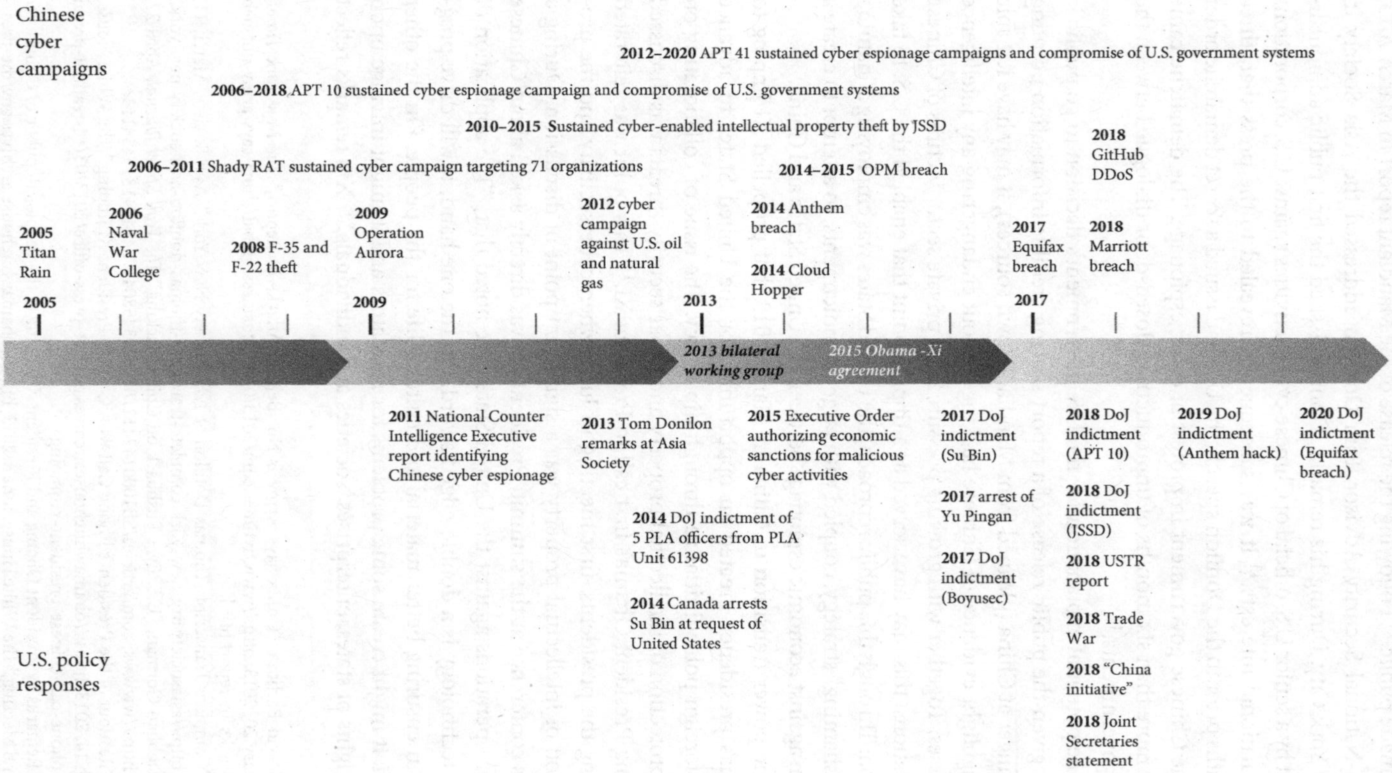

Chinese cyber campaigns

2012–2020 APT 41 sustained cyber espionage campaigns and compromise of U.S. government systems

2006–2018 APT 10 sustained cyber espionage campaign and compromise of U.S. government systems

2010–2015 Sustained cyber-enabled intellectual property theft by JSSD

2006–2011 Shady RAT sustained cyber campaign targeting 71 organizations

2018 GitHub DDoS

2018 Marriott breach

2014–2015 OPM breach

2012 cyber campaign against U.S. oil and natural gas

2014 Anthem breach

2014 Cloud Hopper

2009 Operation Aurora

2008 F-35 and F-22 theft

2006 Naval War College

2005 Titan Rain

2017 Equifax breach

2005   2009   2013   2017

2013 bilateral working group

2015 Obama–Xi agreement

U.S. policy responses

2011 National Counter Intelligence Executive report identifying Chinese cyber espionage

2013 Tom Donilon remarks at Asia Society

2014 DoJ indictment of 5 PLA officers from PLA Unit 61398

2014 Canada arrests Su Bin at request of United States

2015 Executive Order authorizing economic sanctions for malicious cyber activities

2017 DoJ indictment (Su Bin)

2017 arrest of Yu Pingan

2017 DoJ indictment (Boyusec)

2018 DoJ indictment (APT 10)

2018 DoJ indictment (JSSD)

2018 USTR report

2018 Trade War

2018 "China initiative"

2018 Joint Secretaries statement

2019 DoJ indictment (Anthem hack)

2020 DoJ indictment (Equifax breach)

Figure 5.1 Cyber Events in the Context of U.S.–China Rivalry, 2005–2020

and made public.[44] Following the release of the Mandiant report in March 2013, then-National Security Advisor Tom Donilon addressed the Asia Society in New York City. During his remarks, Donilon issued the first public admonishment by a senior U.S. official of Chinese cyber activities against U.S. corporations and national interests.[45] It was subsequently revealed to the press that, three months prior to the Donilon speech, the U.S. had issued a secret demarche order to the Chinese government in protest of cyber espionage. The demarche came after more than six months of unproductive, closed-door dialogue between the two governments.[46]

One potential explanation for the U.S. government's decision to go public is that, given the public release of a report sharing credible information pointing the finger at China (gleaned from Mandiant's own sources), it may have felt able to highlight evidence of Chinese hacking without endangering any intelligence accesses. Together with growing pressure from private sector victims of Chinese operations, this may have served as a tipping point that enabled the U.S. to take action. Through this public reproach, the United States was employing a "naming and shaming" strategy, coupled with targeted indictments, to attempt to create a norm against economic espionage between the United States and China.

The power transition in China in March 2013 that propelled Xi Jinping to China's presidency created an opportunity for the United States to advance this foreign policy initiative through diplomacy. The issue of collaborating on the protection of intellectual property and cyber security threats was discussed during President Obama's first call to President Xi.[47] This point was reiterated during the presidents' first meeting in June, when cybersecurity and the protection of intellectual property was a significant point of discussion. During a press conference at the summit, President Xi was directly asked about Chinese cyber operations against the United States. He noted that, "The application of new technology is a double-edged sword. On the one hand, it will drive progress in ensuring better material and cultural life for the people. On the other hand, it might create some problems for regulators and it might infringe upon the rights of states, enterprises, societies and individuals."[48] Xi's remarks reflect

---

[44] David Barboza, "China Says Army Is Not Behind Attacks in Report," *The New York Times*, February 20, 2013, http://www.nytimes.com/2013/02/21/business/global/china-says-army-not-behind-attacks-in-report.html.

[45] "Complete Transcript: Thomas Donilon at Asia Society New York," Asia Society, March 11, 2013, http://asiasociety.org/new-york/complete-transcript-thomas-donilon-asia-society-new-york.

[46] Siobhan Gorman, "U.S. Eyes Pushback on China Hacking," *The Wall Street Journal*, April 22, 2013, http://www.wsj.com/articles/SB10001424127887324345804578424741315433114.

[47] "Readout of the President's Phone Call with Chinese President Xi Jinping," The White House, March 14, 2013, https://obamawhitehouse.archives.gov/the-press-office/2013/03/14/readout-presid ent-s-phone-call-chinese-president-xi-jinping.

[48] "Remarks by President Obama and President Xi Jinping of the People's Republic of China after Bilateral Meeting," The White House, June 8, 2013, https://obamawhitehouse.archives.gov/the-press-office/2013/06/08/remarks-president-obama-and-president-xi-jinping-peoples-republic-china-.

China's perspective on cyber espionage—as a legitimate means to further the power of the state by enabling innovation and growth across all economic sectors.[49] However, both leaders realized that there was a need to cooperate on cybersecurity related threats and agreed to open a dialogue moving forward. The next month, in July 2013, a bilateral working group for cybersecurity held its first meeting during which the issue of cyber espionage was discussed along with the need to collaborate in future meetings to address related concerns.[50]

Despite the public admonishments and top-level meetings, public reporting from the Office of the National Counter Intelligence Executive indicated that China continued to aggressively target U.S. interests via cyberspace and demonstrated an increasing level of sophistication in doing so.[51] The next public U.S. rebuke of Chinese cyber espionage came in May 2014 with the indictment of five PLA officers for many of the activities identified in the 2013 Mandiant report.[52] China responded to the indictments by again denying its involvement and withdrawing from the bilateral cybersecurity working group in protest.[53]

In mid-2015, Chinese-affiliated actors breached the personnel records of over 21 million U.S. government employees held by the Office of Personnel Management (OPM), even accessing the fingerprints of nearly six million personnel.[54] While this breach was significant due to its scale and the impact it

[49] China's use of cyber espionage as a deliberate means to secure economic and growth and in- dustrialization is well documented. For instance, see Adam Segal, *The Hacked World Order: How Nations Fight, Trade, Maneuver, and Manipulate in the Digital Age* (New York: Public Affairs, 2017), pp. 125–129.

[50] "Senior Administration Officials on the First Day of the Strategic and Economic Dialogue and U.S.-China Relations," U.S. State Department, July 11, 2013, https://2009-2017.state.gov/r/pa/prs/ps/2013/07/211801.htm.

[51] J.J. Green, "Exclusive: NCIX Says Chinese Hackers 'Getting Faster and Smarter,'" *Wtop*, July 10, 2014, http://wtop.com/j-j-green-national/2014/07/exclusive-ncix-says-chinese-hackers-getting-fas ter-and-smarter/.

[52] United States District Court Western District of Pennsylvania, "United States of America v. Wang Dong, Sun Kailiand, Wen Xinyu, Huang Zhenyu, Gu Chunhui," Criminal Number: 14-118, Filed: May 2014, https://www.justice.gov/iso/opa/resources/5122014519132358461949.pdf. But also, see the official press release, Department of Justice, "U.S. Charges Five Chinese Military Hackers for Cyber Espionage against U.S. Corporations and a Labor Organization for Commercial Advantage," Office of Public Affairs, May 19, 2014, https://www.justice.gov/opa/pr/us-charges-five-chinese-military-hackers-cyber-espionage-against-us-corporations-and-labor. Also in 2014, Canada arrested Chinese national Su Bin, at the request of United States, for hacking Boeing between 2008 and 2014. See Garrett Hinck and Tim Maurer, "Persistent Enforcement: Criminal Charges as a Response to Non-State Malicious Cyber Activity," *Journal of National Security Law & Policy* 10 (2020): 528.

[53] Shannon Tiezzi, "China's Response to the US Cyber Espionage Charges," *The Diplomat*, May 21, 2014, http://thediplomat.com/2014/05/chinas-response-to-the-us-cyber-espionage-charges/.

[54] Julie Hirschfeld Davis, "Hacking of Government Computers Exposed 21.5 Million People," *The New York Times*, July 9, 2015, https://www.nytimes.com/2015/07/10/us/office-of-personnel-man agement-hackers-got-data-of-millions.html; David E. Sanger, "Hackers Took Fingerprints of 5.6 Million U.S. Workers, Government Says," *The New York Times*, September 23, 2015, https://www.nyti mes.com/2015/09/24/world/asia/hackers-took-fingerprints-of-5-6-million-us-workers-governm ent-says.html.

could have on ongoing and future intelligence operations, reporting indicates that the Obama Administration was perplexed as to how to respond. This is because the administration had been careful to distinguish between intelligence collection for national security purposes, which is largely accepted as a necessary state practice, and economic espionage and intellectual property theft, which the United States defined as unacceptable. Indeed, James Clapper, the Director of National Intelligence at the time, noted that "you have to kind of salute the Chinese for what they did."[55]

Several months following the U.S. realization of the OPM breach, Presidents Obama and Xi struck a deal in September 2015 in which they mutually agreed to refrain from conducting cyber economic espionage and intellectual property theft and discussed means to create a cyber code of conduct.[56] In addition to public naming and shaming efforts, as well as two sets of Department of Justice (DOJ) indictments against Chinese nationals, the 2015 agreement came on the heels of the Obama Administration's April 2015 issuance of an executive order authorizing economic sanctions against perpetrators of malicious cyber activities, as well as a speech by President Obama at a business roundtable in September 2015 suggesting his administration was contemplating imposing sanctions against the Chinese for cyber espionage.[57] These measures likely brought Xi to the bargaining table and ultimately created the conditions for the 2015 agreement.[58]

Initially, private sector assessments as well as public statements from the U.S. Assistant Attorney for National Security indicated that Chinese cyber espionage decreased in the wake of the accord.[59] A 2016 report by FireEye, a prominent cybersecurity firm, notes a significant decrease in network compromises

[55] David E. Sanger, "U.S. Decides to Retaliate Against China's Hacking," *The New York Times*, July 21, 2015, https://www.nytimes.com/2015/08/01/world/asia/us-decides-to-retaliate-against-chinas-hacking.html.

[56] Julie Hirschfeld Davis and David E. Sanger, "Obama and Xi Jinping of China Agree to Steps on Cybertheft," *The New York Times*, September 25, 2015, https://www.nytimes.com/2015/09/26/world/asia/xi-jinping-white-house.html; David E. Sanger, "U.S. and China Seek Arms Deal for Cyberspace," *The New York Times*, September 19, 2015, https://www.nytimes.com/2015/09/20/world/asia/us-and-china-seek-arms-deal-for-cyberspace.html.

[57] https://obamawhitehouse.archives.gov/the-press-office/2015/04/01/executive-order-blocking-property-certain-persons-engaging-significant-m.

[58] "Red Line Drawn: China Recalculates its Use of Cyber Espionage," *FireEye*, June 2016, p. 8.

[59] John P. Carlin, "Detect, Disrupt, Deter: A Whole-of-Government Approach to National Security Cyber Threats," moderated discussion, Center for Strategic & International Studies, June 28, 2016, https://www.csis.org/events/detect-disrupt-deter-whole-government-approach-natio nal-security-cyber-threats. Also, see the report by the cyber security firm "Redline Drawn: China Recalculated its Use of Cyber Espionage," FireEye Isight Intelligence, June 2016, https://www.fireeye.com/content/dam/fireeye-www/current-threats/pdfs/rpt-china-espionage.pdf. One finding of the report was "a notable decline in China-based groups' overall intrusion activity against entities in the U.S. and 25 other countries. We suspect that this shift in operations reflects the influence of ongoing military reforms, widespread exposure of Chinese cyber operations, and actions taken by the U.S. government."

associated with Chinese threat actors, although FireEye identifies mid-2014 as the start of the decline, prior to the 2015 agreement.[60] FireEye attributes this change in behavior to a number of factors, including "President Xi's military and political initiatives, the widespread exposure of Chinese cyber operations, and mounting pressure from the U.S. government."[61] However, beginning in 2017 our data indicates an uptick in cyber espionage campaigns suspected of being affiliated with the Chinese government, including the Equifax breach in 2017, compromises across the U.S. defense industrial base and other critical infrastructure sectors, and continuing cyber-enabled intellectual property theft carried out by APT10, a threat actor associated with the Chinese government.[62]

Shift from diplomacy to indictments

With the change from the Obama to the Trump Administration, the U.S. shifted from predominantly diplomatic responses to Chinese cyber campaigns toward employing indictments and economic tools (although the Obama Administration did threaten economic sanctions in 2015). On its face, this represented an increase in the strength of U.S. policy responses, but we are skeptical that this should be characterized as any type of escalation—with the exception of the purported "trade war," which we discuss in the next section.

The ostensible increase in Chinese-affiliated malicious cyber campaigns in 2017, following a decline in 2014–2015, is followed by a significant increase in the Trump Administration's use of indictments. In contrast to the Obama Administration, which issued one indictment against five PLA officers in 2015, between 2017 and 2020 the Trump Administration issued six different indictments of Chinese nationals. In 2017, the U.S. DOJ indicted Su Bin on charges of cyber-enabled espionage against U.S. defense contractors and the theft of sensitive military information.[63] The same year, the U.S. arrested Yu Pingan on charges of developing malware that was linked to, among other things, the OPM hack. Notably, however, the charges do not make explicit reference to the OPM incident.[64] In 2017 the U.S. also indicted three Chinese nationals affiliated

[60] Ibid., p. 10.

[61] Ibid., p. 15.

[62] King and Gallagher, "Cyberspace Solarium Commission Report." CSIS list of significant cyber incidents. CFR cyber operations tracker. Also see Adam Segal, "A New Old Threat," *Net Politics*, December 6, 2018.

[63] "Chinese National Pleads Guilty to Conspiring to Hack into U.S. Defense Contractors' Systems to Steal Sensitive Military Information," Department of Justice, March 23, 2016, https://www.justice. gov/opa/pr/chinese-national-pleads-guilty-conspiring-hack-us-defense-contractors-systems-steal-sensitive.

[64] Morgan Chalfant, "FBI Arrests Chinese National Linked to OPM Hack Malware," *The Hill*, June 24, 2017, https://thehill.com/policy/cybersecurity/347897-fbi-arrests-chinese-national-linked-to-opm-hack-malware-report; Hinck and Maurer, "Criminal Charges as a Response to Non-State Malicious Cyber Activity, p. 540.

with Boyusec for cyber espionage against a number of private corporations between 2011 and 2017.[65] The following year, the administration released two additional indictments, including an indictment of two Chinese members of APT
10 for cyber-enabled intellectual property theft from 2006 to 2018, and an indictment of 10 Chinese nationals affiliated with Jiangsu Province Ministry of State
Security for cyber-enabled intellectual property theft from the aviation sector
from 2010 to 2015.[66] In 2019, the DOJ indicted Fujie Wang and John Doe for
the 2014 Anthem hack and, as of this writing, in 2020 it had indicted four PLA
members for the 2017 Equifax breach.[67]

While the more extensive use of indictments is notable, it does not represent any significant escalation between the United States and China. All of the
sanctions were levied against a relatively small number of individuals and were
highly targeted; most of the indicted individuals are living safely in China and
will not face legal punishment within the United States. Moreover, it is difficult to
conceive of how the consequences of these indictments could even be described
as a proportionate, tit-for-tat response. In comparison to the widespread effects
of Chinese cyber campaigns against a range of government and private targets
and the significant economic costs, the U.S. indictments were very tailored and
narrow, affecting only a few individuals and excluding senior Chinese leaders of
any real political importance. Therefore, the U.S. response does not appear to rise
to the level of even a truly proportionate response.

[65] "U.S. Charges Three Chinese Hackers Who Work at Internet Security Firm for Hacking Three
Corporations for Commercial Advantage," *Department of Justice*, November 27, 2017, https://www.
justice.gov/opa/pr/us-charges-three-chinese-hackers-who-work-internet-security-firm-hacking-
three-corporations; Hinck and Maurer, "Criminal Charges as a Response to Non-State Malicious
Cyber Activity, p. 540;Chris Bing, "Arrest of Chinese Malware Suspect Highlights DOJ's Strategy
against Foreign Hackers," *Cyberscoop*, August 31, 2017 https://www.cyberscoop.com/arrest-chinese-
malware-suspect-highlights-dojs-strategy-foreign-hackers/.

[66] "Two Chinese Hackers Associated with the Ministry of State Security Charged with Global
Computer Intrusion Campaigns Targeting Intellectual Property and Confidential Business
Information," Department of Justice, December 20, 2018, https://www.justice.gov/opa/pr/two-
chinese-hackers-associated-ministry-state-security-charged-global-computer-intrusion; "Chinese
Intelligence Officers and Their Recruited Hackers and Insiders Conspired to Steal Sensitive
Commercial Aviation and Technological Data for Years," Department of Justice, October 30, 2018,
https://www.justice.gov/opa/pr/chinese-intelligence-officers-and-their-recruited-hackers-and-
insiders-conspired-steal.

[67] "Member of Sophisticated China-Based Hacking Group Indicted for Series of Computer
Intrusions, Including 2015 Data Breach of Health Insurer Anthem Inc. Affecting Over 78 Million
People," Department of Justice, May 9, 2019, https://www.justice.gov/opa/pr/member-sophistica
ted-china-based-hacking-group-indicted-series-computer-intrusions-including; "Chinse Military
Personnel Charged with Computer Fraud, Economic Espionage and Wire Fraud for Hacking into
Credit Reporting Agency Equifax," Department of Justice, February 10, 2020, https://www.justice.
gov/opa/pr/chinese-military-personnel-charged-computer-fraud-economic-espionage-and-wire-
fraud-hacking.

Economic instruments

The potential exception to these trends is what experts have dubbed the Trump Administration's trade war against China in 2018. In July 2018, the Trump Administration imposed a series of tariffs against billions of dollars of Chinese imports—an initial $34 billion, followed by another $16 billion.[68] The United States also instituted greater restrictions on Chinese visas, particularly due to concerns about the espionage threat posed by Chinese researchers, as well as limitations on Chinese investments within the United States.[69] China responded by imposing more significant tariffs against a range of U.S. goods. Both parties continued to ratchet up reciprocal tariffs over the course of the following year, with the Trump Administration announcing in August 2019 that it would increase tariffs on $550 billion in Chinese goods, in response to increases in Chinese tariffs on U.S. goods.[70]

The public justification for this action was the U.S. accusation that China was conducting unfair trading practices, to include cyber-enabled theft of intellectual property. A 2018 U.S. Trade Representative report, released in March of that year, provided the administration with some of the fodder to justify the tariffs against Chinese goods. The report, subsequently updated in November 2018, accuses China of conducting cyber-enabled theft of intellectual property and sensitive commercial information, despite the 2015 agreement to refrain from such activity.[71] The report estimated that Chinese theft of U.S. intellectual property "currently costs between $225 billion and $600 billion annually."[72] Also in 2018, the U.S. Attorney General unveiled a "China initiative" within the DOJ to address

---

[68] Ana Swanson, "Trump's Trade War With China Is Officially Underway," *The New York Times*, July 5, 2018, https://www.nytimes.com/2018/07/05/business/china-us-trade-war-trump-tariffs. html; "Statement by U.S. Trade Representative Robert Lighthizer on Section 301 Action, Office of the United States Trade Representative, July, 10, 2018 https://ustr.gov/about-us/policy-offices/press-off ice/press-releases/2018/july/statement-us-trade-representative.

[69] Ana Swanson, Alan Rappeport, and Jim Tankersley, "Trump Backs Softer Restrictions on Chinese Investment," *The New York Times*, June 27, 2018, https://www.nytimes.com/2018/06/27/us/ politics/trump-will-back-softer-restrictions-on-chinese-investment.html?rref=collection%2Fbyl ine%2Fana-swanson; Ana Swanson and Keith Bradsher, "White House Considers Restricting Chinese Researchers Over Espionage Fears," *The New York Times*, April 30, 2018, https://www.nyti mes.com/2018/04/30/us/politics/trump-china-researchers-espionage.html.

[70] Aimee Picchi, "Trump Boosting U.S. Tariffs on $550 Billion in Chinese Imports," *CBS News*, August 24, 2019, https://www.cbsnews.com/news/tariffs-china-trump-says-he-is-boosting-tariffs-chinese-imports-in-retaliation-trade-war-2019-08-24/.

[71] "Findings of the Investigation into China's Acts, Policies, and Practices Related to Technology Transfer, Intellectual Property and Innovation Under Section 301 of the Trade act of 1974," Office of the United States Trade Representative, March 22, 2018, https://ustr.gov/sites/default/files/Sect ion%20301%20FINAL.PDF; "Update Concerning China's Acts, Policies, and Practices Related to Technology Transfer, Intellectual Property and Innovation," Office of the United States Trade Representative, November 20, 2018, https://ustr.gov/sites/default/files/enforcement/301Investigati ons/301%20Report%20Update.pdf.

[72] "Findings of the Investigation into China's Acts, Policies, and Practices Related to Technology Transfer, Intellectual Property and Innovation Under Section 301 of the Trade act of 1974," p. 9.

intellectual property theft, and the Secretaries of State and Homeland Security issued a joint statement accusing China of violating the 2015 agreement.[73]

These reciprocal economic actions continued until January 2020, when the United States and China came to an agreement to end the "trade war." The terms of the agreement included Chinese commitments to buy U.S. goods as well as protect intellectual property, especially trade secrets and confidential business information.[74] The economic costs to the United States of the trade war have been significant and were primarily shouldered by U.S. companies.[75] A September 2019 Moody's analysis found that the cost amounted to 0.3% of real U.S. gross domestic product.[76]

At first glance, it may appear that these economic actions confirm arguments that actions in cyberspace can exacerbate escalation between rivals. However, when put into perspective, the evidence strongly corroborates our expectation that interactions between competing states in cyberspace are likely to be characterized by reciprocal, rather than escalating, actions across both cyber and non-cyber instruments; and, importantly, that cyber operations are not useful as tools of escalation, especially in iterative interactions between states. First, the Trump Administration's decision to impose tariffs was not solely a response to Chinese behavior in cyberspace. In fact, the tariffs were not limited to China but, rather, occurred in the context of a broader set of protectionist economic actions taken by the Trump Administration against a number of countries. As a *New York Times* article noted, during this time the administration was "waging trade wars on multiple fronts as it imposes tariffs on foreign steel, aluminum, solar panels and washing machines from countries like Canada, Mexico, the European Union, and Japan."[77] Moreover, these economic actions

[73] "Joint Statement by Secretary Michael R. Pompeo and Secretary of Homeland Security Kistjen Nielsen: Chinese Actors Compromise Global Manages Service Providers," U.S. Department of State, December 20, 2018, https://www.state.gov/joint-statement-by-secretary-of-state-michael-r-pom peo-and-secretary-of-homeland-security-kirstjen-nielsen-chinese-actors-compromise-global-managed-service-providers/; Diane Bartz and Jack Stubbs, "U.S. Allies Slam China for Economic Espionage, Spies Indicted," *Reuters*, December 20, 2018 https://www.reuters.com/article/us-china-cyber-usa/u-s-allies-slam-china-for-economic-espionage-spies-indicted-idUSKCN1OJ1VN. The U.S. was joined by 12 allies in the joint secretaries' statement.

[74] Economic and Trade Agreement B Between the Government of the United States of America and the Government of the People's Republic of China, https://ustr.gov/sites/default/files/files/agr eements/phase%20one%20agreement/Economic_And_Trade_Agreement_Between_The_United_ States_And_China_Text.pdf.

[75] Mary Amiti, Stephen J. Redding, and David E. Weinstein, "Who's Paying for the US Tariffs? A Longer-Term Perspective," National Bureau of Economic Research, working paper, January 2020, https://www.nber.org/papers/w26610.

[76] Mark Zandi, Jesse Rogers, and Maria Cosma, "Trade War Chicken: The Tariffs and the Damage Done," Moody's Analytics, September 2019, https://www.moodysanalytics.com/-/media/article/ 2019/trade-war-chicken.pdf.

[77] Ana Swanson, "Trump's Trade War with China is Officially Underway," *The New York Times*, July 5, 2018, https://www.nytimes.com/2018/07/05/business/china-us-trade-war-trump-tariffs.html.

were consistent with Trump's longstanding policy focus on U.S. trade deficits and originate with his 2016 presidential campaign. Trump used highly inflamma-tory language to describe China's trade policy, stating that, "We can't continue to allow China to rape our country, and that's what they're doing"—ostensibly a reference to Trump's claims about the implications of Chinese currency ma-nipulation, export subsidies, and permissive labor and environmental regulatory environment.[78]

Even if the tariffs were largely a response to Chinese cyber behavior (which is unlikely), the economic costs of the tariffs were generally proportionate to the costs of Chinese cyber operations. Specifically, the magnitude of the tariffs was linked to the U.S. Trade Representative's 2018 findings as a result of the Section 301 investigation of the Trade Act of 1974, and with the explicit claim that the tariffs were intended to be proportionate.[79] The Office of the U.S. Trade Representative stated that the "value of the list [of Chinese goods] is ap-proximately $50 billion in terms of estimated annual trade value for calendar year 2018. This level is appropriate both in light of the estimated harm to the U.S. economy, and to obtain elimination of China's harmful acts, policies, and practices."[80] In this sense, while certainly a more heavy-handed policy action compared to previous U.S. responses, the imposition of tariffs was conveyed as largely proportionate to what the United States assessed to be the impact of Chinese actions.

It is also interesting to note that there is no public reporting of any cyber action taken by the United States against China in response to Chinese cyber activities. While it is impossible to fully ascertain the motivations behind this apparent non-action, it is suggestive of the challenges and trade-offs in cyber op-erations, when so much investment may go into gaining and maintaining access to strategic adversary targets. There is also no evidence that any of the policy actions that were taken risk spilling over into the military realm or sparking a crisis that could spin out of control. The action-reaction cycle was contained to the cyber, economic, and diplomatic realms. Taken together, these interactions are consistent with the argument that cyber operations are unlikely to result in dangerous escalatory spirals between rivals.

---

[78] "Trump Accuses China of 'Raping' US with Unfair Trade Policy," BBC News, May 2, 2016, https://www.bbc.com/news/election-us-2016-36185012.

[79] "Section 301 Investigation Fact Sheet," Office of the United States Trade Representative, June 2018, https://ustr.gov/about-us/policy-offices/press-office/fact-sheets/2018/june/section-301-invest igation-fact-sheet#:~:text=Under%20Section%20301%20of%20the,burden%20or%20restrict%20 U.S.%20commerce.

[80] "China's Acts, Policies, and Practices Related to Technology, Transfer, Intellectual Property, and Innovation," Office of United States Trade Representative, April 6, 2018, https://beta.regulations.gov/ document/USTR-2018-0005-0001.

The United States and Russia

Historically, Russia has been a particularly prolific actor in cyberspace and has been associated with some of the most significant cyber operations in the international system, including the cyber attack against Estonia in 2007, its coupling of cyber operations with conventional military operations in Georgia in 2008 and Ukraine in 2014, cyber attacks against Ukraine's power grid in 2015 and 2016, and the NotPetya cyber attack in 2017 which, according to the U.S. government, was the most costly cyber attack in history.[81] The long-standing rivalry between Russia and the United States traces back to the competition between the two superpowers during the Cold War. More recently, the rivalry has grown more salient and became particularly acute following the 2011 NATO intervention in Libya.[82] President Vladimir Putin has also accused the United States of interfering in the 2011 Russian elections, which saw widespread anti-government protests and demonstrations. Putin specifically blamed then-Secretary of State Hillary Clinton for provoking the protests.[83] Russian officials have also accused the United States of being involved in the color revolutions that saw popular, pro-Western movements in Ukraine, Georgia, and Kyrgyzstan.[84] Tensions were further heightened following Russia's invasion and annexation of Crimea in 2014.[85]

Cyber operations play an important role in the U.S.-Russia rivalry. Our data indicates that Russia has been associated with 102 distinct cyber incidents between 2007 and 2020. These span a wide range of types of cyber operations, including espionage, cyber-enabled information operations/doxing, denial of service attacks, defacements, and data destruction attacks. Government or private entities within the United States were the targets in 21 of these incidents. In turn, according to public reporting, the United States has been associated with two cyber incidents targeting Russia, as well as reports of four incidents where

---

[81] Andy Greenberg, "The White House Blames Russia for NotPetya, the 'Most Costly Cyberattack In History,'" *Wired*, February 15, 2018, https://www.wired.com/story/white-house-russia-notpetya-attribution/. "'Information Troops'—a Russian Cyber Command?" 3rd International Conference on Cyber Conflict, Tallinn, Estonia, NATO CCD COE Publications, 2011; Maria Snegovaya, "Putin's Information Warfare in Ukraine: Soviet Origins of Russia's Hybrid Warfare," Institute for the Study of War, September 2015, p. 9; Janne Hakala and Jazlyn Melnychuk, "Russia's Strategy in Cyberspace," NATO Cooperative Cyber Defence Centre of Excellence, June 2021; Nadiya Kostyk and Yuri M. Zhukov, "Invisible Digital Front: Can Cyber Attacks Shape Battlefield Events?," *Journal of Conflict Resolution* 63, no. 2 (2019): 317–347.

[82] Gleb Bryanski, "Putin Likens U.N. Libya Resolution to Crusades," *Reuters*, March 21, 2011; Marzia Cimmino, "Moscow's Perspectives on War in Libya," Carnegie Endowment for International Peace, March 31, 2011.

[83] David M. Herszenhorn and Ellen Barry, "Putin Contends Clinton Incited Unrest Over Vote," *The New York Times*, December 8, 2011.

[84] Anthony H. Cordesman, "Russia and the 'Color Revolution,'" Center for Strategy & International Studies, May 18, 2014.

[85] Keir Giles, "Russia's 'New' Tools for Confronting the West: Continuity and Innovation in Moscow's Exercise of Power," Chatham House, March 2016.

cyber espionage tools reported to be associated with the United States may have affected Russian targets but were not specifically aimed at Russia.[86] Setting aside cyber espionage, there are two dimensions to the U.S.-Russia rivalry in cyberspace that stand out: first, Russia's use of cyberspace to enable information operations and attempt to interfere in U.S. democratic elections and the U.S. response to these efforts; and second, reciprocal claims that each state has conducted cyber operations to gain access to the other's critical infrastructure. Across both of these sets of interactions, the available evidence largely supports our contentions that cyber operations have not led to escalation, either in cyberspace or through the use of other instruments of power. Rather, similar to the China case described in the previous section, the interactions have been largely limited to tit-for-tat, proportionate responses across cyber and non-cyber capabilities.

Cyber-enabled information operations and election interference

The story of how Russia came to interfere the 2016 U.S. presidential election is widely known.[87] According to U.S. government assessments, as well as the consensus of the information security community and Western intelligence agencies, Putin ordered cyber operations as part of a broader influence campaign against the 2016 elections to undermine confidence in the U.S. democratic process and in Hillary Clinton, her candidacy, and potential presidency.[88] The cyber component of this effort involved Russian-associated threat actors, dubbed Cozy Bear and Fancy Bear, using cyber tools to penetrate Democratic National Committee (DNC) networks beginning in July 2015. In addition, beginning in March 2016, the General Staff Main Intelligence Directorate (GRU) compromised DNC email accounts and exfiltrated volumes of DNC data that was subsequently publicized through Russian-linked personas (e.g., Guccifer 2.0) and websites (e.g., DCLeaks. com and WikiLeaks). Russian intelligence agencies also used cyber means to gain access to state and local election systems, including voter registration information in a number of states.[89] A 2019 Senate Select Committee on Intelligence report found that "Russian government-affiliated cyber actors conducted an unprecedented level of activity against state election infrastructure in the run-up

[86] In this section, we focus on Russia's cyber-enabled information operations and U.S. responses as well as mutual claims about cyber operations to gain access to critical infrastructure, rather than reciprocal reports about cyber espionage efforts ostensibly for national security purposes.

[87] For a concise narrative, see Benjamin Jensen, Brandon Valeriano, and Ryan Maness, "Fancy Bears and Digital Trolls: Cyber Strategy with a Russian Twist," *Journal of Strategic Studies* 42, no. 2 (2019): 212–234.

[88] "Assessing Russian Activities and Intentions in Recent US Elections," Intelligence Community Assessment, January 6, 2017, p. ii; David Sanger, "D.N.C. Says Russian Hackers Penetrated Its Files, Including Dossier on Donald Trump," *The New York Times*, June 14, 2016; Dmitri Alperovitch, "Bears in the Midst: Intrusion into the Democratic National Committee," *CrowdStrike*, June 15, 2016.

[89] "Assessing Russian Activities," pp. 2–3. David E. Sanger and Catie Edmondson, "Russia Targeted Election Systems in All 50 States, Report Finds," *The New York Times*, July 25, 2019.

to the 2016 U.S. elections."[90] The strategic implications of the 2016 influence campaign were significant and continue to persist. According to U.S. intelligence agencies, the 2016 campaign "represented a significant escalation in directness, level of activity, and scope of effort compared to previous operations against US elections."[91] Moreover, similar influence campaigns were replicated across Europe and attempted again in the 2018 U.S. midterm elections.[92]

Given the nature of this cyber campaign, one might expect that this case would be especially ripe for escalation. However, with respect to the response to the 2016 election interference, as well as its efforts to thwart Russian attempts to interfere in the 2018 midterm elections, the United States did not escalate the situation. The Obama Administration's handling of Putin's influence campaign was restrained and largely limited to diplomatic, legal, and economic actions. As the Russian operation was ongoing, President Obama threatened Putin, at the September 2016 G20 summit in Hangzhou, China that there would be "serious consequences" if Russian election interference did not stop.[93] As the release of hacked DNC emails continued, on October 31 Obama used the Nuclear Risk Reduction Center (NRRC) hotline connection with Moscow, bilaterally designated to be used for cyber-related incidents only three years before, to convey to Putin that the laws of armed conflict applied to cyberspace and attempt to deter Russia from directly interfering in the election outcome.[94] In the aftermath of the election in December 2016, the U.S. expelled 35 Russian diplomats, alleging they were Russian agents, and closed two Russian-owned waterfront estates in Maryland and New York that were known to be used for espionage. Furthermore, the Department of Treasury levied targeted economic sanctions against four top Russian officials, a Russian intelligence unit, and three Russian cybersecurity companies that were involved in the operations.[95] Despite initial

[90] "Report of the Senate Committee on Intelligence, United States Senate, on Russian Active Measures Campaigns and Interference in the 2016 U.S. Election," Volume I: Russian Efforts against Election Infrastructure with Additional Views, 116th Congress, First Session, p. 5.

[91] "Assessing Russian Activities," p. 5.

[92] Naja Bentzen, "Foreign Influence Operations in the EU," European Parliamentary Research Service, July 2018; Erik Brattberg and Tim Maurer, "Russian Election Interference: Europe's Counter to Fake News and Cyber Attacks," The Carnegie Endowment for International Peace, May 23, 2018; Julian E. Barnes, "U.S. Begins First Cyberoperations against Russia Aimed at Protecting Elections," The New York Times, October 23, 2018.

[93] Barack Obama, "Press Conference by the President," The White House, December 16, 2016.

[94] William M. Arkin, Ken Dilanian, and Cynthia McFadden, "What Obama Said to Putin on the Red Phone about the Election Hack," NBC News, December 19, 2016; David E. Sanger, "White House Confirms Pre-Election Warning to Russia over Hacking," The New York Times, November 16, 2016.

[95] David E. Sanger, "Obama Strikes Back at Russia for Election Hacking," The New York Times, December 29, 2016. On a related note, Adam Segal noted that during a January 2017 cybersecurity dialogue in Beijing several Chinese representatives did not see any deterrent value in the Obama Administration's response to Russian interference in the election and questioned how it was proportionate for the harm that the administration claimed. See Adam Segal, "The Continued Importance of the U.S.-China Cyber Dialogue," Net Politics, January 23, 2017. Several years later, during the Trump Administration, the Department of Justice issued an indictment against the Internet Research

threats from the Russian foreign minister, Putin responded that he would avoid retaliation and indicated that he looked forward to more favorable relations with the incoming Trump Administration.[96]

It has been reported that the United States considered launching retaliatory cyber attacks against Russia, but ultimately refrained from doing so. Prior to the election, in the summer of 2016, the Cyber Response Group within the National Security Council began to convene recurring meetings to discuss more aggressive response options against Russia, ranging from widespread economic sanctions to offensive cyber attacks, but these were nixed, reportedly due to concerns that this may result in further Russian aggression.[97] Reportedly, one of the more aggressive cyber options was

> to unleash the NSA to mount a series of far-reaching cyberattacks: to dismantle the Guccifer 2.0 and DCLeaks websites that had been leaking the emails and memos stolen from Democratic targets, to bombard Russian news sites with a wave of automated traffic in a denial-of-service attack that would shut the news sites down, and to launch an attack on the Russian intelligence agencies themselves, seeking to disrupt their command and control nodes.[98]

Across these alleged options, the last would have been the most significant because it would have potentially entailed burning access to strategic targets within the Russian government—an operation that likely would have required a significant prior investment in intelligence collection and resources—that could be supporting ongoing intelligence priorities. Such action may not only negate those, but may also foreclose offensive cyber operations in a future contingency. The other reported options were ostensibly more indirect, low-cost cyber responses that, even if they had been carried out, would not have produced the kind of costly effects that one might expect would trigger escalation. Regardless, the Obama Administration purportedly rejected all of these options.[99]

Perhaps more important, an overriding concern was maintaining the integrity of the electoral process itself. In a December 2016 press conference, Obama directly acknowledged this concern, stating that, "What I was concerned about, in

---

Agency and related individuals and entities for interfering in the 2016 elections. See United States v. Internet Research Agency, Case 1:18-cr-00032-DLF, filed 02/16/18.

[96] Neil MacFarquhar, "Vladimir Putin Won't Expel U.S. Diplomats as Russian Foreign Minister Urged," *The New York Times*, December 30, 2016, https://www.nytimes.com/2016/12/30/world/europe/russia-diplomats-us-hacking.html.
[97] Greg Miller, Ellen Nakashima, and Adam Entous, "Obama's Secret Struggle to Punish Russia for Putin's Election Assault," *The Washington Post*, June 23, 2017.
[98] Michael Isikoff and David Corn, "'Stand Down:' How the Obama Team Blew the Response to Russian Meddling," *Huffington Post*, March 9, 2018.
[99] Ibid.

particular, was making sure that [the release of information] wasn't compounded by potential hacking that could hamper vote counting, affect the actual election process itself . . . . And, in fact, we did not see further tampering of the election process."[100] Reportedly, retaliatory options were again proposed after the election and, according to the *Washington Post*, Obama signed a secret finding in the waning days of his administration that authorized a covert program to penetrate and implant Russian networks, but for the purposes of signaling U.S. capabilities and resolve to Russia rather than causing disruptive or destructive effects.[101]

In the lead up to the 2018 midterm elections, Russia again attempted to leverage cyberspace to interfere in U.S. elections.[102] Consistent with the U.S. response in 2016, in October 2018 the Trump Administration brought charges against a Russian national accused of interfering in the 2018 midterm elections.[103] While not directly related to the 2018 elections, a few weeks prior the administration had issued indictments again seven Russia GRU intelligence officers for "international hacking and related influence and disinformation operations."[104] The Trump Administration also issued Executive Order 13848 in September 2018 that allowed the United States to impose economic sanctions against foreign individuals inferring in U.S. elections.[105] One year after the 2018 elections, the Department of Treasury's Office of Foreign Assets Control (OFAC) issued sanctions against four entities and seven people in connection with Russian interference in the 2018 midterms.[106]

---

[100] Barack Obama, "Press Conference by the President," The White House, December 16, 2016, https://obamawhitehouse.archives.gov/the-press-office/2016/12/16/press-conference-president.

[101] Greg Miller, Ellen Nakshima, and Adam Entous, "Obama's Secret Struggle to Punish Russia for Putin's Election Assault," *The Washington* Post, June 23, 2017.

[102] Lara Seligman, "Mattis Confirms Russia Interfered in U.S. Midterm Elections," *Foreign Policy*, December 1, 2018, https://foreignpolicy.com/2018/12/01/mattis-confirms-russia-interfered-in-us-midterm-elections-putin-trump/; Jeremy Herb, "US Intel Unanimous that Russia Is Targeting 2018 Elections," *CNN Politics*, February 13, 2018, https://www.cnn.com/2018/02/13/politics/intelligence-chiefs-russia-2018-elections-target/index.html.

[103] Josh Gerstein, "U.S. Brings First Charge for Meddling in 2018 Midterm Elections," *Politico*, October 19, 2018, https://www.politico.com/story/2018/10/19/first-criminal-case-filed-over-russian-interference-in-2018-midterms-916787; Unites States of America v. Elena Alekseevna Khusyaynova, 1:18-MJ-464, Eastern District of Virginia, September 2, 2018.

[104] "U.S. Charges Russian GRU Officers with International Hacking and Related Influence and Disfromation Operations," Department of Justice, October 4, 2018, https://www.justice.gov/opa/pr/us-charges-russian-gru-officers-international-hacking-and-related-influence-and. The Trump Administration issued a number of indictments against Russian nationals for malicious cyber activities and election interference, though not directly related to the 2018 elections.

[105] "Executive Order on Imposing Certain Sanctions in the Event of Foreign Interference in a United States Election," The White House, September 12, 2018 https://www.whitehouse.gov/presidential-actions/executive-order-imposing-certain-sanctions-event-foreign-interference-united-states-election/.

[106] "Treasury Targets Assets of Russian Financier who Attempted to Influence 2018 U.S. Elections," U.S. Department of the Treasury, September 30, 2019, https://home.treasury.gov/news/press-releases/sm787.

In addition to these measures, it does appear that cyber actions were taken in response to Russian election interference in 2018, which represents an important change from the U.S. response in 2016. This reflected a broader shift in U.S. strategy toward a more prominent role for the military in cyberspace, highlighted in updated strategy and policy documents that were publicized in 2018—especially Cyber Command's new Command Vision, the Department of Defense's revised Cyber Strategy, and new policy that changed how the authority to conduct offensive cyber operations was delegated to the military.[107] In particular, the new Defense Department strategy articulated a concept of "defend forward," which describes a more operational role for the military in cyberspace to "defend forward to disrupt or halt malicious cyber activity at its source, including activity that falls below the level of armed conflict."[108] Senior U.S. military leaders described efforts to address Russian interference in the 2018 midterm elections as an example of the implementation of this strategy.[109] Indeed, the *Washington Post* reported that Cyber Command conducted an offensive cyber operation in the fall of 2018 to block the Internet Research Agency (IRA), a Russian troll farm, from carrying out a cyber-enabled influence operation against the midterms.[110] This appeared to build on a prior cyber operation, reported by the *New York Times* in October 2018, in which Cyber Command directly targeted Russian operations to warn them against meddling in the upcoming midterms.[111]

Yet, even as the United States was apparently stepping up its cyber responses to Russian cyber operations, putting the former into context suggests that the U.S. response was limited and proportionate, rather than escalatory. First, the United States does not appear to have targeted potentially more significant targets within Russia, such as the GRU. Instead, the operation targeted the IRA, a Kremlin-affiliated company that conducts relatively cheap and low-skill social media-based influence campaigns to sow public distrust in U.S. institutions.[112] The United States may have chosen to target the IRA because, from an

[107] Secretary of Defense Mark Esper publicly referred to National Security Presidential Memorandum-13 in July 2019, describing how the new policy would "put our cyber capabilities on a more offensive footing, allowing us to lean forward." See Mark Pomerlau, "What Good Are 'Exceptional' Cyber Capabilities without Authority?," *Fifth Domain*, July 16, 2019.

[108] "Summary: Department of Defense Cyber Strategy," *U.S. Department of Defense*, 2018, p. 1.

[109] William T. Eliason, "An Interview with Paul M. Eliason," *Joint Force Quarterly* 92, January 17, 2019, https://ndupress.ndu.edu/Media/News/News-Article-View/Article/1734461/an-interview-with-paul-m-nakasone/.

[110] Ellen Nakashima, "U.S. Cyber Command Operation Disrupted Internet Access of Russian Troll Factory on Day of 2018 Midterms," *The Washington Post*, February 27, 2019, https://www.washingtonpost.com/world/national-security/us-cyber-command-operation-disrupted-internet-access-of-russian-troll-factory-on-day-of-2018-midterms/2019/02/26/1827fc9e-36d6-11e9-af5b-b51b7ff322e9_story.html.

[111] Julian E. Barnes, "U.S. Begins First Cyberoperation against Russia Aimed at Protecting Elections," *The New York Times*, October 23, 2018.

[112] United States of America v. Internet Research Agency LLC et al., 18 U.S.C. §§ 2, 371, 1349, 1028A, United States District Court of Columbia, 2018

operational perspective, it may have been easier to gain access to their networks. According to Russia's Federal News Agency, Cyber Command's operation relied on remote access through a compromised iPhone that an IRA employee unwittingly connected to a computer.[113] If this reporting is accurate, a plausible explanation for the decision to disrupt the troll farm's influence operations, rather than targeting the GRU, is that it may have been far easier for Cyber Command to gain access to IRA's networks and systems, while the GRU was a considerably more "hardened" target. It is also plausible that the United States may have preferred to maintain access to the networks and systems of more valuable targets within Russian military and intelligence agencies for espionage or potential future military operations, rather than risk revealing it by conducting a cyber operation. Penetration of the GRU's networks could support critical U.S. intelligence priorities. Additionally, the operation targeting the IRA was reportedly disruptive and therefore only achieved temporary effects. As the *New York Times* notes, "Intelligence officials have said it is difficult, if not impossible, to use cyber operations to take an adversary off line permanently . . . . Given time, the target of an operation can find workarounds or fix software problems."[114] Interestingly, rather than use reporting about the operation to justify taking an escalatory response, Russian media attempted to downplay the reported cyber operation, describing it as a "complete failure."[115]

Taken together, the evidence demonstrates that, despite a stronger U.S. cyber response to Russia's cyber-enabled interference in the 2018 midterm elections, this was not an escalatory step and did not trigger further escalatory behavior on the part of Moscow.

Cyber operations targeting critical infrastructure
In tandem with the election interference issue, both Russia and the United States have reportedly conducted cyber operations to gain access to the other's critical infrastructure.[116] If arguments about dangerous security dilemmas in cyberspace are accurate, then we should expect to find that this kind of behavior would

---

[113] "Russian Troll Farm: Yes, the Pentagon Hit Us in Cyber Op. But It Was a 'Complete Failure,'" *The Daily Beast*, February 27, 2018, https://www.thedailybeast.com/russian-troll-farm-yes-the-pentagon-hit-us-in-cyber-op-but-it-was-a-complete-failure.

[114] Julian E. Barnes, "Cyber Command Operation Took Down Russian Troll Farm for Midterm Elections," *The New York Times*, February 26, 2019, https://www.nytimes.com/2019/02/26/us/polit ics/us-cyber-command-russia.html.

[115] "Russian Troll Farm: Yes, the Pentagon Hit Us in Cyber Op. But It Was a 'Complete Failure,'" *The Daily Beast*, February 27, 2018, https://www.thedailybeast.com/russian-troll-farm-yes-the-pentagon-hit-us-in-cyber-op-but-it-was-a-complete-failure.

[116] Russian cyber operations against U.S. critical infrastructure took place around the same time that it was conducting cyber operations to support election interference. While we treat these as separate incidents, it is important to note that decision-making on both sides regarding appropriate responses and concerns about escalation likely took into account both of these incidents.

be uniquely dangerous—even more so than the interactions between the United States and China described earlier, where the objective was clearly espionage. In this case, it's not clear there was communication between the two states regarding these operations and what their intended effects may be. However, existing evidence suggests that actions in this area have been largely reciprocal and contained.

Concerns about Russian penetration of critical infrastructure became public in the United States in March 2018 when the U.S. Department of Homeland Security (DHS) released a report indicating that "Russian government cyber actors" had gained access to industrial control systems in the energy, nuclear, commercial, water, aviation, and critical manufacturing sectors.[117] Russian actors had gained access as early as 2015 and were operating inside U.S. networks. However, according to the *New York Times*, "the hackers never went so far as to sabotage or shut down the computer systems that guide the operations of the plants." Furthermore, "United States officials and private security firms saw the attacks as a signal by Moscow that it could disrupt the West's critical facilities in the event of a conflict."[118] Yet, the evidence to support claims about Russian signaling is ambiguous. It is not immediately apparent that Russia intended the United States to discover its activity against critical infrastructure networks. If it didn't, it could mean that Moscow wasn't signaling at all. According to DHS, the threat actors took actions to cover their tracks once they were inside U.S. networks. For instance, they removed applications that they had installed when they were in the network, as well as logs, and deleted connections made to remote systems. The U.S. discovery of the Russian breach may simply reflect U.S. luck or poor Russian tradecraft.

These patterns illustrate the role of secrecy in cyber operations and how it shapes escalation dynamics. The importance of maintaining secrecy to ensure operational success creates inherent limitations on what a threat actor is able to accomplish, because there are trade-offs between securing a quiet, persistent presence on a network and taking actions that will inevitably reveal it. There is also a significant temporal dimension, which shapes the exigency with which a situation is perceived. It took years from the time Russia reportedly gained access to U.S. critical infrastructure for the United States to uncover its presence. Moreover, the U.S. government's decision to publicly release information that would enable network defenders to take measures to patch vulnerabilities and neutralize threats illustrates how quickly an attacker can go from a position of

---

[117] Alert (TA18-074A), National Cyber Awareness System, March 16, 2018, https://us-cert.cisa.gov/ncas/alerts/TA18-074A.

[118] Nicole Perlroth and David E. Sanger, "Cyberattacks Put Russian Fingers on the Switch at Power Plants, U.S. Says," *The New York Times*, March 15, 2018, https://www.nytimes.com/2018/03/15/us/politics/russia-cyberattacks.html.

advantage to disadvantage—and in a way that can be difficult for an attacker to anticipate in advance. If Russia had been waiting for an opportune time to use a particular, exquisite cyber capability that it had invested significant resources in developing, it may have lost it upon discovery.

Additionally, when Russia's presence was discovered, there was not an immediate, public reaction in the United States suggesting that it would retaliate in a significant manner.[119] However, there has been reporting that suggests the United States also penetrated Russian critical infrastructure through cyber operations, or at the very least is developing plans and capabilities to do so. For instance, in March 2018 confirmation testimony before Congress, then-Lieutenant General Paul Nakasone responded in the affirmative to a question from Senator Jack Reed about whether the United States is "preparing . . . detailed campaign plans with respect to these potential issues," referring to a Defense Science Board recommendation that the country should be developing campaign plans in cyberspace to "go after the key assets of our opponents," to include Russia.[120] In February 2019 testimony before the Senate Committee on Armed Services, General Nakasone, now commander of U.S. Cyber Command, participated in an exchange with Senator Angus King regarding how the United States could shape an adversary's calculus regarding the decision "to launch a cyberattack on our electric grid or a financial system or elections."[121] This question came in the immediate wake of Nakasone's testimony about the Department of Defense's recent efforts to establish a program to collaborate across the agency to defend the energy sector against cyber threats.[122] Responding to King's question, Nakasone responded that part of the U.S. response to adversaries should be "imposing costs," to include responding (in King's parlance in "a forceful way") with "all the elements of our Nation that can be brought to bear on that adversary."[123]

This raises the question: what might those costs be, and could they prompt escalation? The following year, in June 2019, the *New York Times* published an article asserting that since 2012 the United States has "put reconnaissance probes into the control systems of the Russian electric grid" and, more recently, had

---

[119] The primary focus appears to have been on improving the defense and resilience of critical infrastructure, particularly the energy sector. Kate O'Flaherty, "U.S Government Makes Surprise Move to Secure Power Grids from Cyberattacks," *Forbes*, July 3, 2019, https://www.forbes.com/sites/kateoflahertyuk/2019/07/03/u-s-government-makes-surprise-move-to-secure-power-grid-from-cyber-attacks/#3c875aa83191.

[120] Stenographic Transcript before the Committee on Armed Services: United State Senate Nominations, Alderson Court Reporting, Washington, DC, March 1, 2018, pp. 28–29, https://www.armed-services.senate.gov/imo/media/doc/18-19_03-01-18.pdf.

[121] Stenographic Transcript before the Subcommittee on Personnel: Committee on Armed Services in the United States Senate, Alderson Court Reporting, Washington, DC, February 14, 2019, p. 38, https://www.armed-services.senate.gov/imo/media/doc/19-13_02-14-19.pdf.

[122] Ibid., p. 37.

[123] Ibid., pp. 38–39.

implanted malware into Russian systems.[124] Responding on Twitter, Trump denounced the article as being "NOT TRUE!" even as then-National Security Advisor John Bolton stated publicly that the United States was becoming more proactive in cyberspace, in part "to say to Russia, or anybody else that's engaged in cyberoperations against us, 'You will pay a price.'"[125] While the Russian response to this reporting was just bluster—Dmitri Peskov, Putin's official spokesperson, stated that "'there is a hypothetical possibility' of cyberwarfare against Russia"—Russian public statements largely emphasized the security and resilience of the Russian power grid.[126] And, despite reports about U.S. cyber activity, the same month Trump and Putin met in person on the sidelines of the G-20 summit in Osaka, Japan, where Trump reportedly made a joke to Putin about election interference.[127]

Therefore, while some U.S. officials may have issued ambiguous threats about imposing costs against Russia, it's not clear whether and how the U.S. may have actually done so. Regardless, there is no evidence of escalation. This is despite the fact that this case has the hallmarks of what some experts might think would be a dangerous situation: it ostensibly involved two highly capable cyber powers holding each other's critical infrastructure at risk through cyber means, with uncertainty about the intent behind those operations. Furthermore, given Russia's demonstrated history of conducting cyber attacks against critical infrastructure, particularly other countries' power grids (such as in Ukraine), it would be reasonable to expect that the United States might retaliate with escalatory measures in response to discerning Russian threat actors in the energy and other critical infrastructure systems. Instead, the evidence suggests that, over the course of a number of years, both parties participated in reciprocal measures in cyberspace that did not escalate to disruptive or destructive cyber effects against the other's critical infrastructure. Additionally, the public statements on both sides were ambiguous, creating opportunities for both to exercise flexibility rather than

[124] David E. Sanger and Nicole Perlroth, "U.S. Escalates Online Attacks on Russia's Power Grid," *The New York Times*, June 15, 2019, https://www.nytimes.com/2019/06/15/us/politics/trump-cyber-russia-grid.html.
[125] "Trump Calls Newspaper Report on Russia Power Grid 'Treason,'" *Associated Press News*, June 16, 2019, https://apnews.com/ed30a98cafa94ecab4e540ffbd16a385; David E. Sanger and Nicole Perlroth, "U.S. Escalates Online Attacks on Russia's Power Grid," *The New York Times*, June 15, 2019, https://www.nytimes.com/2019/06/15/us/politics/trump-cyber-russia-grid.html; Warren P. Strobel, "Bolton Says U.S. Is Expanding Offensive Cyber Operations," *The Wall Street Journal*, June 11, 2019, https://www.wsj.com/articles/bolton-says-u-s-is-expanding-offensive-cyber-operations-11560266199.
[126] Ivan Nechepurenko, "Kremlin Warns of Cyberwar after Report of U.S. Hacking Into Russian Power Grid," *The New York Times*, June 17, 2019, https://www.nytimes.com/2019/06/17/world/europe/russia-us-cyberwar-grid.html.
[127] "G20 Summit: Trump Jokes to Putin about Russian Election Meddling," *BBC News*, June 28, 2019, https://www.bbc.com/news/world-us-canada-48797485; "Trump Playfully Tells Putin, 'Don't Meddle in the Election," *CBS News*, June 28, 2019, https://www.cbsnews.com/news/trump-putin-meet-g20-summit-japan-today-2019-06-28/.

create a clear pretext for escalatory measures. For all of the experts' fears of security dilemmas in cyberspace, likely reciprocal cyber penetration of critical infrastructure with significant uncertainty about objectives did not result in any spiral dynamics.

The United States and North Korea

One might argue that the United States avoided escalating in response to Russian and Chinese behavior in cyberspace because it feared potential retaliation by those states, given their significant capabilities. By extension, one might expect that United States would be more willing to escalate in contests where it has a clearer advantage; in other words, against rivals over which it has a preponderant military advantage. The United States' interactions with North Korea and Iran meet these characteristics. Indeed, the available, public evidence does suggest that the United States appeared to be more willing to employ cyber capabilities in response to or as part of its strategic interactions with those states. That said, none of the activity could reasonably be characterized as escalatory.

In this section, we evaluate what is arguably the most well-known interaction between the United States and North Korea in cyberspace: the 2014 Sony Hack, carried out by a threat actor known as the Lazarus Group, with links to North Korea.[128] In Chapter 6, we will explore the role of cyber operations in the context of the 2017 crisis between the two states, where there was a real and meaningful risk that the situation would escalate to war. The 2014 Sony Hack was part of a failed coercive attempt by Pyongyang to prevent the release of a film, *The Interview*, that it perceived as portraying the regime in a negative light. The U.S. response to the Sony Hack provides further support for the contention that cyber operations are not likely to cause escalation. However, we acknowledge that this case does not represent a hard test of our theory.

North Korea's cyber operation against Sony Pictures is an example where the risks of escalation are not as salient as in other cases. North Korean threat actors targeted a private company in the entertainment sector, not an essential part of critical infrastructure. And while the Sony hack was the "most elaborate cyberattack from [North Korea] on US soil," it served different strategic purposes than other cyber attacks because it was aimed at preventing a private company from releasing what Pyongyang perceived to be an embarrassing film, rather than

---

[128] "Lazarus Group" MITRE ATT&CK, accessed November 2020, https://attack.mitre.org/groups/G0032/; James Andrew Lewis, "The Likelihood of North Korean Cyber Attacks," The Center for Strategic and International Studies, September 7, 2019, https://www.csis.org/analysis/likelihood-north-korean-cyber-attacks.

achieving a geopolitical objective.[129] Even so, there were some concerns that the threat actors would follow through with threats to carry out a terrorist attack if their demands were not met. Regardless, it is notable that the U.S. response was similar to that in other cases: limited to diplomatic, legal, and economic instruments. Moreover, the situation did not escalate and is consistent with the type of tit-for-tat dynamics that have played out across the other cases.

The Interview depicted two U.S. journalists conscripted by the Central Intelligence Agency to assassinate North Korea's Kim Jong Un. On November 21, several top Sony executives received a cryptic email from a group calling themselves God'sApstls demanding monetary compensation or else "Sony would be bombarded as a whole."[130] Additionally, Sony's Twitter feed was taken over and displayed a message stating that the two co-chairs of Sony were "going to hell." The following Monday, many of the 3,500 Sony employees arrived at the Culver City, California, corporate headquarters to find that they were locked out of their computer systems and left with a virtual banner depicting a skull and a message stating they had been hacked by the Guardians of Peace and threatening to release stolen information to the world.[131] The following day, the first significant data dump occurred with the posting of four yet-to-be released films online.[132] Over the next several weeks, there were at least eight separate leaks of Sony's corporate data, including salary schedules, human resource files, network information, and credentials that could be used by others to gain further access to Sony IT assets, as well as thousands of internal corporate emails.[133] On December 16, Sony's Chief Financial Officer received an email in which the hackers insinuated that "9/11" violence was coming and that employees should seek shelter when the world sees "what an awful movie Sony Pictures Entertainment has made."[134] The coercive tactics worked, causing the studio to cancel their planned release for Christmas Day 2014 as theater chains started to back out of airing the film.[135]

President Obama stated that he respected Sony's decision but felt that the company had "made a mistake" and emphasized that "we cannot have a society in which some dictator someplace can start imposing censorship here in

---

[129] Marie Baezner, "Hotspot Analysis: Cyber Disruption and Cybercrime: Democratic People's Republic of Korea," *Center for Security Studies, ETH Zurich*, June 2018, p. 12.

[130] Mark Seal, "An Exclusive Look at Sony's Hacking Saga," *Vanity Fair*, March 2015, http://www.vanityfair.com/hollywood/2015/02/sony-hacking-seth-rogen-evan-goldberg.

[131] Kim Zetter, "Sony Got Hacked Hard: What We Know and Don't Know So Far," *Wired*, December 3, 2014, https://www.wired.com/2014/12/sony-hack-what-we-know/.

[132] Seal, "An Exclusive Look at Sony's Hacking Saga."

[133] Zetter, "Sony Got Hacked Hard." "Ex-Sony Chief Amy Pascal Acknowledges She Was Fired," *NBC News*, February 12, 2015, http://www.nbcnews.com/storyline/sony-hack/ex-sony-chief-amy-pascal-acknowledges-she-was-fired-n305281.

[134] Zetter, "Sony Got Hacked Hard."

[135] Michael Cieply and Brooks Barnes, "Sony Cyberattack, First a Nuisance, Swiftly Grew into a Firestorm," *The New York Times*, December 30, 2014, https://www.nytimes.com/2014/12/31/business/media/sony-attack-first-a-nuisance-swiftly-grew-into-a-firestorm-.html.

the United States."[136] Obama warned North Korea that the United States would respond, but was careful to articulate that the response would be proportional and did not commit the U.S. to a particular set of responses, preferring flexibility: "They caused a lot of damage, and we will respond. We will respond proportionally, and we'll respond in a place and time and manner that we choose. It's not something that I will announce here today at a press conference."[137] At the same time, the FBI released a report attributing the attack to the North Korean government.[138] The report reflected an unusually high degree of confidence that led some experts to suggest that U.S. likely had preexisting access to the networks from which the attack emanated.[139]

On January 2, 2016 the Obama Administration issued an executive order imposing economic sanctions against ten senior North Korea officials and the intelligence organization linked to North Korean cyber operations.[140] Additionally, in the immediate wake of President Obama's threat to North Korea, several media sources reported that there were unspecified covert actions purportedly taken by the United States against North Korea, but the basis of these allegations has not been reliably substantiated.[141] Specifically, on December 22, 2014, it was reported that North Korea experienced an internet outage for approximately nine hours.[142] According to Reuters, U.S. government officials denied any U.S. involvement. Additionally, Reuters reported that the United States had allegedly "requested China's help, asking Beijing to shut down servers and routers used by North Korea that run through Chinese networks," but the Chinese purportedly

[136] Barack Obama, "Remarks by the President in Year-End Press Conference, The White House, December 19, 2014, https://obamawhitehouse.archives.gov/the-press-office/2014/12/19/remarks-president-year-end-press-conference.

[137] Ibid.

[138] "Update on Sony Investigation," Federal Bureau of Investigation, December 19, 2014, https://www.fbi.gov/news/pressrel/press-releases/update-on-sony-investigation.

[139] David E. Sanger and Martin Fackler, "N.S.A Breached North Korean Networks Before Sony Attack, Officials Say," The New York Times, January 18, 2015, https://www.nytimes.com/2015/01/19/world/asia/nsa-tapped-into-north-korean-networks-before-sony-attack-officials-say.html. Also see, Segal, The Hacked World Order, 51–60, for an accounting of the events surrounding the Sony hack and the resulting attribution.

[140] "Executive Order—Imposing Additional Sanctions with Respect to North Korea," The White House, January 2, 2015, https://obamawhitehouse.archives.gov/the-press-office/2015/01/02/executive-order-imposing-additional-sanctions-respect-north-korea.

[141] David E. Sanger and Michael S. Schmidt, "More Sanctions on North Korea After Sony Case," The New York Times, January 2, 2016, https://www.nytimes.com/2015/01/03/us/in-response-to-sony-attack-us-levies-sanctions-on-10-north-koreans.html. Though the United States has not confirmed or denied the accuracy of this reporting, shortly after Christmas and lasting into January 2016, North Korea's already limited access to the internet was entirely cut off. North Korea quickly blamed the United States as the culprit and leveraged racist insults against President Obama. For more information see, Martin Fackler, "North Korea Accuses U.S. of Staging Internet Failure," The New York Times, December 27, 2014, https://www.nytimes.com/2014/12/28/world/asia/north-korea-sony-hacking-the-interview.html

[142] "Sony Hack: North Korea Back Online after Internet Outage," BBC News, December 23, 2014, https://www.bbc.com/news/world-asia-30584093.

rebuffed the request.[143] The North Korean internet outage could have been the result of a number of events, including a routine disruption stemming from the unreliability of North Korea's infrastructure or an intentional action by Pyongyang to temporarily disable its internet in anticipation of a forthcoming attack. Regardless, if the outage were determined as stemming from an intentional, offensive cyber operation carried out in response to the Sony hack, the magnitude of the incident—a limited duration, disruptive operation that temporarily disabled the internet's functioning in a country with already highly unreliable internet—would not constitute an escalatory action. Instead, it illustrates the limited effects of cyber operations, and the likelihood that the United States may have responded with the capabilities it had at the desired time of employment (given the requirements for more significant cyber operations) or may not have wanted to use and lose valuable accesses that supported other goals. Indeed, as the *New York Times* notes, "any cutoff of Internet services would be mostly symbolic, a warning shot that two can play the game of disruption."[144]

It is not particularly surprising that the United States avoided engaging in escalatory measures, either in cyberspace or using non-cyber instruments of power, to respond to a North Korean cyber attack that targeted a private company outside of the scope of critical infrastructure. However, the dynamics of this case resemble the others we explore in this chapter, both in terms of the policy levers employed to respond to adversary cyber incidents and the trade-offs and limitations of offensive cyber operations as retaliatory options.

The United States and Iran

Strategic interactions in cyberspace between the United States and Iran—a longstanding rivalry in which the threat of military action persistently looms on the horizon—would suggest the case to be prone to escalation. While relations between the United States and Iran have been characterized by an extensive history of proxy warfare, state-sponsored terrorism, risks of nuclear proliferation, and threats of preemptive military strikes, we focus our analysis on actions and reactions in response to the cyber attacks targeting Iran's nuclear program beginning around 2008.[145] While no government has officially taken responsibility for

---

[143] Lesley Wroughton and Megha Rajagopalan, "Internet Outage Seen in North Korea Amid U.S. Hacking Dispute," *Reuters*, December 22, 2014, https://www.reuters.com/article/us-sony-cybersecurity-northkorea/internet-outage-seen-in-north-korea-amid-u-s-hacking-dispute-idUSKBN0K01WA20141222.

[144] Nicole Perlroth and David E. Sanger, "North Korea Loses Its Link to the Internet," *The New York Times*, December 22, 2014, https://www.nytimes.com/2014/12/23/world/asia/attack-is-suspected-as-north-korean-internet-collapses.html.

[145] Muhammet A. Bas and Andrew J. Coe, "A Dynamic Theory of Nuclear Proliferation and Preventive War," *International Organization* 70, no. 4 (Fall 2016): 655–685.

the Stuxnet cyber attack against Iranian atomic centrifuges, extensive reporting has linked this operation to the United States and Israel.[146] On its face, Stuxnet was a counterforce first-strike that was ripe for an escalatory spiral given not only the salience of the U.S.-Iran rivalry but also the level of sophistication of the Stuxnet cyber operation itself, the strategic, high-value nature of the target, and the uniqueness of the operation (the first of its kind in which a digital incident produced tangible effects in the physical environment). However, Iran ostensibly responded to Stuxnet using less escalatory cyber means. It conducted a sustained DDoS attack against the U.S. financial services sector between 2011 and 2012, as well as cyber attacks against Sands Casino in 2014.[147] Similar to other rivalries, actions and responses were largely limited to cyberspace and could be characterized as reciprocal, tit-for-tat actions that did not escalate the situation. In fact, this time period is characterized by a significant diplomatic success in the signing of the Joint Comprehensive Plan of Action (JCPOA) in 2015 between Iran and the permanent members of the UN Security Council plus Germany regarding Iran's nuclear program. Figure 5.2 depicts a general timeline of the events that took place between this set of rivals from 2006 to 2017. In subsequent chapters, we explore other interactions between the United States and Iran in cyberspace in the context of geopolitical crises not triggered by events in cyberspace.

In response to reports of Iran resuming its nuclear weapons program in 2005, Stuxnet (also known as Operation Olympic Games) is said to have begun in 2006, allegedly part of a broader campaign dubbed Nitro Zeus, to surreptitiously undermine Tehran's nuclear efforts.[148] Stuxnet is reported to have caused damage to approximately one fifth of the centrifuges at Natanz, one of the key locations for Iran's uranium enrichment programs. Some assessments claim that the cyber attack delayed Iran's progress toward the development of a functional nuclear weapon by several years.[149] The cyber operation took place in the context of

---

[146] Despite widespread reporting on Stuxnet, neither the U.S. nor Israeli governments have confirmed or denied responsibility for the cyber attack. See, for example, Kim Zetter, *Countdown to Zero Day*; David Sanger, *The Perfect Weapon*; Ellen Nakashima and Joby Warrick, "Stuxnet was Work of U.S. and Israeli Experts, Officials Say," *The Washington Post*, June 2, 2012, https://www.smithsonian mag.com/history/richard-clarke-on-who-was-behind-the-stuxnet-attack-160630516/. This section takes public reporting at face value for hypothetical, academic purposes but does not assume that all or any elements of what exists in the public domain are necessarily accurate.

[147] The 2012 Shamoon cyber attacks against Saudi Aramco and RasGas may have also been part of an Iranian response to Stuxnet, but it did not directly target the United States. However, we briefly explore it in the discussion of the case.

[148] "Implementation of the NPT Safeguards Agreement in the Islamic Republic of Iran," International Atomic Energy Agency, September 24, 2005, https://www.iaea.org/sites/default/files/gov2005-77.pdf; David E. Sanger and Mark Mazzetti, "U.S. Cyberattack Plan if Iran Nuclear Dispute Led to Conflict," *The New York Times*, February 16, 2016, https://www.nytimes.com/2016/02/17/world/middleeast/us-had-cyberattack-planned-if-iran-nuclear-negotiations-failed.html.

[149] Jon R. Lindsay, "Stuxnet and the Limits of Cyber War," *Security Studies* 22, no. 3 (2013): 366; https://www.nytimes.com/2011/01/16/world/middleeast/16stuxnet.html. The campaign reportedly spanned the Bush and Obama administrations, with the former allegedly encouraging the latter to continue operations during the transition. See David E. Sanger, *Confront and Conceal: Obama's Secret Wars and Surprising Use of American Power* (New York: Broadway Paperbacks, 2013), pp. 200–201.

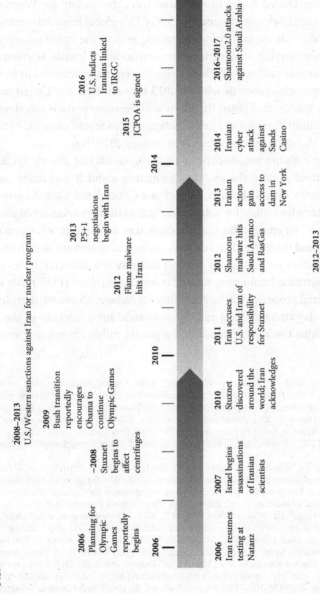

Figure 5.2 Cyber Events in the Context of the U.S.- Iran Rivalry, 2006–2017

U.S.

2006
Planning for Olympic Games reportedly begins

~2008
Stuxnet begins to affect centrifuges

2008–2013
U.S./Western sanctions against Iran for nuclear program

2009
Bush transition reportedly encourages Obama to continue Olympic Games

2012
Flame malware hits Iran

2013
P5+1 negotiations begin with Iran

2015
JCPOA is signed

2016
U.S. indicts Iranians linked to IRGC

Iran

2006
Iran resumes testing at Natanz

2007
Israel begins assassinations of Iranian scientists

2010
Stuxnet discovered around the world; Iran acknowledges

2011
Iran accuses U.S. and Iran of responsibility for Stuxnet

2012
Shamoon malware hits Saudi Aramco and RasGas

2012–2013
Operation Ababil DDoS attacks against U.S. financial sector

2013
Iranian actors gain access to dam in New York

2014
Iranian cyber attack against Sands Casino

2016–2017
Shamoon2.0 attacks against Saudi Arabia

parallel efforts to hobble Iran's nuclear program. This included diplomatic efforts via the UN Security Council to impose increasingly expansive sanctions on Iran for its nuclear weapons program beginning in 2008, as well as a series of sanctions imposed by the Obama Administration between 2011 and 2013 and a successful effort led by the United States to eject Iran from the Society for Worldwide Interbank Financial Telecommunication (SWIFT), a global financial communications network.[150] At the same time, beginning in 2007 the Israeli government was purportedly carrying out a series of assassinations of Iranian scientists involved in its nuclear program.[151] These collective efforts culminated in formal, diplomatic negotiations commencing in 2013 between Iran, the United States, China, Russia, France, the United Kingdom, and Germany to trade sanctions relief for Iranian limitations on its nuclear program. This would ultimately lead to the 2015 JCPOA, which became effective in January 2016.[152]

The Stuxnet malware was discovered in 2010, once it had already spread to computer systems around the world. Information about it was made public by a cybersecurity firm in Belarus. Supervised Control and Data Acquisition (SCADA) systems for critical infrastructure, such as those systems at Natanz, are more "hardened" targets in cyberspace because they are typically not connected to the internet and therefore often require close access operations to gain access. Security researchers found that the Stuxnet malware was deliberately designed to target the Siemens-brand programmable logic controllers (PLCs) that control the industrial processes for the centrifuges at Natanz. Moreover, it exploited multiple zero-day vulnerabilities and, upon establishing a foothold in the network, was designed to surreptitiously self-replicate within the infected systems

---

[150] "Timeline of Nuclear Diplomacy With Iran," *Arms Control Association*, last reviewed September 2020, https://www.armscontrol.org/factsheets/Timeline-of-Nuclear-Diplomacy-With-Iran#2005; "Iran Sanctions," U.S. Department of State, last updated October 30, 2020, https://www.state.gov/iran-sanctions/; Rick Gladstone and Stephen Castle, "Global Network Expels as Many as 30 of Iran's Banks in Move to Isolate Its Economy," *The New York Times*, March 15, 2012, https://www.nytimes.com/2012/03/16/world/middleeast/crucial-communication-network-expelling-iranian-banks.html.

[151] Ronen Bergman, "When Israel Hatched a Secret Plan to Assassinate Iranian Scientists," *Politico*, March 5, 2018, https://www.politico.com/magazine/story/2018/03/05/israel-assassination-iranian-scientists-217223. While Israel has not publicly taken responsibility for the assassinations, Israeli officials have implied an association with these events, "Israel Behind Assassinations of Iran Nuclear Scientists Ya'alon Hints," *The Jerusalem Post*, August 7, 2015, https://www.jpost.com/Middle-East/Iran/Israel-behind-assassinations-of-Iran-nuclear-scientists-Yaalon-hints-411473. During this same time, Israel launched a surreptitious air strike against a Syrian nuclear reactor in 2007, which reportedly contained an electronic warfare component, see Stephen Farrell, "Israel Admits Bombing Suspected Syrian Nuclear Reacter in 2007, Warns Iran," *Reuters*, March 20, 2018, https://www.reuters.com/article/us-israel-syria-nuclear/israel-admits-bombing-suspected-syrian-nuclear-reactor-in-2007-warns-iran-idUSKBN1GX09K; "A Sourcebook on the Israeli Strike in Syria, 6 September 2007," Version 2018-09-08, https://fas.org/man/eprint/syria.pdf. This may have been perceived by Tehran as a signal.

[152] Joint Comprehensive Plan of Action (JCPOA), U.S. Department of State, January 16, 2016, https://2009-2017.state.gov/p/nea/rt/jcpoa/index.htm.

without being detected. The payloads were meant to manipulate the processes that control the centrifuges' functioning to slowly degrade them over time, ideally without being detected. Critically, Stuxnet differs from other cyber attacks in that it was a destructive cyber attack that had effects in the physical environment, rather than being solely contained to the digital realm.[153]

In 2012 it was discovered that Iran—along with a number of other countries— had been hit with malware dubbed Flame that some sources have linked to the United States.[154] Flame was reportedly part of an ongoing cyber espionage campaign and may have been linked to Stuxnet as well as another malware family.[155]

Despite the significance of the Stuxnet cyber operation, it took time for Iran to discern its effects and assess the implications of what was taking place in Natanz. While the effects of Stuxnet had reportedly begun in 2008, it was not until November 2010 that the Iranian government publicly acknowledged that its uranium enrichment program had been targeted by a cyber attack.[156] Then-president of Iran Mahmoud Ahmadinejad aimed to downplay the extent of the impact of the cyber attack, noting that "They succeeded in creating problems for a limited number of our centrifuges with the software they had installed in electronic parts. But the problem has been resolved."[157] Moreover, Iranian government officials did not publicly link the cyber attack to a particular entity until April of the following year, when they claimed that Iran's investigation had revealed that the United States and Israel were responsible for Stuxnet and that the German company Siemans had provided "the enemies with the information about the codes of SCADA software and paved the way for a cyber attack against us."[158]

---

[153] For a full discussion of the technical specification of Stuxnet, see Lindsay, "Stuxnet and the Limits of Cyber War," pp. 380–384. Also see Rebecca Slayton, "What is the Cyber Offense-Defense Balance? Conceptions, Causes, and Assessment," International Security 41, no. 3 (2016): 72–109.

[154] Elinor Mills, "Iran Targeted in New Malware Attack," cnet, April 25, 2011, https://www.cnet.com/news/iran-targeted-in-new-malware-attack/; Caroline Osborne, "Beyond Stuxnet and Flame: Equation 'Most Advanced' Cybercriminal Gang Recorded," Zero Day, February 16, 2015, https://www.zdnet.com/article/beyond-stuxnet-and-flame-equation-group-most-advanced-cyberc riminal-gang-recorded/; "Equation Group," The Council on Foreign Relations, accessed November 2020, https://www.cfr.org/cyber-operations/equation-group.

[155] Nicole Perlroth, "Researchers Find Clues in Malware," The New York Times, May 30, 2012, https://www.nytimes.com/2012/05/31/technology/researchers-link-flame-virus-to-stuxnet-and-duqu.html; "Duqu," The Council on Foreign Relations, accessed November 2020, https://www.cfr.org/cyber-operations/duqu.

[156] David Sanger, Confront and Conceal, ch. 8.

[157] Parisa Hafazi, "Iran Admits Cyber Attack on Nuclear Plants," Reuters, November 29, 2010, https://www.reuters.com/article/us-iran/iran-admits-cyber-attack-on-nuclear-plants-idUSTR E6AS4MU20101129.

[158] "Iran Blames U.S, Israel for Stuxnet Malware," CBS News, April 16, 2011, https://www.cbsn ews.com/news/iran-blames-us-israel-for-stuxnet-malware/#:~:text=TEHRAN%2C%20Iran%20 %2D%20A%20senior%20Iranian,has%20harmed%20Iran's%20nuclear%20program; "Iran Accuses Siiemens over Stuxnet Virus Attack," Reuters, April 17, 2011, https://www.reuters.com/article/us-iran-nuclear-stuxnet-idUSTRE73G0NB20110417.

Iran's initial response to Stuxnet may have followed more than a year after it had publicly linked Stuxnet with the United States and Israel in 2011. In August 2012 a sophisticated, destructive cyber attack occurred against Saudi Aramco, a Saudi Arabian state-owned oil company that at the time produced 10 percent of the global oil supply, as well as RasGas, a Qatari state-owned liquified natural gas company.[159] A relatively unknown hacktivist group calling themselves Cutting Sword of Justice claimed responsibility for the cyber attack and purported that it was a response to Saudi Arabia's policies in the Middle East.[160] The Saudi Aramco attack permanently wiped data from 30,000 computers. Security researchers have suggested that it is likely that the attack was the result of a close access operation, given that "introducing Shamoon onto Aramco's network required physical access to an internal computer."[161] Nevertheless, Saudi Aramco was able to restore operations relatively quickly and, approximately 10 days after the cyber attack, announced that production had resumed.[162]

The link between the Shamoon cyber attack and Stuxnet is ambiguous at best. Some media analysis has suggested that Shamon was Iranian retaliation for Stuxnet, but the connection has never been definitively established by security researchers, analysts, or government officials. Nevertheless, while the United States never formally attributed the Saudi Aramco and RasGas cyber attacks to Iran, officials have implied that the Iranian government is responsible.[163] In October 2012, then-U.S. Secretary of Defense Leon Panetta gave a speech in New York warning of the threat posed by a "Cyber Pearl Harbor" and made specific reference to the Saudi Aramco and RasGas attacks. Panetta described both of these attacks as representing "a significant escalation of the cyber threat. And they have renewed concerns about still more destructive scenarios that could unfold," but did not explicitly link the attacks to Iran (or any actor).[164]

Nonetheless, taking at face value the proposition that Shamoon was a response to Stuxnet, despite Panetta's depiction of the attack as a "significant escalation,"

---

[159] Al Johnson, "Shamoon: Back from the Dead and Destructive as Ever," *Broadcom*, November 30, 2016, https://community.broadcom.com/symantecenterprise/communities/community-home/librarydocuments/viewdocument?DocumentKey=ad6f8259-2bb4-4f7f-b8e1-710b35a4cbed&CommunityKey=1ecf5f55-9545-44d6-b0f4-4e4a7f5f5e68&tab=librarydocuments.

[160] "Shamoon," The Council on Foreign Relations, accessed November 2020, https://www.cfr.org/cyber-operations/search?keys=shamoon.

[161] Christopher Bronk and Eneken Tikk-Ringas, "The Cyber Attack on Saudi Aramco" *Survival* 55, no. 2 (2013): 85.

[162] Daniel Fineren and Amena Bakr, "Saudi Aramco Says Most Damage from Computer Attack Fixed," *Reuters*, August 26, 2012, https://www.reuters.com/article/net-us-saudi-aramco-hacking/saudi-aramco-says-most-damage-from-computer-attack-fixed-idUSBRE87P0B020120826.

[163] Nicole Perlroth, "In Cyberattack on Saudi Firm, U.S. Sees Iran Firing Back," *The New York Times*, October 23, 2012, https://www.nytimes.com/2012/10/24/business/global/cyberattack-on-saudi-oil-firm-disquiets-us.html.

[164] Jason Miller, "Panetta Warns DoD Will Respond to Destructive Cyber Attacks," *Federal News Network*, October 12, 2012, https://federalnewsnetwork.com/tom-temin-federal-drive/2012/10/panetta-warns-dod-will-respond-to-destructive-cyber-attacks/.

available evidence suggests that it does not meet our criteria for escalation. First, the Shamoon attack did not directly target the United States, instead aiming for U.S. regional partners. Additionally, even though the attack included website defacements that depicted the image of a burning U.S. flag, the hackers themselves appeared to obscure the true motivation behind the attack—linking it to Saudi policy rather than to U.S. (and/or Israeli) cyber activities.[165] Given the historic regional rivalry between Iran and Saudi Arabia, it is entirely conceivable that Iran had already developed prepositioned access and tailored capability to conduct cyber operations against Saudi Arabian targets. Assuming this was a retaliatory move, Iran may have chosen to strike with the access and capabilities that it had, rather than with a more direct response. An indirect response against a regional partner, rather than a direct response against the United States, may have also been a deliberate way of retaliating while avoiding escalation. The parallel decisions by Iran to avoid taking responsibility for the attack, and by the U.S. to sidestep directly attributing it to Tehran, suggest a shared (even if not explicitly conveyed) desire to eschew more public actions that may create escalation risks. And, ultimately, despite the destructive nature of the cyber attack, Shamoon caused only a temporary halt in production and did not have a meaningful or sustained impact on Saudi oil production.

Iran's more direct response to Stuxnet likely took place between September 2012 and March 2013 when a group calling itself the Izz ad-Din Al-Qassam Cyber Fighters conducted a multi-phase DDoS cyber attack against U.S. banks.[166] Operation Ababil, as the hackers called it in an online blog post, directed a series of DDoS attacks against dozens of the public-facing websites of U.S. financial institutions.[167] According to the initial DOJ indictment, the attacks began in

---

[165] Nicole Perlroth, "Among Digital Crumbs from Saudi Aramco Cyberattack, Image of Burning U.S. Flag," *The New York Times*, August 24, 2012, https://bits.blogs.nytimes.com/2012/08/24/among-digital-crumbs-from-saudi-aramco-cyberattack-image-of-burning-u-s-flag/.

[166] The Department of Justice indictment of the Iranian Revolutionary Guard Members associated with this attack states that the DDoS attacks started in approximately December 2011 with a significant escalation in September 2012, which was in line with Izz as-Din Al-Qassam Cyber Fighters' blog posts and the commencement of Operation Ababil. For further information see, United States District Court Southern District Of New York, "United States of America v. Ahmad Fathi, Hamid Firoozi, Amin Shokohi, Sadegh Ahmadzadegan, Omid Ghaffarinia, Sina Keissar, and Nader Saedi," 16 Crim 48, https://www.justice.gov/usao-sdny/file/835061/download. In the ensuing years, Iran has been associated with two other cyber attacks: infiltrating a dam in upstate New York in 2013 and the cyber attacks against the Sands Casino in Las Vegas in 2014. The connection between these activities and the action-reaction cycle over Stuxnet is more tenuous, but they are nevertheless important to note as events that took place during this time period. See, Jose Pagilery, "Iran Hacked an American Casino," *CNN Business*, February 27, 2015, https://money.cnn.com/2015/02/27/technology/security/iran-hack-casino/index.html; Joseph Berger, "A Dam, Small and Unsung, Is Caught Up in an Iranian Hacking Case," *The New York Times*, March 25, 2016, https://www.nytimes.com/2016/03/26/nyregion/rye-brook-dam-caught-in-computer-hacking-case.html.

[167] Nicole Perlroth, "U.S. Banks Again Hit by Wave of Cyberattacks," *The New York Times*, January 4, 2013, https://bits.blogs.nytimes.com/2013/01/04/u-s-banks-again-hit-by-wave-of-cyberattacks/ ; Nicole Perlroth and David E. Sanger, "Cyberattacks Seem Meant to Destroy, Not Just Disrupt," *The*

December 2011 and occurred on an occasional basis until September 2012 when their frequency increased to almost weekly and their intensity also increased. The U.S. government estimates that at least 46 major U.S. financial institutions and other financial sector entities were targets of DDoS attacks over a period of at least 176 days. They note that, "[o]n certain days during these attacks, hundreds of thousands of customers were unable to access their banks accounts online" and that "[a]s a result of these attacks, those victim institutions incurred tens of millions of dollars in remediation costs as they worked to mitigate and neutralize the attacks on their computer servers."[168] Given the technical specifications of the attack and other intelligence, the United States assessed Iran was the culprit and that it was a probable response to U.S.-led sanctions against Iran as well as Stuxnet.[169] Overall, the impact of the DDoS attacks was relatively limited. The disruptive nature of DDoS attacks, in general, mean that their effects are transient. Even though Operation Ababil was "considered one of the largest DDoS attack[s] at the time," the financial sector was able to rapidly recover as "banks were quick to apply countermeasures, and the final waves of DDoS attacks only had limited consequences."[170]

It took the United States three years to respond to Operation Ababil. In 2016, the Justice Department indicted seven individuals linked to the Iranian Revolutionary Guard Corps for their involvement in the attacks.[171] Of course, it is theoretically possible that the United States could also have responded with covert operations.[172] However, there is no public evidence suggesting this occurred, and it seems unlikely because even if information about an attack were not made public, the implications would have been likely to exacerbate tensions between the United States and Iran. Instead, in 2013 Iran began diplomatic negotiations with the United States and other countries over its nuclear program.

New York Times, March 28, 2013, http://www.nytimes.com/2013/03/29/technology/corporate-cyb erattackers-possibly-state-backed-now-seek-to-destroy-data.html.

[168] United States District Court Southern District Of New York, "United States of America v. Ahmad Fathi, Hamid Firoozi, Amin Shokohi, Sadegh Ahmadzadegan, Omid Ghaffarinia, Sina Keissar, and Nader Saedi," p. 4.

[169] Nicole Perlroth and Quentin Hardy, "Bank Hacking Was the Work of Iranians, Officials Say," *The New York Times*, January 8, 2013, http://www.nytimes.com/2013/01/09/technology/online-bank ing-attacks-were-work-of-iran-us-officials-say.html.

[170] "Hotspot Analysis: Iranian Cyber-activities in the Context of Regional Rivalries and International Tensions," ETH Zurich, May 2019, p. 15.

[171] Department of Justice, "Manhattan U.S. Attorney Announces Charges against Seven Iranians for Conducting Coordinated Campaign of Cyber Attacks against U.S. Financial Sector on Behalf of Islamic Revolutionary Guard Corps-Sponsored Entities," U.S. Attorney's Office, Southern District of New York, March 24, 2016, https://www.justice.gov/usao-sdny/pr/manhattan-us-attorney-announ ces-charges-against-seven-iranians-conducting-coordinated.

[172] David E. Sanger and Mark Mazzetti, "U.S. Had Cyberattack Plan if Iran Nuclear Dispute Led to Conflict," *The New York Times*, February 16, 2016, https://www.nytimes.com/2016/02/17/world/mid dleeast/us-had-cyberattack-planned-if-iran-nuclear-negotiations-failed.html.

The available evidence strongly suggests that this situation ultimately lacked the features that would otherwise give rise to a precarious, escalatory spiral for reasons anticipated by our theory. First, available evidence suggests that Iran did not know the Stuxnet attack was impending, so it could not have taken measures to mount a preemptive response. Stuxnet was deliberately designed to evade detection and slowly degrade the functioning of Iran's centrifuges over time, rather than deliver an immediate, decisive effect. This demonstrates one pathway through which the secrecy surrounding cyber operations can dampen the potential for escalation. This temporal aspect also played a role in mitigating the situation's escalatory potential through other pathways. For instance, it took time for the Iranians to ascertain that the effects on its centrifuges were the result of a cyber attack and then to ascribe intent and attribution. It reportedly took two years from when centrifuges were first affected, in 2008, to when the Iranians publicly acknowledged and attributed the attack, in 2010.[173]

Moreover, even if Iran had warning, it most likely lacked a comparable ability to mount a relevant disarming counterforce strike with cyber means against the United States or Israel. This is because a cyber operation comparable in scale and effects to Stuxnet would have taken years to develop and implement and required a level of organizational maturity and human capital skill available only to the most capable states.[174] It reportedly took a number of years to develop Stuxnet as well as a highly skilled team of experts.[175] And, despite the code underlying Stuxnet existing in the public domain for nearly a decade, it "has not been repurposed since its discovery in 2010. Neither have new versions of the malware appeared in the wild, most likely because zero-day exploits used by Stuxnet have since been patched and repurposing malware designed for such a specific target demands significant expertise and resources."[176] This demonstrates the high barriers a state such as Iran would confront if it sought to launch a retaliatory cyber attack proportionate in its level of sophistication and effects. The relatively low level of skill and organizational capability of Iranian advanced persistent threat actors at the time suggests this would have been far beyond their capacity.[177] This may be the reason why Iran conducted a cyber attack against Saudi Aramco and RasGas in 2012.

The DDoS attacks against the financial services sector, Iran's purportedly retaliatory response to the cyber attack against it, took place at least one year following its public attribution of Stuxnet. Moreover, Iran's DDoS response was disruptive,

---

[173] Kim Zetter, *Countdown to Zero Day*. David Sanger, *The Perfect Weapon*.
[174] Slayton, "What is the Cyber Offense-Defense Balance?."
[175] Ibid., p. 99.
[176] "Hotspot Analysis: Iranian Cyber-Activities in the Context of Regional Rivalries and International Tensions," *Center for Security Studies, ETH Zurich*, May 2019, p. 16.
[177] Ibid., p. 15.

transient, and not destructive in nature. In terms of the level of sophistication and magnitude of effects, this was orders of magnitude less costly than the attack Iran absorbed. Thus, any escalatory responses would not be under time pressure and would involve redoubling efforts toward a nuclear program or hitting back at an opportune time against different targets using different forces, leaving plenty of latitude in the meantime to pursue de-escalatory diplomatic options. Because the attack did not cross a threshold of civilian collateral damage, there was no pressing motive based on prestige or emotion for an urgent riposte.

Furthermore, it took time for the United States to publicly attribute Iran's response to the Iranian Revolutionary Guard Corps (IRGC) and indict the individuals involved. Moreover, not only was the U.S. response limited to highly tailored indictments against a limited number of individuals—in itself, arguably at a magnitude far less than the effects of the DDoS attacks—Washington waited until after the multilateral diplomatic efforts had already succeeded to release the indictments. Ultimately, the broader strategic issue was resolved through dip-lomatic means—the Iran nuclear deal—rather than by escalating a tense situa-tion to conflict. Indeed, there are a number of reports suggesting that the cyber option in particular provided the United States with an opportunity to restrain the Israeli government and avoid what would have been a significant and dan-gerous escalation of the crisis—a preventive Israeli air strike against Iranian nuclear facilities.[178] According to David Sanger, the United States purportedly conveyed to Israel that, "if you bomb Natanz, it will take the Iranians two years to replace it—but they will be so deep underground; you won't be able to get it the next time . . . . But if you do it this way, they won't see it."[179] Thus, rather than triggering escalation, even a sophisticated cyber attack that was launched at a strategic target in the context of salient international hostilities between historic rivals was able to work as part of a broader escalation-avoidance strategy.

Conclusion

A review of patterns of behavior between rivals provides scant evidence of es-calation dynamics in cyberspace. Moreover, the case studies demonstrate how the characteristics of offensive cyber operations—their limited effects, the role of secrecy, the intelligence value of cyber operations, and the resources involved in gaining access to and developing capabilities against strategically important targets—shape both the impact of cyber operations on interactions between

---

[178] Ronen Bergman and Mark Mazzetti, "The Secret History of the Push to Strike Iran," *The New York Times*, September 4, 2019, https://www.nytimes.com/2019/09/04/magazine/iran-strike-isr ael-america.html.

[179] Sanger, *Confront and Conceal*, p. 190.

rivals and how states use cyber operations in response. Rather than being characterized by high-tempo crisis scenarios in which both parties escalate in response to perceived aggressions by the other, even in instances where the stakes are high, rival states instead preferred to respond to cyber incidents with proportional measures—and often with non-cyber instruments of power—rather than taking escalatory steps in cyberspace or beyond it. When states do respond in cyberspace, they appear to be constrained by either the less sophisticated capabilities they may have at their immediate disposal or their willingness to expend valuable cyber resources that serve both intelligence and military purposes and that are diminished, or even negated, in their employment. Time also shapes how these interactions play out and dampens the cycle of action and reaction. Across many of these cases, there are significant gaps in between when a cyber incident takes place, when it may be observed by the target, and when a response occurs.

There are, of course, caveats and limitations to our case studies given the predominant focus on the United States and its interactions with four rivals states. But the evidence in this deeper dive is consistent with general patterns that researchers have uncovered about behavior in cyberspace more broadly. Taken together, this provides strong support for our argument that states are not likely to respond to cyber operations with escalatory actions either within or outside of cyberspace. The available evidence also does not match up to prominent arguments in the literature about security dilemma dynamics in cyberspace, especially the contention that espionage or penetration of a target in cyberspace causes escalation because states cannot distinguish between espionage and attack. Next, we extend our arguments about escalation to explore whether cyber operations may not only be non-escalatory but may also help contribute to de-escalation and crisis resolution.

6

Cyber Operations and the De-Escalation of International Crises

Evaluating Evidence for De-Escalation

In the previous chapter, we explored cases involving offensive cyber operations that took place between rival states to evaluate the extent to which they may lead to escalation. We found little evidence that they do, and the patterns that presented across the case studies are consistent with our argument that the characteristics of cyber operations shape these dynamics. The limited effects of cyber operations, coupled with the inherent difficulty of cyber operations of strategic significance, mean that most of the activity that has taken place between rivals has been at a low level that would be unlikely to cause a situation to escalate in the first place. Moreover, in cases where a cyber operation was more sophisticated or caused greater effects, plausible deniability created breathing room for tensions to dissipate as states took time to better understand the situation, ascertain responsibility, and develop response options. Finally, even if a cyber-capable state may have been able to act offensively in cyberspace, the intelligence value of cyber operations forced leaders to weigh the trade-offs of doing so. In this chapter, we take the logic of our argument one step further. If cyber operations do not cause escalation, is it also possible that they could help crises peacefully resolve in some circumstances?

Specifically, here we explore whether the limited effects of cyber operations coupled with plausible deniability—some of the same factors that reduce the likelihood that cyber operations will trigger escalation—may also facilitate crises de-escalation. We find that some cyber operations that take place in the context of geopolitical crises appear to allow states to respond to perceived transgressions by rivals in a way that placates domestic audiences and express concern or disagreement with a particular issue, while not taking such forceful action that would escalate the situation. These dynamics can provide a window for crises to resolve. In this chapter we conduct process tracing across six different case studies that vary according to the presence or absence of cyber operations, as well as the type of cyber operation. Specifically, we focus our analysis on cases where we assessed de-escalation was not particularly likely. Overall, we find convincing evidence

Escalation Dynamics in Cyberspace. Erica D. Lonergan and Shawn W. Lonergan, Oxford University Press.
© Oxford University Press 2023. DOI: 10.1093/oso/9780197550885.003.0006

consistent with our claim that some types of cyber operations, when employed in the context of geopolitical crises, are associated with crisis de-escalation.

Some Challenges of Testing Signaling Hypotheses

Our analysis raises two critical questions: First, how can we know that states deliberately choose cyber tools for signaling purposes rather than other, non-signaling, reasons? And second, does it matter if a state intends for a cyber operation to be a form of signaling, or is it simply the effects of cyber operations alone that affect crisis dynamics?

One alternative explanation could be that states do not intend for cyber operations to serve as signals—accommodative or otherwise. Instead, cyber operations may simply be a "low cost" option for states to pursue strategic objectives that are unrelated to the crisis. This is probably the case for ongoing, long-term cyber espionage campaigns that support intelligence collection priorities, take a significant amount of time to develop and implement, and are likely to continue alongside other geopolitical events like crises. The discovery of an adversarial espionage campaign during a crisis, therefore, should in most cases not be interpreted as a signal. By way of example, if the U.S. government had been made aware during a crisis that Russia had compromised dozens of government and private sector networks and exfiltrated sensitive data—which occurred in December 2020 in the SolarWinds supply chain breach, but not during a crisis—it would be a mistake for policymakers to interpret this as a form of Russian signaling.[1] The exception, of course, is if there were evidence that a rival was intentionally making itself discoverable during the course of a crisis.

But, setting aside the unique category of most cyber espionage campaigns, we are skeptical of the argument that *visible* cyber operations that occur during crises are unrelated to signaling. That's because most states are likely to anticipate that there is a good chance that all forms of observable behavior that take place during a crisis will be interpreted as signals. Therefore, it is reasonable to infer that, in evaluating response options during a crisis, decision makers will consider how the actions they take—specifically, those that are seen by the other side—will be interpreted as an intentional act meant to convey something. Alternatively, while cyber attacks may indeed be low-cost measures or some other byproduct unrelated to signaling, it is precisely this ambiguity that makes the signal useful for saving face. There may be uncertainty about whether a government is deliberately encouraging cyber proxies to take action during a crisis

---

[1] Lily Hay Newman, "A Year after the SolarWinds Hack, Supply Chain Threats Still Loom," *Wired*, December 8, 2021.

or leaving something to chance, but a willingness to take measures to then curtail these activities to exit a crisis could act as a form of accommodation.

Two factors can guide researchers in assessing whether a cyber operation is intended to be a signal: its observability and the extent to which it is linked to the signaling state. Regarding the former, a deliberate signal is one that is intended to be received by the target; it must be conducted in such a way that it is meant to be visible at least to the target—even if it is not observable to others. In terms of the latter, the target should be able to associate the signal in some way to the signaling state. Not all forms of cyber behavior satisfy these two conditions. For instance, some cyber operations, such as espionage operations as we noted above, are intended to be kept secret. In these cases, states employ tradecraft to obscure their presence on an adversary's or third-party network. Similarly, a state could go to considerable lengths to disassociate itself from a cyber operation: it could publicly denounce the operation; avoid using tactics, techniques, and procedures that are linked to other types of cyber operations that the state conducts; or refrain from coupling its cyber operations with other signals or communications. It's unlikely that these types of cyber operations are forms of deliberate signaling.

One could also argue that the effects of cyber tools impact crisis dynamics, regardless of intent. According to this reasoning, cyber operations could facilitate the de-escalation of a crisis not necessarily because a state intends to do so but, rather, because the relatively limited effects of cyber operations happen to prevent crises from spiraling out of control, holding all else constant, or otherwise have a marginal impact on crisis dynamics. However, effects are only one aspect of our argument; it is effects coupled with how decision makers approach choices about secrecy that shape crisis dynamics. If effects alone determined the implications of cyber operations for international crises then, holding effects constant, we should not expect to observe variation in how parties to a crisis approach secrecy—a more obvious signaling choice than the effects of operations in themselves—nor should we expect to observe changes in subsequent crisis behavior. We explore this variation in our case studies.

Case Selection

To test whether cyber operations can contribute to the de-escalation of international crises, we reviewed our aggregated datasets to identify cases in which cyber operations occurred in the context of a geopolitical crisis between rival states.[2] We specifically looked for crises involving a contested political issue

---

[2] The datasets we explored were Ryan C. Manness, Brandon Valeriano, and Benjamin Jensen, "The Dyadic Cyber Incident and Dispute Data," Version 1.5, https://drryanmaness.wixsite.com/cyberconfl ict/cyber-conflict-dataset; the Council on Foreign Relations Cyber Operations Tracker, https://www.

(such as a dispute over territory or a perceived political threat to a regime) that raised the risk of military hostilities.[3] Intentionally, unlike the case studies in the previous chapter, here we chose cases where the trigger of a crisis was not a cyber event but a broader political issue. We also deliberately selected cases so that there would be variation in the type of cyber operation that took place during the crisis. Specifically, we examined differences between low-cost, disruptive cyber operations and more sophisticated, destructive cyber operations. This helps to shed light on the different ways states use cyber operations during crises, providing a means of distinguishing between when cyber operations might be used for conciliatory purposes to de-escalate a crisis and when they might be used as signals of resolve or deterrence.

We excluded instances of tit-for-tat exchanges between rivals that were caused by an initial cyber incident or campaign (which we explored in greater depth in the previous chapter) or cases where the employment of cyber power did not appear to be connected to an international crisis. An example of the former are the extensive cyber espionage campaigns that have been conducted over a decade between China and its rivals in Southeast Asia; an example of the latter is the U.S. government's revelation in 2018 that Russian government-affiliated cyber actors were conducting cyber operations targeting critical infrastructure.[4] This allows us to examine within-case variation in crisis behavior over time, to assess whether the conduct of a cyber operation in the context of an ongoing crisis that contains some meaningful risk of escalation precipitates a change in the crisis behavior of the parties, in any direction: escalation of the crisis, de-escalation of the crisis, or maintenance of the status quo.

Finally, as a means of comparison, we selected several cases where crises occurred without any observable cyber operations, but that are otherwise similar to crises where cyber operations did take place. This allows us to evaluate the extent to which the presence or absence of cyber operations may affect crisis dynamics. While there is an inherent logic to the argument that cyber operations

cfr.org/cyber-operations/; the Center for Strategic & International Studies list of significant cyber incidents, https://www.csis.org/programs/technology-policy-program/significant-cyber-incidents; and Jason Healey, Neil Jenkins, and J.D. Work, "Defenders Disrupting Adversaries: Framework, Dataset, and Case Studies of Disruptive Counter-Cyber Operations," 2020 12th International Conference on Cyber Conflict, https://ccdcoe.org/uploads/2020/05/CyCon_2020_14_Healey_Jenkins_Work.pdf.

[3] Our definition of crisis follows from Michael Brecher and Jonathan Wilkenfeld, *A Study of Crisis* (Ann Arbor: University of Michigan Press, 2000), pp. 3–5.

[4] "APT30 and The Mechanics of a Long-Running Cyber Espionage Operation: How a Cyber Threat Group Exploited Governments and Commercial Entities across Southeast Asia and India for Over a Decade," *FireEye*, April 2015, https://www.mandiant.com/sites/default/files/2021-09/rpt-apt30.pdf; "Alert (TA18-074A) Russian Government Cyber Activity Targeting Energy and Other Critical Infrastructure Sectors," *Cybersecurity and Infrastructure Security Agency*, March 15, 2018, https://us-cert.cisa.gov/ncas/alerts/TA18-074A.

as accommodative signals could facilitate crisis de-escalation, the overwhelming tendency of most crises, particularly involving nuclear powers, to resolve short of major escalation makes it more difficult to establish a clear causal relationship between cyber operations and de-escalation—or to find cases with meaningful variation across escalation outcomes. Therefore, because cyber operations take place in some crises but not others, analyzing non-cyber crises in comparison to cyber crises helps to validate our argument that some cyber operations are, in fact, deliberate signals rather than superfluous noise. This is particularly true for closed regimes, which monitor (and in some cases control) the online activity that occurs within their cyber borders. This gives us greater confidence that, during a crisis, parties are likely to surmise that observable cyber attacks originating from a closed state occur with some level of implicit permission by the central government and are therefore a form of signaling.[5]

The vast majority of observed cyber behavior associated with states takes place outside of the context of international crises. However, we identified 18 cases of geopolitical crises that contained one or more cyber operations conducted by parties to the crisis, listed in Table 6.1.

Of these cases, 13 stand out as being more likely to escalate and, therefore, represent hard tests of our argument (denoted in the table by an asterisk next to the name of the crisis). These cases are more conducive to escalation because they involved death, the use of physical/kinetic force, or significant invocation of national honor or prestige.

A few patterns stand out across these cases. First, cyber operations did not prompt an escalatory response in any of them. Instead, cyber operations were typically followed either by a reciprocal cyber operation or the de-escalation of the crisis.[6] Additionally, most of these cases involved relatively low-cost cyber operations, such as website defacements and DDoS attacks perpetrated by proxy groups or patriotic hackers, rather than highly sophisticated operations that targeted adversary critical infrastructure or had destructive effects. There are only two exceptions to this observation: the Strait of Hormuz crisis between the United States and Iran in June 2019, and the Abqaiq-Khurais attack that led to a crisis between the United States/Saudi Arabia and Iran in September 2019. According to the Council on Foreign Relations, in June 2019 the United States

[5] Suzy Hansen, "Finding Truth Online Is Hard Enough. Censors Make It a Labyrinth," *The New York Times*, November 13, 2019; Darrell M. West, "Internet Shutdowns Cost Countries $2.4 Billion Last Year," Center for Technology Innovation at Brookings, October 2016, p. 3; Carolina Vendil Pallin, "Internet Control through Ownership: The Case of Russia," *Post-Soviet Affairs* 33, no. 1 (2017): 16–33; Alina Polyakova and Chris Meserole, "Exporting Digital Authoritarianism: The Russian and Chinese Models," *Foreign Policy at Brookings* (2019): 1–22.

[6] However, as of this writing the Galwan Valley dispute was ongoing, so the situation may change. For further information on this dispute, see Jin Wu and Steven Lee Myers, "Battle in the Himalayas," *The New York Times*, July 18, 2020, https://www.nytimes.com/interactive/2020/07/18/world/asia/china-india-border-conflict.html.

Table 6.1 Cyber Operations in Geopolitical Crises

Crisis	Rivals	Date	Description
U.S./NATO bombing of Chinese embassy in Belgrade during Kosovo War*	U.S./NATO/ China	May 1999	Chinese patriotic hackers deface U.S. government websites in response to accidental bombing of Chinese embassy. This occurred in conjunction with nationalist protests in Chinese cities. Crisis de-escalates when President Clinton's apology is broadcast in China.
Hainan Island Incident*	U.S./China	April 2001	U.S. Navy EP-3 spy plane and Chinese fighter jet collide near Hainan Island, leading to death of Chinese pilot and detention of EP-3 crew. Chinese patriotic hackers conduct website defacements. Crisis defused when U.S. issues apology letter.
Mumbai terrorist attacks*	India/ Pakistan	November 2008	After Pakistani-sponsored terrorist organization attacks a number of targets in Mumbai, Indian-affiliated actors deface Pakistani websites and Pakistani-affiliated actors respond by defacing Indian websites.
Paracel and Spratly Islands Dispute	China/ Vietnam	June– October 2011	Vietnam accuses Chinese patrol boats of cutting cables of a Vietnamese ship in Vietnam's EEZ. Chinese and Vietnamese hackers both conduct website defacements and DDoS attacks against the other. In October, both parties sign an agreement regarding how to address maritime disputes.
Scarborough Shoal Dispute	China/ Philippines	April–May 2011	Chinese Coast Guard prevents fishing boats from the Philippines from accessing Scarborough Shoal. Patriotic hackers affiliated with China and Philippines conduct website defacements and DDoS attacks.
Senkaku/ Diaoyu Islands Dispute*	China/Japan	September 2012	Japan purchases disputed islands from a Japanese family on the anniversary of the Japanese invasion of Manchuria in 1931. There are major anti-Japanese protests across China. Chinese affiliated hackers conduct DDoS attacks and website defacements against Japanese targets. China suppresses domestic protests. U.S. and Japanese forces conduct planned amphibious landing drill in Guam. China eventually establishes an Air Defense Identification Zone in November 2013.

(continued)

Table 6.1 Continued

Crisis	Rivals	Date	Description
North Korea nuclear test*	South Korea/ North Korea	February– March 2013	North Korea reports it had conducted a nuclear test in February 2013, prompting South Korea to go on heightened military alert. UN Security Council condemns the test. North Korea accuses South Korea of conducting cyber attacks. The UN Security Council imposes sanctions and U.S. flies B-52s over South Korea. South Korean banks and media suffer a cyber attack, using DarkSeoul malware, which its government blames on North Korea. DDoS and website defacements occur against North Korea. North Korea launches DDoS attack against South Korea media and government websites.
Guang Da Xing No. 28 Incident*	Taiwan/ Philippines	May 2013	Incident between Taiwanese fishing boat and Filipino coast guard leads to shooting death of Taiwanese fisherman. Taiwan imposes sanctions on Philippines and demands an apology. Filipino and Taiwanese hackers conduct DDoS attacks and website defacements. Philippines issues an apology in August.
Hai Yang Shi You 981 Standoff	China/ Vietnam	May–July 2014	Chinese state-owned oil company moves oil rig into disputed waters near the Paracel Islands. Vietnam and China send ships to the area, each accuses the other of ramming and spraying ships. Large anti-China protests in Vietnam take place. Chinese patriotic hackers conduct website defacement attacks; the group Goblin Panda targets Vietnamese government entities. China withdraws oil rig.
Fiery Cross Reef	China/ Vietnam/ Philippines	May 2015	China installs military infrastructure on the disputed Fiery Cross Reef, including building an airfield and deploying artillery, and conducts dredging in the Spratly Islands. Vietnamese and Filipino patriotic hackers conduct DDoS attacks and website defacements against Chinese websites.

Table 6.1 Continued

Crisis	Rivals	Date	Description
Turkish downing of Russian jet*	Russia/ Turkey	November 2015– January 2016	A Turkish jet shoots down a Russian jet in Syria near the Syrian-Turkish border, with Turkey claiming the jet had violated its airspace. Turkey and Russia mobilize forces in the region. Russia breaks off military communications with Turkish military. Turkish targets experience DDoS attacks, DNS attacks, and hacktivist activity. In January 2016, Russian banks experience DDoS attacks and Russian government social media accounts experience website defacement. There are reports of a breach of Russia's security services.
Terrorist attack in Kashmir*	India/ Pakistan	September– October 2016	After Pakistani-backed group launches attack in Kashmir, India responds with air strikes. Pakistani-affiliated actors deface Indian websites. Indian actors claim to have gained access to Pakistani critical infrastructure.
North Korea nuclear test*	U.S./North Korea	February– September 2017	North Korea conducts a sixth nuclear test. There is an emergency UN Security Council meeting, and the United States responds with escalating rhetoric. There are reports of a U.S. denial of service cyber attack against North Korea.
Iran nuclear agreement withdrawal	U.S./Iran	May 2018	Immediately after the United States announces it will withdraw from the Iran nuclear agreement, Iran increases cyber activities against U.S. government and critical infrastructure entities, including sending spear-phishing emails with malware.
Pulwama attack*	India/ Pakistan	February 2019	A suicide bombing kills 40 Indian security personnel in Jammu and Kashmir. Pakistan denies responsibility. Pakistani hackers target government websites, and Indian hackers conduct website defacements. India conducted an airstrike across the Line of Control against terrorist training camps.

(continued)

Table 6.1 Continued

Crisis	Rivals	Date	Description
Strait of Hormuz crisis*	U.S./Iran	June–July 2019	Iran downs a U.S. drone and launches attacks on oil tankers in the Strait of Hormuz. There are reports that the United States hacked Iranian rocket and missile launch systems in response. At the same time, the United States calls off kinetic strikes against Iranian targets. U.S. Cyber Command issues warning about Iranian malware targeting government networks.
Abqaiq-Khurais attack*	U.S./Saudi Arabia/Iran	September–October 2019	Attacks on Saudi Arabian oil facilities are blamed on Iran. There were reports of a U.S. cyber attack against Iran's ability to spread propaganda. United States announces it will send additional troops to Saudi Arabia. Microsoft reports Iranian attempts to hack Trump campaign and other U.S. email accounts.
Galwan Valley Dispute*	China/India	June 2020	Indian and Chinese troops clashed in the Galwan Valley along the Line of Actual Control, leading to the deaths of 20 Indian soldiers. Indian government and bank entities claim DDoS attacks from China.

* Case considered more likely to escalate

reportedly "hacked Iranian rocket and missile launch systems in retaliation for the downing of a U.S. drone and attacks on oil tankers in the Strait of Hormuz."[7] The *New York Times* reported that this cyber operation took place at "the same time President Trump called off a strike on Iranian targets like radar and missile batteries."[8] Similarly, CSIS reported that in September 2019 the United States "carried out cyber operations against Iran in retaliation for Iran's attacks on Saudi Arabia's oil facilities. The operation affected physical hardware and had the goal of disrupting Iran's ability to spread propaganda."[9]

[7] "Attack on Iranian Computer Systems," CFR Cyber Operations Tracker, https://www.cfr.org/cyber-operations/attack-iranian-computer-systems .

[8] Julian E. Barnes and Thomas Gibbons-Neff, "U.S. Carried Out Cyberattacks on Iran," *The New York Times*, June 22, 2019. Also see Jenna McLaughlin, Zach Dorfman, and Sean D. Naylor, "Pentagon Secretly Struck Back against Iranian Cyberspies Targeting U.S. Ships," *Yahoo! News*, June 21, 2019.

[9] "Significant Cyber Incidents," Center for Strategic and International Studies, https://www.csis.org/programs/technology-policy-program/significant-cyber-incidents. Also see Idrees Ali

While there have been no official statements from the U.S. government confirming or denying these reports, the fact that there are only two observations of alleged cyber operations targeting critical infrastructure with destructive effects during crises is not surprising. As we've argued, these types of operations are difficult to conduct and may not be available for most states to employ at the desired time during a crisis. Nevertheless, when they do occur, these kinds of highly sophisticated cyber operations, especially those against strategic targets like weapon systems, are more easily attributable—given their complexity and resources required—to powerful state actors. Therefore, it is reasonable to expect that they could serve signaling purposes. We examine one of those cases—the Strait of Hormuz crisis—in greater detail as a point of comparison to the other instances of cyber operations during international crises.

Additionally, we explore patterns of state behavior in 3 additional cases out of the 13 identified in Table 6.1 where escalation risks were particularly salient: the 2012 Senkaku/Diaoyu Islands dispute between China and Japan; the 2015 crisis between Turkey and Russia after Turkey downed a Russian jet; and North Korea's nuclear test in 2017 that caused a crisis between it and the United States. We also chose these cases because they exhibit variation across the dyads in terms of the participants involved, the specific type of event that triggered the crisis, and the cyber behavior that is observed. In the course of our analysis, we briefly compare two of these cases with the most convincing evidence in support of cyber operations as accommodative signals—the crises between China/Japan and Russia/Turkey—to similar cases that did not involve cyber operations. These are a crisis in 2013 between China, the United States, and several states in the region over China's Air Defense Identification Zone (ADIZ), and a 2018 crisis between the United States and Russia over inadvertent military confrontations in Syria. This helps us assess whether it is really cyber operations that help facilitate de-escalation, or other factors about a crisis.

If some cyber operations can indeed function as accommodative signals in a crisis that provide opportunities for de-escalation to occur, then we should expect to observe the following behavior across the cases: first, cyber operations should occur in parallel to diplomatic and government efforts—in other words, they are part of the dynamics of crisis interaction; second, cyber operations should be observed following more escalatory non-cyber moves in a crisis; third, domestic political dynamics should play a role in the use of cyber operations, particularly in circumstances where domestic political audience or

and Phil Stewart, "Exclusive: U.S. Carried out Secret Cyber Strike on Iran in Wake of Saudi Oil Attack: Officials," *Reuters*, October 16, 2019.

veto players are expressing more hawkish views, raising the chances of escalation; fourth, the lower the costs and sophistication of the cyber operation, the more it should serve accommodative signaling rather than coercive purposes; fifth, rather than trigger further escalation, de-escalation should follow from cyber operations; and finally, we should observe mutual, implicit accepting by both parties of the plausible deniability associated with attribution of cyber operations.

Summary of the Cases

In two of the case studies—the 2012 crisis between China and Japan and the 2015 crisis between Russia and Turkey—the crises triggered domestic nationalist sentiments and private backchannels failed to resolve the issues at hand. In this context, low-level, disruptive cyber operations carried out by hacktivist groups or proxies loosely affiliated with the government functioned as accommodative signals. There were two sets of audiences for these cyber signals: nationalist or hawkish domestic constituencies and the adversary government. The limited effects of these attacks, coupled with their highly visible nature and tenuous connection to the government, enabled leaders to manage domestic sentiments while avoiding more aggressive action that could further escalate the situation. In response, the targets avoided publicly linking the cyber attacks with the adversarial government, and the crises were resolved.

In contrast, in two similar cases that did not contain cyber operations—the 2013 ADIZ crisis and the 2018 crisis between the United States and Russia in Syria—the crises were resolved through a combination of diplomacy and military maneuvers, both public and private. The absence of cyber operations in these instances demonstrates that the choice to conduct or allow cyber operations in some cases but not others is deliberate, providing inherent plausibility to our argument that cyber operations could be signals.

Finally, in two of the cases, both of which involved the United States—the 2017 crisis between the United States and North Korea over the latter's missile tests and the 2019 crisis between the United States and Iran over the Strait of Hormuz—the evidence suggests that cyber operations were used more as part of a coercive signaling approach than as a means of demonstrating restraint and accommodation. Both of these cases involved a real, credible threat of a kinetic military strike, which was purportedly followed by a cyber operation instead. In the Iran case, the cyber operation appears to have been more sophisticated and destructive, while in the North Korea case it was more disruptive. Moreover, unlike the first two cases containing cyber operations, in these instances a cyber attack was reportedly directly conducted by government forces and was covert (only made public due to anonymous leaks by officials to the media) and more tailored to the adversary. This is suggestive of a cyber signal of resolve rather than accommodation. Nevertheless, these crises also did not escalate, which reinforces our findings from the previous chapter. Also distinct from the first two cases, in both of these cases it does not appear that domestic audiences were pushing for a more strident stance. If anything, it was the reverse, and there were real fears of unnecessary military conflict.

Altogether, the six cases provide some granularity in terms of how states may see different types of cyber operations as serving varying signaling purposes, illustrating the characteristics of cyber operations as signals of accommodation versus resolve. They also suggest the conditions under which accommodative cyber signaling is more likely to be observed: in a crisis where leaders strive to balance nationalist domestic sentiments while avoiding actions that would exacerbate the situation and where other forms of private communication may not be as viable. Table 6.2 depicts a summary of the cases and the core findings.

In the following section, we discuss two cases that are strongly suggestive of cyber operations serving as accommodative signals: the 2012 crisis between China and Japan and the 2015 crisis between Russia and Turkey. Next, we briefly compare these cases to two similar examples of international crises where cyber operations were not observed. This helps validate our claim that cyber operations can function as signals. Finally, we compare the dynamics of the first two cases to the two cases where cyber operations took place, but which are more suggestive of signaling for resolve: the 2017 crisis between the United States and North Korea and the 2019 crisis between the United States and Iran. This helps to distinguish between characteristics of cyber signals for accommodation, rather than resolve.

International Crises with Cyber Operations as Accommodative Signals

The 2012 crisis between China and Japan and the 2015 crisis between Turkey and Russia share similar contextual features: the mobilization of domestic publics for nationalist purposes and the inability of leaders to resolve the crisis through traditional private communication. They are also characterized by similar forms of cyber behavior: noisy but low-cost cyber operations carried out by proxy or hacktivist groups loosely affiliated with the government. In both cases, leaders appeared to leverage cyber operations to placate mobilized domestic constituencies while avoiding more escalatory actions.

Table 6.2 Case Studies Summary

Crisis	Presence and Type of Cyber Operations	Nationalism/Hawkish Domestic Audiences	Public vs. Private Statements/Actions	Role of Cyber Operations in Crisis
International Crisis with Cyber Operations as Accommodative Signals				
2012 Crisis between China and Japan over the Senkaku/ Diaoyu islands	Yes; public, temporary, widespread disruptive cyber attack by nationalist proxies affiliated with Chinese government	Yes; sustained anti-Japanese protests in China; nationalist activity in Japan; power transitions in China and Japan	Failed private backchannel; public statements, public diplomatic actions, and military maneuvers. For cyber attacks, both sides maintain plausible deniability; China does not acknowledge cyber attacks, and Japan does not publicly attribute cyber operations to China.	Cyber operations appear to function as accommodative signals; audience is domestic public and the opposing government
2015 Crisis between Russia and Turkey over Turkish downing of Russian jet	Yes; public, temporary, widespread disruptive cyber attack by hacktivist proxy groups affiliated with both Russia and Turkey	Yes; anti-Turkish protests in Russia; nationalist sentiments in Turkey and Russia	Failed private backchannels; public statements, public diplomatic actions, and military maneuvers. For cyber attacks, both sides maintain plausible deniability; Turkey privately links cyber attacks to Russia but does not publicly attribute; Russia does not publicly attribute cyber attacks to Turkey.	Cyber operations appear to function as accommodative signal; audience is domestic public and the opposing government
International Crisis without Cyber Operations				
2018 Crisis between Russia and the United States in Syria over inadvertent military engagements	None	Not significant	Direct, private communication via military hotline; both parties publicly disassociate attack from Russian government; United States conducts military strike against proxy force in Syria	n/a

2013 Crisis between China, the United States, and reginal states over China's declaration of an Air Defense Identification Zone	None	Not significant	Absence of private backchannels with potential exception of China and South Korea; public statements, public diplomatic actions, and military maneuvers	n/a

International Crises with Cyber Operations as Signals of Resolve

2017 Crisis between United States and North Korea over ballistic missile tests	Yes; covert, tailored denial of service cyber attack reportedly by U.S. government against North Korea's Reconnaissance General Bureau	On the U.S. side, little evidence of domestic pressure for military conflict with North Korea; however, crisis did occur shortly after inauguration of new U.S. administration	Status of direct private communication unknown, but unlikely; both parties make very bellicose public statements and conduct military exercises and weapons tests, with United States threatening military action against North Korea. For cyber attacks, both sides maintain plausible deniability; neither the United States nor North Korea publicly acknowledges cyber attacks, but media reports unattributed comments from U.S. officials.	Cyber operations appear to function as signal of resolve/coercion; audience is largely the opposing government
2019 Crisis between Iran and the United States over oil tanker attacks in the Strait of Hormuz	Yes; covert, tailored cyber attacks reportedly by U.S. government against opposing government targets; more long-term, more destructive effects	No evidence of U.S. domestic political pressure for military conflict with Iran, while administration is more hawkish on Iran than prior administration	Status of direct private communication unknown, but unlikely; both parties make public statements and conduct military maneuvers, with United States threatening a military strike against Iran. For cyber attacks, both sides maintain plausible deniability; neither Iran nor U.S. publicly acknowledge cyber attacks, but media reports unattributed comments from U.S. officials	Cyber operations appear to function as signal of resolve/coercion; audience is largely the opposing government

The 2012 crisis between China and Japan

The 2012 Senkaku/Diaoyu islands dispute represents a difficult case for our argument because conditions were ripe for escalation. Historically, crises between China and its regional rivals over disputes about territorial sovereignty have been more likely than others to escalate to violence.[10] A number of crises have been triggered by contests over disputed territorial islands and maritime rights, especially concerning the Senkaku/Diaoyu islands.[11] While Japan has administered these islands since 1972, their sovereignty has been contested by China and Japan since 1970.[12] Sovereignty disputes over these islands have "introduced significant uncertainty and risk into the most volatile flashpoint between the world's second and third largest economies."[13] Indeed, there have been "major escalations in 1978, 1990, 1996, and 2004–2005, which involved significant incidents and escalatory actions (both diplomatic and military)."[14] Moreover, there is an enduring history of rivalry between China and Japan that dates back to the Japanese invasion of mainland China during World War II. This historical memory (particularly narratives of national humiliation) has significance for political and strategic purposes in China.[15] Anti-Japanese sentiment has served a "rally 'round the flag" effect for Beijing and as a "safety valve" to direct domestic discontent away from Chinese Communist Party (CCP) leadership and toward a perceived foreign adversary.[16] This has played out in cyberspace as well, "in the form of Chinese hacktivists DDoS'ing and defacing Japanese government websites," often during historically significant calendar dates.[17]

---

[10] Alastair Iain Johnston, "The Evolution of Interstate Security Crisis-Management Theory and Practice in China," *Naval War College Review* 69, no. 1 (Winter 2016): 41. For a general discussion, see Stephan A. Kocs, "Territorial Disputes and Interstate War, 1945–1987," *The Journal of Politics* 57, no. 1 (1995): 159–175; and John Vasquez and Marie T. Henehan, "Territorial Disputes and the Probability of War, 1816–1992," *Journal of Peace Research* 38, no. 2 (2001): 123–138.

[11] James Manicom, *Bridging Troubled Waters: China, Japan, and Maritime Order in the East China Sea* (Washington, DC: Georgetown University Press, 2014), p. 42.

[12] M. Taylor Fravel, "Explaining Stability in the Senkaku (Diaoyu) Islands Dispute," in Gerald Curtis, Ryosei Kokubun, and Wang Jisi, eds., *Getting the Triangle Straight: Managing China-Japan-US Relations* (Washington, DC: Brookings Institution Press, 2010), p. 145. They are also contested by Taiwan.

[13] Adam P. Liff and Andrew S. Erickson, "From Management Crisis to Crisis Management? Japan's post-2012 Institutional Reforms and Sino-Japanese Crisis (In)stability," *Journal of Strategic Studies* 40, no. 5 (2017): 604.

[14] Hyun Joo Cho and Anjin Choi, "Why Do Territorial Disputes Escalate? A Domestic Political Explanation for the Senkaku/Diaoyu Islands Dispute," *Pacific Focus* 31, no. 2 (2016): 255.

[15] Zheng Wang, *Never Forget National Humiliation: Historical Memory in Chinese Politics and Foreign Relations* (New York: Columbia University Press, 2014).

[16] See James Reilly, "A Wave to Worry About? Public Opinion, Foreign Policy, and China's Anti-Japan Protests," *Journal of Contemporary China* 23, no. 86 (2014): 197–215. Also see Jack Levy, "A Diversionary Theory of War: A Critique," *Handbook of War Studies* 1 (1989): 259–288.

[17] Stefan Soesanto, *A One-Sided Affair: Japan and the People's Republic of China in Cyberspace: Hotspot Analysis*, Center for Security Studies, ETH Zurich, January 2020, p. 3.

However, implicit agreements between Beijing and Tokyo from the 1970s through the late 1990s enabled both sides to avoid very dangerous crisis escalation and control domestic nationalist sentiments that otherwise could have derailed regional stability.[18] One important mechanism for doing so was the fact that "China has avoided mobilizing the public around the dispute."[19] For instance, examining publication patterns in official Chinese media outlets between 1987 and 2005, particularly in comparison to state-sanctioned articles on other disputed territories (such as Taiwan or the Spratly Islands), M. Taylor Fravel has noted an apparently deliberate Chinese effort to eschew leveraging the Senkaku/ Diaoyu islands to fan domestic nationalist flames.[20]

This shared understanding began to unravel in 2010, and disputes with regional states over contested territories began to generate risks that Chinese nationalist sentiments could lead to escalation.[21] This coincided with China's increased military spending, pursuit of military modernization programs, and more assertive exercising of what Beijing perceives to be its legitimate sovereignty claims, particularly maritime claims.[22] In September 2010, for instance, after a Chinese fishing boat collided with Japanese coast guard vessels, Tokyo detained the captain of the vessel. This was followed by the eruption of nationalist protests in China and the arrest by the Chinese government of four Japanese citizens in China.[23]

Similar events in September 2012 precipitated a crisis between China and Japan. Coinciding the with anniversary of the Japanese invasion of Manchuria in 1931—in itself a politically significant date for Chinese nationalism—on September 11, 2012, the Japanese government effectively nationalized the Senkaku/Diaoyu islands, purchasing three islands in the group from a private Japanese citizen.[24] The crisis took place during a time of domestic political

---

[18] James Manicom, *Briding Troubled Waters: China, Japan, and Maritime Order in the East China Sea* (Washington, DC: Georgetown University Press, 2014), pp. 42, 52–53.

[19] Fravel, "Explaining Stability in the Senkaku (Diaoyu) Islands Dispute," 153.

[20] Ibid, 153–155. Also see Erica Strecker Downs and Phillip C. Saunders, "Legitimacy and the Limits of Nationalism: China and the Diaoyu Islands," *International Security* 23, no. 3 (1999): 114–146.

[21] Paul J. Smith, "The Senkaku/Diaoyu Island Controversy: A Crisis Postponed," *Naval War College Review* 66, no. 2 (2013): 38. These concerns have dated back to the 1990s, even prior to major Chinese military modernization programs. See, for instance, Thomas J. Christensen, "China, the U.S.-Japan Alliance, and the Security Dilemma in East Asia," *International Security* 23, no. 4 (Spring 1999): 49–80.

[22] Cho and Choi, "Why Do Territorial Dispute Escalate?," p. 257.

[23] Soesanto, "A One-Sided Affair," p. 4.

[24] Smith, "The Senkaku/Diaoyu Island Controversy," p. 27. The origins of the crisis trace back to April 2012, when the governor of Tokyo announced his intentions to buy the islands. See Sanaa Yasmin Hafeez, "The Senkaku/Diaoyu Islands Crises of 2004, 2010, and 2012: A Study of Japanese-Chinese Crisis Management," *Asia-Pacific Review* 22, no. 1 (2015): 84. Initially, it appears that Tokyo attempted to resolve the crisis privately through backchannels to Chinese officials, but this became inviable when the purchase was made public. See Tod Hall, "More Significance than Value: Explaining Developments in the Sino-Japanese Contest over the Senkaku/Diaoyu Islands," *Texas National Security Review* 2, no. 4 (August 2019): 24.

transition for both states, with upcoming elections in Japan and a historic leadership transition in China from Hu Jintao to Xi Jinping.[25] Immediately, Japan's purchase of the islands triggered a crisis between Beijing and Tokyo, with China's official military newspaper warning that Japan was "playing with fire" and that "The Chinese government and military are unwavering in their determination and will defend national territorial sovereignty. We are closely following developments, and reserve the power to adopt corresponding measures."[26] On September 14, 2012, China sent six surveillance ships into waters in the vicinity of the disputed islands. Two of the ships entered Japanese waters and were issued warnings by the Japanese Coast Guard. Moreover, between September 18 and 24 the Japanese Coast Guard claimed that 20 Chinese vessels entered Japanese territorial waters.[27]

Large-scale anti-Japanese protests broke out across 85 cities in China, beginning on September 15, and were accompanied by physical threats to the safety of Japanese citizens and businesses in China and economic boycotts of Japanese goods.[28] The CCP clearly tolerated and implicitly condoned anti-Japanese protests, with an editorial in the People's Daily on September 15 expressing empathy with nationalist protesters and noting that "No one would fail to understand the compatriots' hatred and fights when the country is provoked; because a people that has no guts and courage is doomed to be bullied, and a country that always hides low and bides its time will always come under attack."[29] At the same time, Beijing strove to gingerly balance allowing domestic dissent while preventing nationalist protests from spiraling out of control, taking measures such as deploying police to the Japanese embassy and sending text messages to Chinese citizens warning them to steer clear of certain protest areas.[30] Beyond potential concerns about inadvertent crisis escalation, leaders in Beijing were also concerned about, "striking a balance between tolerating and controlling nationalist sentiment against Japan . . . in order to complete the once-in-a-decade leadership transition smoothly."[31] On September 18, two Japanese activists

---

[25] Cho and Choi, "Why Do Territorial Disputes Escalate?," pp. 272–274.

[26] Kiyoshi Takenaka, "Japan Buys Disputed Islands, China Sends Patrol Ships," Reuters, September 11, 2012.

[27] There were also reports that Chinese People Liberation Army Navy conducted a naval exercise in the area; Cho and Choi, "Why Do Territorial Disputes Escalate?," p. 270; Carlyle A. Thayer, "The Senkaku Islands Dispute: Risk to U.S. Rebalancing in the Asia-Pacific?," USNI News, October 16, 2012. Also see Hafeez, "The Senkaku/Diaoyu Islands Crises of 2004, 2010, and 2012," p. 85.

[28] Thayer, "The Senkaku Islands Dispute."

[29] Ian Johnson and Thom Shanker, "Beijing Mixes Messages Over Anti-Japan Protests," The New York Times, September 16, 2012. Apparently, Japan did not anticipate that China's response would be that strong. See Hall, "More Significance than Value," 29.

[30] Cho and Choi, "Why Do Territorial Disputes Escalate?," p. 276.

[31] Ibid., 278.

landed on the Senkaku/Diaoyu islands, coinciding with the exact date of Japan's 1931 invasion of China.[32]

The cyber portion of the crisis began during the same weekend that the anti-Japanese protests commenced. First, distinct from cyber attacks that may serve as a form of signaling, Chinese nationalist discourse proliferated on social media sites, most notably on Weibo.[33] There was some element of central control over social media discourse because during this time the Chinese government prohibited specific terms associated with the protests from showing up on online searches, such as "anti-Japan," "protest," and "demonstrate."[34] This was a form of "selective censoring" to ratchet up or down "anti-Japanese sentiment, depending on the political needs and objectives of the government."[35]

More relevant for our analysis, cyber proxy groups played an important role in this crisis.[36] During the period in question, the Chinese government had moved from granting freer rein to domestic hacker groups, often dubbed patriotic hackers or hacktivists, toward "tighten[ing] its control over non-state actors wielding cyber capabilities" to establish a more organized and formalized system of cyber militias.[37] These groups typically engaged in website defacement and DDoS activities—highly visible, but not particularly sophisticated attacks with relatively low costs for a target to absorb—although they were increasingly moving toward more sophisticated data theft and espionage operations.[38]

Beginning on September 15, Japan's minister of internal affairs and communication reported a spate of DDoS attacks against Japanese websites, peaking on September 16; 95% of the traffic associated with the DDoS attacks originated from China.[39] The Honker Union, a Chinese patriotic hacker group, posted on YY Chat, a Chinese blog, "its plan to attack Japanese websites, distributed information about attack vectors and software vulnerabilities, and congratulated itself on successfully striking Japan via cyberspace. It also claimed Chinese ownership over the Senkaku/Diaoyu Islands and boasted about having awakened

[32] Sheila A. Smith, "The History behind China and Japan's Anger over a Few Empty Islands," *The Atlantic*, September 22, 2012.

[33] Christopher Cairns and Allen Carlson, "Real-world Islands in a Social Media Sea: Nationalism and Censorship on Weibo during the 2012 Diaoyu/Senkaku Crisis," *The China Quarterly* 225 (2016): 23–49.

[34] Cho and Choi, "Why Do Territorial Disputes Escalate?," p. 278.

[35] Kieran Richard Green, "People's War in Cyberspace: Using China's Civilian Economy in the Information Domain," *Military Cyber Affairs* 2, no. 1 (2016): 5.

[36] Erica D. Borghard and Shawn W. Lonergan, "Can States Calculate the Risks of Using Cyber Proxies?," *Orbis* 60 no. 3 (2016): 408–409.

[37] Tim Maurer, *Cyber Mercenaries: The State, Hackers, and Power* (Cambridge: Cambridge University Press, 2017), p. 107.

[38] Ibid., p. 114.

[39] Soesanto, "A One-Sided Affair," p. 11.

the patriotic spirit of Chinese youth."[40] Patriotic hackers associated with the Honker Union conducted a number of DDoS attacks, website defacements, and doxing campaigns—publicly releasing private or damaging information gleaned through cyber exploitation—against targets such as Japan's Ministries of Defense and Internal Affairs, Supreme Court, and Tokyo Institute of Technology.[41] Given the CCP's ability to suppress or permit nationalist protests, whether in person or online, this cyber campaign was not long-lasting.[42] Following a swell of activity in cyberspace perpetrated by actors ostensibly sympathetic to the political objectives of the government in Beijing—which was demonstrably able to control the magnitude of online behavior if not implicitly direct it—domestic protests dissipated by mid-September.

On the Japanese side, the cyber campaign carried out by Chinese patriotic hacker groups occurred at the same time that important changes were taking place in Tokyo regarding cyberspace that created potential conditions for the crisis to escalate. As cyber threats and attacks against Japan have grown, particularly since 2009, Japan has "moved responsibility for cybersecurity to military institutions, namely the Japan Ministry of Defense (JMOD) and Japan Self-Defense Forces (JSDF)."[43] In July 2012, the JMOD published an interim Defense Posture Review report (just before the crisis with China), which identified responding to cyber attacks as one of its top ten priorities. Then, while the crisis over the Senkaku/Diaoyu Islands was unfolding, JMOD published *Toward Stable and Effective Use of Cyberspace* that, among other things, directed JMOD and JSDF to "prepare for cyberattacks as part of an armed attack" and identified "cyberspace as a domain for defense operations in the same way as land, sea, air, and outer space."[44] Despite this, there was no meaningful Japanese cyber response to the Chinese cyber campaign.[45]

[40] Scott W. Harold, Yoshiaki Nakagawa, Junichi Fakuda, John A. Davis, Keiko Kono, Dean Cheng, and Kazuto Suzuki, "The U.S.-Japan Alliance and Deterring Gray Zone Coercion in the Maritime, Cyber, and Space Domains," RAND Corporation, 2017, p. 67.

[41] Scott W. Harold, Yoshiaki Nakagawa, Junichi Fakuda, John A. Davis, Keiko Kono, Dean Cheng, and Kazuto Suzuki, "The U.S.-Japan Alliance and Deterring Gray Zone Coercion in the Maritime, Cyber, and Space Domains," RAND Corporation, 2017, pp. 7–8; Soesanto, "A One-Sided Affair," p. 11; Phil Muncaster, "Chinese Hactivists Launch Cyber Attack on Japan: Government Sites Sink in Dispute over Islands," *The Register*, September 21, 2012; Thayer, "The Senkaku Islands Dispute."

[42] Jessica Chen Weiss, *Powerful Patriots: Nationalist Protests in China's Foreign Relations* (Cambridge, UK: Oxford University Press, 2014), pp. 222–223.

[43] "Japan's Cybersecurity Strategy: Deterring China with Selective Engagements," Japan Studies Program, University of Washington, May 22, 2017.

[44] Paul Kallender and Christopher W. Hughes, "Japan's Emerging Trajectory as a 'Cyber Power': From Securitization to Militarization of Cyberspace," *Journal of Strategic Studies* 40, nos. 1–2 (2017): 130.

[45] "Japan's Cybersecurity Strategy: Deterring China with Selective Engagements"; and Soesanto, "A One-Sided Affair."

Public diplomatic efforts by China, Japan, and the United States ultimately resulted in the immediate crisis dissipating.[46] Japanese Prime Minister Yoshihiko Noda publicly asked Beijing to temper anti-Japanese protests, and on September 17 U.S. Secretary of Defense Leon Panetta made a public statement that the United States would meet its treaty obligations to come to Japan's aid if the latter were attacked, before meeting with Chinese leaders on September 18.[47] In a January 2013 meeting between Chinese President Xi Jinping and Japanese lawmaker Natsuo Yamaguchi, Xi struck a conciliatory tone in the context of seeking to mitigate tensions between China and Japan over the East China Sea, stating that, "The Chinese government remains committed to China-Japan relations."[48]

China did not capitulate to Japan's sovereignty claims over the Senkaku/Diaoyu islands and continues to contest them to this day, but both parties were able to avoid crisis escalation during this particular incident. China's use of cyber operations in this context is strongly consistent with the objectives of accommodative signaling. Cyber operations followed what were otherwise more escalatory non-cyber moves undertaken by Beijing and the situation calmed down following the employment of cyber capabilities. Moreover, sending ambiguous signals for the purpose of promoting crisis stability is consistent with Chinese strategic thinking on crisis management and deterrence.[49] Permitting Chinese patriotic hackers—implicitly under the direction of the central government, but absent the exertion of direct command and control—to conduct highly visible but, nevertheless, low-cost cyber attacks against Japanese targets enabled Beijing to signal displeasure with the political situation and provide a safety valve to discontented Chinese nationalists, all while eschewing more provocative measures that might escalate the crisis. Indeed, the military maneuvers preceded, rather than followed, Chinese activities in cyberspace.

Moreover, the Japanese government did not use Chinese-affiliated cyber attacks as a pretext for escalation. Despite the clear link to China, as well as recent policy changes elevating the significance of cyber attacks in Japanese strategy and defense guidance, the Japanese government did not make a significant public issue out of the cyber attacks.[50] Rather, it capitalized on the ambiguous association of the attacks with Beijing, their relatively low impact, and their reduction over time (along with

---

[46] However, this remains a contested issue and there have been flare-ups subsequent to the 2012 crisis. See Hafeez, "The Senkaku/Diaoyu Islands Crises of 2004, 2010, and 2012," pp. 86–87. Also see Hall, "More Significance than Value," pp. 13–14.

[47] Smith, "The History behind China and Japan's Anger over a Few Empty Islands."

[48] Jane Perlez, "Chinese Leader Takes Conciliatory Tone in Meeting with Japanese Lawmaker," *The New York Times*, January 25, 2013.

[49] Johnston, "The Evolution of Interstate Security Crisis-Management Theory and Practice in China," p. 49.

[50] "Japan's Cybersecurity Strategy: Deterring China with Selective Engagements"; Kallender and Hughes, "Japan's Emerging Trajectory as a 'Cyber Power,'" 130.

the reduction in public protests) in conjunction with public diplomatic activities to de-escalate the crisis.

Even after the crisis had concluded, official accounts published by the Japanese Ministry of Defense acknowledged the cyber attacks against government and private websites and implied a link to Chinese proxy groups and hacktivists, but did not directly name the Chinese government—even as it attributed cyber attacks conducted against other states, such as the United States and South Korea, to China.[51] In a 2013 volume published by the Ministry of Defense, in the section devoted to detailing trends and threats in cyberspace, there is a significant focus on cyber threats stemming from the Chinese government and the various "private hacker groups that have been involved" in cyber attacks.[52] Among a number of cyber incidents, the document acknowledges cyber attacks against government and private websites "after the Japanese government made a cabinet decision concerning the acquisition of ownership of three Senkaku islands in September 2012."[53]

More so than the acknowledgement by Japan's Ministry of Defense that a cyber attack took place in conjunction with the Senkaku islands dispute, what is fascinating about this aside is what it omits. While nearly the entire section on cyber threats specifically draws attention to Chinese cyber threats and enumerates a history of Chinese-affiliated cyber attacks, including a 2006 attack against companies in the United States and a 2009 attack against U.S. and South Korean government websites, the document does not explicitly attribute the September 2012 attack against Japan to China. Of course, responsibility is implied—the section begins by linking Chinese hackers and their activities in cyberspace to the central government and concludes by referencing a series of cyber events targeting Japan that were carried out by patriotic hacker groups in China. However, it does not explicitly make the connection between the two, even though any informed reader would understand the implication. This is consistent with our argument that states can be strategic about the extent they are willing to go public about attribution—alluding to attribution without outright "naming and shaming."

The 2015 crisis between Russia and Turkey

An incident between Russia and Turkey in November 2015, in which Turkey shot down a Russian warplane in the context of the Syrian civil war, created the

---

[51] "Chapter 2: Issues in the International Community," in Japan Ministry of Defense, *Defense of Japan 2013*, 2013, 81–82.
[52] Ibid., 81.
[53] Ibid, 82.

potential conditions for crisis escalation. These concerns were particularly acute given that the crisis occurred during an ongoing conflict in which rival states and their treaty allies—notably, members of NATO—had already intervened with military force.[54] Moreover, since the beginning of the Syrian conflict in 2011 a number of military clashes took place around the Syrian-Turkish border, including an incident in June 2012 when Syria shot down a Turkish jet and another in September 2013 when Turkey shot down a Syrian helicopter.[55] There were also increasing tensions between Turkey and Russia and, a month prior to the crisis at hand, Turkey issued a warning to Russia when a Russian fighter jet violated Turkish airspace.[56]

During the course of the November 2015 crisis, both Russia and Turkey also suffered various types of cyber attacks in conjunction with the diplomatic, economic, and military activity in which both parties were engaged. In fact, the penultimate event prior to the peaceful resolution of the crisis in June 2016 was an ostensibly retaliatory cyber operation allegedly conducted by Turkish-affiliated cyber actors against Russian targets. Given the limitations of the available evidence, we must note some caveats in drawing direct links between the cyber attacks and the definitive resolution of the crisis. That said, the patterns in this case offer further confirmatory evidence that cyber operations, even during heated geopolitical crises, are unlikely to cause escalation and, rather, may operate as accommodative signals that facilitate crisis de-escalation.

The crisis began on November 24 when a Turkish F-16 jet shot down a Russian Su-24 jet that Turkey claimed had entered its airspace from Syria. Turkey stated that the F-16 pilots had issued a number of warnings to the Russian warplane, which were all ignored. This was the first time a NATO member state had shot down a Russian jet since the Korean War.[57] At the time this incident occurred, Russia, Turkey, and several NATO members were conducting ongoing military operations in Syria. Moreover, in the weeks leading up to the incident, tensions between Turkey and Russia had intensified in response to Turkish government objections to Russia's bombing of Turkmen tribes in northern Syria. These Turkmen tribes claimed that they had shot the Russian crew as they ejected from the plane over Syria. Turkey

---

[54] In the context of this particular crisis, Syria and Turkey had disputes over the border, the Hatay Province, which is where Turkey shot down the Russian jet. See Keith Bradsher, "Range of Frustrations Reaches Boil as Turkey Shot Down Russian Jet," *The New York Times*, November 25, 2015.

[55] "Syria-Turkey Tension: Assad 'Regrets' F-4 Jet's Downing," *BBC News*, July 3, 2012; and Kareem Fahim and Sebnem Arsu, "Turkey Says it Shot Down Syrian Military Helicopter in its Airspace," *The New York Times*, September 16, 2013.

[56] Erşen, Emre, "Evaluating the Fighter Jet Crisis in Turkish-Russian Relations," *Insight Turkey* 19, no. 4 (2017): 85–104.

[57] Thomas Gibbons-Neff, "The Last Time a Russian Jet was Shot Down by a NATO Jet was in 1952," *The Washington Post*, November 24, 2015.

immediately called for a NATO meeting, while Putin publicly denounced the downing of the Russian jet as a "stab in the back delivered by the accomplices of terrorists" and warned that there would be "serious consequences for Russian-Turkish relations."[58]

Over the next few days, Russia retaliated with a number of diplomatic, economic, and military responses, including canceling the visit of Russian foreign minister Sergey Lavrov to Turkey, suspending tourism to Turkey, announcing economic sanctions and visa restrictions for Turkish citizens traveling to Russia that would take effect in January 2016, detaining Turkish businessmen traveling in Russia, continuing to bombard Turkmen areas in northern Syria, and announcing the emplacement of its S-400 missile defense system in Latakia (30 miles south of the Syrian border).[59] It was also reported that Russia's Federal Security Service (FSB) prevented Turkish ships from entering Russian ports and Turkish vehicles from crossing the land border into Russia.[60]

There was also significant domestic political protest surrounding the events of the crisis. On November 25, a large, violent demonstration took place outside Turkey's embassy in Moscow, with some claims in the media that local authorities did not take measures to control the protests but, rather, tacitly permitted them.[61] Russia also leveraged media to disseminate propaganda about Turkey. In particular, Russian media capitalized on uncertainty among NATO allies about Turkey's commitment to fighting terrorism to "aggressively [craft] narratives that portrayed Turkey and its leaders as supporters of terrorism that funded ISIS through illegal oil purchases."[62] There was also significant domestic political pressure on Turkish president Recep Tayyip Erdogan to take a more hawkish stance on Russian activities in Syria, particularly Russia's bombardment of the Turkmen tribes. An emphasis on ethnic Turkish identity was central to Erdogan's political messaging in the election victory he had secured just prior to this crisis.[63] And anti-Russian protests broke out in Istanbul in the wake of anti-Turkish protests in Moscow, with Turkish protestors calling for Putin's assassination.[64]

---

[58] Neil MacFarquhar and Steven Erlanger, "NATO-Russia Tensions Rise after Turkey Downs Jet," *The New York Times*, November 24, 2015.

[59] MacFarquhar and Erlanger, "NATO-Russian Tensions Rise after Turkey Downs Jet"; Natasha Bertrand, "Russia is Already Exacting its Revenge on Turkey for Downing a Russian Warplane," *Business Insider*, November 26, 2015. "Russia 'Playing with Fire,' Warns Turkey, as Moscow Imposes Visa Regime," *The Guardian*, November 27, 2015.

[60] Adam Meyers, "Cyber Skirmish: Russia v. Turkey," *CrowdStrike*, April 13, 2016.

[61] Etienne Henry, "The Sukhoi Su-24 Incident between Russia and Turkey," *Russian Law Journal* 4, no. 1 (2016): 8–25.

[62] Katherine Costello, "Russia's Use of Media and Information Operations in Turkey," RAND Corporation, 2018, 3.

[63] Keith Bradsher, "Range of Frustrations Reached Boil as Turkey Shot Down Russian Jet," *The New York Times*, November 25, 2015.

[64] "Russia 'Playing with Fire,' Warns Turkey, as Moscow Imposes Visa Regime," *The Guardian*, November 27, 2015. "Turkey, Russia Continue War of Words," *VOA News*, November 27, 2015.

Erdogan stated on French television that he had called Russian president Vladimir Putin, seeking to meet with the Russian leader to resolve the crisis, but received no response.[65] Russia indicated that Putin would only meet with Erdogan under the condition that he apologize for Turkey's actions, which Erdogan refused to do.[66] Nevertheless, at the same time, Lavrov publicly stated that "We do not intend to wage a war on Turkey."[67] Erdogan retorted that Russia was "playing with fire" and said that Russia was supporting a "terrorist state" in Syria.[68] It is notable that Lavrov's public statement of reassurance was not sufficient to bring both parties to the bargaining table or resolve the crisis.

Approximately two weeks into the crisis, the private cybersecurity firm CrowdStrike noted that it had "observed Distributed Denial of Service (DDoS) attacks targeting Turkish state-owned banks, government sites, and hacking forums. Soon hacktivists operating under Anonymous-style monikers began targeting the Turkish root DNS [Domain Name System] and threatening to destroy the banking infrastructure."[69] The cyber attacks against Turkish DNS—the system that converts domain names into IP addresses so that an individual can use the internet—affected between 300,000 and 400,000 websites and lasted for one week.[70] In response to the DDoS attack, Turkey "cut off all foreign Internet traffic to .tr," essentially blocking all incoming traffic from outside of the Turkish-controlled internet.[71] While the hacking group Anonymous, which is not affiliated with any government, publicly claimed responsibility for the attacks and observers have made connections between the DDoS attacks and Russia. CrowdStrike describes the attacks as taking place "under the guise of hacktivism" and notes that the cyber attacks "may be a subtle way for opposing countries with tightly linked economies to draw blood against each other without escalating to full-scale combat."[72]

More importantly for the dynamics of the crisis, Turkey appeared to have linked the attacks to Russia. Media reports claimed that, privately, "the Turkish military concluded that Russia was [behind] a series of recent attacks on Internet infrastructure, the finance industry and health care sector in Turkey."[73] Furthermore, in early January 2016, Turkey's technology minister publicly implied a link between the cyber attacks and Russia, stating that "[t]he crisis with

---

[65] Natasha Bertrand, "Russia is Already Exacting its Revenge on Turkey for Downing a Russian Warplane," *Business Insider*, November 26, 2015.

[66] "Russia to Wage Electronic Warfare against Turkey," *Defense World*, November 30, 2015.

[67] "Russia Will Not Wage War on Turkey after it Downed Russian Jet–Foreign Minister," *Reuters*, November 25, 2015.

[68] "Russia 'Playing with Fire.'"

[69] Meyers, "Cyber Skirmish: Russia v. Turkey."

[70] "Hackers Block Russian Minister's Cyber Account with Turkish Symbols," *Reuters*, January 3, 2016; and Cory Bennett, "Turkey: Rift with Russia Inciting Hackers," *The Hill*, January 4, 2016.

[71] Ibid.

[72] Meyers, "Cyber Skirmish: Russia v. Turkey."

[73] Abdullah Bozkurt, "Russia Targeted Turkey with Offensive Cyber Operations," *Nordic Monitor*, December 16, 2019.

Russia and other developments in the region could have incited this," referring to the cyber attacks.[74] Turkey's statement exploits the plausible deniability of cyber operations—while Turkey ostensibly holds Russia responsible for the cyber attacks, it chose to avoid directly connecting them to Russia in public. Turkey's statement not only demonstrates the uncertainty associated with attributing cyber operations in the first place, but also the ways in which both parties to a crisis can mutually leverage the inherent ambiguity of cyber operations (especially those conducted by proxy or hacktivist groups). Specifically, this kind of hedging statement in response to ambiguous cyber attacks can help implicitly signal that both sides will keep these dynamics outside of the public realm, creating the conditions for potential de-escalation of a crisis.

Turkey's public statement in January 2016 implying a link between cyber attacks the prior month and Russia is also notable because, at the exact same time, Turkish-affiliated hacktivist groups appeared to have mounted a response to Russia's cyber attacks. On January 3, 2016, a group known as the Börteçine Cyber Team blocked the Instagram account of Russia's communications minister, "presenting themselves as a Turkish activist group and parading images of a warplane and Turkish flags."[75] Additionally, CrowdStrike observed cyber attacks targeting Russian banking infrastructure and Russia's FSB.[76] There were no subsequent reports of Russia acknowledging or responding to these cyber incidents. While we do not have access to the internal deliberations of Russian or Turkish leaders, the timing of these events and the particular choice of language in public statements is strongly suggestive of both sides employing relatively low-impact cyber operations to signal a combination of displeasure at the events taking place and a shared interest in keeping responses in the plausibly deniable realm and avoiding escalation—in other words, some form of accommodative signaling. Both leaders could have chosen to go public about events taking place in cyberspace, but apparently refrained from doing so. The crisis finally resolved in June 2016, after a (peaceful) stalemate lasting a number of months, when Turkey apologized to Russia for the downing of the jet, with Erdogan sending a message to Putin offering "sympathy and deep condolences."[77]

Discussion

The 2012 crises between China and Japan and the 2015 crisis between Russia and Turkey share a number of similar characteristics. The cyber aspect of both crises

---

[74] Bennett, "Turkey: Rift with Russia Inciting Hackers," 2016.
[75] "Hackers Block Russian Minister's Cyber Account," 2016.
[76] Meyers, "Cyber Skirmish: Russia v. Turkey."
[77] "Turkey 'Sorry for Downing Russian Jet,'" *BBC News*, June 27, 2016.

commenced when private diplomatic backchannels failed, and also after more escalatory non-cyber moves were taken. Moreover, the crises drew in domestic audiences on both sides and created a risk that nationalist pressures would drive leaders to escalate—even when, especially in the Turkey-Russia crisis, it was clear that neither government sought escalation. These factors made the crisis ripe for policy tools, such as cyber operations, that have the advantage of being able to straddle the line between the public and private realms; manage the pressure from more nationalist domestic audiences pushing for a more aggressive response to the crisis; and not cause high-level costs against an adversary that would unnecessarily exacerbate an ongoing situation.

In the Russia-Turkey crisis, while there were a number of very senior-level, strident public statements by leaders on both sides regarding perceived culpability and expressing respective national interests at stake, as well as highly visible economic and military activities, there was far more public ambiguity about the cyber operations that took place concurrent with these more overt moves. This is consistent with observed patterns in the China-Japan crisis, where cyber operations functioned as plausibly denial signals, while at the same time other actions took place in the public domain. There are also similarities between the crises in terms of the extent to which China, Russia, and even Turkey can monitor (and in some cases even control) a good portion of the online activity that occurs within their cyber borders, such that, during a geopolitical event, parties may surmise that cyber attacks originating from a given state likely take place with some level of implicit permission by the central government and, therefore, function as a form of signaling.[78]

Additionally, the cases are similar in terms of the type and impact of the cyber operations that took place. Specifically, the effects of the cyber operations across both cases were relatively indiscriminate but not particularly costly. They caused only minimal, short-lived disruptions. Importantly, they were also immediately visible to their targets—they were "noisy" cyber operations that would reasonably be interpreted as being linked to the dynamics of the crisis, either because of their overt political content (such as with website defacements) or the nature of the specific entities that were targeted (government or critical infrastructure). And across both cases, the targets of the cyber attacks made deliberate choices to refrain from publicly blaming the other side, instead opting for ambiguous public statements that only made inferences about responsibility. In the Turkish

[78] Suzy Hansen, "Finding Truth Online Is Hard Enough. Censors Make It a Labyrinth," *The New York Times*, November 13, 2019. In 2015, prior to the crisis with Russia, Turkey blocked Twitter and Facebook. See Darrell M. West, "Internet Shutdowns Cost Countries $2.4 Billion Last Year," Center for Technology Innovation at Brookings, October 2016, p. 3; Carolina Vendil Pallin, "Internet Control through Ownership: The Case of Russia," *Post-Soviet Affairs* 33, no. 1 (2017): 16–33; and Alina Polyakova and Chris Meserole, "Exporting Digital Authoritarianism: The Russian and Chinese Models," *Foreign Policy at Brookings* (2019): 1–22.

case, the public statement was coupled with a proportionate, tit-for-tat cyber response against Russian targets—to which Russia responded with silence.

However, there are also some important differences between the crises. First, the link between hacktivist activity and the Chinese government is noticeably clearer than the connection between Russia and the cyber attacks against Turkey. Nevertheless, both Japan and Turkey expressed similarly ambiguous public statements about attribution. Second, Japan did not respond in cyberspace to Chinese-affiliated cyber attacks, but in the Russia-Turkey case there appear to have been tit-for-tat, reciprocal cyber attacks against both Turkish and Russian targets. Nevertheless, in both cases cyber attacks did not cause any meaningful escalation of the crises and, in fact, were the events immediately preceding their resolution.[79]

International Crises without Cyber Operations

The evidence from the cases we analyzed above strongly suggests that cyber operations functioned as a form of accommodative signaling during the crises. However, it's also possible that cyber operations were simply background noise and did not have a meaningful effect on how the crises played out. Therefore, to explore whether cyber operations that take place during crises are meant to be signals, we briefly compare the two crises above to two similar crises where cyber operations were not observed: the 2013 crisis between the United States, China, and other states in the region over China's declaration of an ADIZ and the 2018 crisis between Russia and the United States over unintended military engagement in Syria. This variation in the presence or absence of cyber operations across similar types of crises provides plausible support for our argument that visible cyber operations can be a deliberate choice and function as signals. Moreover, the attributes of the non-cyber cases—particularly the absence of significant domestic political pressure—provides greater context for assessing the conditions under which states may turn to cyber operations for accommodative signaling.

The 2013 ADIZ crisis

On November 23, 2013, a crisis was precipitated when China announced that it would establish an ADIZ in the East China Sea (ECS) that would go into effect

---

[79] One challenge with the Russia-Turkey case is ascertaining what ultimately prompted Erdogan to issue an apology to Putin. Unlike the China-Japan case, where cyber and non-cyber actions took place in tandem and where the crisis ended shortly after the cyber attacks, in this case there is a six-month gap between the last observed cyber attacks and the ultimate cessation of the crisis.

the following morning. This declaration required all civilian and military aircraft entering the zone to provide flight plan information, among other administrative data, to China or be subjected to "defensive emergency measures" from China's armed forces.[80] The declaration also featured a map depicting the boundaries of the zone, which crossed over the existing ADIZs of Japan, South Korea, and Taiwan, as well as a number of contested geographical features in the region.[81]

Unlike the events that took place in the lead up to the 2012 crisis between China and Japan, in this case there is no evidence of private backchannels, diplomatic communications, or consultations between China, Japan, and the United States, with the potential exception of South Korea, where China reportedly used private diplomatic channels to notify South Korea in advance that its ADIZ would cover the Socotra Rock.[82] Instead, China's announcement largely "surprised everyone—both inside and outside China."[83]

China's declaration immediately provoked an outcry from political leaders of the affected countries, as well as the United States, and caused concerns about increasing the overall risk of conflict—a sentiment directly expressed by the U.S. secretaries of state and defense.[84] In the end, affected parties reproached China through diplomatic action and military maneuvers, such as scrambling fighter jets to intercept Chinese patrols and conducting military exercises.[85] The United States' response aimed to balance refusing to accept the legitimacy of China's ECS ADIZ, while at the same time avoiding inadvertent escalation. The United States flew bombers over the Senkaku/Diaoyu islands (now within the ECS ADIZ) without prior notification of China, as well as made public reaffirmations of its security guarantees to Japan.[86] In January 2014, a series of

[80] "Announcement of the Aircraft Identification Rules for the East China Sea Air Defense Identification Zone of the P.R.C.," *ChinaDaily.com.cn*, November 23, 2013.

[81] "Statement by the Government of the People's Republic of China on Establishing the East China Sea Air Defense Identification Zone," *ChinaDaily.com.cn*, November 23, 2013.

[82] Michael Green, Kathleen Hicks, Zack Cooper, John Schaus, and Jake Douglas, "Counter-Coercion Series: East China Sea Air Defense Identification Zone," *CSIS*, June 13, 2017.

[83] Feng Zhang, "Should Beijing Establish an Air Defense Identification Zone Over the South China Sea?" *Foreign Policy*, June 4, 2015; "Daily Press Briefing—December 2, 2013," U.S. Department of State; Michael D. Swaine, "Chinese Views and Commentary on the East China Sea Air Defense Identification Zone (ECS ADIZ)," Carnegie Endowment for International Peace, 2014, pp. 3–4.

[84] Green et al., "Counter-Coercion Series."

[85] For an in-depth review of the ensuing actions see, Ian E. Rinehart and Bart Elias, "China's Air Defense Identification Zone (ADIZ)," Congressional Research Service, January 30, 2015. Swaine, "Chinese Views and Commentary on the East China Sea Air Defense Identification Zone (ECS ADIZ)," 11; Green et al., "Counter-Coercion Series"; Kim Eun-jung, "S. Korea, Japan Conduct Search, Rescue Drill in East China Sea," *Yonhap*, December 12, 2013; Ankit Panda, "The East China ADIZ and the Curious Case of South Korea," *The Diplomat*, November 28, 2013. "Executive Yuan Responds Firmly to Mainland China's East China Sea ADIZ Declaration," Office of Information Services, Executive Yuan, November 29, 2013; Lily Kuo, "Will a Tiny, Submerged Rock Spark a New Crisis in the East China Sea?," *The Atlantic*, December 9, 2013.

[86] Craig Whitlock, "U.S. Flies Two Warplanes over East China Sea, Ignoring New Chinese Air Defense Zone," *The Washington Post*, November 26, 2013. "Remarks to the Press by Vice President

high-level, bilateral meetings between U.S. and Chinese officials continued as planned and focused on cooperation and the need to reduce tensions.[87]

Notably absent during this strategic interaction was any evidence of a cyber component which, given China's control over domestic cyber hacktivist groups and proxy organizations, suggests was a deliberate choice. Relatedly, the inflamed domestic political tensions that were present during the 2012 crisis, including nationalist sentiments expressed in online chat forums, appear to have been largely absent in this case. Instead, available evidence indicates that escalation was avoided through a combination of diplomatic actions, military maneuvers, and China's decision not to intercept military aircraft that traversed the ECS ADIZ without prior warning, as well as stepping back from complete and consistent enforcement, particularly in disputed areas.

The 2018 Russia-U.S. crisis in Syria

In a similar case to the 2015 Russia-Turkey crisis, which involved Russia and a NATO member state, a crisis was triggered during the Syrian conflict when proxy forces affiliated with the Russian government attacked U.S. forces in Syria on February 7, 2018, leading to a protracted four-hour battle.[88] The Battle of Khasham occurred at a Conoco oil refinery in Syria's Deir al-Zour province where a small U.S. outpost manned by a 40-person special operations force was attacked by a pro-Assad force. Prior to and as the battle unfolded, the U.S. military command in Syria contacted the Russian military command via an established deconfliction line, only to be met with repeated denials that the attacking forces were Russian.[89] However, U.S. intelligence collection reportedly indicated that the pro-Assad force was speaking Russian.[90] The United States was able to suppress the attacking force by calling in repeated air strikes that killed an estimated 300 personnel, including an estimated 200 who were a mix of Russian and former Soviet Union nationals.[91]

Joe Biden and Prime Minister Shinzo Abe of Japan," The White House, Office of the Vice President, December 3, 2013.

[87] Ian E. Reinhart and Bart Elias, "China's Air Defense Identification Zone (ADIZ)," Congressional Research Service, January 30, 2015, pp. 17–18.

[88] Thomas Gibbons-Neff, "How a 4-Hour Battle between Russian Mercenaries and U.S. Commandos Unfolded in Syria," The New York Times, May 24, 2018.

[89] "Department of Defense Press Briefing by Lieutenant General Harrigian via Teleconference from Al Udeid Airbase, Qatar," Department of Defense, February 13, 2018.

[90] Gibbons-Neff, "How a 4-Hour Battle between Russian Mercenaries and U.S. Commandos Unfolded in Syria."

[91] Ivan Nechepurenko, Neil MacFarquhar, and Thomas Gibbons-Neff, "Dozens of Russians Are Believed Killed in U.S.-Backed Syria Attack," The New York Times, February 13, 2018.

At a press conference on February 8, then-Defense Secretary James Mattis expressed uncertainty about the links between the attacking force and the Russian government, stating, "I don't think [Russian] contractors were involved—I think the Russians would've told us."[92] U.S. military leaders similarly refused to blame Russia.[93] A former deputy assistant secretary of defense for Russia, Ukraine, and Eurasia noted that the statement likely reflected an effort to signal to Russia, "My guess is [Mattis] said he was perplexed because he was sending a signal to the Russians: 'I am willing to give you a little time to cut this out, but don't do it again.'"[94] This case is fraught with considerable ambiguity about the command and control of Russian proxy forces in Syria. Despite initial denials that Russians were involved, leaked phone calls indicated that the Wagner Group, a Russian-backed paramilitary organization, directly led the attack.[95]

Despite what could have been a dangerous escalation, the crisis ultimately resolved following the use of the military hotline between Russian and U.S. forces, Russia's denial of involvement and, most importantly, Russia's willingness to sacrifice its proxy forces.[96] Russia's decision to absorb those casualties, coupled with ambiguous statements from senior U.S. officials that avoided placing blame on the Russian government, ultimately allowed the crisis to dissipate and both parties to avoid escalation. Furthermore, absent from this crisis was any major domestic political aspect (such as widespread anti-U.S. protests or Russian state-sponsored media capitalizing on the events), as well as any cyber incidents.

Discussion

Given the prolific cyber behavior of the parties to these crises, the events surrounding the 2013 ADIZ crisis and the 2018 crisis between Russia and the United States stand out in terms of the lack of cyber activity. Compared to the 2012 and 2015 crises, this suggests that some types of cyber operations— specifically, those that are visible to domestic or adversary audiences—can act as

[92] James Mattis, "Media Availability with Secretary Mattis," US Department of Defense, February 8, 2018.

[93] "Department of Defense Press Briefing by Lieutenant General Harrigian via Teleconference from Al Udeid Airbase, Qatar."

[94] Eli Lake, "Don't Be Fooled: Russia Attacked U.S. Troops in Syria," *Bloomberg Opinion*, February 16, 2018.

[95] Fatima Tlis, "Zakharova Downplays Armed Clash with Americans in Syria, Kremlin-linked Audio Recordings Contradict Her Story," *Polygraph.info*, February 16, 2018.

[96] Nathaniel Reynolds, "Putin's Not-So-Secret Mercenaries: Patronage, Geopolitics, and the Wagner Group," Carnegie Endowment for International Peace, July 8, 2019; Kimberly Marten, "Into Africa: Prigozhin, Wagner, and the Russian Military," *PONARS Eurasia Policy Memo*, January 4, 2019, https://www.ponarseurasia.org/into-africa-prigozhin-wagner-and-the-russian-military/.

signals during crises. This is especially the case in the context of closed regimes where the government exerts significant control over activity that takes place in and through cyberspace. In the 2013 ADIZ crisis, events unfolded almost entirely in public and decision makers on all sides apparently did not perceive a need for strategic ambiguity. There is also scant evidence of domestic nationalist sentiments being provoked by the crisis. Taken together, this suggests that the context was not particularly conducive for cyber operations as accommodative signals. In the 2018 crisis, events took place in the more private and ambiguous realm. There were private military communications between U.S. and Russian militaries, and the crisis itself was caused by a Russian proxy group with vague links to the Russian government. That said, the absence of a salient domestic political dimension to the crisis and the rapid success of direct, private communication suggests there was not a clear role for cyber operations as accommodative signals.

International Crisis with Cyber Operations as Signals of Resolve

Not all cyber operations that take place during crises necessarily serve accommodative purposes. In fact, differences in how states employ cyber tools to signal to adversaries help illuminate the attributes of accommodative cyber signals versus those used to convey resolve. Two crises, both of which involved the United States, illustrate these differences: the 2019 crisis between Iran and the United States over the Strait of Hormuz and the 2017 crisis between the United States and North Korea over the latter's missile tests. In both of these crises, media reports suggest that the United States conducted covert cyber operations targeting specific government or military assets, as distinct from the noisy, less discriminate cyber operations that were carried out by hacktivist and proxy groups in the 2012 and 2015 crises discussed above. Moreover, these crises differ from the others in that tensions between the United States and Iran and North Korea, respectively, remained high rather than dissipating, even after the immediate events.

The 2019 Strait of Hormuz crisis

In the lead-up to the crisis in the spring and summer of 2019 between Iran and the United States, tensions between the rivals had significantly increased. In May 2018, President Donald Trump withdrew from the 2015 nuclear deal, the Joint Comprehensive Plan of Action, as part of the administration's strategy of "maximum pressure" on Iran.[97] The following month, the United States designated the Islamic Revolutionary Guard Corps (IRGC), a core part of Iran's military organization, a foreign terrorist organization—the first time the United States has applied that label to another state's military, rather than to a non-state actor.[98] As threats to U.S. forces in the region began to increase, the United States announced it was sending a carrier group and bombers to the Persian Gulf to "send a clear and unmistakable message" to Iran, in the words of then-National Security Advisor John Bolton, that "any attack on United States interests or those of our allies will be met with unrelenting force."[99] The United States also imposed a new round of economic sanctions against Iran.[100]

These events set the stage for the crisis that began in May 2019, when four oil tankers, owned by Saudi Arabia, the United Arab Emirates (UAE), and a Norwegian company, were attacked in waters in the region, including the Strait of Hormuz.[101] While it was not immediately clear who was responsible for the attacks, the U.S. government blamed Iran, while other states, such as the UAE more ambiguously stated that the attacks were likely perpetrated by a "state actor" given the level of sophistication.[102] A few days after the oil tanker incident, the United States announced it was sending an additional 1,500 troops to the region to deter Iran and, according to then-Acting Assistant Secretary of Defense for International Security Affairs Katheryn Wheelbarger, "to be responsive to [Iran's] aggressive behavior."[103] However, another attack occurred against two oil tankers in June 2019, this time in the Gulf of Oman. The United States released video that appeared to show an IRGC patrol boat removing a mine from one of the tankers, which led the U.S. government to attribute the attack to Iran. President Donald Trump stated that the mining had, "Iran written all over it," but other U.S. allies expressed skepticism that Iran was responsible.[104] Tensions continued to rise as the United States deployed an additional 1,000 troops to the region, and Iran announced it was at the precipice of breaching existing limits

[97] Mark Landler, "Trump Abandons Nuclear Deal He Long Scorned," The New York Times, May 8, 2018.

[98] Edward Wong and Eric Schmitt, "Trump Designates Iran's Revolutionary Guards a Foreign Terrorist Group," The New York Times, April 8, 2019.

[99] Quint Forgey, "Navy Strike Group Deployed to Send 'Message' to Iran," Politico, May 5, 2019.

[100] For a detailed discussion of U.S. sanctions against Iran, see Kenneth Katzman, "Iran Sanctions," Congressional Research Service, April 6, 2021.

[101] Vivian Yee, "Claim of Attacks on 4 Vessels Raises Tension in the Middle East," The New York Times, May 13, 2019.

[102] "UAE Tanker Attacks Blamed on 'State Actor,'" BBC, July 7, 2019.

[103] Paul Sonne and Missy Ryan, "Trump Approves Sending More Forces to the Middle East Amid Tensions with Iran," The Washington Post, May 24, 2019; Sasha Ingber, "Trump Orders an Additional 1,500 Troops To the Middle East," NPR, May 24, 2019.

[104] Mark Landler, Julian E. Barnes, and Eric Schmitt, "U.S. Puts Iran on Notice and Weighs Response to Attacks on Oil Tankers," The New York Times, July 14, 2019.

on enriched uranium. Then, on June 20, Iran shot down a U.S. surveillance drone that it claimed had violated Iranian airspace, while the U.S. government maintained that the drone was shot down in international waters over the Strait of Hormuz.[105]

Both U.S. and Iranian officials made strident public statements in response to this incident, with each condemning the other side and disputing the other's depiction of the course of events. At the same time, both sides conveyed a desire to avoid war. In response to the shooting down of the drone, President Trump offered an ambiguous statement about how the United States would respond, tweeting, on the one hand, that "Iran made a very big mistake," but also saying, "Let's see what happens." However, Trump also seemed to imply that a "loose and stupid" person may have been responsible for shooting down the U.S. drone, rather than a deliberate attack ordered by Iranian leaders. Iran's ambassador to the United Nations said that Iran was committed to defending its sovereignty but "does not seek war."[106] Nevertheless, the next day President Trump revealed that his administration had initiated, but then walked back, plans to carry out a military strike against Iranian military assets, while publicly implying that military options would remain on the table. Trump tweeted, "We were cocked & loaded to retaliate last night on 3 different sights (sic) when I asked, how many will die. 150 people, sir, was the answer from a General. 10 minutes before the strike I stopped it."[107]

What stands out about this crisis is that it appears that cyber operations were conducted as an alternative to the U.S. military strike against Iran. Given Trump's repeated, public emphasis on concerns about the likely casualties that would follow a kinetic strike and the lack of proportionality, it is reasonable to infer that cyber operations may have been seen as a proportionate response that would not cause death or unnecessarily provoke further escalation. Yet, based on public statements by senior officials, it does not appear that the cyber operations were intended to serve as an accommodative signal. Instead, it is more plausible that they were meant to convey resolve without unduly precipitating a military conflict with Iran.

---

[105] David D. Kirkpatrick, Richard Pérez-Peña, and Stanley Reed, "Tankers Are Attacked in Mideast, and U.S. Says Video Shows Iran Was Involved," *The New York Times*, June 13, 2019; "Strait of Hormuz: US Confirms Drone Shot Down by Iran," *BBC News*, June 20, 2019; Joshua Berlinger, Mohammed Tawfeeq, Barbara Starr, Shirzad Bozorgmehr, and Federik Pleitgen, "Iran Shoots Down US Drone Aircraft, Raising Tensions Further in Strait of Hormuz," *CNN*, June 20, 2019.

[106] Jeremy Diamond, Barbara Starr, Jamie Gangel, and Kate Sullivan, "Trump Says US Was 'Cocked and Loaded' to Strike Iran before He Pulled Back," *CNN*, June 21, 2019; Michael D. Shear, Eric Schmitt, Michael Crowley, and Maggie Haberman, "Strikes on Iran Approved by Trump, Then Abruptly Pulled Back," *The New York Times*, June 20, 2019.

[107] Diamond et al., "Trump Says US Was 'Cocked and Loaded.'"

The day after the United States called off the military strike, media reported that U.S. Cyber Command had conducted a cyber operation against Iran on June 20.[108] Purportedly, it was a targeted, covert cyber operation against Iranian military computer systems that was meant to disable Iran's ability to carry out attacks against marine traffic in the region.[109] Neither the U.S. government nor Iran publicly acknowledged the cyber attacks, but media reports on the cyber operation were based on leaks by anonymous U.S. government officials while the crisis was ongoing.[110]

According to the *New York Times*, the cyber attacks were more long-lasting than DDoS attacks or other short-term disruptions. The attacks, "wiped out a critical database used by Iran's paramilitary arm to plot attacks against oil tankers and degraded Tehran's ability to covertly target shipping traffic in the Persian Gulf." Months later, Iran was purportedly still attempting to recover. They were described by U.S. officials as a signal of resolve to Iran in the context of the crisis, as well as being intended to degrade Iran's ability to conduct attacks in the future.[111] Moreover, unlike the relatively unsophisticated, low-cost cyber attacks that occurred in the 2012 and 2015 crises, according to anonymous U.S. officials the cyber operations that took place against Iran "were in the works for weeks if not months." And while the U.S. government refused to directly comment on reports about the purported cyber operation, Thomas Bossert, who had just recently served as a homeland security advisor in the Trump Administration, publicly stated that, "This operation imposes costs on the growing Iranian cyber threat, but also serves to defend the United States Navy and shipping operations in the Strait of Hormuz."[112]

The crisis did not escalate following the cyber operation. However, it's not clear that the operation served as an effective signal of resolve because tensions remained high and additional incidents occurred in the wake of the June cyber operation. In July, British authorities seized an Iranian tanker; in July and August, Iranian officials seized British and Iraqi tankers; and in September, yet another crisis—also reportedly involving another U.S. cyber operation against Iran—unfolded when an attack took place against a Saudi Aramco oil facility in Saudi Arabia, which the Americans and Saudis blamed on Iran.[113]

---

[108] Julian E. Barnes, "U.S. Cyberattack Hurt Iran's Ability to Target Oil Tankers, Officials Say," *The New York Times*, August 28, 2019.

[109] Ellen Nakashima, "Trump Approved Cyber-strikes against Iranian Computer Databases Used to Plan Attacks on Oil Tankers," *The Washington Post*, June 22, 2019.

[110] Julian E. Barnes and Thomas Gibbons-Neff, "U.S. Carried Out Cyberattacks on Iran," *The New York Times*, June 22, 2019.

[111] Julian E. Barnes, "U.S. Cyber Attack Hurt Iran's Ability to Target Oil Tankers, Officials Say," *The New York Times*, August 28, 2019.

[112] Nakashima, "Trump Approved Cyber-strikes against Iranian Computer Databases Used to Plan Attacks on Oil Tankers."

[113] Ben Hubbard, Palko Karasz, and Stanley Reed, "Two Major Saudi Oil Installations Hit by Drone Strike, and U.S. Blames Iran," *The New York Times*, September 14, 2019; Idris Ali and Phil Stewart,

The 2017 North Korean missile crisis

The crisis that broke out between the United States and North Korea in February 2017 shares a number of key similarities to the 2019 crisis with Iran. As in the 2019 crisis, public reporting suggests the United States conducted a targeted, covert cyber operation against North Korean military assets to signal resolve, while avoiding dangerously escalating the situation, as part of a coercive bargaining strategy coupled with other non-cyber instruments of power, such as diplomatic pressure, economic sanctions, and military exercises and shows of force.[114] Furthermore, the patterns observed in this crisis suggest that, as for the 2019 Iran crisis, this form of cyber signaling may not have been effectively perceived by the target.[115]

A crisis between the United States and North Korea was sparked in February 2017 when, following President Trump's inauguration in January 2017, North Korea began a series of missile tests.[116] The first took place in February 2017 when North Korea successfully launched a medium-range ballistic missile into the Sea of Japan. This was followed by an additional eight missile launches between March and May.[117] In response to North Korea's missile launches, in March 2017 the United States deployed a Terminal High-Altitude Area Defense missile battery system in South Korea (over Chinese objections) and announced in April that the missile defense system was on the cusp of being operational.[118]

"Exclusive: U.S. Carried Out Secret Cyber Strike on Iran in Wake of Saudi Oil Attack: Officials," *Reuters*, October 16, 2019.

[114] Karen DeYoung, Ellen Nakashima, and Emily Rauhala, "Trump Signed Presidential Directive Ordering Actions to Pressure North Korea," *The Washington Post*, September 30, 2017.

[115] Erica D. Borghard, "Lost in Cyber Translation? U.S. Cyber Signaling to North Korea," *Net Politics*, October 16, 2017.

[116] Chloe Sang-Hun, "North Korea Fires Ballistic Missile, Challenging Trump," *The New York Times*, February 11, 2107, https://www.nytimes.com/2017/02/11/world/asia/north-korea-missile-test-trump.html.

[117] "North Korea Missile Tests—a Timeline," *CBS News*, September 6, 2017, https://www.cbsnews.com/news/north-korea-missile-tests-a-timeline/. It's notable that during this time period, the Lazarus Group, the APT associated with the regime in North Korea, is reported to have conducted a number of different cyber attacks, including the WannaCry cyber attack, compromises of cryptocurrency exchanges in South Korea, the compromise of Far Eastern International Bank, and spear phishing attempts against U.S. electrical companies. See CFR Cyber Operations tracker for a further description of each of these. However, these do not appear to be connected to the crisis dynamics unfolding on the Korean peninsula pertaining to the Democratic People's Republic of Korea's (DPRK) missile launches. This demonstrates how cyber operations are a tool of statecraft with a diversity of uses and applications.

[118] Gerry Mullany, "U.S. Antimissile System in South Korea Is Said To Be Nearly Operational," *The New York Times*, April 27, 2017, https://www.nytimes.com/2017/04/27/world/asia/north-korea-thaad-missile-defense-us-china.html. During this time, there was also miscommunication regarding whether the movement of the U.S.S. Carl Vinson was part of the U.S. response to North Korea. Despite President Trump's statement, "We're sending an armada" to the Sea of Japan, this was not the case. See Mark Landler and Eric Schmitt, "Aircraft Carrier Wasn't Sailing to Deter North Korea, as

In the lead-up to a Security Council meeting at the United Nations in April 2017 to address North Korea's missile launches, President Trump stated in an interview that "There is a chance that we could end up having a major, major conflict with North Korea. Absolutely."[119]

On July 4, 2017, a significant incident occurred when the U.S. government confirmed that Pyongyang had, for the first time, successfully conducted an intercontinental ballistic missile launch of the Hwasong-14 into the Sea of Japan.[120] This considerably ratcheted up tensions. The United States stated that it would employ "the full range of capabilities at our disposal against the growing threat." This statement followed a tweet from President Trump the day before stating that "Perhaps China will put a heavy move on North Korea and end this nonsense once and for all."[121] Beyond making statements, the United States also took a number of other steps in response. The following day, U.S. bombers flew over the Korean peninsula and the commander of U.S. Pacific Air Forces released a public statement: "Let me be clear, if called upon we are trained, equipped and ready to unleash the full lethal capability of our allied air forces."[122] U.S. and South Korean forces also conducted a joint military exercise, and U.S. Forces in Korea issued a statement indicating that the alliance had conducted a "combined event exercising assets countering North Korea's destabilizing and unlawful actions" and emphasizing that "U.S. commitment to the defense of the ROK in the face of threats is ironclad."[123]

Nevertheless, North Korea continued to conduct a series of missile launches throughout July and August of 2017, prompting President Trump to threaten on August 8 that North Korea would be "met with fire and fury like the world has never seen" if Pyongyang endangered the security of the United States.[124] A few days later, on August 11, Trump tweeted that "Military solutions are now

U.S. Suggested," *The New York Times*, April 18, 2017, https://www.nytimes.com/2017/04/18/world/asia/aircraft-carrier-north-korea-carl-vinson.html.

[119] "Trump Fears 'Major, Major Conflict,' with North Korea," *BBC News*, April 28, 2017, https://www.bbc.com/news/world-asia-39741671.

[120] "North Korea Missile Activity in 2017," Center for Arms Control and Non-Proliferation, November 30, 2017, https://armscontrolcenter.org/fact-sheet-north-korea-missile-activity-2017/.

[121] Choe Sang-Hun, "U.S. Confirms North Korea Fired Intercontinental Ballistic Missile," *The New York Times*, July 4, 2017, https://www.nytimes.com/2017/07/04/world/asia/north-korea-miss ile-test-icbm.html; https://twitter.com/realDonaldTrump/status/882062572081512449.

[122] Chieu Luu, Brad Lendon, and Zachary Cohen, "US Bombers Fly over Korean Peninsula in Response to N.Korea's ICBM test," *CNN*, July 8, 2017, https://edition.cnn.com/2017/07/08/asia/us-bombers-north-korea-icbm-test/index.html.

[123] "ROK-US Alliance Demonstrates Precision Firing Capability," United States Forces Korea, July 4, 2017, https://www.usfk.mil/Media/News/Article/1236985/rok-us-alliance-demonstrates-precis ion-firing-capability/.

[124] Peter Baker and Chloe Sang-Hun, "Trump Threatens 'Fire and Fury' against North Korea if It Endangers U.S," *The New York Times*, August 8, 2017, https://www.nytimes.com/2017/08/08/world/asia/north-korea-un-sanctions-nuclear-missile-united-nations.html.

fully in place, locked and loaded, should North Korea act unwisely. Hopefully Kim Jong Un will find another path!"[125] In August 21–31, U.S. and South Korean forces conducted an annual military exercise, Exercise Ulchi Freedom Guardian, which, as noted by the U.S. Department of Defense in an official press release on August 18, was "designed to enhance readiness, protect the region and maintain stability on the Korean peninsula [and] highlight the longstanding military partnership, commitment and enduring friendship between the two nations."[126] North Korea responded by launching three more short-range ballistic missiles on August 26, and on August 29 "carried out one of its most provocative missile tests in recent years [by] hurling a ballistic missile directly over Japan."[127] On August 31, in a show of force to North Korea, the United States flew two B-1B bombers and four F-35 fighter jets over South Korea.[128]

The crisis reached its height on September 3, when North Korea conducted its sixth nuclear test, which it claimed was a successful hydrogen bomb test, prompting the UN Security Council to impose additional sanctions on the regime and President Trump to publicly state that even the threat by North Korea to use nuclear weapons would be "met with a massive military response."[129] Following North Korea's launch of a missile over Japan on September 15, President Trump addressed the UN General Assembly on September 19 and threatened that if the U.S. were "forced to defend itself or its allies, we will have no choice but to totally destroy North Korea."[130] A few days later, the administration issued an executive order imposing additional sanctions on North Korea in response to "[t]he provocative, destabilizing, and repressive actions and politics of the Government of North Korea, including its intercontinental ballistic

---

[125] Donald Trump, Twitter post, August 11, 2017, 7:29AM, https://twitter.com/realdonaldtrump/status/895970429734711298?lang=en.

[126] "Exercise Ulchi Freedom Guardian 2017," U.S. Dept of Defense, August 18, 2017, https://www.defense.gov/Newsroom/Releases/Release/Article/1282786/exercise-ulchi-freedom-guardian-2017/.

[127] "North Korea Fires Three Missiles into Sea," *BBC News*, August 26, 2017, https://www.bbc.com/news/world-asia-41058152; Chloe Sang-Hun and David E. Sanger, "North Korea Fires Missile Over Japan," *The New York Times*, August 28, 2017, https://www.nytimes.com/2017/08/28/world/asia/north-korea-missile.html.

[128] Chloe Sang-Hun, "2 Days after North Korea Missile Test, a Show of U.S. Airpower," *The New York Times*, August 31, 2017, https://www.nytimes.com/2017/08/31/world/asia/north-korea-south-korea-us-joint-exercises.html.

[129] "Sixth Nuclear Test Detected at Punggye-ri, Declared to be a Hydrogen Bomb" *38 North*, September 3, 2017, https://www.38north.org/2017/09/nuke090317/; David E. Sanger and Choe Sang-Hun, "North Korean Test Draws U.S. Warning of 'Massive Military Response,'" *The New York Times*, September 2, 2017, https://www.nytimes.com/2017/09/03/world/asia/north-korea-tremor-possible-6th-nuclear-test.html.

[130] Remarks by President Trump to the 72nd Session of the United Nations General Assembly, The White House, September 19, 2017, https://trumpwhitehouse.archives.gov/briefings-statements/remarks-president-trump-74th-session-united-nations-general-assembly/.

missile launches . . . and nuclear tests."[131] North Korea responded with belli-
cose language, with Kim Jong Un declaring President Trump to be a "mentally
deranged U.S. dotard" and Foreign Minister Ri Yong-ho describing President
Trump's comments about North Korea as equivalent to a declaration of war that
would justify the them shooting down U.S. bombers—which had just flown to
their northernmost point near North Korea's coast in decades.[132]

On September 30, the *Washington Post* reported that President Trump had
signed a secret presidential directive to pursue a strategy of maximum pressure against North Korea, which allegedly "led to the use of military cyber-
capabilities."[133] This reportedly included a denial of service cyber operation
against the Reconnaissance General Bureau (RGB), North Korea's military intelligence organization, to temporarily disrupt RGB computers' internet access. At
the time the article was published, the journalists claimed that the cyber operation was ongoing, slated to end that day, and "part of the overall campaign set in
motion many months ago."[134] If this report is true, this type of cyber operation
had only temporary, disruptive effects. It reportedly had "a limited effect on the
RBG's networks and capabilities. It is not the equivalent of a disarming offensive
first strike in the cyber realm. Rather, the U.S. had ostensibly chosen to deliberately use relatively unsophisticated tools—a denial-of-service attack—to take the
cyber equivalent of a shot across North Korea's bow, presumably signaling that it

[131] Presidential Executive Order Imposing Additional Sanctions with Respect to North Korea, The
White House, September 21, 2017, https://trumpwhitehouse.archives.gov/presidential-actions/presi
dential-executive-order-imposing-additional-sanctions-respect-north-korea/.

[132] Chloe Sang-Hun, "Kim's Rejoinder to Trump's Rocket Man: 'Mentally Deranged U.S. Dotard,'"
The New York Times, September 21, 2017, https://www.nytimes.com/2017/09/21/world/asia/
kim-trump-rocketman-dotard.html; Paul Mcleary, "North Korea Threatens to Shoot Down U.S.
Bombers," *Foreign Policy*, September 25, 2017, https://foreignpolicy.com/2017/09/25/north-korea-
threatens-to-shoot-down-u-s-bombers/. There was some mixed messaging on the part of the Trump
Administration during this time, with then-Secretary of State Rex Tillerson seeming to walk back
some of the president's more strident statements and noting that the United States was holding
"probing" talks with North Korea. See David E. Sanger, "U.S. in Direct Communication with North
Korea, Says Tillerson," *The New York Times*, September 30, 2017, https://www.nytimes.com/2017/09/
30/world/asia/us-north-korea-tillerson.html.

[133] DeYoung et al., "Trump Signed Presidential Directive Ordering Actions to Pressure North
Korea." Separately, in March 2017, the *New York Times* published a long article claiming that
the United States had conducted a long-term cyber campaign, that began during the Obama
Administration, to sabotage North Korea's missile program. See David E. Sanger and William J.
Broad, "Trump Inherits a Secret Cyberwar against North Korean Missiles," *The New York Times*,
March 4, 2017, https://www.nytimes.com/2017/03/04/world/asia/north-korea-missile-program-
sabotage.html. It is not clear how much, if any, of this reporting is accurate and what the impact may
have been, if any, on North Korea's program. See Andy Greenberg, "Hacking North Korea Is Easy. Its
Nukes? Not So Much," *Wired*, October 10, 2017, https://www.wired.com/story/cyberattack-north-
korea-nukes/.

[134] DeYoung et al., "Trump Signed Presidential Directive Ordering Actions to Pressure North
Korea."

has the requisite access to North Korean networks to deliver considerably more significant damage in wartime."[135]

The sequence of a denial of service cyber operation coupled with an informal, ambiguous post-hoc claim of responsibility from the U.S. government via a leak by an unnamed "senior administration official" linking the operation to a broader maximum pressure campaign, likely represented an attempt by the Trump Administration to send a signal of resolve to North Korea.

Following the purported cyber operation, there was a temporary lull in the crisis. There were some concerns that North Korea might launch cyber attacks against U.S. critical infrastructure during this time period, but this did not occur.[136] Furthermore, for the next two months, North Korea did not conduct a missile test. It is difficult to ascertain the meaning behind this calming of tensions and whether it represented an attempt by Kim Jong Un to implicitly provide an opportunity for the United States to pursue a more diplomatic approach rather than continue to implement the maximum pressure campaign. It is also not clear the extent to which the cyber operation may have played a role in contributing to this breathing room. Indeed, the U.S. special envoy to South Korea remarked in November 2017 regarding the pause in the North's missile that "I hope that they will stop forever. But we had no communication from them so I don't know whether to interpret it positively or not. We have no signal from them."[137]

Given the limited information about North Korean decision-making, we can only speculate as to whether the regime may have (mis)interpreted the actions coming from the United States—such as the denial of service cyber operation coupled with Secretary of State Rex Tillerson's multiple, public statements during this time period about the United States' willingness to pursue diplomatic negotiations and assure North Korea that it was not seeking to conduct regime change, promote the North's collapse, invade, or force the reunification of the peninsula—as an opportunity for de-escalation;[138] whether the regime was simply regrouping only to resume missile launches; or whether there were domestic or unrelated reasons behind the lull in aggressive activity. Regardless, this brief suspension of tension ended when North Korea launched an intercontinental ballistic missile into Japan's exclusive economic

[135] Ankit Panda, "How to Make Sense of Offensive US Cyber Operations against North Korean Military Intelligence," *The Diplomat*, October 2, 2017, https://thediplomat.com/2017/10/how-to-make-sense-of-offensive-us-cyber-operations-against-north-korean-military-intelligence/.

[136] James A. Lewis, "North Korea and Cyber Catastrophe—Don't Hold Your Breath," *38 North*, January 12, 2018, https://www.38north.org/2018/01/jalewis011218/.

[137] "U.S. Envoy Says No Communication, No Signal from North Korea Amid Nuclear Crisis," *Reuters*, November 16, 2017, https://www.reuters.com/article/us-northkorea-missiles-southkorea-usa/u-s-envoy-says-no-communication-no-signal-from-north-korea-amid-nuclear-crisis-idUSKBN1DH0F7.

[138] Spencer D. Bakich, "Signalling Capacity and Crisis Diplomacy: Explaining the Failure of 'Maximum Pressure' in the 2017 U.S.-North Korea Nuclear Crisis," *Journal of Strategic Studies* 45, no. 5 (2020): 15.

zone on November 29, and in December the Trump Administration implied that the United States was considering a "bloody nose" limited airstrike against North Korea to signal U.S. resolve to go to war if Pyongyang refused to renounce its nuclear weapons program.[139]

The crisis continued into the following year, despite North and South Korea establishing a hotline and engaging in diplomatic discussion, as the United States pursued its maximum pressure approach and imposed additional sanctions on North Korea. The United States also raised the specter of military action once again through President Trump's comment in February 2018 that "[i]f sanctions don't work, we'll have to go to phase two. Phase two may be a very rough thing, may be very, very unfortunate for the world."[140] While the crisis did not ultimately escalate to military conflict, the two diplomatic summits between President Trump and Kim Jong Un in the spring of 2018 did not lead to any meaningful steps toward North Korean denuclearization, representing a failure of maximum pressure.[141]

Discussion

Cyber operations played a different role in these crises than in the others we examined, illustrating the differences between cyber operations conducted to convey resolve rather than accommodation. Nevertheless, it is notable that none of these crises escalated, despite the differential uses of cyber operations. In the 2012 and 2015 crises, proxy and hacktivist groups conducted low-cost but highly visible cyber attacks against a wide array of government and private sector targets, in the context of mobilized domestic publics and sustained—even violent—protests. However, in the 2017 and 2019 crises the cyber operations were reportedly directly conducted by government forces, highly tailored to their targets (and specifically targeted networks used by government and military organizations), and involved some level of prior planning, suggesting they were more sophisticated. However, one key difference between the cyber operations that occurred during the latter crises, as they were reported by prominent medias outlets, is that in the Iran case the cyber operations had a more significant and sustained impact on Iranian military and intelligence capabilities, while in the North Korea case public evidence suggests the effects were more transient and short-lived.

[139] Bakich, "Signalling Capacity and Crisis Diplomacy," pp. 13, 17.
[140] Steve Holland and Christine Kim, "U.S. Imposes More North Korea Sanctions, Trump Warns of 'Phase Two,'" *Reuters*, February 23, 2018, https://es.reuters.com/article/idUSKCN1G71RD.
[141] Bakich, "Signalling Capacity and Crisis Diplomacy"; Victor Cha and Katrin Fraser Katz, "The Right Way to Coerce North Korea: Ending the Threat Without Going to War," *Foreign Affairs* (2018): 87–100.

Moreover, the cyber operations that took place during the course of both of these crises were covert and not immediately visible to domestic audiences. These factors, in conjunction with the absence of hawkish domestic political constituencies in the United States pressuring the Trump Administration to take an *even* harder stance on Iran or North Korea, suggests accommodative signaling mechanisms to assuage nationalistic domestic audiences while eschewing escalation were likely not at play in this case. Instead, it is far more plausible that the intended audience was the adversary government itself and that the leaks by U.S. government officials about the cyber operations during the course of the crises were likely meant to enable the Iranian and North Korean governments to understand that their networks were degraded or disrupted as a result of U.S. government actions in cyberspace—a signal of resolve. Another shared feature of these crises is that direct, private communications were not viable given the lack of diplomatic relations between the United States and Iran and North Korea. Moreover, the crises did not quickly resolve in the wake of the cyber operations; instead, despite temporary lulls, friction between the two sides persisted, and tensions flared up again a few months later.

These episodes demonstrate that states perceive different utilities for cyber operations during international crises and also that a state's aim to use cyber operations to signal resolve is complicated by plausible deniability, limitations on generating costs, and the challenges of conducting strategic, decisive cyber operations. First, signals need to be perceived as such by a target to be effective. However, the United States was likely facing competing incentives regarding the extent to which it should go public about cyber operations against both North Korea and Iran for signaling purposes. Secrecy is important for operational success, which may account for anonymous government officials leaking information to the press about the cyber operations after they had already occurred— especially if both operations had been months in the making, as was reported. Moreover, in the case of North Korea, given the unreliability of that country's rudimentary internet infrastructure, it is plausible that the leak may have been necessary to ensure North Korea actually received the signal and linked it to the United States, rather than it getting lost in the noise. It is also plausible that similar dynamics were at play in the Iran case; computer malfunctioning may not have been easily attributed to a deliberate cyber operation, necessitating coupling the cyber operation with other forms of communication.

The North Korea case in particular illustrates how sending costly signals to convey resolve is difficult in cyberspace. A denial of service attack, such as that purportedly launched against North Korea's RGB, may have disrupted system functioning for a period of time but would not have had permanent effects and was likely not costly for the target to absorb. This contrasts with the cyber operation reportedly conducted against Iran, which degraded Iranian computer systems for a longer period of time. In the immediate wake of the alleged denial of service operation, there were reports that North Korea had established a new means of access to the internet through Russia, ostensibly increasing its resilience to denial of service attacks and reducing dependence on China, which had been the sole source of internet traffic routed to and from North Korea.[142] This would have further reduced the impact of the operation and illustrates how targets can adapt to mitigate the consequences of cyber operations, especially disruptive ones.

Finally, in both cases, there was a significant mismatch between the cyber signal and other signals that were being sent at the time in terms of the scale and costs—especially the looming threat of military conflict, which shaped interactions between adversaries during both crises. Therefore, while a cyber operation inherently conveys less resolve than, for example, a limited military strike, it also is far less likely to cause a crisis to escalate.[143]

Conclusion

Taken together, the two cases most illustrative of accommodative cyber signaling share marked similarities in terms of how the crises unfolded. They began with unsuccessful attempts at resolution through private backchannels, coupled with agitated domestic constituencies. This was followed by cyber operations with ambiguous attribution and public statements by both sides that strove to balance the need to satisfy domestic interests while avoiding actions that might further escalate ongoing events. Comparing these to similar crises without cyber operations enables us to draw inferences about when states perceive a utility in using cyber operations as accommodative signals. Specifically, cyber-capable states, such as Russia and China, do not always employ or permit cyber attacks during international crises. This suggests the use of cyber operations is a deliberate choice meant to convey some intent. Moreover, the crises between the United States and Iran and between the United States and North Korea, which involved different types of cyber operation, illustrates the distinction between cyber signals for resolve versus accommodation—even as all of these crises ultimately did not lead to military conflict. Accommodative cyber signals are characterized by widespread but lost-cost and transient effects, coupled with deliberate decisions

[142] Martyn Williams, "Russia Provides New Internet Connection to North Korea," *38 North*, October 1, 2017, https://www.38north.org/2017/10/mwilliams100117/.

[143] Contradictory signals between the president and secretary of state likely further muddied the waters in the North Korea case. See Peter Baker and David E. Sanger, "Trump Says Tillerson Is 'Wasting His Time' On North Korea," *The New York Times*, October 1, 2017, https://www.nytimes.com/2017/10/01/us/politics/trump-tillerson-north-korea.html.

by both parties to strategically use the ambiguity of attribution to avoid further inflaming domestic sentiments. In contrast, cyber signals of resolve are more tailored, directed against government or military targets in a way that is more specifically linked to the ongoing crisis, require greater investments in planning, and are likely to be carried out by entities more directly affiliated with the government (such as military or intelligence units). The audience for these cyber signals is the adversary government.

Taken together, these cases provide strong support for our argument that the factors that make cyber operations unlikely to trigger escalation have implications for their utility as signaling tools. However, the fact that cyber operations have not received as much consideration in policy circles as signaling tools for accommodation and de-escalation suggests that policymakers should give careful attention to how cyber operations might be employed in this capacity, a subject we explore further in the conclusion to this book.

7

Plausible Escalation Scenarios for the Future

Cyber Operations in a Warfighting Context

The Link between Cyberspace and Conflict

Throughout this book we have argued that cyber operations are unlikely to cause escalation between rival states. We have also argued that some of the same factors that mitigate the risks of cyber operations leading to escalation can sometimes make them useful for de-escalating international crises. But this does not mean that cyber operations will *never* lead to escalation. Therefore, in this chapter we explore the very narrow set of plausible circumstances under which cyber operations are more likely to result in escalation. Specifically, we contend that cyber escalation risks are most salient when cyber operations have an effect on a state's warfighting capabilities—especially during the course of conflict. In other words, escalation is most likely to take place not through the independent employment of cyber power but, rather, when cyber operations are perceived to affect the use of kinetic military capabilities. Our analysis in this chapter is hypothetical, based on scenarios that could conceivably take place between rival states, but which have not yet occurred. Moreover, the highly contingent nature of these scenarios—coupled with what we know about the difficulties of cyber operations and their limited effects—strongly suggests caution about drawing overly pessimistic assessments about escalation risks. That said, systematically examining some plausible use cases is important for policymaking, especially given their potential consequences.

Scholars have explored how escalation from cyber to kinetic military operations could occur through incentives to strike first and the emergence of windows of vulnerability. We provide some additional nuance to this literature to develop different scenarios for cyber operations during wartime versus in the lead-up to conflict and argue that once hostilities have commenced, the escalation risks stemming from cyber operations that target critical military capabilities are likely to be far more significant than cyber operations that occur short of war. We also further refine the literature to distinguish between different types of military targets of cyber operations, evaluating how variation across target sets may affect

Escalation Dynamics in Cyberspace. Erica D. Lonergan and Shawn W. Lonergan, Oxford University Press.
© Oxford University Press 2023. DOI: 10.1093/oso/9780197550885.003.0007

the likelihood of an escalatory response. Finally, our scenarios take into account the form that escalation may take—whether a state escalates with the specific military capability that a cyber operation is targeting (through a "use it or lose" it calculation) or with other military capabilities. These plausible scenarios are meant to serve as a guide for policymakers to help inform risk assessments and decision-making around the conduct of cyber operations, which we explore further in the next chapter.

Cross-Domain Escalation Pathways

Theoretically, there are a few circumstances in which cyber operations could lead to escalation when they affect a state's conventional warfighting or nuclear deterrence capabilities. However, the universe of potential cases is relatively narrow. For one, there is an enormous amount of cyber activity that routinely targets a states' military capabilities that has not risen to a level that would prompt escalation. This type of activity generally falls under the category of cyber espionage and intelligence property theft. Media reports, for instance, have described the U.S. Navy as being "under siege" by Chinese-backed cyber operators; for years the U.S. defense industrial base has been beset by large-scale cyber-enabled exploitation and intellectual property theft; and multiple U.S. government reports have highlighted the persistent cyber vulnerabilities of advanced weapon systems.[1]

Separate from cyber espionage against military targets, there are two potential sets of scenarios in which cyber operations that threaten a state's military capabilities could conceivably lead to escalation. The first involves escalation *to* war. Following traditional arguments in the security studies literature about the link between first strike incentives and the onset of war, a cyber operation could lead to escalation when it is perceived by a target state as being a precursor to imminent war—where the attacking state is seen as using cyber operations to prepare the battlefield for a forthcoming kinetic strike. For example, when Russia began to mass troops along the border with Ukraine in the winter of 2021–2022, these moves were accompanied by an increase in cyber intrusions against Ukrainian targets, and some commentators warned that Russia's actions

---

[1] Gordon Lubold and Dustin Volz, "Navy, Industry Partners Are 'Under Cyber Siege' by Chinese Hackers, Review Asserts," *The Wall Street Journal*, March 12, 2019; Erica D. Borghard and Shawn W. Lonergan, "Chinese Hackers Are Stealing U.S. Defense Secrets: Here Is How to Stop Them," *Council on Foreign Relations: NetPolitics*, March 11, 2019. See, for example, "Weapon Systems Cybersecurity: DOD Just Beginning to Grapple with Scale of Vulnerabilities," Government Accountability Office, October 9, 2018; Erica D. Borghard and Madison Creery, "Persistent Vulnerabilities: Strengthening Cybersecurity Requirements for the Department of Defense," *Council on Foreign Relations: NetPolitics*, June 17, 2020.

in cyberspace were a precursor to an invasion of Ukraine. In particular, cyber operations were seen as shaping the information environment to influence the Ukrainian population's perception of the situation, as well as potentially holding targets at risk to attack in cyberspace in tandem with or in support of battle-field operations—as Russia did when it annexed Crimea in 2014.[2] The second potential scenario involves escalation *within* war, once the fighting has already commenced. This may occur when cyber operations create a perceived window of vulnerability that threatens to shift the balance of power during a conflict in a way that would meaningfully disadvantage one side.

Across both of these potential situations, escalation risks are likely to be con-tingent on organizational, strategic, and contextual variables. Assuming that an attacking state is able to carry out a cyber operation against an adversary's military capabilities and that the target is able to discern that operation within the timeframe of a crisis or conflict—two critical conditions that may only rarely be satisfied—we argue that there are several factors that shape escalation risks. One is how the observed cyber operation maps onto the target's percep-tion of its *adversary's* strategy and doctrine of force employment (for instance, whether an adversary promulgates strategic concepts that rely on cyber opera-tions as a precursor to conventional strikes). Another is how dependent a state's *own* warfighting strategy is on the military capabilities being targeted in cyber-space. A related factor is the extent to which the target perceives a cyber attack as changing the wartime balance of power. And a final factor is the extent to which command and control decisions for force employment are delegated down the chain of command. This means that *any* cyber operation against *any* military capability does not automatically increase the chances of escalation—even with respect to cyber operations targeting nuclear forces or nuclear command and control.

Furthermore, both in the lead-up to and during conflict, we hypothesize that the nature of escalation should be different depending on the particular weapon systems being targeted. Specifically, when cyber operations are conducted against offensive and nuclear capabilities, escalation is likely to occur through a use it or lose it dynamic. In this context, a state employs the capability it assesses as being targeted in cyberspace before the adversary can carry out the cyber operation against that capability. Alternatively, for defensive capabilities and command, control, communications, computers, intelligence, surveillance, and reconnais-sance (C4ISR) capabilities, what we term escalation by other means is likely to

[2] Nadiya Kostyuk and Yuri M. Zhukov, "Invisible Digital Front: Can Cyber Attacks Shape Battlefield Events?," *Journal of Conflict Resolution* 63, no. 2 (2019): 317–347; Maggie Miller, "Russia Invasion of Ukraine Could Redefine Cyber Warfare," *Politico*, January 28, 2022; Maggie Miller, "US Concerns Grow over Potential Russian Cyber Targeting of Ukraine Amid Troop Buildup," *The Hill*, December 16, 2021.

take place. In other words, the targeted state is likely to escalate by increasing the level of violence or scope of a conflict through employing military capabilities that are not being targeted by adversary cyber activity. Taken together, these factors (the distinction between the lead-up to conflict and warfighting and the type of capability being targeted through cyber means) create four potential escalation scenarios with different expectations about behavior, summarized in Table 7.1. Across all of the potential outcomes in the table, the less critical the capability or the more resilient or redundant measures a target possesses, the lower the probability is of escalation.

Importantly, a number of factors, discussed at length in the prior chapters, raise the threshold at which these kinds of scenarios are likely to unfold in the first place, which likely accounts for why our analysis, at this point, is hypothetical. For instance, while cyber operations are typically stealthy, they must be perceived by the target during a potential crisis or conflict to generate the expected outcomes described in Table 7.1. Additionally, an observed cyber operation must be attributed with some level of confidence to an adversary. While this threshold is likely lower during conflict and hostilities, states may be even more attuned to the risks of inadvertent escalation stemming from ambiguous

Table 7.1 Escalation Pathways When Cyber Operations Target Warfighting Capabilities

	Cyber Operations Targeting Offensive Conventional or Nuclear Capabilities	Cyber Operations Targeting Defensive Conventional or C4ISR Capabilities
Lead Up to Conflict	Escalation is likely to take place if the cyber operation is *perceived as a precursor to war*, based on force employment strategies. Escalation will occur through a *use it or lose it* logic.	Escalation is likely to take place if the cyber operation is *perceived as a precursor to war*, based on force employment strategies. Escalation will occur through an *escalation by other means* logic.
During Conflict	Escalation is likely to take place if the cyber operation is *perceived as changing the battlefield balance of power*. Escalation will occur through a *use it or lose it* logic. Risk is heightened during wartime because authority is likely to delegated down.	Escalation is likely to take place if the cyber operation is *perceived as changing the battlefield balance of power*. Escalation will occur through an *escalate by other means* logic. Risk is heightened during wartime because authority is likely to delegated down.

attribution or even false flags during crises. For instance, when Ukraine experienced a cyber attack in January 2022 involving defacements of government websites and evidence of potential future cyber attacks in the middle of a crisis with Russia—where the threat of Russian invasion loomed large—the Ukrainian government attributed it to a group linked to Belarus. While Russia and Belarus have close ties, the extent of Russia's responsibility for the attack remained uncertain, and there was no immediate escalation on Ukraine's part.[3] Finally, much of the discussion in this chapter rests on propositions about what might be technologically feasible. However, elsewhere in the book we have described how cyber operations are highly imperfect, unpredictable, and limited in their ability to reliably cause intended effects at precise times. Altogether, these aspects of cyber operations reduce the likelihood that the scenarios described here may unfold.

How Vulnerable Are Weapon Systems to Cyber Operations?

In technologically advanced states, conventional and nuclear capabilities often depend on digital infrastructure for critical functions and processes. This provides an indirect pathway for adversaries to hold these capabilities at risk. Cyber operations could, in theory, manipulate, degrade, or otherwise undermine the effectiveness and intended employment of key military systems and functions that buttress state security, warfighting capabilities, and regime survival. This includes cyber operations against conventional offensive and defensive capabilities (e.g., integrated air defenses or cruise missiles), C4ISR capabilities, and nuclear forces, including nuclear command, control, and communications (NC3).[4] For a number of years, policymakers and practitioners have been sounding the alarm about cyber risks to conventional and nuclear weapon systems, but the specific mechanisms through which cyber operations targeting these capabilities could trigger escalation have not yet been fully understood or explicated.

The proliferation of these advanced capabilities began in earnest in the wake of the Persian Gulf War as they were demonstrated with stunning effect when the United States rapidly defeated the Iraqi army 1991. In the ensuing decades, modern militaries have pursued technologically advanced capabilities that rely on a complex "system of systems" of information technologies—what some have

---

[3] Pavel Polityuk, "EXCLUSIVE Ukraine Suspects Group Linked to Belarus Intelligence over Cyberattack," *Reuters*, January 15, 2022. Pavel Polityuk and Steve Holland, "Cyberattack Hits Ukraine as U.S. Warns Russia Could Be Prepping for War," *Reuters*, January 14, 2022.

[4] For a more detailed discussion of cyber threats to NC3, see Andrew Futter, "Cyber Threats and Nuclear Weapons: New Questions for Command and Control, Security and Strategy," *RUSI Occasional Paper* (July 2016), https://nsarchive.gwu.edu/sites/default/files/documents/3460884/Document-07-Andrew-Futter-Royal-United-Services.pdf.

called a revolution in military affairs.[5] These innovations have enabled, "long-range, precision-guided munitions (PGMs), C4I (command, control, communications, computers, and information), and RSTA (reconnaissance, surveillance, targeting acquisition) in a form that completely changed the combat environment and altered the way militaries think about the aims and methods of conventional warfare."[6]

However, an unanticipated consequence of these military technological advances is the numerous and often unknown vulnerabilities and access points that exist across modern weapon systems. These could provide adversaries a surreptitious means of gaining access to these systems for the purposes of espionage or attack. Furthermore, as weapon systems become increasingly complex and networked, to include the interaction of legacy and modern platforms, otherwise highly capable militaries may find themselves stymied in even assessing and understanding the full scope of cyber vulnerabilities, let alone developing and implementing measures to remediate them.[7]

States are attuned to these vulnerabilities. In the United States, for example, the defense and energy departments have been concerned about cyber vulnerabilities and the acquisition process for emerging technologies for over a decade.[8] An unclassified 2018 Government Accountability Office (GAO) report to the Senate Armed Services Committee examined cyber threats to specific weapons systems and highlighted ongoing deficiencies in efforts by the Department of Defense to remedy them as well as incorporate cybersecurity considerations into the entire acquisition lifecycle.[9] In 2019, the National Security Agency created the Cybersecurity Directorate to address cyber threats to national security systems

[5] See, for example, Eliot A. Cohen, "A Revolution in Warfare," *Foreign Affairs* 75, no. 2 (March–April 1996): 37–54; Michael Horowitz, *The Diffusion of Military Power: Causes and Consequences for International Politics* (Princeton, NJ: Princeton University Press, 2010), pp. 13–16; Andrew F. Krepinevich, Jr., "The Military-Technical Revolution: A Preliminary Assessment," Center for Strategic and Budgetary Analysis, 2002; Robert O.Work and Greg Grant, "Beating the Americans at Their Own Game," Center for a New American Security, June 6, 2019. "Remarks by Deputy Secretary Work on Third Offset Strategy," https://www.defense.gov/Newsroom/Speeches/Speech/Article/753482/remarks-by-d%20eputy-secretary-work-on-third-offset-strategy/.
[6] Dima Adamsky, *The Culture of Military Innovation: The Impact of Cultural Factors on the Revolution in Military Affairs in Russia, the US, and Israel* (Stanford, CA: Stanford University Press, 2010), p. 2. But see Stephen Biddle, *Military Power: Explaining Victory and Defeat in Modern Battle* (Princeton, NJ: Princeton University Press, 2006), for a different take on how "revolutionary" this new RMA may actually be.
[7] Robert Koch and Mario Golling, "Weapons Systems and Cyber Security—A Challenging Union," Paper Presented at the 2016 8th International Conference on Cyber Conflict, NATO CCDCOE, https://www.ccdcoe.org/uploads/2018/10/Art-12-Weapons-Systems-and-Cyber-Security-A-Challenging-Union.pdf.
[8] Office of Inspector General, "Progress and Challenges in Securing the Nation's Cyberspace," edited by Department of Homeland Security, Office of Information Technology, July 2004, pp. 1–36, https://nsarchive2.gwu.edu/NSAEBB/NSAEBB424/docs/Cyber-019.pdf.
[9] Christina Chaplain, "Weapon Systems Cybersecurity: DoD Just Beginning to Grapple with Scale of Vulnerabilities," GAO Report No. GAO-19-128, 2018, p 2.

and the defense industrial base (which comprises tens of thousands of private companies that contract with the Department of Defense).[10]

Beyond conventional weapon systems, policymakers have also recognized cyber threats to nuclear forces and NC3. The latter encompass a vast and diverse system of early warning, information collection, and communications capabilities that provide notice about impending nuclear strikes and support the maintenance of positive and negative control of nuclear weapons during peacetime and conflict.[11] In the United States, a 2017 Defense Science Board report highlighted the importance of ensuring the resilience of nuclear forces, with a particular emphasis on NC3. The report recommended that the Secretary of Defense "conduct an annual assessment of the cyber resilience of the U.S. nuclear deterrent including all essential nuclear 'Thin Line' components (e.g., NC3, platforms, delivery systems, and warheads)."[12] Similarly, the 2018 Nuclear Posture Review highlighted concerns about adversary cyber threats to NC3 systems, noting that "[t]he emergence of offensive cyber warfare capabilities has created new challenges and potential vulnerabilities for the NC3 system. Potential adversaries are expending considerable effort to design and use cyber weapons against networked systems."[13]

These concerns have not been limited to the United States. For example, a 2016 White Paper published by the Australian Department of Defense warned that "[c]yber attacks are a direct threat to the ADF's [Australian Defense Forces] warfighting ability given its reliance on information networks."[14] Similar concerns have been prevalent in the United Kingdom for nearly a decade, given the reliance of the its armed forces on advanced information and communications technologies and the potential for adversaries to exploit vulnerabilities.[15]

Yet, much of the policy focus has been on how cyber threats could affect mission assurance—ensuring the functioning of capabilities, particularly under degraded, wartime conditions—or reducing the scale of cyber-enabled espionage and intellectual property theft. Relatively little policy attention has been devoted to the risks of escalation stemming from cyber vulnerabilities to

[10] Frank Konkel, "Inside the NSA's New Cybersecurity Directorate," *Nextgov*, October 11, 2019, https://www.nextgov.com/cybersecurity/2019/10/inside-nsas-new-cybersecurity-directorate/160 566/; Defense Industrial Base Sector, *Cybersecurity and Infrastructure Security Agency*, accessed November 2020, https://www.cisa.gov/defense-industrial-base-sector.

[11] "The Nuclear Matters Handbook 2020," *Office of the Deputy Assistant Secretary of Defense for Nuclear Matters*, 2020, ch. 2.

[12] "Task Force on Cyber Deterrence," p. 24, https://dsb.cto.mil/reports/2010s/DSB-CyberDete rrenceReport_02-28-17_Final.pdf.

[13] "Nuclear Posture Review," *U.S. Department of Defense*, 2018, p. 57, https://media.defense.gov/ 2018/Feb/02/2001872886/-1/-1/1/2018-NUCLEAR-POSTURE-REVIEW-FINAL-REPORT.PDF.

[14] "2016 Defence White Paper," *Australian Government, Department of Defense*, 2016, p. 52.

[15] Nick Hopkins, "British Military at Risk of 'Fatal' Cyber-attack, MPs Warn," *The Guardian*, January 9, 2013, https://www.theguardian.com/politics/2013/jan/09/armed-forces-cyber-strategy-criticised.

conventional and nuclear weapon systems and plausible scenarios where escalation could occur.

Cyber Scholarship on Cross-Domain Escalation

In contrast, scholars have homed in on this potential for cross-domain escalation. A good portion of this literature specifically focuses on cyber threats to nuclear command and control—arguably, the most exigent threat. We build on and refine this foundation to develop plausible scenarios to inform policymaking. Specifically, much of the literature does not explore potential differences in escalation risks in the lead-up to war versus once conflict has already commenced, or consider how the type of target, states' strategies for force employment, and delegation of authority could affect escalation. In the remainder of this chapter, we review the current state of the field and then present our framework for categorizing different cross-domain escalation mechanisms.

Cyber threats to nuclear capabilities

Much of the contemporary security studies literature on inadvertent nuclear escalation overlooks cyber operations as a potential trigger.[16] However, as cyber scholars have noted, many modern nuclear systems, especially NC3, depend on cyberspace—and this creates a potential for escalation and instability that "arises not from the cyber domain itself but through its interaction with forces and characteristics in other domains (land, sea, air, etc.)."[17] Compounding these risks, the development of interoperable, common systems can create additional vulnerabilities with the potential for cascading effects. For example, James Acton notes that if "a design flaw in a common receiver . . . left it vulnerable to being disabled by a cyberattack, then all the nuclear-weapon delivery systems that used the receiver could be simultaneously compromised."[18] In a different vein, Paul Bracken argues that "the integration of cyber weapons and other technologies— especially drones, precision strike, and data analytics" can undermine nuclear

---

[16] Caitlin Talmadge, "Would China Go Nuclear? Assessing the Risk of Chinese Nuclear Escalation in a Conventional War with the United States," *International Security* 41, no. 4 (2017): 50–92; Josh Rovner, "AirSea Battle and Escalation Risks," Changing Military Dynamics in East Asia, Policy Brief 12, U.S. Naval War College, January 2012, pp. 1–5. Talmadge, for instance, only mentions cyber once, in the context of potential Chinese cyber attacks against Taiwan as one of the triggers of a conventional war with the United States, p. 65. Rovner's piece does not mention cyber at all.

[17] Erik Gartzke and Jon R. Lindsay, "Thermonuclear Cyberwar," *Journal of Cybersecurity* 3, no. 1 (March, 2017): 37. Also see James M. Acton, "Cyber Warfare & Inadvertent Escalation," *Daedalus* 149, no. 2 (Spring 2020): 61–62.

[18] Acton, "Cyber Warfare & Inadvertent Escalation," p. 62.

stability by making it easier for states to find and fix targets, such as the dispersed, mobile missile delivery systems that newer nuclear powers rely on for their secure second strike deterrent capabilities.[19] There are, of course, some skeptics. Martin Libicki briefly touches on and dismisses the potential for cyber operations causing escalation through targeting a state's nuclear capabilities. His analysis focuses on a direct cyber attack to destroy or "disconnect" a target's nuclear weapons. Because most nuclear forces are air-gapped and analog, Libicki argues that these risks are overblown.[20] However, his scenario does not address cyber threats to dual-use and vulnerable early warning systems that are part of the architecture of nuclear command and control, distinct from the nuclear forces themselves.

The cyber literature identifies three pathways through which the dependence of nuclear systems on digital infrastructure could cause escalation: secrecy, misperception, and communication problems. First, some focus on the clandestine nature of cyber operations and whether penetration of NC3 systems is even detected by the target state. Erik Garzke and Jon Lindsay, for instance, argue that, on the one hand, stealthily gaining access to adversary NC3 through cyber means could give a state an asymmetric information advantage that destabilizes nuclear deterrence and increases the potential for war.[21] On the other hand, if a target uncovers a heretofore secret cyber operation, this could lead to escalation through a use it or lose it incentive—the target, fearing an impending cyber operation, may elect to preemptively employ nuclear weapons.[22] However, secrecy may also circumscribe the conditions under which escalation is likely to occur. Acton notes that a decision to escalate following a cyber intrusion to NC3 depends on whether the state detected the cyber intrusion in the first place and whether it could discern the intent behind the operation.[23] Unlike physical attacks on NC3, "cyberattacks on early-warning systems might go undetected and have no escalation consequences."[24]

A second pathway to escalation could occur through misperceiving the intent behind a cyber operation, which may also generate a use it or lose it incentive. Acton notes the detection of a cyber espionage operation could be misperceived as threatening a state's nuclear capabilities, given the indistinguishability between espionage and offense, prompting it to escalate to nuclear employment.[25]

---

[19] Paul Bracken, "The Cyber Threat to Nuclear Stability," *Orbis* 60, no. 2 (Spring 2016): 189.
[20] Martin C. Libicki, *Crisis and Escalation in Cyberspace* (Santa Monica, CA: RAND, 2012), pp. 125–126.
[21] Erik Gartzke and Jon R. Lindsay, "Thermonuclear Cyberwar," *Journal of Cybersecurity* 3, no. 1 (2017): pp. 43–44.
[22] Ibid., p. 44. However, the authors note that this does not necessarily mean that escalation is predetermined. Rather, it will depend on other contextual factors, such as risk aversion and how decision makers address uncertainty, and the relative capabilities of rival states.
[23] Acton, "Cyber Warfare & Inadvertent Escalation," pp. 90–91.
[24] Ibid., p. 92.
[25] Ibid., pp. 134, 141.

Even routine espionage activities could potentially lead to inadvertent nuclear escalation should a state misidentify an adversary's cyber operations to collect intelligence about its nuclear forces or manipulate command and control as a damage limitation strategy that presages a forthcoming attack.[26] Similarly, Andrew Futter argues that a cyber attack on dual-use systems, such as those that control both conventional and nuclear forces, could be misperceived as heralding an impending attack on a state's nuclear capabilities.[27] Or, a state may be unable to exert control over malware it implants in adversary systems, leading to the unanticipated result that the target misperceives this operation as escalatory.[28] Furthermore, the mere cognizance of cyber vulnerabilities within NC3 and the fear they may induce could cause states to take actions, such as dispersing forces, raising the level of nuclear alerts, or threatening to use nuclear weapons, that lower the barriers to escalation or increase the chance those actions are perceived as preparations for war.[29]

Finally, cyber operations may disrupt the communications systems for a state's nuclear forces, creating uncertainty about the integrity of the chain of command.[30] In separate pieces, Futter and Stephen Cimbala both argue that this uncertainty could give rise to a use it or lose it incentive, which may be heightened by the temporal pressures of a nuclear crisis.[31] In a different vein, cyber operations could complicate how adversaries communicate with one another during crises, "muddy[ing] the signals being sent from one side to the other" and creating a general environment of confusion and uncertainty that could lead to escalation.[32]

In addition, some researchers have noted that cyber operations could affect nuclear stability through non-technical means. Cyber-enabled mis- and disinformation operations could distort the information environment in which decisions about nuclear employment are made. Herbert Lin, for example, discusses how states could corrupt the information environment through the weaponization of social media, or even provoke false flag attacks through creating and amplifying belligerent messages.[33] Lindsay also notes that the cybersecurity of nuclear command and control should include addressing

---

[26] Ibid., pp. 137–140.

[27] Andrew Futter, *Hacking the Bomb: Cyber Threats and Nuclear Weapons* (Washington, DC: Georgetown University Press, 2018), p. 118.

[28] Acton, "Cyber Warfare & Inadvertent Escalation," pp. 141–142.

[29] Ibid., p. 134.

[30] Futter, *Hacking the Bomb*, pp. 118–119; Stephen J. Cimbala, "Nuclear Cyberwar and Crisis Management," *Comparative Strategy* 35, no. 2 (2016): 125.

[31] Futter, *Hacking the Bomb*, p. 119; Cimbala, "Nuclear Cyberwar and Crisis Management," p. 126.

[32] Cimbala, "Nuclear Cyberwar and Crisis Management," p. 124.

[33] Herbert Lin, *Cyber Threats and Nuclear Weapons* (Stanford, CA: Stanford University Press, 2021), pp. 114–117.

non-technical threats, such as "social engineering or blackmailing targeting operators, administrators, or their families."[34]

While all of these pathways contain inherently plausible logics, they do not specify the conditions under which they are more or less likely to occur. For instance, while it is reasonable to infer that a cyber espionage operation targeting a state's nuclear command and control may create uncertainty about underlying intent, scholars must also tease out the causal logic that would prompt a policymaker to make the significant decision to cross the nuclear threshold.

Cyber threats to conventional capabilities

Unlike cyber threats to nuclear weapons, the mechanisms through which cyber operations targeting conventional defensive and offensive weapon systems may cause escalation is a less-theorized area.[35] David Gombert and Martin Libicki explore how the mutual first strike incentives inherent in both the United States' AirSea Battle concept (subsequently renamed the Joint Concept for Access and Maneuver in the Global Commons, or JAM-GC), and China's anti-access area denial (A2/AD) strategy, which includes offensive cyber capabilities, could create the conditions for crisis instability.[36] In a more systematic assessment, Jacquelyn Schneider assesses cyber threats to conventional weapon systems. Specifically, Schneider argues that the reliance on technologically sophisticated military capabilities creates a "capability/vulnerability paradox", that in turn creates incentives to strike first and increases the risk of war.[37] First, less-capable states are incentivized to strike first and exploit the vulnerabilities of more advanced states because they assess that they cannot prevail in a conflict with the latter. Second, more-capable states have an incentive to strike first because, cognizant of their vulnerabilities, they feel they must employ their advantageous capabilities before less-capable states can target them.[38]

---

[34] Jon Lindsay, "Digital Strangelove: The Cyber Dangers of Nuclear Weapons," *Lawfare*, March 12, 2020.

[35] Michael Fischerkeller, for instance, reviews various options for how cyber operations could be employed in an increasingly escalatory fashion to demonstrate resolve and capabilities. He categorizes offensive cyber operations against defensive weapons systems as a less escalatory move than targeting offensive systems but does not present a cohesive theory for cyber operations triggering escalation dynamics through their effects on conventional weapon systems. See Fischerkeller, "Incorporating Offensive Cyber Operations into Conventional Deterrence Strategies," *Survival* 59, no. 1 (2017): 111.

[36] David D. Gombert and Martin Libicki, "Cyber Warfare and Sino-American Crisis Instability," *Survival* 56, no. 4 (2014): 9.

[37] Jacquelyn Schneider, "The Capability/Vulnerability Paradox and Military Revolutions: Implications for Computing, Cyber, and the Onset of War," *Journal of Strategic Studies* 42, no. 6 (2019): 842.

[38] Ibid., p. 848.

The capability-vulnerability paradox, however, contains some caveats when applied to cyberspace. The more-capable state may not be fully aware of the extent of the cyber vulnerabilities in its conventional weapons systems, especially for complex systems with large surface areas of attack or systems that integrate legacy and modern platforms.[39] And the less-capable state may not possess the organizational sophistication and capability to gain access to adversary systems, develop a means of identifying and exploiting vulnerabilities, and then cause a desired cyber effect at a defined time. And, even so, the cyber effects are likely to be short lived. This significantly narrows the conditions under which this logic is likely to play out in cyberspace. Indeed, Schneider notes that "[a]s long as states are uncertain about their ability to conduct effective first strikes against adversary information resources, the incentive to conduct attacks will be mitigated." Nevertheless, she cautions that first strike incentives may become more appealing as states' conventional military capabilities become increasingly dependent on digital systems.[40]

Building on this work, we seek to integrate arguments about potential escalation pathways from cyber operations against nuclear and conventional systems to build a general framework that accounts for when we would expect these risks to be more or less acute.

Reframing Cyber Causes of Cross-Domain Escalation

While cyber vulnerabilities proliferate across states' weapon systems, and their adversaries seek to take advantage of these on a routine basis, states have not yet responded by escalating to conventional or nuclear force employment.[41] This is because, we argue, there are specific contextual factors that must come into play to cause states to choose to escalate. The discernment of a cyber operation, in itself, does not automatically cause escalation.

In developing our argument, we draw from traditional arguments in the security studies literature about causes of cross-domain escalation. First, we make an important distinction between escalation to war and escalation within war. In this sense, we rely on Glenn Snyder and Paul Diesing's conceptualization of a crisis as "an intermediate zone between peace and war," where "[a]lmost all wars

---

[39] Borghard and Creery, "Persistent Vulnerabilities."

[40] Schneider, "The Capability/Vulnerability Paradox and Military Revolutions," p. 857.

[41] Sarah Kreps and Jacquelyn Schneider, "Escalation Firebreaks in the Cyber, Conventional, and Nuclear Domains: Moving Beyond Effects-Based Logics," *Journal of Cybersecurity* 5, no. 1 (2019): 1–11; Henry Farrell and Charles L. Glaser, "The Role of Effects, Saliences and Norms in US Cyberwar Doctrine," *Journal of Cybersecurity* 3, no. 1 (2017): 7–17.

are preceded by a crisis of some sort, although of course not all crises eventuate in war."[42] Almost all of the cross-domain cyber escalation literature focuses on escalation *to* war—the conditions under which a cyber operation could trigger a violent military response. However, just as compelling is the question of escalation *within* war—how the employment of cyber capabilities during a military conflict could escalate the severity of the conflict itself.[43] Moreover, the issue of escalation during wartime traces its roots to the traditional escalation literature, which is less focused on crisis dynamics. While Herman Kahn, for example, does address what he terms "traditional crises" in his treatise on escalation, the primary question he tackles is the conditions under which limited war (or "agreed battle") might further escalate to unlimited war.[44] Additionally, Barry Posen's work on inadvertent escalation addresses escalation pathways that occur *during* conventional conflict, rather than during international crises before war has begun.[45]

There are intuitive reasons to expect that escalation dynamics may manifest differently in the lead-up to than during hostilities. Most importantly, during a conflict the inherent restraint or hesitation that decision makers may exhibit when deliberating whether to use force has already been overcome. Furthermore, the fog of war may make the use of force more difficult to control and military commanders (who may already be offensively inclined by virtue of their organizational culture and bureaucratic incentives) are likely to have greater autonomy and discretion.[46] In the following sections, we separately explore escalation pathways both leading up to and during conflict. Within each context, we discuss how strategies for force employment and delegation of authority shape the likelihood of escalation, as well as the form escalation may take. Our argument is summarized in Table 7.2.

---

[42] Glenn Herald Synder and Paul Diesing, *Conflict Among Nations: Bargaining, Decision Making, and System Structure in International Crises* (Princeton, NJ: Princeton University Press, 1977), p. 10. Also see Michael Brecher and Jonathan Wilkenfeld, *A Study of Crisis* (Ann Arbor, MI: University of Michigan Press, 1997).

[43] For the effectiveness of cyber operations as a tool of coercion during wartime, see Kostyuk and Zhukov, "Invisible Digital Front."

[44] Herman Kahn, *On Escalation: Metaphors and Scenarios* (New Brunswick, NJ: Transaction Publishers, 2010), pp. 4–6. Also see Richard Smoke, *War: Controlling Escalation* (Cambridge, MA: Harvard University Press, 1977), p. 32.

[45] Barry R. Posen, *Inadvertent Escalation: Conventional War and Nuclear Risks* (Ithaca, NY: Cornell University Press, 1991), p. 1. This is often overlooked by scholars who rely on Posen's framework to draw inferences about crisis escalation, which may in fact present with dynamics that are different from wartime escalation.

[46] Posen identifies the fog of war as an important variable in causes of inadvertent nuclear escalation, see *Inadvertent Escalation*, pp. 19–20. For military organizational culture and the offense, see Barry R. Posen, *The Sources of Military Doctrine: France, Britain, and Germany Between the World Wars* (Ithaca, NY: Cornell University Press, 1984).

Table 7.2 How Cyber Operations Could Cause Escalation

	Key Question	Nuclear Forces	Conventional Forces
Escalation is Less Likely			
Crisis	When does an adversary cyber operation look like preparation for impending war?	Cyber operations targeting adversary nuclear forces, particularly NC3 that may be more vulnerable to cyber attack, can lead to inadvertent nuclear escalation if the target assesses its adversary has a counterforce/damage limitation strategy. However, escalation risks are attenuated by time to detection, attribution, and level of readiness of nuclear forces.	Cyber operations that target a state's conventional forces are likely to cause escalation when they are perceived as heralding an impending attack; when the target assesses that its adversary has a force employment strategy that rests on cyber operations as the opening phase of an attack. Of particular concern are fears that defenses are being suppressed or the target is being blinded in the lead-up to conflict. However, escalation risks are attenuated by time to detection, attribution, and level of delegation of authority.
Escalation Is More Likely			
Conflict	When does an adversary cyber operation imperil the target's ability to carry out core warfighting functions and/or state survival during conflict?	Cyber operations targeting adversary nuclear forces during wartime are more likely to trigger inadvertent nuclear escalation if the target assesses its adversary has a counterforce/ damage limitation strategy. Confidence thresholds for attribution are likely to be lower, forces are likely to already be on higher alert.	Cyber operations targeting conventional capabilities during wartime as part of the attacking state's denial or decapitation strategy could cause escalation when the target perceives that this threatens its core warfighting functions. This is more likely when the target lacks secondary and tertiary capabilities, which can occur in forward-deployed environments for certain functions.

Cyber Operations and Escalation to War

Prior to the onset of conflict, cyber operations against conventional and nuclear weapons systems could provoke inadvertent escalation through the related logics of a perceived window of vulnerability and an incentive to strike first.[47] This follows arguments in the traditional security studies literature that, if a state anticipates that it is vulnerable to adversary attack within some constrained period of time, it may feel it faces an incentive to strike first rather than cede advantage to the adversary. A number of factors could prompt a state to perceive this incentive. Glenn Snyder, for example, argues that first strike incentives could occur if one state develops a first-strike capability that threatens the other state's ability to respond; if one state has a military/technological advantage over the other that provides it with an ability to strike first; or if there is reciprocal fear that the other side is likely to strike first.[48] Similarly, Stephen Van Evera's work on the causes of war identifies first-mover advantages and perceived windows of vulnerability as triggers of escalation from crisis to war.[49] Van Evera notes that escalation to war could occur if one side mobilizes its forces or attacks because "they fear they will soon be attacked." This could occur because a state accurately perceives the intentions of its adversary, or because of "misinformation or misinterpretation of evidence [that] could create false warning of attack, sparking preemption of a nonexistent threat."[50] Windows of vulnerability could also emerge when a state perceives that the balance of power is changing in favor of its adversary.[51] This could prompt the vulnerable state to "launch an early war before the power shift is complete, either to avoid a later war waged under worse conditions or to avoid later being compelled to bargain from weakness."[52] There is an important temporal dimension to this logic; it rests on some level of imminence of threat that provokes a perceived need to act within a defined period of time or suffer the consequences.

First strike incentives and windows of vulnerability are often confused with use it or lose it incentives, but these are not always interchangeable. Strategic conditions may exist that generate perceived windows of vulnerability and

---

[47] For an important critique of this logic, see Dan Reiter, "Exploding the Powder Keg Myth: Preemptive Wars Almost Never Happen."

[48] Glenn Herald Snyder, *Deterrence and Defense: Toward a Theory of National Security* (Princeton, NJ: Princeton University Press, 1991), pp. 97–98. Also see Thomas C. Schelling, *The Strategy of Conflict* (Cambridge, MA: Harvard University Press, 196), ch. 9. For an alternative perspective on surprise, see Richard K. Betts, *Surprise Attack: Lessons for Defense Planning* (Washington, DC: The Brookings Institution, 1982).

[49] Stephen Van Evera, *Causes of War: Power and the Roots of Conflict* (Ithaca, NY: Cornell University Press, 1999).

[50] Ibid., pp. 41–42.

[51] Ibid., p. 74.

[52] Ibid., p. 76.

incentives to strike first, but this does not necessarily mean that the state will escalate with the particular capabilities that its adversary appears to be threatening
(which would be a use it or lose it scenario). It could also be the case that the state
will strike first with other capabilities, including those that may be in a different
theater or that are forward positioned.

Extending this logic to cyberspace, a key question for assessing potential escalation pathways from crisis to conflict is: What are the conditions under which a
state is likely to perceive an adversary cyber operation as preparation for imminent war? Prior instances of state behavior in cyberspace suggest cyber operations are sometimes used as a shaping tool in the lead-up to a conventional strike
or conflict. For instance, Israel now acknowledges having conducted an airstrike
against a Syrian nuclear reactor in 2007, dubbed Operation Orchard.[53] Experts
have noted that a cyber operation (and/or an operation using the electromagnetic
spectrum) to disable Syria's air defenses likely preceded the airstrike.[54] Similarly,
Russia-linked groups conducted a wave of cyber operations against Georgia in
the summer of 2008 to shape the battlefield prior to Russia's invasion.[55] However,
these were DDoS attacks and website defacements, rather than tailored cyber
attacks against Georgia's conventional military capabilities. Nevertheless, they
were timed to coincide with Russia's conventional invasion of South Ossetia in
early August 2008 and illustrate how cyber operations could be a prelude for a
forthcoming kinetic attack.[56] Finally, it has been widely reported, but never confirmed by the United States government, that since 2014 the United States has
conducted cyber operations targeting North Korean ballistic missile delivery
systems.[57] If this reporting is accurate, it is plausible that during a crisis North
Korea could perceive the operation to be a prelude to a conventional strike.[58]

However, unlike other military operations that may be seen as presaging war,
secrecy, attribution challenges, and the limited effects of cyber operations narrow
the conditions under which cyber operations are likely to cause escalation from

[53] Anna Ahronheim, "After a Decade Israel Admits: We Bombed Syria Nuclear Reactor in 2007,"
The Jerusalem Post, March 21, 2018.
[54] See, for example, Mohan B. Gazula, "Cyber Warfare Conflict Analysis and Case Studies,"
Massachusetts Institute of Technology, May 2017, pp. 55–58; David A. Fulghum and Douglas Barrie,
"Israel Used Electronic Attack in Air Strike against Syrian Mystery Target," *ABC News*, October
8, 2007.
[55] John Markoff, "Before the Gunfire, Cyberattacks," *The New York Times*, August 12, 2008.
[56] Sarah P. White, "Understanding Cyberwarfare: Lessons from the Russia-Georgia War," Modern
War Institute, March 20, 2018, p. 1. Also see David J. Smith, "Russian Cyber Strategy and the War
against Georgia," Atlantic Council, January 17, 2014.
[57] David E. Sanger and William J. Broad, "Trump Inherits a Secret Cyberwar against North Korean
Missiles," *The New York Times*, March 4, 2017; Patricia Lewis and Beyza Unal, "The Destabilizing
Danger of Cyberattacks on Missile Systems," Chatham House, July 2, 2019.
[58] But see Erica D. Borghard, "Lost in Cyber Translation? US Cyber Signaling to North Korea,"
Council on Foreign Relations, October 16, 2017, https://www.cfr.org/blog/lost-cyber-translation-us-
cyber-signaling-north-korea.

crisis to conflict. For a cyber operation to create the perception of imminent war, it must be discernable to the target. The secretive nature of cyber operations—the fact that states typically deliberately go to great lengths to conceal their presence on a network and can leverage the obfuscating nature of cyberspace to do so—creates barriers to observing adversary behavior. Moreover, given the fleeting nature of cyber effects and their limits on cost generation, a target may not even realize that it is experiencing an adversarial cyber operation, rather than a benign disruption in service. Additionally, while a number of states have incorporated cyber operations as part of their military strategies to prepare the battlefield for conflict, moving from strategic concept to military reality requires a level of skill, sophistication, and reliability of cyber operations that is exceedingly difficult and precarious to achieve. Absent decisive effects against critical military targets at the appropriate time, escalation pressure is attenuated. Finally, an observed cyber operation also has to be attributed with some level of confidence to an adversary within a relatively short time. If a state is highly uncertain about the source of a cyber operation against a critical military capability, the drive to escalate is less potent.

Therefore, under these very limited conditions—when a state discerns and attributes a significant cyber operation during a crisis—escalation risks are greatest when the target state perceives the cyber operation as being consistent with its adversary's concept for force employment that involves cyber operations to prepare the environment for a forthcoming attack.[59] This could comprise, for example, the use of cyber operations to temporarily suppress or degrade a target's air defenses, early warning, or C4ISR capabilities. In this instance, a state may perceive an incentive to strike first to take out its adversary's offensive capabilities to prevent their anticipated use or to initiate the first phase of a conflict that it now perceives as inevitable.

Additionally, the potential for escalation is further heightened when authority for the use of force is delegated down to lower levels in the chain of command or through technical means that enable launch on warning (although, as we note below, delegation is far more likely once conflict has already commenced).[60] Delegating authority to military organizations could increase

[59] In theory, it is possible that an adversary cyber operation that directly threatens a critical military function or capability on which the targeted state relies for its defenses could create pressures to strike first, even if the target does not assess this to be part of the attacking state's strategy for force employment. However, we find this scenario to be highly implausible. Cyber operations rarely have permanent, decisive effects on the balance of power. Rather, most operations have time-bound, reversible effects, making it unlikely that they would independently prompt an impending decisive shift in the balance of power that would generate first strike incentives.

[60] Samuel P. Huntington, *Solider and the State* (Cambridge, MA: Harvard University Press, 1981); Peter D. Feaver, *Armed Servants: Agency, Oversight and Civil-Military Relations* (Cambridge, MA: Harvard University Press, 2005); Biddle, *Military Power*, p. 49. Also see Kenneth M. Pollack, *Arabs at War: Military Effectiveness, 1948–1991* (Lincoln, NE: University of Nebraska Press, 2002). For a comprehensive overview of this in the nuclear context, see Eric Schlosser, *Command and*

the risk of escalation to conflict given the proclivity of militaries toward offensive action—especially when observed adversary behavior is seen as confirming the expectations of military leaders about how a conflict is likely to unfold. Moreover, for highly technical areas, such as cyberspace, expertise is more likely to reside within military organizations. Civilians, therefore, may be more willing to defer to the assessments of military leaders regarding how to interpret the intent behind a cyber operation.[61]

While hypothetical, this type of escalation scenario is theoretically plausible given current strategies for force employment among a number of great power rivals. Several states have developed strategies and operational concepts in which cyber operations are part of the initial phases of a conventional campaign. One example is the United States' JAM-GC concept, mentioned above.[62] This joint concept is intended to surmount adversary A2/AD capabilities, enabling the United States to project force and maneuver in a theater of operations.[63] Many scholars have assessed the escalatory potential of implementing this concept in a crisis involving China. Potentially, this could involve the United States conducting a first strike against Chinese military capabilities that serve dual purposes for anti-access area denial operations as well as nuclear command and control and early warning.[64] Specifically, the concept includes first strike targeting of "Chinese command and control networks, missile sites, intelligence, surveillance, and reconnaissance (ISR) assets, air defense systems, and submarines."[65]

JAM-GC includes, potentially, cyber operations. It involves integrating "capabilities from all five warfighting domains (land, sea, air, space, and

---

Control: Nuclear Weapons, the Damascus Incident, and the Illusion of Safety (New York: Penguin Press, 2013); Paul J. Bracken, The Command and Control of Nuclear Forces (New Haven, CT: Yale University Press, 1983); Thomas J. Schelling, Arms and Influence (Westport, CT: Praeger, 1977), pp. 39–40; Bruce Blair, "Loose Cannons: The President and US Nuclear Posture," Bulletin of Atomic Scientists 76, no. 1 (January 2020): 14–26; Peter Feaver and Kenneth Geers, "'When the Urgency of Time and Circumstances Clearly Does Not Permit . . . :' Pre-delegation in Nuclear and Cyber Scenarios," in Understanding Cyber Conflict.

[61] Posen, Sources of Military Doctrine.

[62] For a review of the JAM-GC concept, see Michael E. Hutchens, William D. Dries, Jason C. Perdew, Vincent D. Bryant, and Kerry E. Moores, "Joint Concept for Access and Maneuver in the Global Commons: A New Joint Operational Concept," Joint Forces Quarterly 84, no. 1 (2017): 134–139. While JAM-GC builds on the AirSea Battle concept, it reflects a recognition that AirSea Battle's primary focus on overcoming adversary A2/AD may not always be possible and, therefore, the focus of JAM-GC is on not only destroying adversary A2/AD capabilities when possible but also defeating "the adversary's plan and intent," p. 136. Also see Tom Greenwood and Pat Savage, "In Search of a 21st-Century Joint Warfighting Concept," War on the Rocks, September 12, 2019.

[63] Erica D. Borghard and Shawn W. Lonergan, "Will Air-Sea Battle Be 'Sunk' By Cyberwarriors?," The National Interest, December 8, 2014.

[64] Rovner, "AirSea Battle," p. 4.

[65] Caitlin Talmade, "Would China Go Nuclear? Assessing the Risk of Chinese Nuclear Escalation in a Conventional War with the United States," International Security 41, no. 4 (Spring 2017): 53.

cyberspace)," to include "interoperable land, naval, air, space, and cyber forces having the necessary capabilities to overcome and defeat the increasingly sophisticated threats that potential competitors are now fielding."[66] Therefore, there could be scenarios in which China perceives and attributes U.S. cyber operations targeting key nodes in its command and control capabilities during a potential crisis, such as in the Taiwan Straits. Given U.S. force employment concepts, China could interpret U.S. behavior in cyberspace as a prelude to a conventional assault and take steps to escalate first to thwart a U.S. attack or gain an operational advantage.

Another plausible scenario could involve cyber operations targeting a state's space-based capabilities, which serve a range of important military functions, including early warning systems, space-based C4ISR, and position, navigation, and timing systems.[67] The United States, Russia, and China all conceptualize space as essential for warfighting.[68] According to U.S. government assessments, actors can "use offensive cyberspace capabilities to enable a range of reversible to nonreversible effects against space systems, associated ground infrastructure, users, and the links connecting them."[69] Moreover, major powers may also perceive an incentive to strike first in the lead-up to conflict to neuter adversary space-based capabilities and gain a momentary advantage. Benjamin Bahney et al. note that Chinese strategic writing focuses on "gaining 'mastery by striking first'" and there are apparent "Russian and Chinese fears that U.S. military operations may neuter a state's ability to conduct space strikes once a conflict has begun."[70] The vulnerability of space-based assets to cyber operations, coupled with perceived first-mover advantages and the interdependence between space capabilities and other key military capabilities, could mean that a cyber operation that leads to a "failure of deterrence in space could prompt cascading deterrence failures across other domains, resulting in crisis escalation."[71]

In the case of cyber operations targeting NC3 systems, escalation could occur if the target associates these operations with an adversary's counterforce or damage limitation strategy. Damage limitation relies on reducing the effectiveness of another state's nuclear forces—the amount of pain it can inflict via nuclear weapons. In the United States, the concept of damage limitation emerged in the early Cold War as an alternative to assured destruction. According to then-Secretary of

---

[66] Hutchens et al., *Joint Concept for Access and Maneuver in the Global Commons*, pp. 136, 139.

[67] Benjamin W. Bahney, Jonathan Pearl, and Michael Markey, "Antisatellite Weapons and the Growing Instability of Deterrence," in Erik Gatzke and Jon R. Lindsay, *Cross Domain Deterrence: Strategy in the Era of Complexity* (New York, NY: Oxford University Press, March 2019), p. 129.

[68] "Challenges to Security in Space," Defense Intelligence Agency, January 2019. Dean Cheng, "China's Military Role in Space," *Strategic Studies Quarterly* 6, no. 1 (Spring 2012): 55–77.

[69] "Challenges to Security in Space," p. 9.

[70] Bahney et al., "Antisatellite Weapons and the Growing Instability of Deterrence," p. 135.

[71] Ibid., p. 137.

Defense Robert McNamara, if deterrence failed, the United States had to ensure it possessed the capabilities to limit the damage the Soviet Union could inflict on the United States. In a 1965 memorandum, McNamara articulated the logic as follows: should deterrence fail, "it is essential that forces be available to limit the damage of such an attack to ourselves or our Allies. Such forces include not only anti-aircraft defenses, anti-ballistic missile defenses, anti-submarine defenses, and civil defense, but also offensive forces, i.e., strategic missiles and manned-bombers, used in a Damage Limiting role."[72] A counterforce strategy, organized around targeting adversary nuclear forces to disarm them, is "damage-limitation by offensive action."[73] However, the threshold for escalation in this scenario is quite high. A decision maker would likely demand very high confidence that an observed cyber operation against its nuclear forces or command and control truly represents the first stages of a damage limitation or counterforce strategy, justifying the first use of nuclear weapons. One exception would be if a state had pre-delegated authority to launch nuclear forces on warning *and* if the cyber operation had a direct effect on those early warning systems that would trigger nuclear launch.

Cyber Operations and Escalation during War

While the same factors that shape decisions to escalate during crises also affect escalation in wartime, in the latter context those risks are more salient. In fact, much of the traditional security studies literature is concerned with processes of escalation of, rather than to, conflict.[74] Indeed, George Smoke describes escalation as, "an act [that] has consequences and meaning for the overall pattern or nature of the ongoing war: its ground rules or limits."[75] Specifically, wartime escalation involves an action that "noticeably intensifies or widens the area of violence [or carries] the possibility of sparking an open-ended action-reaction cycle."[76]

---

[72] Draft Memorandum from Secretary McNamara to President Johnson, Washington, November 1, 1966. Foreign Relations of the United States, 1964–1968, Volume X, National Security Policy, p. 299.

[73] William A. Stewart, *Counterforce, Damage-Limiting, and Deterrence* (Santa Monica: The RAND Corporation, 1967), pp. 10–11. For further discussion of counterforce strategies during the Cold War, see Charles L. Glaser, *Analyzing Strategic Nuclear Policy* (Princeton, NJ: Princeton University Press, 1990), ch. 7.

[74] Kahn, *On Escalation: Metaphors and Scenarios* (New York: Praeger, 1965), pp. 4–6. Also see Smoke, *War*; and Morton H. Halperin, *Limited Wars in the Nuclear Age* (New York: Wiley, 1963).

[75] Smoke, *War*, p. 32.

[76] Ibid., 32–33.

Escalating during wartime could occur deliberately—as a means of gaining an advantage over the enemy or ending a conflict in one's favor.[77] Thomas Schelling, for example, describes how states can intentionally manipulate the risks of a limited war turning into a total war to their advantage.[78] Or, during a conflict one side could attempt a fait accompli as part of a limited aims strategy to seize and solidify a territorial advantage.[79] In doing so, the attacking side runs the risk that its adversary could escalate rather than capitulate.[80]

But wartime escalation could also occur through inadvertent pathways, as a byproduct of changes in the perceived vulnerability of one party or the balance of power on the battlefield.[81] Much of this literature has focused on inadvertent escalation to nuclear war during conventional conflict. Barry Posen argues that the security dilemma dynamics that often characterize relations between states short of war are even more exacerbated during conflict itself.[82] Specifically, inadvertent nuclear escalation is likely to take place during conventional conflict when conventional operations "come into direct contact with the nuclear forces of an adversary and substantially affect the victim's confidence in his future ability to operate these forces in ways that he had counted upon."[83] This could include direct conventional attacks on a state's second-strike nuclear capabilities, as well as operations targeting a state's early warning systems, command and control systems, or forces that protect nuclear forces.[84] When a state's second strike forces are at risk during war, it may perceive a window of vulnerability, assessing that it is better off escalating rather than risking the integrity of its second strike nuclear forces—especially if the attacking state has a damage limitation or counterforce doctrine.[85]

---

[77] This is essentially extending the bargaining literature to warfare. Kahn, *On Escalation*, p. 6. Van Evera discusses "windows of opportunity" as a cause of war, rather than escalation in war, but the same logic could be extended to conflict dynamics. In his parlance, windows of opportunity represent a "fading offensive opportunity," *Causes of War*, p. 74.

[78] Schelling, *Arms and Influence*, p. 105. The introduction of nuclear weapons, of course, would be a dramatic act that would escalate any otherwise limited conflict, pp. 106–107.

[79] John J. Mearsheimer, *Conventional Deterrence* (Ithaca, NY: Cornell University Press, 1985), pp. 53–58.

[80] Dan Altman, "By Fait Accompli, Not Coercion: How States Wrest Territory from Their Adversaries," *International Studies Quarterly* 61 (2017): 882.

[81] The most notable of these is Posen's work on inadvertent escalation of conventional conflicts. See Barry R. Posen, *Inadvertent Escalation: Conventional War and Nuclear Risks* (Ithaca, NY: Cornell University Press, 1991).

[82] Posen, *Inadvertent Escalation*, pp. 13–15.

[83] Ibid., p. 2.

[84] Ibid., p. 3. The latter is an acute concern of contemporary security studies scholars, who fear that conventional conflict between the United States and China could lead to inadvertent escalation given the dual-use nature of many Chinese early warning and command and control capabilities. See James M. Acton, "Escalation through Entanglement: How the Vulnerability of Command-and-Control Systems Raises the Risks of Inadvertent Nuclear War," *International Security* 43, no. 1 (Summer 2018): 57–59.

[85] Posen, *Inadvertent Escalation*, p. 3.

However, this logic also applies to conventional escalation during war. Wartime dynamics may cause states to perceive an unfavorable change in the balance of power on the battlefield, exposing them to windows of vulnerability where they fear critical warfighting capabilities will be degraded or imperiled. This may also cause incentives to escalate to regain the advantage, to use conventional capabilities before they can be rendered inert.

These escalation risks are made more salient by the greater autonomy that military organizations enjoy during war, as well as the proverbial fog of war. The uncertainties and information asymmetries that are routinely present in international politics are only amplified during wartime. In the middle of conflict, "the great difficulty of gathering and interpreting the most relevant information about a war in progress and using it to understand, control, and orchestrate the war" creates additional conditions for inadvertent escalation.[86]

The cyber dimensions of wartime escalation

How might this logic apply to cyber operations targeting conventional or nuclear capabilities? On the one hand, several factors limit a state's ability to employ cyber operations in a manner that is likely to escalate an ongoing conflict.[87] For instance, in addition to the relatively limited and transient effects of cyber operations, the difficulties of developing new accesses and exploits and sustaining cyber effects are even greater in a battlefield environment than during a crisis. Put simply, there are significant constraints in the "combat power" of cyber operations to cause meaningful and decisive changes in the level of violence of a conflict or the balance of power on a battlefield.

The evidence from past conflict largely bears out these expectations. Nadiya Kostyuk and Yuri Zhukov, analyzing unique data from the 2014–2016 conflict in Ukraine and the Syrian civil war between 2011 and 2016, find that cyber attacks employed as an independent coercive tool on the battlefield have minimal coercive utility.[88] Similarly, in our dataset we identified 238 cyber incidents that took place between August 2005 and May 2020 in which government and/or military entities were targeted. Of those cases, only 14 took place during an ongoing conflict. Eight of those involved cyber espionage operations, and two entailed relatively unsophisticated denial of service attacks, one by Hamas against Israel's

---

[86] On information asymmetries, see James D. Fearon, "Rationalist Explanations for War," *International Organization* 49, no. 3 (Summer 1995): 379–414; Posen, *Inadvertent Escalation*, p. 19.

[87] On warfighting strategies, also see Erica D. Borghard and Shawn W. Lonergan, "The Logic of Coercion in Cyberspace," *Security Studies* 26, no. 3 (2017): 452–481.

[88] Nadiya Kostyuk and Yuri Zhukov, "Invisible Digital Front." In particular, the authors find that "cyber operations have not created forms of harm and coercion that visibly affect their targets' actions," p. 3.

internet infrastructure that disrupted service to Israeli government websites during the 2009 Gaza offensive[89] and the other by Russian entities during the invasion of Georgia in 2008.[90]

Altogether, we identified four cases that may be candidates for escalation during conflict, because they involved sabotage. Nevertheless, upon closer examination, none of them represents an instance in which cyber operations were used against military capabilities to shift the balance of power on the battlefield. Three of these cases were Russian cyber operations against Ukraine's civilian infrastructure—the power grid in 2015 and 2016 and a chemical plant in 2018—rather than against military targets as part of a military engagement.[91] Therefore, these represent examples of cyber operations used as a tool of coercion rather than to shape battlefield dynamics. Finally, one case involved a cyber campaign conducted by the United States in 2016 to deny the Islamic State the ability to use the internet for recruitment, coordination, and propaganda.[92] This example comes closest to the type of scenario that we expect might affect the escalation of a conflict. However, this case is also problematic: it involved a cyber campaign against a non-state actor, rather than a state rival, in a context with significant power asymmetries between belligerents. Moreover, even in this instance, the effectiveness of the cyber campaign was reportedly questionable. According to a report by the *New York Times*, "[t]he effectiveness of the nation's arsenal of cyberweapons hit its limits, they have discovered, against an enemy that exploits the internet largely to recruit, spread propaganda and use encrypted communications, all of which can be quickly reconstituted after American 'mission teams' freeze their computers or manipulate their data."[93]

This suggests caution is warranted about the likelihood of cyber operations causing wartime escalation. That said, there are some theoretical reasons to

[89] Anshel Pfeffer, "Israel Suffered Massive Cyber Attack during Gaza Offensive," *Haaretz*, June 15, 2009, https://www.haaretz.com/1.5065382.

[90] John Markoff, "Before Gunfire, Cyberattacks," *The New York Times*, August 12, 2008, https://www.nytimes.com/2008/08/13/technology/13cyber.html.

[91] Michael Assante, "Confirmation of Coordinated Attack on the Ukrainian Power Grid," *SANS*, January 6, 2016, https://ics.sans.org/blog/2016/01/09/confirmation-of-a-coordinated-attack-on-the-ukrainian-power-grid; https://ics.sans.org/media/E-ISAC_SANS_Ukraine_DUC_5.pdf; Andy Greeberg, " How an Entire Nation Became Russia's Test Lab for Cyber War," *Wired*, May 20, 2017, https://www.wired.com/story/russian-hackers-attack-ukraine; "Analysis of the Cyber Attack on the Ukrainian Power Grid," Electricity Information Sharing and Analysis Center, March 18, 2016, https://dragos.com/blog/20180716UkraineChemicalPlantEvent.html.

[92] For a phenomenal resource containing declassified documents from the United States on Joint Task Force ARES and OPERATION GLOWING SYMPHONY detailing the cyber effort to combat the Islamic State's use of the Internet, see https://nsarchive.gwu.edu/briefing-book/cyber-vault/2018-08-13/joint-task-force-ares-operation-glowing-symphony-cyber-commands-internet-war-against-isil.

[93] David E. Sanger and Eric Schmitt, "U.S. Cyberweapons Used against Iran and North Korea, Are a Disappointment against ISIS," *The New York Times*, June 12, 2017, https://www.nytimes.com/2017/06/12/world/middleeast/isis-cyber.html.

expect that the factors that limit cyber escalation risks in competition and crisis may have inverse effects in wartime. For instance, given the ambiguous nature of cyber signals, the fog of war may generate even greater uncertainty with respect to discerning the intent behind cyber operations. And military organizations, already more empowered during wartime, are likely to enjoy even greater leeway with respect to evaluating and developing responses for cyber operations during conflict, given their authority in a theater of operations and monopoly on technical expertise. Research has shown that it is precisely during conflicts that military organizations' proclivities to the offense kick in.[94]

Moreover, some of the dampening mechanisms present during crises that diminish the likelihood of escalation are less present during conflict. For instance, confidence thresholds for attribution are likely to be lower during conflict; during ongoing hostilities, when the stakes are higher and an adversary has already demonstrated a willingness to use force, states are more likely to assign malicious behavior to that adversary. This increases not only a state's willingness to escalate based on less than reliable evidence but also the chances of false flag cyber operations and catalytic escalation.[95] Relatedly, incentives to maintain secrecy around cyber operations may be less important in a warfighting context when belligerents are conducting overt military operations. Moreover, in considering the trade-offs between quiet and stealthy intelligence operations versus loud military cyber operations, decision makers are likely to favor military demands during times of war.

The reality is that the scenarios most likely to exhibit the types of escalation pathways during wartime described above have not actually occurred, making it difficult to test these arguments. Specifically, there has not been a direct military conflict between great powers—let alone one in which cyber operations have been seamlessly integrated into conventional campaign plans, which requires a certain level of organizational maturity and skill. Along these lines, some researchers have noted that cyber escalation may not have taken place because the geopolitical conditions have not been ripe for escalation—in cyberspace or other domains.[96] One implication of this argument is that if the geopolitical environment were to deteriorate and become more unstable, there is a greater chance that cyber operations may cause escalation.

Changes in the stability of international politics do not affect the characteristics of cyber operations, which forms the core of our argument in this book.

[94] See, for example, Richard Betts, *Soldiers, Statesmen, and Cold War Crises* (New York, NY: Columbia University Press, 1991).

[95] Herb Lin, "Escalation Dynamics and Conflict Termination in Cyberspace," *Strategic Studies Quarterly* 6, no. 3 (Fall 2012): 46–70.

[96] See, for example, Jason Healey and Robert Jervis, "The Escalation Inversion and Other Oddities of Situational Cyber Stability," *Texas National Security Review* 3, no. 4 (Fall 2020): 30–53.

Shifting geopolitics would not change, for instance, the fact that cyber operations have limited effects, or that there are significant operational challenges associated with planning and implementing cyber campaigns and sustaining effects over time. These aspects of cyber operations severely limit the circumstances in which they are likely to cause escalation—during peacetime or in crises and conflicts. However, geopolitical changes may increase the likelihood of militarized conflict between states and, in doing so, the chances that states employ cyber operations during a conflict. While the overall risks of cyber escalation are low, wartime conditions are the most conducive to cyber operations causing escalation.

During conflict, cyber operations could cause perceived windows of vulnerability when the target assesses that its adversary's strategies for force employment imperil its own key warfighting functions, portending a shift in the balance of power and threatening to meaningfully disadvantage one party to a conflict.[97] In particular, when one state employs cyber operations against an adversary's conventional forces for the purposes of denial (preventing its adversary from achieving battlefield objectives) or decapitation (causing strategic paralysis through undermining a target's C4ISR capabilities), or against its nuclear forces as part of a counterforce/damage limitation strategy, such that the target believes its own abilities to continue to fight or survive are undermined, then the chances of escalation are the highest. It is the fear of a deleterious shift in the balance of power—stemming from a cyber operation causing some core capability or function to be degraded or eroded within a period of time—that changes the nature of the conflict and drives states to escalate to stave off defeat.[98]

In terms of cyber operations leading to inadvertent nuclear escalation, one important difference between Posen's model and the cyber realm is that, in the former, nuclear forces and conventional capabilities are not deeply intertwined or interconnected. Rather, the threat to nuclear forces is a byproduct of otherwise independent conventional operations on the battlefield. In the modern era, however, some elements of NC3, especially dual-use systems, are interconnected with cyber infrastructure. This interdependence is only increasing with nuclear modernization efforts, such as those reflected in the United States' 2018 Nuclear Posture Review, where NC3 systems are growing more reliant on digital

---

[97] Other arguments about escalation during conflict are important but less relevant for this specific context. For instance, Austin Carson's work on the political causes of escalation and how the visibility or secrecy of actions taken during a conflict can create political pressure to escalate is important for our earlier arguments about signaling, but less relevant for this particular topic. See Carson, "Facing Off and Saving Face: Covert Intervention and Escalation Management in the Korean War," *International Organization* 70, no. 1 (2016): 112–113.

[98] Thus, this shares logic with the idea of gambling for resurrection. See George W. Downs and David M. Rocke, "Conflict, Agency, and Gambling for Resurrection: The Principal-Agent Problem Goes to War," *American Journal of Political Science* 38, no. 2 (May 1994): 362–380.

technologies.[99] Therefore, contingent on a state actually being able to conduct a cyber operation that disrupts or degrades NC3 systems, there are reasons to expect Posen's proposed inadvertent nuclear escalation pathway to be more heightened in the context of cyber operations.

Beyond nuclear escalation, cyber operations carried out as part of various warfighting strategies could, in some cases, lead to inadvertent conventional escalation during wartime through fears about the shifting balance of power on the battlefield. Specifically, we focus on those strategies that directly target adversary military capabilities: denial, decapitation, and attrition.[100] A denial strategy entails thwarting an adversary from "attain[ing] his goals on the battlefield" or "preventing battlefield success."[101] Robert Pape notes that denial strategies aim to "deny the opponent hope of achieving the disputed territorial objectives."[102] Leveraging the dependence of warfighting capabilities on digital infrastructure, cyber operations could be conducted on the battlefield to deny or degrade an adversary's ability to employ a key non-cyber capability at a desired time—even if the effect is temporally bound. Perhaps even more likely in modern combat, cyber operations could play an integral role in decapitating an adversary's ability to sense its environment, maintain command and control, communicate with forces, and collect intelligence against adversary movements and maneuvers. Decapitation rests on paralyzing an adversary's C4ISR capabilities.[103] This is because C4ISR capabilities are deeply intertwined with and reliant on cyberspace. Finally, it is important to note that while cyber capabilities may be used as part of an attrition strategy—to erode a target's military capabilities over time—it is less likely that they will lead to windows of vulnerability dynamics given the fact that attrition occurs over longer periods of time and therefore does not give rise to temporally bound pressures or the perception of a surprise or sudden shift in the conflict's dynamic.

Our argument that cyber operations that are part of denial or decapitation strategies during conflict could trigger escalation through windows of vulnerability logics rests on the extent to which these operations may threaten a state's key warfighting functions. Windows of vulnerability only exist when

---

[99] Jon Lindsay, "Digital Strangelove: The Cyber Dangers of Nuclear Weapons," *Lawfare*, March 12, 2020.

[100] Joseph S. Nye, Jr., "Deterrence and Dissuasion in Cyberspace," *International Security* 41, no. 3 (2016): 56–57; Jacquelyn G. Schneider, "Deterrence in and through Cyberspace," in Erik Gartzke and Jon R. Lindsay eds., *Cross-Domain Deterrence: Strategy in an Era of Complexity* (New York: Oxford University Press, 2019), pp. 112–115.

[101] John J. Mearsheimer, *Conventional Deterrence* (Ithaca, NY: Cornell University Press, 1985), pp. 14–15; Daniel Byman and Matthew Waxman, *The Dynamics of Coercion: American Foreign Policy and the Limits of Military Might* (Cambridge, UK: Cambridge University Press, 2002), p. 50.

[102] Robert A. Pape, *Bombing to Win: Air Power and Coercion in War* (Ithaca, NY: Cornell University Press, 1996), p. 19. While this is also a discussion of coercion, the same logic holds for deterrence.

[103] Ibid., p. 79.

there is a meaningful, imminent threat to a target's ability to fight and wage war. Importantly, cyber operations may only be able to generate this perception under very limited conditions, given the difficulties of conducting them. Additionally, the magnitude of the threat will further rest on the extent to which a target has redundant and robust secondary and tertiary capabilities.

Warfighting functions are those "tasks and systems united by a common purpose that commanders use to accomplish missions and training objectives."[104] These functions comprise a commander's combat power in war and disrupting them can serve tactical and operational objectives. U.S. military doctrine holds that these functions include command and control, intelligence, fires, movement and maneuver, protection, sustainment, and information, with C4ISR essentially being a combination of the command and control and intelligence functions.[105] Each of these functions is underpinned by a set of core capabilities that could be potential targets of a cyber operation. For instance, disrupting the satellite communications architecture that buttresses a commander's ability to communicate with forces at sea or in a remote operating environment would undermine a warfighting function and support a decapitation or denial strategy. However, it may be far from decisive if the operation does not also target the secondary and potentially tertiary means of communications that may exist and enable the force to overcome the disruption. In the satellite communications example, these include well-tested radio capabilities, wired networks, couriers, and even indigenous telecommunications networks. Indeed, it is exceedingly difficult to conduct a decisive strike against a warfighting function of an adversary with cyber power alone.

That being said, the temporal aspects of such an operation should not be diminished. It takes a force time to adjust to a redundant or less-preferred means of operating and in that moment of reset, a tactical advantage may be conferred to the attacker. Additionally, for some warfighting functions, particularly in deployed environments where redundant capabilities may not be readily available, it may be possible for an attacker to conduct a cyber operation that can have decisive impacts in a way that effectively deny the target the ability to achieve a battlefield objective. It would be conceivable, for instance, that a belligerent could conduct a cyber attack that paralyzes a missile defense system that provides protection for troops in the field and exploits this vulnerability to conduct a synchronized air raid. Under these circumstances the attacker would have a tactical

---

[104] Headquarters, Department of the Army, "ADP 3-0: Operations," October 2017. While this is definition is based on the United States' approach to warfighting functions, the basic logic of the concept is generalizable across modern militaries.

[105] See "Joint Publication 1: Doctrine for the Armed Forces of the United States," *U.S. Joint Chiefs of Staff*, March 25, 2013, Incorporating Change 1, July 12, 2017. Other states may define these differently. This example is for illustrative purposes.

advantage until the disruption could be overturned or a compensating system brought into service, further shifting the relative balance of combat power on the battlefield and creating the conditions to provoke an escalatory response.

Conclusion

At this point, the analysis presented here is entirely hypothetical. Secrecy, the difficulties of conducting strategic cyber operations, and the limitations on the costs that can be generated through them mean that cyber operations are unlikely to cause escalation under most circumstances—including when they target an adversary's conventional or nuclear capabilities during crisis or conflict. However, there is a small set of potential pathways through which cyber operations could cause the kind of dangerous escalation dynamics that initial academic work on cyberspace feared—albeit through different mechanisms than the early cyber literature anticipated and under highly circumscribed conditions. Of particular concern is a potential scenario involving peer state adversaries in direct military conflict, where cyber operations are effectively employed as part of conventional campaigns.

An important implication of our analysis is that states that are at the cutting edge of military technology are more susceptible to escalation pressures than those with military forces that are less modernized. Moreover, it is precisely because of these asymmetries that less technologically advanced states may be more likely to exploit these vulnerabilities in adversaries with more modernized capabilities.[106] Therefore, despite the low probability that the scenarios discussed in this chapter will unfold, the potentially high consequences suggest that technologically advanced states should deliberately assess and consider how their warfighting and deterrence capabilities may be held at risk in cyberspace and take measures to reduce vulnerabilities and increase cybersecurity. In the following chapter we discuss a number of policy recommendations that follow from this analysis, with specific applications for the United States in terms of increasing the cybersecurity and resilience of key conventional warfighting systems and NC3.

---

[106] This concern drives debates within U.S. defense policy circles regarding appropriate strategies and concepts for overcoming adversary anti-access area denial (A2/AD) capabilities. See, for example, Andrew Krepinevich, Barry Watts, and Robert Work, "Meeting the Anti-Access and Area-Denial Challenge," Center for Strategic and Budgetary Analysis, 2003; Stephen Biddle and Ivan Oelrich, "Future Warfare in the Western Pacific: Chinese Antiaccess/Area Denial, U.S. AirSea Battle, and Command of the Commons in East Asia," *International Security* 41, no. 1 (Summer 2016): 7–48.

8

Implications for Policymaking

Bridging the Theory-Policy Gap

Despite longstanding concerns of many academics and practitioners, we find little evidence that cyber operations lead to escalatory spirals between rival states. Instead, the evidence overwhelmingly demonstrates that interactions in cyberspace—even between adversarial states—is characterized by tit-for-tat, proportionate responses that leverage both cyber and non-cyber instruments of power, but do not meaningfully increase the intensity of crises or escalate to the use of kinetic military force. We argue that this is due to core characteristics of cyber operations: the technical realities that make strategic cyber operations difficult and unreliable; limits on the costs that can be inflicted on a target through cyber means; and characteristics such as secrecy and the value of cyber operations for espionage that shape leaders' decision calculus regarding the risks and benefits of using cyber operations. Our analysis also suggests that the same factors that dampen escalation risks can also make cyber operations useful for accommodative signaling, creating space for crises to de-escalate. Deliberate decisions to maintain plausible deniability around cyber operations allow parties to avoid domestic political pressure to escalate. Moreover, the limited effects of cyber operations in comparison to alternative actions in a crisis can serve as a signal of restraint. Furthermore, states can leverage the importance of secrecy to share information about capabilities and operations to demonstrate reassurance.

However, this does not mean that cyber escalation is impossible. There is a narrow set of conditions under which cyber operations may trigger cross-domain escalation and, while the probability of this occurring is low, the potential consequences are high. This hypothetical escalation pathway stems from the dependence of conventional warfighting and nuclear deterrent capabilities on digital systems and the potentially unknown set of cyber vulnerabilities to which these systems are exposed. Following the logic of windows of vulnerability and incentives to strike first, a state may perceive that an adversary cyber operation during a crisis that targets its core warfighting and deterrence functions represents the initial salvo of an impending conflict. Or, during wartime, a cyber operation targeting these same capabilities could generate incentives to escalate if the target perceives a change in the balance of power on the battlefield.

Escalation Dynamics in Cyberspace. Erica D. Lonergan and Shawn W. Lonergan, Oxford University Press.
© Oxford University Press 2023. DOI: 10.1093/oso/9780197550885.003.0008

Taken together, our analysis suggests a number of important policy recommendations, particularly for the United States. First, there are important implications for the role of offensive cyber operations in U.S. strategy, especially in the wake of the Department of Defense's shift to a more assertive strategic concept of "defend forward."[1] Second, the role of cyber operations in signaling is highly underdeveloped in U.S. cyber strategy, despite its potential for escalation and crisis management. Finally, the potential consequences of inadvertent cyber escalation stemming from cyber operations conducted against critical conventional and nuclear systems, and the existing gaps in U.S. efforts to secure those systems against cyber adversary operations, suggest action should be taken to enhance the cybersecurity and resilience of these systems.

Offensive Cyber Operations and Escalation

In 2018, the U.S. Department of Defense issued a new cyber strategy that articulated a more engaged role for the military in cyberspace, epitomized in the concept of defend forward. The strategy states that the military will "defend forward to disrupt or halt malicious cyber activity at its source, including activity that falls below the level of armed conflict."[2] The strategy was published right after Cyber Command released its Command Vision, which calls for gaining and maintaining U.S. cyber superiority through "continuously engaging and contesting adversaries and causing them uncertainty wherever they maneuver."[3] Since then, the United States has reportedly taken measures to impose costs against adversaries in cyberspace in support of election defense and countering ransomware, among other missions.[4] This shift toward a more offensively inclined approach in cyberspace reflects a substantial change in approach from the Department of Defense's 2015 cyber strategy, which was focused on defending

---

[1] "Summary: Department of Defense Cyber Strategy," U.S. Department of Defense, 2018, https://media.defense.gov/2018/Sep/18/2002041658/-1/-1/1/CYBER_STRATEGY_SUMMARY_FINAL.PDF.

[2] Ibid., p. 1.

[3] "Achieve and Maintain Cyberspace Superiority: Command Vision for U.S. Cyber Command," *U.S. Cyber Command*, 2018, p. 6. Fischerkeller and Harknet elaborate on the concept of persistent engagement, which they define as "operational persistence . . . in an environment of constant activity." In their view, persistent engagement entails "continuous tactical, operational, and strategic interaction in cyberspace, which, over time, can begin to moderate and normalize into an environment of competition without nearing the threshold of armed conflict or the undermining of fundamental sources of power." See Michael P. Fischerkeller and Richard J. Harknett, "Persistent Engagement, Agreed Competition, Cyberspace Interaction Dynamics, and Escalation," *Institute for Defense Analysis* (May 2018): 12.

[4] Julian E. Barnes, "Cyber Command Operation Took Down Russian Troll Farm for Midterm Elections," *The New York Times*, February 26, 2019; Julian E. Barnes, "U.S. Military Has Acted against Ransomware Groups, General Acknowledges," *The New York Times*, December 5, 2021.

the department's networks and developing capabilities to defend the United States against cyber attacks of significant consequences, rather than more routinely conducting cyber operations beyond the networks controlled by the military, outside of the scope of war or conflict.[5]

This move to be more operationally engaged in cyberspace grew out of an evolution of thinking within the Department of Defense regarding the nature of the threat environment in cyberspace and the perceived insufficiency U.S. policy. In particular, there was a growing belief that organizing U.S. cyber forces around a response and retaliatory posture for adversary activity that does not rise to the level of warfare, but may nevertheless have significant implications, had been ineffective in preventing adversary campaigns; and initiatives that leverage nonmilitary instruments of power, such as sanctions, indictments, and attribution, had insufficiently altered the adversary's cost and risk calculus to dissuade them from conducting these campaigns.[6] The 2018 strategy reflects the view that, to thwart malicious adversary behavior, especially that occurring below the level of armed conflict, military cyber forces should operate beyond the military's own networks in what the U.S. military terms "gray" and "red" space—those parts of cyberspace that are owned or controlled by the adversary or third party entities.[7] This includes positioning forces forward in the virtual environment, as well as dispatching cyber teams to allied and partner nations, with their consent, to assist with cybersecurity efforts against shared threats.[8] The purpose of these activities is to deny, disrupt, and degrade adversary cyber operations and capabilities as close as possible to the source, to stop impending threats or reduce their effects. Defend forward could also enable early warning of forthcoming threats and support improved understanding of adversary intent and capabilities.[9]

---

[5] "The DoD Cyber Strategy," *U.S. Department of Defense*, 2015.

[6] Paul M. Nakasone, "A Cyber Force for Persistence Operations," *Joint Forces Quarterly* 92, no. 1 (2019): 10–14; Paul M. Nakasone and Michael Sulmeyer, "How to Compete in Cyberspace," *Foreign Affairs*, August 25, 2020.

[7] As stated in "Cyberspace Operations," Joint Publication 3–12, Joint Chiefs of Staff, June 2018, the term 'blue cyberspace' denotes areas in cyberspace protected by the US, its mission partners, and other areas DOD may be ordered to protect." While DoD has standing orders to protect the DODIN, forces will be prepared to defend or secure other USG networks. The term "red cyberspace" refers to "those portions of cyberspace owned or controlled by an adversary or enemy." Finally, "all cyberspace that does not meet the description of either 'blue' or 'red' is referred to as 'gray' cyberspace," pp. I-4–I-5.

[8] Mark Pomerleau, "How 'Hunt Forward' Teams Can Help Defend Networks," *Fifth Domain*, February 12, 2020, https://www.fifthdomain.com/dod/2020/02/12/how-hunt-forward-teams-can-help-defend-networks/; "DoD Has Enduring Role in Election Defense," *U.S. Department of Defense*, February 10, 2020, https://www.defense.gov/Explore/News/Article/Article/2078716/dod-has-endur ing-role-in-election-defense/#:~:text=%22In%20a%20hunt%20forward%20operation,'re%20pote ntially%20concerned%20about.%22.

[9] United States, Congress, Senate Armed Services Committee, Advance Policy Questions, Nomination Hearing, July 16, 2019, 116th Congress, Washington, 2019 (Advance Policy Questions for Dr. Mark T. Esper, Nominee for Appointment to be Secretary of Defense); United States, Congress, Senate Armed Services Committee, February 14, 2019, 116th Congress, Washington, 2019 (Statement of General Paul M. Nakasone, Commander United States Cyber Command); "An

In tandem with changes in the Department of Defense's strategy, there were also changes to law and policy that enabled the military to be more offensively engaged in cyberspace. The Trump Administration, for example, issued National Security Presidential Memorandum (NSPM) 13, which has been reported to further enable the implementation of defend forward. The contents of NSPM 13 remain classified, but public statements by senior officials have broadly confirmed that the memorandum addresses the decision-making process for conducting offensive cyber operations and the delegation of decision-making to lower levels.[10] According to the Department of Defense's General Counsel, the memorandum "allows for the delegation of well-defined authorities to the Secretary of Defense to conduct time-sensitive military operations in cyberspace."[11] And as then-U.S. Secretary of Defense Mark Esper noted in Congressional testimony in July 2019, "last year the [sic] put out a new NSPM-13, which really put our cyber capabilities on a more offensive footing, allowing us [sic] lean forward," and noted that "[o]n the offensive side, I think we have a lot of capabilities, but policy had not caught until, as you [sic] the passage of NSPM-13."[12]

Changes in law also enabled greater military activity in cyberspace. As part of the 2019 National Defense Authorization Act (NDAA), Congress defined cyber operations as "traditional military activity," distinct from covert action. This delegates authority to the Secretary of Defense to conduct unattributable cyber operations under a specific set of conditions. Relatedly, in the same piece of legislation, Congress pre-delegated authority to the commander of U.S. Cyber Command to take proportional action in response to active, systematic, and ongoing campaigns by Russian, Chinese, Iranian, and North Korean cyber attacks, as determined by the National Command Authority, and defines these responses as constituting traditional military activities.[13]

Interview with Paul M. Nakasone," *Joint Force Quarterly* no. 92 (2019): 4–9; Nakasone, "A Cyber Force for Persistent Operations," pp. 10–14.

[10] Ellen Nakashima, "White House Authorizes 'Offensive Cyber Operations' to Deter Foreign Adversaries," *The Washington Post*, September 20, 2018, https://www.washingtonpost.com/world/national-security/trump-authorizes-offensive-cyber-operations-to-deter-foreign-adversaries-bolton-says/2018/09/20/b5880578-bd0b-11e8-b7d2-0773aa1e33da_story.html.

[11] Hon. Paul C. Ney, Jr., "DOD General Counsel Remarks at U.S. Cyber Command Legal Conference," Department of Defense, March 2, 2020, https://www.defense.gov/Newsroom/Speeches/Speech/Article/2099378/dod-general-counsel-remarks-at-us-cyber-command-legal-conference/.

[12] Stenographic Transcript Before the Committee on Armed Services, United States Senate Hearing to Conduct a Confirming Hearing on the Expected Nomination of: Honorable Mark T. Esper to be Secretary of Defense, July 16, 2019, Washington, DC, pp. 37, 60. Also see Nakashima, "White House Authorizes 'Offensive Cyber Operations' to Deter Foreign Adversaries."

[13] John S. McCain National Defense Authorization Act for Fiscal Year 2019, H.R. 5515, 115th Congress, 2018, p. 18.

What are the escalation risks of U.S. offensive cyber operations?

External observers have raised a number of concerns about more offensive turn in U.S. cyber strategy, including ambiguity regarding how to define the desired end state and measure success; the feasibility of its implementation; and implications for allies, partners, and the private sector.[14] More pertinent to this analysis, there is a significant omission in U.S. strategy documents: they make absolutely no mention of the concept of escalation, despite the fact that a more proactive U.S. posture in cyberspace involving military cyber forces should raise concerns about whether this shift is likely to increase that.[15] It is not clear whether the absence of explicit references to escalation in the strategy is because policymakers simply did not consider these risks or because they did so but dismissed them.[16] Regardless, a critical question for U.S. policymakers is: What are the conditions under which the implementation of the defend forward strategy, or similar military cyber strategies involving offensive operations, might cause escalation?

Our finding that cyber operations are unlikely to trigger escalatory responses suggests some optimism is warranted, and the United States could conduct some offensive cyber operations without substantially increasing the risks of escalation. However, there are several caveats to this assessment. It requires that a strategy such as defend forward be clearly scoped; greater consistency in U.S. strategy and actions across the government; and improve communication with external parties about U.S. strategy and behavior in cyberspace. Ultimately, escalation is a function of a target's perception of an event, regardless of the intent

---

[14] Jacquelyn Schneider, "Persistent Engagement: Foundation, Evolution, and Evaluation of a Strategy," *Lawfare*, May 10, 2019, https://www.lawfareblog.com/persistent-engagement-foundat ion-evolution-and-evaluation-strategy; Jason Healey and Neil Jenkins, "Rough-and-Ready: A Policy Framework to Determine if Cyber Deterrence is Working or Failing," Paper presented at the 2019 11th International Conference on Cyber Conflict: Silent Battle, Tallinn; Brandon Valeriano and Benjamin Jensen, 2019, "The Myth of the Cyber Offense: The Case for Restraint," Cato Institute Policy Analysis No. 862, January 15, 2019; Rose McDermott, "Emotional Dynamics of Cyber Conflict," *forthcoming*; Emily Goldman and Michael Warner, "History of Persistent Engagement and Defend Forward," Minutes of Cyberspace Solarium Commission meeting 23 September 2019, Cyberspace Solarium Commission Main Office, Arlington, VA; Max Smeets, "U.S. Cyber Strategy of Persistent Engagement & Defend Forward: Implications for the Alliance and Intelligence Collection," *Intelligence and National Security* 35, no. 3 (2020): 444–453; Max Smeets, "Cyber Command's Strategy Risks Friction with Allies," *Lawfare*, May 28, 2019, https://www.lawfareblog.com/cyber-commands-strategy-risks-friction-allies.

[15] Jason Healey, "The Cartwright Conjecture: The Deterrent Value and Escalatory Risk of Fearsome Cyber Capabilities," in Herbert Lin and Amy Zegart, eds., *Bytes, Bombs, and Spies: The Strategic Dimensions of Offensive Cyber Operations* (Washington, DC: Brookings Institution Press, 2018), pp. 173–194,. Interestingly, the 2015 DoD Cyber Strategy describes cyber operations as useful for managing conflict escalation, p. 14. However, the discussion of escalation management is more about preserving escalation dominance and advantage for the United States, rather than preventing the risks of inadvertent escalation.

[16] Nina Kollars and Jacquelyn Schneider, "Defending Forward: The 2018 Cyber Strategy is Here," *War on the Rocks*, September 20, 2018, https://warontherocks.com/2018/09/defending-forward-the-2018-cyber-strategy-is-here/.

230 ESCALATION DYNAMICS IN CYBERSPACE

of the initiating party. Therefore, communication and signaling are essential to managing escalation risks. We address the latter issues more fully in a separate discussion of signaling.

With respect to scoping the strategic concept, public discussions of the concept by U.S. government officials have not clarified the left and right limits of defend forward beyond what exists in strategy documents and in law through the 2019 NDAA. For instance, then-National Security Advisor John Bolton described in September 2018 how the United States had "authorized offensive cyber operations" against adversaries.[17] Similarly, in September 2019 Esper described how the U.S. needs "to do more than just play goal line defense . . . . As such, the department's 2018 Cyber Strategy articulates a proactive and assertive approach to defend forward of our own virtual boundaries."[18] While it is clear that defend forward includes offensive cyber operations, an important question is whether the concept refers to any and all types of offensive cyber operations writ large, or some subset of clearly defined offensive cyber operations. We argue they should involve the latter, rather than the former.[19] Even setting aside concerns about escalation, our findings suggest that cyber operations have limited utility as instruments of coercion and to gain and maintain escalation dominance, and are resource intensive. This suggests that cyber operations conducted as part of defend forward, or other similar strategies in the future that rely on offensive cyber operations, should be comprised of two core elements.

First, defend forward should be conceptualized—and communicated—as a counter-cyber strategy aimed at disrupting, denying, and degrading the offensive cyber capabilities and supporting infrastructure and organizations that enable their offensive campaigns against the United States. A direct effect of these operations would be to make it more difficult for these actors to conduct cyber operations and campaigns. Additionally, a secondary effect could be to increase the indirect costs of such activity by forcing adversaries to shift to secondary and tertiary lines of effort and divert resources from other areas. This conceptualization of defend forward would deliberately exclude offensive cyber operations employed as part of a coercive strategy, particularly against adversary civilian critical infrastructure during peacetime.

Second, the bulk of activity associated with defend forward should, from our perspective, include operations to gain access to and maneuver where adversaries operate for the purposes of gathering information about evolving

---

[17] Nakashima, "White House Authorizes 'Offensive Cyber Operations' to Deter Foreign Adversaries."

[18] Jim Garamone, "Esper Describes DOD's Increased Cyber Offensive Strategy," U.S. Department of Defense, September 20, 2019, https://www.defense.gov/Explore/News/Article/Article/1966758/esper-describes-dods-increased-cyber-offensive-strategy/.

[19] Jacquelyn Schneider, "A Strategic Cyber No-First-Use Policy?," *The Washington Quarterly* 43, no. 2 (2020): 61–162.

adversary organizations, capabilities, tactics, techniques, procedures, and personas. Cyber operations fundamentally rest on intelligence collection, and their success is often a function of private information about vulnerabilities and capabilities. Therefore, actors that can cultivate better intelligence, improved situational awareness, and enhanced understanding of the threat environment are better positioned not only to carry out offensive operations but also to defend their own networks and systems. Prioritizing these lines of effort would enable the U.S. to develop comprehensive profiles of key threat actors and treat them as living, evolving organizations. Moreover, gaining access and pursuing adversaries can reduce the effects of adversary cyber campaigns through providing intelligence that can enable better situational awareness and support more tailored defensive efforts; serving as an early warning function that can enable counter-cyber operations to disrupt impending attacks; and passing information about impending adversary activity to owners and operators of the targeted infrastructure, including private sector entities.

Additionally, the United States should take care to avoid the kinds of cyber operations that adversaries might perceive as precursors to conflict or to a kinetic strike. If there is a pressing operational or strategic imperative to conduct these types of operations, this should occur in tandem with efforts to balance operational requirements with communication and transparency to avoid misunderstandings. This demands that institutionalized communication mechanisms be established in advance to address potential crises, which we discuss further later in this chapter. Being deliberate about refraining from engaging in the kind of activity in cyberspace that could generate perceptions of windows of vulnerability requires prioritizing strategic intelligence collection against adversary perception of the cyber threat environment, U.S. strategy and force employment concepts, and the relationship between cyberspace and adversary regime survival and stability—and having these assessments inform U.S. cyber campaign planning.

Cyber operations alone are insufficient to shape adversary behavior

Our analysis also demonstrates that cyber operations alone are likely to be insufficient to shape adversary behavior. This is because cyber operations are limited in their ability to generate costs against targeted entities, and cyber capabilities are not highly reliable in the sense of being able to employ them at the desired time against a specific set of targets. This means that cyber operations, conducted independently of other actions, are likely to be insufficient to induce adversary behavior to shift in a desired direction. Cyber operations could be used to frustrate adversaries' cyber operations, making it more difficult for them to carry out their campaigns. And they could allow the United States to gain better information about adversaries to improve defensive efforts across the government and private sector. However, this essentially leverages cyberspace as a limited tool to meet a very specific set of tactical and operational objectives in support of a campaign plan or contingency operation, rather than as an independent capability that can cause decisive and strategic effects. Put simply, counter-cyber operations in themselves are not sufficiently decisive to impose the costs necessary to generate effects at scale and to meaningfully change the decision calculus of adversary states. Rather, conducting cyber operations may require coordination across other elements within the U.S. government that employ other instruments of national power.[20]

The inherent limitations of offensive cyber operations is one reason why, for example, the Cyberspace Solarium Commission—created by Congress in 2019 to develop a cyber strategy for the United States—recommended integrating defend forward into a broader government strategy that incorporates the full range of instruments of national power.[21] The commission's March 2020 report specifically calls for the U.S. government to update its national cyber strategy to "clearly express that defend forward is an integral part of a comprehensive approach that encompasses all of the instruments of national power beyond the employment of strictly military capabilities; these include trade and economic efforts, law enforcement activities, and diplomatic tools."[22]

One critical area where coordination is important is across military and diplomatic efforts in cyberspace. The State Department takes the lead in leveraging diplomacy and working through various international fora to promote norms of acceptable behavior for cyberspace and deter cyber attacks. However, it's not clear the extent to which the State Department and Department of Defense are coordinating on efforts to shape behavior in cyberspace—even though proponents of a more proactive military approach in cyberspace advocate for concepts that are grounded in an implicit argument about how norms of acceptable behavior develop in cyberspace.[23] Indeed, Emily Goldman, who spent 2018–2019 as a cyber

---

[20] Nicole Perlroth and David E. Sanger, "White House Eliminates Cybersecurity Coordinator Role," *The New York Times*, May 15, 2018, https://www.nytimes.com/2018/05/15/technology/white-house-cybersecurity.html. The recent U.S. campaign to secure the 2018 midterm elections, which did involve a number of different executive branch departments and agencies, was based on an ad hoc task force organizational construct, rather than driven by a top-down, institutionalized role that would play a coordination and integration function.

[21] Erica D. Borghard and Mark Montgomery, "Defend Forward as a Whole-of-Nation Effort," *Lawfare*, March 11, 2020, https://www.lawfareblog.com/defend-forward-whole-nation-effort.

[22] Angus King and Mike Gallagher, co-chairs, "United States of America Cyberspace Solarium Commission," *U.S. Cyberspace Solarium Commission*, March 2020, p. 33.

[23] Michael P. Fischerkeller and Richard J. Harknett, "Persistent Engagement and Tacit Bargaining: A Path toward Constructing Norms in Cyber Space," *Lawfare*, November 9, 2018,

advisor to the director of policy planning at the State Department, noted this mismatch.[24]

Offensive cyber operations are not inherently inimical to U.S. efforts to shape norms of acceptable behavior in cyberspace. However, diplomatic efforts and military cyber operations should be more closely coordinated to ensure that strategic messaging is consistent with and continuously reinforced by action. This requires a coherent, national-level strategy that articulates how diplomatic and military instruments of power can and should work together, identifies the conditions under which operational imperatives and norms may be in tension, and defines a process for adjudicating priorities. There are similar concerns about coordinating military and law enforcement efforts, particularly given the historical independence of law enforcement bodies in choosing how and when indictments and other law enforcement actions that may be in tension with military priorities are pursued.[25] This is increasingly important given the growing overlap of military and law enforcement cyber operations, especially in the realm of cyber criminal activity, such as ransomware, conducted with the implicit or explicit direction of state adversaries.

A Strategy for Signaling and De-Escalation

Relatedly, an important implication of our research is that the United States should more systematically address how it communicates about its cyber strategy and operations, as well as develop viable pathways for de-escalation and crisis management. Currently, there is a significant amount of strategic ambiguity about the role of offensive cyber operations in U.S. strategy; how new concepts such as defend forward relate to traditional deterrence and warfighting concepts; and what types of cyber activities constitute (or do not constitute) defend forward. Moreover, policymakers and practitioners have publicly described the military's cyber strategy as being more "aggressive" or "offensive," which raises concerns about misperceptions that may have implications for escalation.[26] By

https://www.lawfareblog.com/persistent-engagement-and-tacit-bargaining-path-toward-constructing-norms-cyberspace.

[24] Emily O. Goldman, "From Reaction to Action: Adopting a Competitive Posture in Cyber Diplomacy," *Texas National Security Review*, September 3, 2020, https://tnsr.org/2020/09/from-reaction-to-action-adopting-a-competitive-posture-in-cyber-diplomacy/.
[25] Tim Maurer and Garrett Hinck, 2019, "What's the Point of Charging Foreign State-Linked Hackers," *Lawfare*, May 24, 2019, https://www.lawfareblog.com/whats-point-charging-foreign-state-linked-hackers; Christopher Ashley Ford, "Cyberspace Security Diplomacy: Deterring Aggression in Turing's Monument," Department of State, May 13, 2020, https://www.state.gov/cyberspace-security-diplomacy-deterring-aggression-in-turings-monument/.
[26] For instance, in his 2019 confirmation hearing General Mark Milley testified that, in cyberspace, the best defense is a good offense. See "Stenographic Transcript Before the Committee on Armed

way of example, in 2018 the Trump Administration released its National Cyber Strategy, the Department of Defense delivered its updated Cyber Strategy, and Cyber Command promulgated its Command Vision.[27] However, there is marked tension across these documents. For instance, the 2018 National Cyber Strategy does not even refer to the concepts of defend forward or persistent engagement.[28] Therefore, a priority action for the U.S. government should be to define and clarify defend forward and better communicate the strategy to external audiences, both domestic and international. Without a coherently articulated strategy that its allies, partners, and adversaries alike understand, the United States risks strategic disintegration, with political ends and the means to carry them out poorly integrated, incoherent, or at odds with one another.[29]

Our research has also demonstrated that, while cyber operations have marginal utility for signaling resolve, they can be useful for accommodative signaling to create opportunities for escalation during international crises. But U.S. cyber strategy has not paid meaningful attention to the role and nature of signaling in cyberspace. This includes using cyber operations themselves as signals and coupling cyber operations with more traditional forms of signaling (through both public and private diplomacy, as well as actions utilizing other instruments of power) to bring greater clarity to U.S. cyber strategy and convey intent to external parties. Indeed, as Jason Healey notes, "there are almost zero out-of-band means to signal and de-escalate cyber tensions, complicating efforts to convince other nations a mistake is not an intentional attack."[30]

In particular, while cyber operations have properties that sometimes make them conducive for de-escalation, it's not apparent that the United States has deliberately incorporated cyber operations into its strategy for these purposes.

Services, United States Senate, Hearing to Consider the Nomination of: General Mark A. Milley, USA, for Reappointment to the Grade of General and Be Chairman of the Joint Chiefs of Staff," Washington, DC, July 11, 2018, pp. 64–65 https://www.armed-services.senate.gov/imo/media/doc/19-58_07-11-19.pdf.

[27] "National Strategy of the United States of America," The White House, September 2018; "U.S. Department of Homeland Security Cybersecurity Strategy," Department of Homeland Security, May 15, 2018; "Summary of the 2018 National Defense Strategy of the United States of America: Sharpening the American Military's Competitive Edge," Department of Defense, 2018; "Summary: Department of Defense Cyber Strategy"; "Achieve and Maintain Cyberspace Superiority: Command Vision for U.S. Cyber Command," United States Cyber Command, 2018.
[28] "Recommendations to the President on Protecting American Cyber Interests through International Engagement," Office of the Coordinator for Cyber Issues, U.S. Department of State, May 31, 2018; "Recommendations to the President on Deterring Adversaries and Better Protecting the American People from Cyber Threats," Office of the Coordinator for Cyber Issues, U.S. Department of State, May 31, 2018.
[29] Barry R. Posen, The Sources of Military Doctrine (Ithaca, NY: Cornell University Press, 1984), pp. 24–29.
[30] Jason Healey, "The Implications of Persistent (and Permanent) Engagement in Cyberspace," Journal of Cybersecurity 5, no. 1 (2019): 8.

Instead, defend forward appears to rely on a tacit, implied bargaining and communication process between adversarial states to keep actions contained within acceptable (but ambiguously defined) boundaries.[31] While case studies reveal reported instances of cyber operations carried out by entities associated with the U.S. government during recent crises, they do not indicate that this was part of an intended signaling strategy to help manage or de-escalate international crises. Developing the capability to provide cyber options to decision makers to support signaling in the context of geopolitical crises requires prior planning and preparation. This may be distinct from planning requirements for cyber options as part of operations or contingency plans, although accesses developed in support of these could be leveraged for an unanticipated crisis event.

At the strategic level, the United States could develop and implement a signaling strategy that leverages existing, non-cyber communications mechanisms, such as public and private diplomatic communications and confidence-building measures (CBMs), as well as military-to-military channels. CBMs play an important role in reassurance, crisis stability, and escalation management. They are "a form of reassurance that seeks to demonstrate intent among rivals, therefore (ideally) conveying a desire to maintain the status quo and foster a sense of security between otherwise threatened states."[32] As the 2015 United Nations Group of Government Experts (UN GGE) report suggests, CBMs "can increase interstate cooperation, transparency, predictability and stability."[33] As previously discussed in this book, an example of a bilateral CBM for cyberspace is the agreement between the United States and Russia to use the Nuclear Risk Reduction Center (NRRC), the "nuclear hotline," as a forum for inquiring about cybersecurity incidents.[34] At present, it is not clear in what way existing U.S. strategy conceptualizes the role of CBMs in relation to offensive cyber

---

[31] Michael P. Fischerkeller, "Persistent Engagement and Tacit Bargaining: A Strategic Framework for Norms Development in Cyberspace's Agreed Competition," Institute for Defense Analysis, November 2018; Michael P. Fischerkeller and Richard J. Harknett, "Persistent Engagement and Tacit Bargaining: A Path toward Constructing Norms in Cyberspace," *Lawfare*, November 9, 2018; Michael P. Fischerkeller and Richard J. Harknett, "What Is Agreed Competition in Cyberspace?" *Lawfare*, February 19, 2019, https://www.lawfareblog.com/persistent-engagement-and-tacit-bargaining-path-toward-constructing-norms-cyberspace.

[32] Erica D. Borghard and Shawn W. Lonergan, "Confidence Building Measures for the Cyber Domain," *Strategic Studies Quarterly* 12, no. 3 (2018): 12.

[33] United Nations, Group of Government Experts on Developments in the Field of Information and Telecommunications in the Context of International Security, *Report of the Group of Governmental Experts on Developments in the Field of Information and Telecommunications in the Context of International Security*, A/70/174, 22 July 2015, https://www.un.org/ga/search/view_doc.asp?symbol=A/70/174.

[34] "Fact Sheet: U.S.-Russian Cooperation on Information and Communications Technology Security," Office of the Press Secretary, June 17, 2013, https://obamawhitehouse.archives.gov/the-press-office/2013/06/17/fact-sheet-us-russian-cooperation-information-and-communications-technol.

operations. However, CBMs can offer one avenue to manage escalation concerns, particularly if they are synchronized with cyber operations.

Furthermore, signaling is typically conceived of as existing at the strategic level. The most notable examples of signaling—diplomatic communications, the movement of carrier groups, testing a thermonuclear weapon, or public ultimatums—are all instances in which the intended audience of a signal is the decision maker on the receiving end. However, a significant amount of signaling also occurs in international politics at the tactical and operational level, where the immediate intended audience is the operator, even if the ultimate audience is a national decision maker. Examples of this type of signaling include communications by the Chinese People's Liberation Army Navy sailors to U.S. sailors conducting freedom of navigation operations in contested waters; signaling to establish standoff distances between troops of foreign countries operating in Syria; or fighter jets conducting maneuvers (such as "headbutting") or engaging in direct radio communications with other aircraft. Like strategic signaling, tactical signaling is meant to shape decision-making, perception, and behavior. In cyberspace, there is some evidence that the United States may already be directly engaging adversary operators to directly communicate or convey messages.[35] However, to be effective, this kind of stealthy, direct communication should be deliberately designed to be consistent with how the United States seeks to convey intentions and images to adversaries. Currently, there is little public information about the extent to which this kind of effort is part of a comprehensive strategy of using cyber operations for tactical signaling.

Finally, our research shows that there is value in being strategic about the use of attribution as a policy tool. Specifically, an important implication of our research is that public attribution may not always be the best policy choice, particularly during a crisis. This runs contrary to an implicit assumption in U.S. cyber policy circles that more public, more rapid attribution is an unalloyed good.[36] However, this ignores some compelling evidence that secrecy, particularly in some crisis situations, could help reduce domestic political pressure and enable crises to de-escalate. Rather than default to rapid, public attribution under all circumstances, the U.S. government should consider how it could strategically leverage the plausible deniability of cyber operations in some contexts, specifically with respect to decisions surrounding the timing and means of attribution. Our analysis suggests the United States should develop a framework that would determine when and under what conditions cyber operations and campaigns should be attributed, whether to domestic or adversarial operations.

---

[35] Julian E. Barnes, "U.S. Begins First Cyberoperation against Russia Aimed at Protecting Elections," *The New York Times*, October 23, 2018.

[36] See, for example, "Executive Order on Improving the Nation's Cybersecurity," The White House, May 12, 2021.

Clarifying thresholds in cyberspace

The role of thresholds in U.S. cyber strategy is related to these issues of signaling and escalation management.[37] Thresholds represent some type of explicit or implicit boundary that, if crossed by one or both parties, leads to a qualitative change in the nature of their interactions. They are "socially constructed and, ultimately, exist in the minds of the actors rather than in objective reality."[38] Thresholds are integral to the concept of escalation and were the defining feature of Herman Kahn's escalation ladder.[39] Given that what counts as escalation ultimately rests in the perception of the targeted entity, clarifying where thresholds exist and how they are delineated is an important aspect of escalation management and an area where signaling and communication should play a key role. Research by Sarah Kreps and Jacquelyn Schneider has demonstrated that cyber operations are currently perceived to exist below the threshold of use of conventional military force.[40] However, below that threshold, U.S. policy is ambiguous about distinguishing between various forms of cyber behavior, even though they may have different strategic implications.

One clear threshold is that which distinguishes between cyber operations and the use of kinetic force, which is alternatively (and interchangeably) referred to as a "use of force" threshold or an "armed conflict" threshold.[41] International law distinguishes between a lower "use of force" threshold in Article 2(4) of the United Nations charter and a higher threshold of "armed attack" in Article 51. However, the United States has long maintained a policy that "there is no distinction between a use of force and an armed attack, and that any unlawful use of force qualifies as an armed attack triggering the right of self-defense" and has extended this notion to cyber operations.[42] Further, similar to other domains, the United States promulgates an ambiguous declaratory policy for cyberspace around the use of force threshold in which it reserves the right to respond to a

---

[37] Sarah Kreps and Jacquelyn Schneider, "Escalation Firebreaks in the Cyber, Conventional, and Nuclear Domains: Moving Beyond Effects-Based Logics," *Journal of Cybersecurity* 5, no. 1 (2019): 1–11. Also see Schneider, "A Strategic Cyber No-First-Use Policy?"

[38] Forrest E. Morgan, Karl P. Mueller, Evan S. Medeiros, Kevin L. Pollpeter, and Roger Cliff, *Dangerous Thresholds: Managing Escalation in the 21st Century* (Santa Monica, CA: RAND Corporation, 2008), p. 11.

[39] Kreps and Schneider, "Escalation Firebreaks in the Cyber, Conventional, and Nuclear Domains," p. 2.

[40] Ibid.

[41] See, for example, "Achieve and Maintain Cyberspace Superiority," p. 3; "Summary: 2018 Department of Defense Cyber Strategy," pp. 1–4. "The North Atlantic Treaty," NATO, April 1949, https://www.nato.int/cps/en/natolive/official_texts_17120.htm; Jens Stoltenberg, NATO Secretary General, 2019, "NATO Will Defend Itself," NATO, August 2019.

[42] Catherine Lotrionte, "Reconsidering the Consequences for State-Sponsored Hostile Cyber Operations Under International Law," *The Cyber Defense Review* 3, no. 2 (2018): 87.

cyber attack at a time, place, and manner of its choosing.[43] In a recent example of this ambiguous declaratory policy, the 2018 National Cyber Strategy states that "All instruments of national power are available to prevent, respond to, and deter malicious cyber activity against the United States. This includes diplomatic, information, military (both kinetic and cyber), financial, intelligence, public attribution, and law enforcement capabilities." It goes further to state that the United States and its allies and partners will "attribute and deter malicious cyber activities with integrated strategies that impose swift, costly, and transparent consequences when malicious actors harm the United States or our partners."[44] This is consistent with prior statements, such as President Obama stating in 2014 in response to the Sony hack that the United States would respond "in a place and time and manner that we choose."[45]

Some observers might contend that the current, ambiguous declaratory policy has been successful because there has not yet been an instance of a cyber attack against the United States that breached a use of force threshold, as most would define it (and certainly not an armed attack). However, U.S. adversaries are clearly exploiting this threshold to conduct a range of cyber campaigns below that level, suggesting that, despite the strategic value in maintaining flexibility, the current U.S. approach to communicating about thresholds may be insufficient to address the bulk of adversarial cyber behavior.[46]

For instance, the United States may find some cyber behavior objectionable and seek to reduce its occurrence, but nevertheless begrudgingly accept it as state practice in cyberspace. This could include intelligence, counter-intelligence, and information-gathering cyber operations. Conversely, there may be a set of cyber activities that do not rise to a use of force level, but for which the United States may reserve the right to employ counter-cyber and other proportional actions to reduce their magnitude and effects. This could include cyber campaigns that seek to interfere in democratic elections or disrupt the functioning of critical infrastructure. There may then be a further set of actions for which more aggressive responses are reserved, such as cyber attacks that have significant,

---

[43] Erik Gartzke and Jon Lindsay, "The Cyber Commitment Problem and the Destabilization of Nuclear Deterrence," in *Bytes, Bombs, and Spies*, p. 212. The concept of a "declaratory policy" grew out of Cold War strategies of nuclear deterrence. The underlying logic was that, to promote the credibility of deterrence, the U.S. had to publicly define the conditions under which it would use nuclear weapons, to include reserving the right to use these capabilities first in a conflict. See Alexander L. George and Richard Smoke, *Deterrence in American Foreign Policy* (New York: Columbia University Press, 1974). NATO has a similar declaratory policy for cyberspace in which a "cyber attack" can trigger the invoking of Article V by members. See, Stoltenberg, "NATO Will Defend Itself."

[44] 2018 National Cyber Strategy, p. 21.

[45] David E. Sanger, Michael S. Schmidt, and Nicole Perlroth, "Obama Vows a Response to Cyberattack on Sony," *The New York Times*, December 19, 2014.

[46] Schneider suggests defining two thresholds, "strategic cyber attack" and "status quo cyber competition." See "A Strategic Cyber No-First-Use Policy?," p. 162.

permanent, or destructive effects on critical infrastructure and key resources, or that lead to loss of life.[47] Elucidating how to categorize these cyber operations with respect to existing thresholds, and potentially defining new thresholds, as well as clarifying how its strategies and response options broadly map onto these different categories, would help the United States more accurately convey intent, set expectations, and manage escalation risks. This does not mean that such communications should function as red lines that bind decision makers to rigid stances and foreclose the possibility of flexible and adaptive approaches. However, greater clarity than the current level of ambiguity would have strategic benefits.

How the U.S. communicates about its cyber strategy should match how it operates in the virtual environment and the image it seeks to project to external audiences. This requires a coherent, rather than an ad hoc (or absent), approach to signaling, and that the various elements of U.S. cyber strategy to be coordinated and support mutually reinforcing and shared objectives.

Securing Conventional and Nuclear Weapon Systems

Finally, our analysis of the interdependence between the digital environment and conventional and nuclear weapon systems raises questions about the extent to which core U.S. warfighting and deterrence capabilities may be vulnerable to adversary cyber operations. During conditions of crisis and conflict, it is certainly plausible that an adversary may seek to use offensive cyber capabilities to disrupt or degrade the functioning or command and control of U.S. military capabilities. While this is likely to require a significant level of organizational maturity and skill, which currently only a handful of states possess, changes in the geopolitical environment make it more likely that the United States will face conflict with more capable adversaries.

In previous chapters, we described how cyber operations that target military capabilities may lead to inadvertent escalation through perceived windows of vulnerability and first strike advantages during a crisis or in a wartime situation. Institutionalizing and strengthening CBMs, as discussed in the previous section, to facilitate communication and transparency about these kinds of activities so a to avoid escalation is critical. While reaching a clear consensus with adversaries about cyber operations targeting, for example, nuclear command and control may be a bridge too far for the United States, deliberate engagements that aim to sensitize decision makers on all sides about the issues and risks of

---

[47] See Jacquelyn G. Schneider, "The Cyberspace Solarium Commission: From Competing to Complementary Strategies," *Lawfare*, April 1, 2020.

these types of cyber operations can help clarify potential areas of concern and reduce misperceptions. Relatedly, in conducting offensive cyber operations during peacetime and developing operation and contingency plans for conflict, the United States should take into account how adversaries are likely to perceive cyber operations targeting sensitive military capabilities and infrastructure. Incorporating plausible use cases into war games and exercises could help identify potential flash points and areas of greatest risk.

Furthermore, with respect to cyber threats to weapon systems, the U.S. technological edge in the conventional realm is a core comparative advantage. Indeed, this is why U.S. adversaries typically prefer to contest the United States below the use of force threshold in the "gray zone" and eschew direct confrontation. At the same time, U.S. adversaries are making substantial investments in technology and innovation in an attempt to directly erode that edge, while also shielding themselves by developing asymmetric capabilities, such as anti-access area-denial capabilities.[48] Moreover, U.S. adversaries are engaging in cyber espionage to discern where key military capabilities and systems may be vulnerable, so they can not only develop similar or offset capabilities but also ostensibly so that they can hold them at risk and potentially blind and paralyze the United States in a time of crisis or conflict.[49]

From a policymaking perspective, while there has been considerable emphasis on assessing the merits of defend forward and offensive cyber operations, this should not come at the expense of efforts to address the cyber defense and resilience of the capabilities that support deterrence and warfighting, and crafting measures to avoid the escalation risks that may emerge from adversary—and U.S.—cyber operations in these systems. This suggests that the United States should not only invest in bolstering CBMs for transparency, but also dedicate resources toward improving the cybersecurity and resilience of critical conventional and nuclear military systems and functions. The scope and challenge of doing so is immense and, despite recent laudable efforts to enhance weapon system cybersecurity, significant gaps remain. This is perhaps most prominent for so-called super weapons, such as the as the F-35 Joint Strike Fighter and its

---

[48] See, for example, "Overview of the State of the U.S. S&E Enterprise in a Global Context," National Science Board, Science & Engineering Indicators, 2018, p. 1; Scott Boston et al. "Assessing the Conventional Force Imbalance in Europe: Implications for Countering Russian Local Superiority," RAND Corporation, 2018.

[49] Gordon Lubold and Dustin Volz, "Navy, Industry Partners are 'Under Cyber Siege' by Chinese Hackers, Review Asserts," *The Wall Street Journal*, March 12, 2019, https://www.wsj.com/articles/navy-industry-partners-are-under-cyber-siege-review-asserts-11552415553; Zak Doffman, 2019, "Cyber Warfare: U.S. Military Admits Immediate Danger is 'Keeping Us Up at Night," *Forbes*, July 21, 2019, https://www.forbes.com/sites/zakdoffman/2019/07/21/cyber-warfare-u-s-military-adm its-immediate-danger-is-keeping-us-up-at-night/#7f48cd941061.

unparalleled technology, sensors, and situational awareness.[50] But the reality is that the increasingly computerized and networked nature of weapon platforms is a systemic challenge that is not confined only to a select category of advanced weapon platforms.

Concerns about vulnerabilities and the acquisition process for emerging technologies are longstanding.[51] However, clear and consistent mechanisms to identify and assess cyber vulnerabilities and determine the risk to U.S. weapon systems have significant room for maturation.[52] A number of independent reports have documented ongoing gaps and highlighted persistent risks. For instance, in 2020 a Government Accountability Office (GAO) report found significant delays in the Department of Defense's compliance with cybersecurity vulnerabilities assessments that had been mandated by Congress. The 2020 report highlights how major defense acquisition programs are characterized by "inconsistent implementation of leading software development approaches and cybersecurity practices;" that the Department of Defense is behind in conducting cybersecurity vulnerability assessments and cybersecurity assessments; and that it often fails to factor cybersecurity requirements into acquisitions at the outset.[53]

These challenges suggest that the United States should institutionalize a recurring process to assess and remediate the cyber vulnerabilities of individual weapon platforms and systems that are comprised of multiple (legacy and new) capabilities. In particular, this process should prioritize cyber threats to NC3 as well as space-based systems, given the dual-use of the latter in enabling the employment of both conventional and nuclear forces, and the essential role of the former in ensuring the effective functioning of nuclear deterrence. Space-based assets, for instance, are critical for U.S. precision strike capabilities. During the 2003 invasion of Iraq, 68% of U.S. munitions used outer space-based capabilities for precision targeting.[54] Moreover, there are new and under-researched challenges stemming from the interdependence of cyber- and space-based

---

[50] Valerie Insinna, "Inside America's Dysfunctional Trillion-Dollar Fighter-Jet Program," *The New York Times Magazine*, August 21, 2019, https://www.nytimes.com/2019/08/21/magazine/f35-joint-strike-fighter-program.html.

[51] Office of Inspector General, "Progress and Challenges in Securing the Nation's Cyberspace," edited by Department of Homeland Security, Washington DC: Office of Information Technology, July 2004, pp. 1–36, https://nsarchive2.gwu.edu/NSAEBB/NSAEBB424/docs/Cyber-019.pdf.

[52] See Erica D. Borghard, "Congress Should Act to Ensure Weapon Systems' Cybersecurity," *Net Politics*, September 10, 2020, https://www.cfr.org/blog/congress-should-act-ensure-weapon-systems-cybersecurity.

[53] "Defense Acquisitions Annual Assessment: Drive to Deliver Capabilities Faster Increases Importance of Program Knowledge and Consistent Data for Oversight," Government Accountability Office, June 2020, pp. 24, 41–47.

[54] Beyza Unal, "Cybersecurity of NATO's Space-Based Strategic Assets," Chatham House, July 2019, p. 2, https://www.chathamhouse.org/sites/default/files/2019-06-27-Space-Cybersecurity-2.pdf.

systems that inevitably generate complex and systemic vulnerabilities that threat actors could exploit.[55]

Looking Ahead

Despite longstanding concerns that cyberspace poses unique escalatory risks, there is little empirical support to back up these claims. However, this does not mean that practitioners should be sanguine about the risks of cyber operations. It is plausible that some actions in cyberspace may trigger inadvertent escalation under very narrow—but highly consequential—conditions due to the interdependence of conventional and nuclear weapon systems with the digital world. Given these concerns, policymakers in the United States should take due care to scope the conditions under which offensive cyber operations are employed, be more transparent about communicating these limits to external parties, and invest in measures that facilitate clearer signaling of intent and promote crisis stability. Ultimately, if escalation is in the eye of the beholder, the United States needs to do a better job of understanding how adversaries perceive its own activities and leverage that knowledge to conduct cyber operations while minimizing the risks of unintended escalation.

Looking ahead, some may argue that a compelling explanation for the general absence of escalation in cyberspace between interstate rivals is the reality that the current international system is characterized by an overall absence of territorial conquest and interstate war. Therefore, by extension, if the stability of the international system deteriorates and great power competition becomes more salient, one might expect that instances of cyber escalation would increase. Nevertheless, our argument would suggest that, under conditions of heightened geopolitical instability, cyber operations are still not particularly useful as tools of coercion and escalation. In fact, there could be a benefit to cyber operations in a more unstable world, given their lack of physical violence. As international politics becomes more dangerous, cyber operations that enable states to respond to perceived aggressions without causing physical destruction or loss of life could provide much-needed stability, rather than stoke instability.

That said, a change in the underlying characteristics of cyberspace that currently minimize escalation could portend a change in the risks associated with

---

[55] David A Deptula, William LaPlante, and Robert Haddick, "Modernizing U.S. Nuclear Command, Control and Communications," Mitchell Institute for Aerospace Studies, February 2019; Jon Lindsay, "Digital Strangelove: The Cyber Dangers of Nuclear Weapons," *Lawfare*, March 12, 2020, https://www.lawfareblog.com/digital-strangelove-cyber-dangers-nuclear-weapons.

cyber operations. But it's not clear that these dynamics will change in favor of increased escalation. In fact, a number of trends suggest greater fragmentation of cyberspace rather than increased interdependence and, by extension, greater ease of access and a larger surface area of attack. Internet Balkanization—the splintering of the global internet into more closed, often regional or state-based systems—may make it more rather than less difficult for states to gain access to adversary networks and systems.[56] This would likely increase the relative costs of offense over defense. It may also make it easier for states to spot anomalous traffic on their networks. Furthermore, efforts to cultivate cyber resilience— the ability to withstand and rapidly recover core functions and services in the wake of a cyber incident—may further reduce the impact of offensive cyber operations. Building domestic resilience to cyber attacks is at the foundation of U.S. domestic cyber strategy.[57] Russia has experimented with an indigenous alternative to the global internet.[58] China is undertaking a "multi-year effort [to] control information flows, physical devices, software, and internet services in the country [as part of] an effort to increase China's resilience . . . to hostile cyber attack and politically-motivated information manipulation."[59] States may make even greater investments in highly customized software, rather than relying on commercial off the shelf technologies that may be less secure, such as the joint effort between China and Microsoft for the latter to develop a customized version of Windows 10.[60] Efforts to improve supply chain risk management approaches may make backdoors even more difficult to emplace. States could work to develop strategies to secure foundational internet protocols, such as the Domain Name System and the Border Gateway Protocol, and implement measures to improve email security.[61] The list goes on.

Therefore, while there is certainly a wide range of plausible alternative futures, it is not preordained that the system will become less secure and more dangerous

---

[56] Michael A. Spence, "Preventing the Balkanization of the Internet," Council on Foreign Relations, March 28, 2018, https://www.cfr.org/blog/preventing-balkanization-internet; Mark Scott, "Goodbye Internet: How Regional Divides Upended the World Wide Web," *Politico*, December 15, 2017, https://www.politico.eu/article/internet-governance-facebook-google-splinternet-europe-net-neutrality-data-protection-privacy-united-states-u-s/.

[57] See King and Gallagher, "Solarium," pp. 54–70; "U.S. Department of Homeland Security Cyber Security Strategy," *U.S. Department of Homeland Security*, May 15, 2018.

[58] Jane Wakefield, "Russia 'Successfully Tests' Its Unplugged Internet," *BBC News*, December 24, 2019, https://www.bbc.com/news/technology-50902496.

[59] John Costello, "China's Strategic Support Force: A Force for a New Era," Testimony to the U.S-China Economic and Security Review Commission, February 15, 2018.

[60] Craig Miller, "Security Considerations in Managing COTS Software," Cybersecurity and Infrastructure Security Agency, December 14, 2006, https://us-cert.cisa.gov/bsi/articles/best-practices/legacy-systems/security-considerations-in-managing-cots-software; Tom Warren, "Microsoft Finalizes Its Custom Version of Windows 10 for China," *The Verge*, March 21, 2017, https://www.theverge.com/2017/3/21/14998644/microsoft-windows-10-china-custom-version.

[61] King and Gallagher, "Solarium," p. 86.

over time. That being said, states have an important role to play in these efforts. The United States, specifically, should make a concerted effort in the present to reduce its own vulnerabilities and invest in CBMs and other communications mechanisms to enhance the stability of the international cyber system. As the global balance of power inevitably shifts, this imperative becomes even more pressing.

Index

For the benefit of digital users, indexed terms that span two pages (e.g., 52–53) may, on occasion, appear on only one of those pages.
Tables and figures are indicated by *t* and *f* following the page number

Izz ad-Din Al-Qassam Cyber Fighters, 149–50, 149n.166

Japan
Coast Guard, 169–70
lack of cyber escalation and, 115
Manchuria, invasion of, 169–70
Ministry of Defense (JMOD), 171–72, 174
Ministry of Internal Affairs, 171–72
Self-Defense Forces (JSDF), 172
Senkaku/Diaoyu Islands dispute, 168–74 (*see also* Senkaku/Diaoyu Islands dispute)
Jenkins, Neil, 109
Jensen, Benjamin, 23–24, 83–84, 93–94, 109–10
Jervis, Robert, 18, 63, 64, 89, 89n.17
Joint Comprehensive Plan of Action (JCPOA), 143–46, 159t, 184–85
Joint Concept for Access and Maneuver in the Global Commons (JAM-GC), 207, 214–15, 214n.62
Joint Publication for Cyberspace Operations, 15–16
Joyce, Rob, 6–7
Justice Department, 103–4, 125–26, 127–28, 149–50, 149n.166

Kahn, Herman, 11–12, 12n.41, 12n.43, 83–84, 88, 208–9, 237
Kashmir attack, 159t
Kaufmann, Chaim, 66–67, 68, 71–72
Kello, Lucas, 15n.56, 29, 47, 61–62
Kennedy, John F., 11–12
Kim Jong Un, 141, 189–91, 192, 193
King, Angus, 138
Kosovo War, 86
Kostyuk, Nadiya, 4–5, 13n.47, 218–19
Kreps, Sarah, 6, 237
Kyrgyzstan, pro-Western movement in, 130

Lashakr-e-Taiba, 113–14
Lavrov, Sergei, 176, 177
Libicki, Martin, 4–5, 21–22, 46–47, 54–55, 61–62, 93–95, 204–5, 207
Libya, NATO intervention in, 130
Lieber, Kier, 67–68
Lin, Herbert, 15, 27, 47, 51–52, 206–7
Lindsay, Jon, 24, 77, 205, 206–7
"logic bomb," 72–73
Long, Austin, 56, 62–63, 94–95
Lynn, William, 73
Lynn-Jones, Sean, 64

Maersk, 6
malware. *See also specific country or incident*

generally, 28
gaining access to target and, 39–42, 40t
host security and, 69t
"inoculation," 104–6
non-universal lethality of, 46–47
nuclear weapons and, 205–6
operational information, revealing, 102, 103–4
time considerations, 49
Mandiant, 118–19, 120–22, 123
Maness, Ryan, 109–10
maneuver, offensive advantage in cyberspace and, 66–71
Mattern, Troy, 48
Mattis, James, 183
Mayorkas, Alejandro, 36–37n.12
McAfee, 118–19
McNamara, Robert, 215–16
Merck, 6
Microsoft, 44, 99–100, 242–43
militarization of cyberspace, assumption regarding, 23–26
Militarized Interstate Disputes (dataset), 110n.5
Miller, Matthew, 47
Milley, Mark, 233–34n.26
MITRE, 68–70
mobility, offensive advantage in cyberspace and, 66–71
Montenegro, NATO cyber operations and, 25–26
Most, Benjamin, 97
Mumbai terrorist attacks, 113–14, 159t
Munich Security Conference, 6–7
mutual deterrence, 2–3

Nakasone, Paul, 49, 81–82, 138
National Command Authority, 228
National Cyber Strategy, 233–34, 237–38
National Defense Authorization Act (NDAA), 228, 230
National Hurricane Center, 52
National Security Agency, 45–46, 202–3
National Security Council, 133
National Security Presidential Memorandum (NSPM) 13, 228
NATO. *See* North Atlantic Treaty Organization (NATO)
Navy, 198
Netherlands
cult of cyber offense in, 26
cyber operations defined in, 15–16
Defence Cyber Strategy, 15–16
malware and, 105–6
network architecture and management, 69t